TIME ON ICE

A WINTER VOYAGE TO ANTARCTICA

■ ■ ■

DEBORAH SHAPIRO AND ROLF BJELKE

INTERNATIONAL MARINE
Camden, Maine

International Marine/
Ragged Mountain Press

A Division of The **McGraw·Hill** Companies

10 9 8 7 6 5 4 3 2 1

Copyright © 1998 text and photos, Northern Light Inc.

Library of Congress Cataloging-in-Publication Data

Shapiro, Deborah, 1951–
 [Vinterskepp. English]
   Time on ice : a winter voyage to Antarctica / Deborah Shapiro and
 Rolf Bjelke.
     p. cm
   ISBN 0-07-006399-0
   1. Northern Light (Yacht) 2. Antarctica. I. Bjelke, Rolf.
 II. Title.
 G850.S47513 1997
 910'.9163'1—dc21   97-25715
                                           CIP

Questions regarding this book should be addressed to:

The McGraw-Hill Companies
Customer Service Department
P.O. Box 547
Blacklick, OH 43004
Retail customers: 1-800-262-4729
Bookstores: 1-800-722-4726

This book is printed on 60-pound Renew Opaque Vellum, an acid-free paper containing 50 percent recycled waste paper (preconsumer) and 10 percent consumer waste paper.

Printed by R.R. Donnelley

Project Management by University Graphics, Inc.

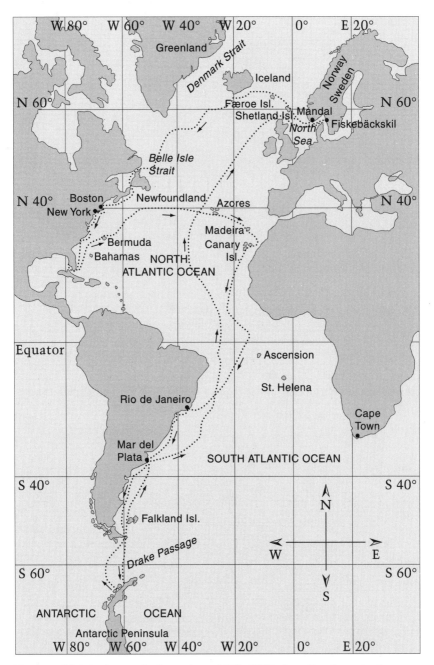

Northern Light's Antarctic Overwinter 1989–1992, from Sweden, via the
United States, Azores and Canary Islands, South America, to the Antarctic
Peninsula and back to Sweden was a total of 28,000 nautical miles. The last
leg: Mar del Plata, Argentina to Fiskebäckskil, Sweden was 7,900 nautical
miles, which we sailed non-stop in 60 days and 18 hours.

CONTENTS

■ ■ ■

INTRODUCTION

Deborah

■ ■ ■

Rolf's first boating adventure, at age five, was paddling a cupboard door across a creek. He grew up in Örebro, a small city in southern Sweden. There is a castle on the river there, but otherwise, the landlocked town is Sweden's Pittsburgh.

I was born in the Steel City and grew up outside it. But as our rural home was nowhere near any of Pittsburgh's three rivers, I had to leave to get my first chance at boating. It finally happened when I was in my twenties. I was working in the music industry in Los Angeles when a friend called to ask if I would help crew a boat to Hawaii. And it wasn't just any boat—it was a newly renovated 160-foot J-class racing sailboat from the 1920s, the *Invader*.

The passage was an enormous experience, the boat and its gigantic sail area glorious to behold, and the crew congenial, but a huge boat is *not* the place to learn to sail. The forces involved and the orchestration required to keep disaster at arm's length are all too overwhelming to sort out in a few weeks. Still, my appetite was whetted. I enjoyed being at sea and the teamwork involved.

My ears remained open for another opportunity. Five years later, I signed on the 110-foot wooden brigantine *Romance*—a museum piece cared for and maintained, state of the art 1800s-style, with absolute dedication by its owners. I hired on as cook for eighteen people, sailing the tradewind route through the South Pacific.

Sadly, a ship's cook can't learn to sail. As a matter of fact, it was forbidden for my valuable fingers to even participate in line-handling! Still, the skipper, recognizing my interest, was sympathetic. Once, while I stood with him at the wheel in heavy weather as he steered his flaxen-sailed vessel, my senses absorbing the rhythm and harmony of his response to each gust and lull, wave and trough, and relaxing after a marathon of Thanksgiving cooking and baking in my enclosed, steamy slave-cave, Skipper said to me: "Well Deborah, if you can cook meals like that in conditions like these, you can certainly sail. If you ever want to learn, my suggestion is that you sign on an undermanned vessel." Prophetic words.

I soon became one of a four-person delivery crew on a 50-footer from Tahiti to Fiji, but sailing in constant tradewinds, with an autopilot and electronic navigation, didn't really do the trick either. I started to think that sailing and my life just weren't meant to mix. Once a farmer. . . .

In the meantime, Rolf had traded in his door for a sailing canoe—a butterfly with oversized wings, a delicate slip of a thing with two masts. Sailing it, with sheet in one hand and tiller in the other, he satisfied his teenage curiosity and wanderlust by venturing farther and farther from home. He first explored every nook and cranny of the nearby lake, then transited a canal system to the seemingly endless archipelago outside Stockholm. As an adult, while working as a goldsmith and designer in his own shop, he bought a 24-foot sloop, a midget ocean racer. He and friends sailed and raced *Gunita* coastally, then tried the North Sea, reaching the Orkney Islands. Rolf and his friend Bengt then sailed to the Canary Islands and from there onward to Barbados, setting a speed record for the passage.

The thrashing that *Gunita* had taken in her 12,000 nautical miles of open ocean sailing took its toll. The bow of the fiberglass boat became pliable, almost soft. At home, while repairing it, Rolf started dreaming of a stronger boat: a seaworthy, disciplined boat that could be sailed anywhere.

When he was about to take his ideas to a marine architect, an article fortuitously appeared in the Swedish Cruising Club's magazine describing a double-ended boat so like the one he wanted that he immediately contacted Meta, the boatyard mentioned in the article. Oddly situated in the French countryside just outside Lyon, the yard, run by metallurgist Joseph Fricaud, had been building steel road-working machinery until the day Bernard Moitessier ordered a hull to be welded. It was drawn by Jean Knocker but based on a wooden pleasure craft hull designed in 1914 by the legendary Colin Archer, a genius who solved the problem of how and why a boat must be shaped in a certain way to react harmonically to the seas that build when gale-strength wind has been blowing days on end. Perhaps his best-known designs are the sturdy rescue boats that plied the Norwegian coast to aid the small, engineless, and often open boats the fishermen used year-round.

Moitessier, famous for breaking out of his leading position in the flock of singlehanders in the first around-the-world singlehanded race and continuing another half-turn around the world to settle in Polynesia, named his boat *Joshua*, in honor of the first man to sail singlehanded around the world: American Joshua Slocum. The boat type therefore became known as Joshua, and the hull Rolf ordered was the 68th in the series of approximately 100 built.

Rolf had originally planned to call the boat "Norrsken," the Swedish word for *aurora borealis*. But, as the word's pronunciation is all but impossible for non-Scandinavians, she became *Northern Light*. In 1977, Rolf and two crew left Sweden. After becoming the first Swedish yacht to round Cape Horn, he also found his way to Fiji. . . .

We met there because my friends Susie and Charlie Donnelly, who were giving their four children a sabbatical learning-voyage around the Pacific, pointed at the red boat in the anchorage and told me that its skipper was the finest navigator they had ever met. I rowed over to ask him about Cape Horn—to find out if the literature I had pored over aboard the brigantine was exaggerated or to be believed.

In the long conversations that followed, we found out that we were both serious amateur photographers turned amateur filmmakers. We shared many views on life. And there was a spark there. But as we were both unsettled, traveling, searching, neither of us wanted to fan it. I can only speak for myself, but I was afraid of turning the spark to ashes. I felt Rolf could be an important person in my life, and still, walked away from him and went home, leaving him to finish his circumnavigation. It was the toughest decision I had ever made.

I stayed in touch via letters to general delivery addresses he had given me on his planned route. But I got no answer. My last try was to send a letter to an address he had given me in Sweden, asking that it be forwarded. I poured special energy into that letter. As it turned out, it was the only one he ever received.

Two years later, in 1982, we set out together on a voyage we called "North Ice—South Ice" a 33,000-mile Arctic-to-Antarctic expedition. Originally, Rolf had planned an expedition to Elephant Island off the Antarctic Peninsula and then to South Georgia. His intention was to chronicle Earnest Shackleton's heroic story of survival in the Southern Ocean after his ship *Endurance* was crushed in pack ice. But a new idea emerged. We decided to try to chronicle our own lives instead—to show what it's like living aboard a small boat in the wilderness.

We were told that such a documentary couldn't be done by just two people. After all, while standing "watch and watch" (two people alternating watch responsibilities), working together to take pictures at sea would necessitate one of us sacrificing needed sleep. Many before us had set out to accomplish a self-documentary and come back with as many stories and excuses as rolls of undeveloped film. And yet we set a second, more difficult goal—to take pictures of *Northern Light* sailing through various scenes, using her to give the viewer an object of known size by which to comprehend the scale of a landscape or seascape they might otherwise misjudge. People said (so encouragingly), "That's impossible! One of you will have to singlehand while the other leaves to take pictures."

Though unspoken, we both knew (or at least I *thought* I did) what challenges would be entailed. I suggested that, since we planned to leave for the Antarctic Ocean from Sweden, it would perhaps be prudent to head north first, so that I could learn to sail *Northern Light* along the Norwegian coast. If, for whatever reason, it was a total fiasco, I could hightail it home, and Rolf would still be able to go back or get other crew. If things turned out okay, we could continue north to Svalbard, an island group north of Norway.

In the summer north of the Arctic Circle, where nighttime is magically suspended and delicate wildflowers grow between rocks and snow, where birds gather in the millions to raise their chicks, where blue whales blow and polar bears teach their cubs to hunt, I was changed—bitten, as it were, by the bug of "high latitude fever." Sure there were challenges, but the rewards—the beauty, the majesty, the new sounds and light, the expanded view of my world—all entranced me.

We sailed north from Svalbard to the edge of the polar pack ice, and along it until we found a gap and headed north again, reaching N80° 25'—less than 600 miles from the north pole! Then we turned the bow south, enduring gales in areas of iceberg risk and fog. My eyes turned feverish from staring out hour after hour with nothing to focus on. It was gray, dull, yet paradoxically tinged in my imagination with danger's bright-white. And we continued south, to Greenland, Labrador, to the Caribbean, through the Panama Canal and to Chilean Patagonia, through ever-increasing wind and decreasing temperatures, until, blanketed by snow flurries that didn't melt on deck, we left Cape Horn astern.

Before a white man set eyes on the Antarctic Continent, it was proposed that perhaps what we now call Drake Passage was the border between our world and purgatory. That perhaps, even, the fires of hell burned at the south pole. The strangeness of the place hasn't yet left our collective imagination. Nor had the dread been purged from my personal realm either. As we headed into Drake Passage toward Antarctica, I thought back to the weather-creased face of a retired Swedish fisherman who asked me just prior to our departure for Svalbard if I had any inkling of what I was getting myself into. The answer, of course, was no.

We sailed south of the Antarctic Circle before making landfall. The steep mountains, an extension of the Andes, craggy, glaciated, rose before us, there for the viewing pleasure of no one but us. Rolf wrote in our first book: "I feel I am going through the kind of change that only those who have risked disaster to reach an unknown destination and succeeded can know. I sense a special freedom, an explorer's privileged rebirth." And me? I was awestruck. And then, for the first time in my life, I heard a penguin call.

There is something to be said for experiencing brand-new things as an adult. Just when you think you know the routines, have made the same yearly cycle so many times, even feel (one thinks) justifiably blasé about some things, everything one "knows" and takes for granted is suddenly set on its ear. I think it is for that reason that so many of us from temperate or tropical zones liken our arrival to Antarctica to traveling to a new planet.

Rolf and I coined a new descriptor for ourselves: aquanauts. As we sailed in, the wind intensified. I went off watch and lay myself down, as much to rest my overstimulated sensors as my weary body. Rolf started to sail us north on the inside route. I had hardly fallen asleep when he woke me again. "Dress and come quickly. I need your help."

On deck I looked forward. From the low-to-the-water perspective of a small boat, any ice ahead always looks more tightly packed than it is. Knowing that fact didn't really make me feel any better. I couldn't see any opening. But it was so beautiful that I became breathless, frozen to the spot. In the low twilight of the mustard-colored midnight sun just grazing the horizon, each vertical surface on each iceberg was lilac. Lilac! Yet every horizontal plane was iridescent green, like the waves the *aurora borealis* had once shown me in the northern sky—a fresh, shimmering, silvery-green, like the back side of a blade of dew-covered spring grass in the yard of my childhood home. But instead of my dog barking, as I almost expected in the instant of the thought, a humpback whale exhaled somewhere nearby.

The images and associations had flowed by as fast as only thoughts can. The last of the series was: "And they call this the white continent—ha!" But Rolf broke the spell by superimposing danger on my appreciation. He said, "You steer while I see if I can find this route." His finger traced a zig-zag line on the chart, then pointed at a cluster of islands before he continued, "I haven't been able to spot these islands yet. Icebergs must be hiding them. I'll climb the mast." Adrenally aided, he moved at top speed, and climbed to spy ahead. One mistaken turn and we would be in uncharted water. One rock and. . . .

It wasn't worth pressing on. I suggested that we beat a hasty retreat the way we had come, get back to open water and heave-to there until the blow was over. Three days later, it was calm enough to try again.

Danger, beauty, newness, and raw power are components of the alluring potion Antarctica proffers. We sailed there seven weeks, two weeks longer than planned, documenting what we saw and experienced. We were tough when we started, having come from the cold and wind of Patagonia. But without respite, even below-decks, as our heater refused to function on the kerosene bought in South America, and due to the endless decisions made without certain experience to draw from, the time there drained our reserves. Living with the treachery of ice—what we came to call "moving rocks"—and either too little or too much wind, all sapped our energy. Then killer whales attacked and destroyed the better of our two dinghies, which was crucial for getting shore lines in place, and then nighttime reappeared and then a crack opened in the fitting at the top of the mainmast (which provides the attachment point for the fore- and backstays that hold up the mast). And we still had Drake Passage ahead of us. . . .

Some pitch-black nighttime maneuvers later, we were forced by a wind shift to leave a now-untenable anchorage in gale-force winds, for a poorly charted place we had never been before. Hearing the umpteenth piece of ice "ca-chunk" into the hull, wondering if whatever ate the dinghy would eat me the next time I had to get ashore, and taking pictures with frozen fingers for the viewing pleasure of I knew not who anymore, all started to take its toll. The continent was no longer beautiful. It had become a demanding monster, a place of pain and constant worry. When we made it out successfully, we both sighed and agreed we would never go back.

What we hadn't counted on was one fantastic trait of the human species: the inability to retain a sensory memory of pain—that is, to conjure it up and actually *hurt* when remembering it. Instead, like a siren's song, our memories lured us back with images of what we had seen, felt, smelled, touched, experienced, and learned as enthusiastically as kids sucking a milkshake glass dry with a straw. We had accomplished what we set out to do, knew we now had experience to draw from, and had developed and honed a special teamwork. People at home enjoyed what we had to share, and seemed never to get enough information from us about our lives and the way we survived out on the edge.

We also started to place a special value on a lifestyle that has a music all its own. The wind, no matter its strength—wafting, blowing, or howling a hurricane—had become a lullaby of a sort. The most important verse told us: in the wilderness you, and only you, will determine if you survive or not. Your capabilities, judgment, heart, bravery, and creativity will enjoy full use, and indeed blossom as you blend into the magical, mystical scene.

And we realized that the window we had opened onto Antarctic summer gave us but a glimpse of what the place was all about. To actually understand it, we would have to stay a full cycle, a year or more, call it home. We would arrive in summer and enjoy it in anchorages we knew. The season would quickly become winter. Oddly enough, we thought winter would be a respite— for when the boat was frozen to the spot, it would not need the usual constant tending, and we would therefore be able to relax and meditate, ruminate. And at winter's end, but before people can normally approach in their ships or planes, we would experience spring. Assuming all was well, we would take a six-week ski trip along the Peninsula.

That became our plan, the grand plan. Our minds, our energy, everything was put to the preparation of the project. And that is where you, dear reader, now join us.

Put yourself in our shoes, or come along as the third person aboard. You don't know exactly where you are going, because you will have to decide after a series of tests whether the project is on or off. So much depends on your health, your gear, your preparation, the ice conditions you find in the South. You will not be allowed to falter along the way. And remember that at the first stage, your journey's start, you never know if you will reach Ithaca again. As a matter of fact, at this very moment, though you've been working hard, you can't even be sure the boat will ever leave the dock. . . .

1

NO TIME
TO TALK

DEBORAH

■ ■ ■

Without any warning whatsoever, I lose contact with the world. As though anesthetized, all sensory information simply evaporates, and consciousness is whisked away. The blackout breaks a step intended to take me from the dock to the boat. With one foot midair and water below, I wither and drop.

Although I am unaware of it, my free fall is almost immediately interrupted as I clip the corner of the dock. Taking the brunt of the impact, my pelvic bone cracks. Pain sears a comet trail through the darkness, cleaving the inky black nothingness with a bright white flash.

Conscious. Injured. Falling. Superawareness suddenly reigns. More information than usual is available, as if I can process more frames per second. Everything in my field of vision is crystal clear and oddly highlighted. Rolf's confused, concerned expression dominates the picture. His hand, though too far away, reaches out to me. Noises and smells expand. Thoughts and feelings become one and the same, lumped together in wordless clusters.

And although I haven't the foggiest clue *why* I happen to be bouncing off the edge of the dock, I arrest my fall. One hand goes to the wooden edge, the other grabs the rail of the boat. My feet never touch water. Feeling light as a feather, I push myself up and roll to my noninjured side. Sweat beads on my pain-tensed upper lip and brow. I tell myself to get up.

While forcing movement over pain, the part of me that still *must think* can't help wondering what's just happened and what the consequences will be. I know all too well that five weeks past our intended departure date, both Rolf and I are overworked, exceedingly tired, and anxious. But to add a physical problem to that list means that our voyage may have just ended without one mile ever slipping past the keel.

Rolf is at my side and wants to know how badly I'm hurt. I grimace inwardly but manage a weak smile and tell him it's not too bad, then accept his outstretched hand and climb gingerly aboard. Rolf clears tools off a bench in the main cabin so that I can lie down. Silence envelops us as he brews a pot of tea. Quite sure that calamity has just obliterated our plans and feeling guilty that I proved to be the weak link, all the work we've accomplished roils in my mind.

The goal of the rebuild in progress is to turn our 40-foot sailboat into a polar base camp. The final phase of the ambitious transformation had begun nearly seven months earlier—the day after New Year's—on a rather raw Swedish winter day.

The first job we accomplished that day was to inspect already completed work. The previous summer, we had reconditioned the entire inside of the boat. Every square inch of the steel hull and deck had been sandblasted, zinc sprayed, and epoxy painted. As we finished looking over the work, Rolf commented: "The treatment looks positively fantastic. It may have been a bear of a job, but we've extended the lifetime of the boat at least a hundred years. Though, come to think of it, half that will suffice."

We laughed and dug in. It was time to put the interior back together. We traced exact paper patterns for each section of the hull and from them cut out new polyurethane insulation $2\frac{1}{3}$ inches (6 cm) thick. Each sheet was carefully pushed into place, tight to the hull between the steel frames, from stem to stern and deck to bilge. A perfect job was a necessity: Our lives could depend on it. Done right, the temperature inside the boat would stay above freezing during a polar winter, even if the heater failed.

We made cardboard patterns for a watertight bulkhead and a new companionway and delivered them to a workshop to be made in aluminum. We installed a diesel heater and seven radiators throughout the main cabin and navigation desk area. To build in the heater required appropriating space from the head. That in turn meant moving and replumbing the toilet and sink. Adjoining the heater in the main cabin, we built a new bookshelf that immediately became known as "Bosse's bookshelf" because its frame was cut from a gorgeous teak plank that Bosse, our friendly neighbor, had given us.

As part of another big plan—to improve the way *Northern Light* sails—we redesigned the anchor chain stowage system. Too much weight in the ends of a boat will exaggerate its pitching, or hobbyhorsing, which not only slows it down but makes its motion uncomfortable. To move the weight of the chain as far from the bow as possible, we added a pipe below deck through which the 825 pounds (375 kg) of chain travels 6 feet (1.75 m) farther aft for storage. Furthermore, so that the wet chain could no longer drip salt water on the steel hull and perhaps lead to corrosion, we designed a storage tank for the chain. It was ordered along with another stainless steel tank needed to complete Rolf's new invention: a waterproof ventilation system. The basic idea was that any water coming in through the Dorade air vents on deck would end up in the tank, meaning that the vents could always be left open, even in such bad weather that turning upside down was a possibility.

We started to reinstall some of the old furniture modules. Then we cut new plywood ceiling sections and treated them against mold and covered them with new white material. We were so pleased. Everything would soon be nice and fresh.

As the rebuild was proceeding on schedule in a normal working week's hours, we also had time to exercise. Three times a week we briskly walked the roads and paths through our little island community for 55 minutes, all the while vigorously pumping hand weights above chest height. We endured onlookers' stares, which became giggles, which became comments behind our backs, which finally turned to questions such as, "Whatever are you two doing, walking around imitating hyperactive railroad-crossing booms?" And even though we twice increased the weights, we improved our time and eventually made it around the loop in under fifty minutes. Walking at a fast jogging pace and lifting weights above heart level made for a great aerobic workout.

In addition, on Saturdays and Sundays we went for four-hour and then six-hour trail hikes to build endurance. The short-range goal for this training was a spring cross-country skiing trip in the Swedish mountains. There we'd test both the recently bought winter camping equipment and me; I had no prior experience living out of doors in a winter landscape or skiing while pulling a sledge. The supply-bearing sledge is called a *pulka*; the name comes from the language of the Saame, the native seminomadic inhabitants of the high north of Sweden. For this test, my pulka would be loaded with 145 pounds (66 kg) of gear, 5 percent more than my body weight.

Boy oh boy, did I train hard! I had a feeling that once we were in the mountains, I would be thankful for every strand of newly built muscle fiber, every cubic inch of lung capacity, and every ounce of endurance. And was I ever right. I never regretted one second of training, not even the longest blistering walk.

A marathon distance wasn't actually part of our original training scheme. But when our friends Inger and Ernst invited us to dinner one Saturday night in March, I suggested to Rolf that we accept as long as we added the time that we wouldn't spend making dinner to our normal outdoor time and walk the 26 miles (42 km) to their house.

Yes, were it not for every iota of training, I think I may have collapsed in a puddle of tears the first minutes of our three-week mountain skiing trip. As the train started to pull away and its passengers stared at us through the windows, we harnessed up. I moved a ski forward for the very first stride, jubilantly jerking my hips to get the fully packed pulka going and ... well, it didn't even budge. *Uh oh,* I thought to myself, *what do I do now?*

Although his opinion leaked through elevated superciliary arches, Rolf calmly advised: "It's no problem, Deborah. Just plant both poles in close to your feet, and then, as you bend your body forward, use your entire weight to jerk the pulka to a start."

Oh, I love that word *just.* Especially as the technique Rolf described was the one I thought I had just tried. In all honesty, I was worried, really worried. I looked up. The train had chugged out of sight, leaving us to our own devices in the middle of absolutely nowhere. There was only one alternative. "Mush," I muttered to myself. And I got going, slowly but surely.

Even though Rolf's pulka was loaded with 15 percent more than his body weight and he was breaking the trail, he quickly forged ahead. That was discouraging. I started to feel sorry for any animal ever harnessed. The flat terrain near the train tracks gave way to an uphill grade. Because every step that first day would include altitude gain, I was thankful that the mountain's upper contours were demurely ensconced in fog. Without seeing the top, I could at least fantasize that the pull wouldn't be all that bad. Recalling a bit of Inuit advice about self-propelled travel in cold climes, I went as fast as I could without sweating.

Higher up, the snow became windpacked and icy, and my skis started backsliding. I was suddenly burning lots of energy to go nowhere. Rolf turned and skied back to me to impart more advice: "It's time to attach climbing skins to the bottom of your skis. With them on, you'll be able to walk uphill."

To my amazement, the furry things worked just fine. I no longer needed a death grip on my poles nor be ready to plant them at an instant's notice to halt the tendency of being pulled backward. We continued at a faster pace up and up. I could practically match Rolf's speed.

After a few hours we poked our heads through to the clear. The reward for the climb was a dazzling sight: an entire range of craggy, jagged mountaintops. Wow! What challenges lay ahead. The array of peaks dangled in front of my nose like so many carrots! And the snow was sparkling and glittering, like so many carats!

Although it was a juvenile pun, I had to laugh. Tired as I was, I was ready to grab onto anything to detour my thoughts from the long uphill slog still ahead. I had already tried every trick I knew to divert my concentration from whatever hurt the most and to keep from counting each step, all to no avail. It was all too new. *But don't worry*, I told myself. *Every process of a new endeavor can grind in the beginning.*

After 12 miles (20 km), we pitched our tent beside a frozen lake. We were within sight of a public hut that had a border of skis planted around the porch.

Dumb me suggested that we go over for a fireside chat with the hut's occupants. Dumb, because once inside, the first question asked of us was about our route, and after hearing it outlined, the obvious leader of the other group told Rolf in no uncertain terms, "That's no pulka route." Then he turned his deep gaze on me and explained, "The descent to Lake Alisjávri is far too steep."

Those were the most discouraging words I could ever hear. Going up is one thing; although it may be hard work, it's not scary. But careening downhill out of control, with the pulka tending to push or rather emphasize the gravity of the situation, as well as forcing a yang when its leader is trying her best to yin . . . no, "far too steep" was not something I needed to hear, especially from an experienced, male skier. But Rolf was not fazed. "We can handle it," he responded unblinkingly.

Back in the privacy of our tent, poring over topographical maps, I heard that one design finesse of our route was that particular descent to Lake Alisjávri. Not accidentally, it was in the second half of the trip. Rolf explained that he had planned a route that would provide a succession of increasingly difficult challenges to find out what I could handle.

But what Rolf didn't divulge then was that he actually expected the day-long uphill before that steep descent to be the toughest part. In particular, to climb to the saddle 3,936 feet (1,250 m) above sea level, we would need to gain 1,968 feet (600 m) in one day. And the altitude gain included one *very* steep grade. He thought the pulkas might not track well traversing such a steeply canted incline.

Rolf's concern proved right. My new pulka had Teflon runners that didn't grip the hill as well as his older model with brass runners. We therefore had to switchback more times than usual, and catastrophe loomed the entire hour. When we finished, I was drenched in sweat, but I never lost control. And Rolf was right: I made it both up and down. To top that, a few days later we climbed Kebnekaise, Sweden's highest peak. I had never climbed a mountain before.

Rolf's first arctic training and experience came during his mandatory military stint in the Swedish Army. For more than a year he trained to be a solo operative. He lived outdoors, slept in hand-dug snow caves, and traveled exclusively on skis, carrying everything he needed. A Saame taught him how to survive in the high north, in summer as well as winter. During the two decades following his discharge, Rolf in turn taught winter survival techniques to others and led many high-latitude expeditions.

On our excursion, I found Rolf to be a thorough and capable teacher. Perhaps most important, but not unexpected, I adored the outdoor experience. At least most of it. Above the sighs and scrapes of our skis and the measured beat of our ever-strengthening hearts was all-too-often superimposed the out-of-place noise of snowmobiles and helicopters. Except for those oppressive sounds, I enjoyed every moment.

If we weren't well trained when we started, we were by the end of the three weeks of pulling. At rest, Rolf's heart beat forty-eight times per minute and mine fifty-two. Full of energy and with metabolisms in high gear, we went stir crazy sitting still an entire day, cooped up in an overheated train, clickety clacking our way south to our rebuilding project. We were so very ready to finish and get under sail.

Back at the marina in Fiskebäckskil, all was as we had left it, except the air. Spring, a magical time everywhere but especially in high latitudes, had arrived. The light continued to increase by leaps and bounds day after day, until sleepiness had to be encouraged by going indoors and pulling down the window shades.

The lengthening daylight and the invigoration that long days impart were surely in our favor as we were forced to lengthen our work hours. The first in a string of disappointments was the custom stainless steel work we had ordered. It was not ready as promised. As a consequence, we were forced to rearrange the way the puzzle pieces of the interior were to be reassembled. As we waited, we continued to craft the new navigation desk and various other cabinets and doors, laminating curved trim and frames and applying the prime coats of varnish. But with the loss of a logical progression, our time plan started to crack.

We started working seven days a week, trying as best we could to stay on schedule. We worked longer days and slept less, but we knew better than to ever fudge on food. Three squares a day and as many snack pauses kept us fueled. My favorite break was eleven o'clock coffee, a serious tradition in Sweden. Each day we'd meet with the five others working in the marina to chat over a cup of the world's blackest brew and an open-faced sandwich.

With spring's arrival, more and more folks showed up at the marina café until there were too many to adhere to one conversation. At that point the carpenter, the smithy, Rolf, and I cleared out the rearmost corner of the motor workshop and began meeting there instead, to talk work or politics or philosophize during the break. Going into our hideout reminded me of my childhood, when I'd truck down to the basement with my siblings to watch the *Mickey Mouse Club* on television. Although I can't be sure my Swedish counterparts really understood the reference, that name became attached to our coffee klatch.

Our industrious island neighbors were at least as busy as we were. They had winter to clean away, houses to spruce up, gardens to turn over and plant, and boats to ready and launch so that as soon as possible every free minute could be devoted to outdoor pleasure. I had the impression that they saw spring and summer as a sort of daylight savings plan. It was as if they could gather and store the sun's rays and the nice mood to mete out through the next winter. Being as frantically busy as they were, just a nod or a wave was considered a fine greeting.

But on the first nice Saturday, motor vehicles disgorged flocks of people who clustered around their boats to rip off the tarps and canvas covers and start readying for launch day. Beside the tools in their trunks were blankets, picnic baskets, and thermoses of steaming coffee. And as soon as possible they stopped to chat about boats and spring. "Ah, spring. . . ."

Oh, the conflict this presented for us. Although we wanted to be friendly, we couldn't possibly stop several times each hour to talk. Doing so would jeopardize our project. Rolf became better at extricating himself from conversation than I. In fact, once we began working every waking hour of every day (and sleeping only six), people could not finish their opening statement before he was begging their pardon. And on July first, when Sweden's nationwide five-week vacation started and the crowds arrived, every person meandering by had an abundance of time and questions. I had to do something, figure out some way of becoming "invisible." Finally I asked my friend Cilla, who has the nicest handwriting on the island, to paint a message on my sweatshirt: NO TIME TO TALK announced my dilemma loud and clear. Person after person chortled when they saw it, then nodded as they backed off and said: "OK, OK, I understand."

But then our schedule took a succession of blows. First, measurements of tanks and sails ordered long ago were declared lost. Redoing the specs and delivering them chewed up days of Rolf's time. And big chunks of work had to remain on hold until the tanks arrived. Then came the straw that broke the camel's back: our new wingkeel, declared ready by the welder, looked like a twisted banana. The man had not had the skill to make the keel, which Rolf had designed to fit like a handmade shoe over *Northern Light*'s integral, ramrod-straight long keel.

Because vacation had already started, no one else was willing to take over the job and build us a functional keel. We had no choice but to have the welder take a torch to his unusable steel abomination and cut it back to the frame stage. Then Rolf and I took over. We shaped the keel in steel mesh and finished it with ferrocement, microballoons, and fiberglass. This additional project took us nearly three weeks. We would have had to sail away with an unfinished interior had Gunilla and Ulf not arrived, tied their boat up to ours, and announced, "We are good at sanding and varnishing and we can stay five days, so put us to work." Sometimes there are no words to express one's gratitude.

On the day we had originally planned to leave, we moved instead from the marina to a shipyard farther up the fjord. While the old cockpit and part of the aft cabin were being cut away, a new horseshoe-shaped aluminum cockpit frame was manufactured. Its installation and finish work were up to us. Among many advantages, the new cockpit would allow us to move the companionway to a safer center position and raise the height of the interior passageway from the galley to the aft cabin.

Returning to the marina, *Northern Light* was lifted so that we could attach the new keel and paint the bottom. Back in the water, we thoroughly inspected the previous summer's installation of new furling masts and their standing and running rigging. Then Rolf began to build the cockpit benches in plywood and dress them in teak, and he mounted the new steering gear. Meanwhile, I varnished and sanded and varnished—until today, when sheer exhaustion caused me to black out, fall, and injure myself.

After a short break and a cup of tea, I press on with my work. Although the assumed pelvic fracture hurts to the point that painkillers would help, I don't want to risk working while medicated. Therefore, and because I don't want any bad news, there's no visit to the doctor's office for me. Fortunately, Rolf and I are working on separate projects for the most part, so I figure to be able to keep my problems to myself these last few days on shore. I can only hope that continuing to work will not worsen the injury and that the pain will be manageable when we're ready to sail.

Ingrid and her sister Krisy have a summer place nearby, built in what used to be a herring-oil factory. Weeks ago they told us of their plan to throw a going away party for us. They have an incredible sphere of friends, and we are always stimulated by the intriguing variety of conversations and activities at their gatherings. But on the day of the party, when they call to say they are driving over to pick us up, we have to tell them how sorry we are that we can't possibly stop working. Nonetheless, the party goes on, with us there in spirit only. Later that evening, Björn shows up at the boat, bringing us our portions of the dinner and gifts from the gang, including a toy mascot for the trip from Gunnel. It's a stuffed platypus that for some reason she thinks looks just like her. And Björn presents us with a full medical kit that he and Olav (both physicians) have assembled for us.

Finally, August the eighth at 0800, we hear the unmistakable sound of the one-cylinder engine in *Turbulent*, our friend Bernt's sturdy little boat, arriving to lead us and a little parade of well-wishers out of the harbor. Fiskebäckskil is quiet, the hum gone with the summer guests. As we motor past the cliff under Bernt's house, we look up as we always do, to see if his parents are looking out a window. They are indeed up there, but not in the house. Today they stand side by side on the lawn, waving white handkerchiefs in formal farewell.

Reaching open water, we start to set sail. Horns blow, and everyone waves and shouts jubilantly as they start to turn around. Everyone, that is, except Bernt. He neither moves nor makes any sound. In fact, he's not even smiling. He stands in the stern of his boat, his gaze riveted on us.

Like many islanders, Bernt has been working at sea all his adult life. Unlike the well-intentioned summer sailors, who have been repeatedly but mistakenly reminding us that once the grind is over, our "long vacation" would start, Bernt realizes that just because we'll be sailing doesn't mean it'll be fun. He knows that crossing the North Atlantic this late in the season will be tough. And he's been keeping tabs on us through the entire seven months' work. Bernt knows of our trials and tribulations, he knows just how ragged tired we are, and he is the only one who commented that I seemed to be walking oddly. He told me that were it not for our experience and routine at sea, he would have thought it prudent to stop us from departing.

All sails unfurled, *Northern Light* picks up speed. The distance between our two boats increases. But before Bernt starts to turn *Turbulent* homeward, he raises his right hand, palm out, and holds it there, steady, like he's carved from stone. It's a serious final statement, this good-bye. Rolf and I look at one another. Rolf smiles ever so slightly; I reciprocate and nod to him. Knowing that someone else really does understand is a true and meaningful support and the best boost we could have gotten as the long voyage starts to unfold.

2

CROSSING
THE
NORTH ATLANTIC

ROLF

■ ■ ■

That we have left our home harbor doesn't mean that everything's in order. Far from it. Consequently, as we daysail north along the Swedish coast and then westward in southern Norway, we continue working. Day after day we either mount new winches or move the old ones, along with their respective blocks and cleats, so that coupled to the sweeping changes that we've already made to both the rigging and the cockpit, everything will end up a functional whole.

Only now, under sail, can we determine where each individual fitting should be mounted. The placement must be decided underway, after assessments have been made in different winds. From experience we know that solutions developed in harbors seldom function well at sea. It doesn't seem to matter how much time or energy has been put into the thinking.

While one of us sails, the other works. When Deborah has the watch, hours can pass without my ever looking up to see where we are, and when I do, it's more a reflexive check of wind, weather, and sail trim than to appreciate the surroundings.

For the first ten days out, we continue working as though we'd never left the harbor. Only when it becomes too dark to work do we anchor and sleep. The feeling of being underway and heading out on a long voyage doesn't come before all the work is finally accomplished and we embark from Mandal, on the southwestern coast of Norway.

This is my seventh Atlantic crossing in my own boat, but that doesn't mean that in the moment of departure I am blasé. I know that each voyage, even if traveling a route sailed many times before, is unique. The excitement carries with it a little tingling feeling that also underscores how wonderful it is to be under sail. I analyze the details of everything I see and hear. While listening to the bow waves murmuring, I inhale the salty smell of the sea. Each cell in my body slowly gains new strength.

I've felt this way on earlier voyages as well. Each time the boat has been readied—with enough water, fuel, and provisions brought aboard to allow months of independence—the moment of departure has felt magical. Trust in the future has been created through preparation. When the wind first fills the sails, it fills me with optimism. And that's the way it should be.

But after some hours at sea, I start to realize that this time, things are different. As soon as all the new impressions have been sorted out, I realize that it was only the magic of change itself that affected me. The good feeling of being compensated for all the work accomplished starts to dwindle. Worry for the future creeps in. It's as if I can't escape a bad dream.

Even though there's only a light breeze and it's not particularly cold, I start to shiver. On my way down into the boat to get a sweater, I pause on the ladder. It's seven hours since we left Norway, and to the east I can see the permanently snow-covered mountain peaks about to drop below the horizon. We are leaving our home waters. And as far as I am concerned, it's just as well; we certainly experienced more than our fill of shoddy workmanship and disreputable behavior in the past months.

When I come down inside the boat, I pad as quietly as possible. I don't want to disturb Deborah, who is off watch and lying in the seaberth, but she apparently has difficulty sleeping. After I take a few steps, she turns around and opens her eyes. Her look discloses that she's also uneasy, pondering something. Normally, I would have said something to her, to assess recent events before becoming fully absorbed by the voyage. But I'm too preoccupied with my own thoughts now to have anything sensible to say. The only contact we have with each other is a smile I manage to force, which I hope she will interpret as meaning that all is well with me. Then I look away.

From the beginning, our intention was to leave around midsummer and cruise through the Shetland and Færoe Islands. We figured that a month's vacation would allow a peacefully paced readjustment to being aboard. We also planned to make it to the United States by the beginning of September to attend Deborah's brother's wedding. But all those plans were foiled. Due to the delayed departure, we are now heading out toward approaching fall storms. Our new plan is to sail north for a few days. Once we sight Iceland, we will decide what route to take across the Atlantic. Everything depends on weather, wind, and how we feel.

We entertain the hope that despite everything, we will have gained enough strength to be able to continue on a northerly route. We want to hold as close as we can to the Great Circle course, pass the southern tip of Greenland, continue through Belle Isle Strait, go west of Newfoundland, and then proceed to the east coast of the United States. That's 3,400 nautical miles nonstop. After a pause in New England, we plan to sail more or less directly to Argentina. There, we'll choose our next project from three we have in mind.

One project is to go to the Antarctic Peninsula and stay there for more than a year. With that expedition in mind, we have skis and pulkas on board and a mountain of vacuum-packed expedition food that will remain "fresh" for two years. But if the ice conditions along the Peninsula are too severe, or if we can't find an acceptable winter harbor, we'll attempt project two: sail around the entire continent, in the latitude of the Antarctic Convergence, and visit a dozen or so islands that abound in wildlife. If for one reason or another that voyage is not possible, our third option is to spend a year in southern Argentina and Chile, the two Patagonias.

But before making the choice, we must know that the boat indeed functions properly after all the changes we've made. Specifically, we must be sure that the new rig will be able to withstand the severe conditions existing in the Antarctic Ocean. Thus, even though we are actually on our way south, we choose to detour north first. This passage is to be a test, a shakedown, done for the sake of safety.

In our original plan, this crossing would have been made in July to August when the weather is most suitable, following the rule that says: If taking the northern route across the Atlantic Ocean, pass the longitude of Greenland's southern point before August has ended. In August, there is a 4 percent risk of getting hit by a real storm; in September, 9 percent, a doubling; and in October, as much as 16 percent. Because we have been so delayed, it is now likely that during this crossing, we will have to drive *Northern Light* against gale- or storm-force winds twice a week and, perhaps, for days on end. To put it mildly, due to other peoples' sloppiness and inability to deliver on time what they promised, we have ended up in a very unpleasant situation.

On my way back up to the cockpit, Deborah clears her throat and says, "Rolf, I have to talk to you." Her tone divulges that this isn't going to be an ordinary "Is everything OK?" conversation. Deborah tells me that she hasn't been able to sleep. I see that she has properly adjusted the angle of the sea berth to compensate for the boat's heel and is therefore lying horizontally. I ask what the problem is. She tells me that she can only lie on her left side. If she tries to sleep on the injured side, her hip aches unbearably; If she tries to lie on her back, the pain shoots along her spine each time the boat pitches. On top of that, she informs me that during her watch she couldn't sit down; the pain was too great. Instead, she was forced to stand, leaning toward the wheel and holding onto the handrail above the compass. In the beginning of her watch when the wind came in a little aft of abeam, everything was all right. But when it shifted to westerly and the sea started to come against us, it got progressively tougher and more tiring for her.

It's been months since Deborah and I have had any real conversation. All talk between us has concerned work on the boat. Therefore, what she now tells me comes as an absolute shock. We have left port without even knowing the status of one another's health! Of course, I understood that just like me, Deborah must be very tired, but I had no clue that she was still in so much pain. But then I remember that since her fall, Deborah has usually stood while eating, or sometimes she half-sat, resting lightly against a corner of the seat while supporting her upper body on the table.

Deborah has related her problem without any trace of complaint in her voice. All was said in the same matter-of-fact tone as everything else that she's reported during the last few months. But when she finishes off with "So, how are you doing?" I just don't know how to respond.

If Deborah's situation doesn't improve, she will be forced to stand during her four-hour watches, without any possibility of moving around to stay warm. The unpleasantness will stretch her watches to eternity. But we have no choice. Our own comfort must be set aside. We have to sail *Northern Light* hard enough to get answers to all the questions we have about the equipment.

I know just what Deborah has ahead of her, but I can't address it right now. Eventually, I manage an answer to her question, which is actually no answer at all. "Right now," I tell her, "it's unbelievably nice sailing. The wind has turned against us a little more, but we are still making fine speed, over 7 knots. And half an hour ago, I saw the first gannet. What a beautiful bird. It has a cream-colored body and pastel rainbow pattern around its beak and eyes. During your watch, you will most certainly see a lot of them. If the wind remains steady, we will pass less than 20 miles east of the Shetland Islands, and that's one of their nesting places." That's the extent of the exchange I can manage before dismissing myself to go on deck again.

I knew that our first week at sea would be difficult. We have been on shore far too long to have sea legs left. It's the same for everyone: the body quickly adjusts to being ashore. There, one doesn't have to coordinate one's steps with the ground, which is rigid and lifeless. After just a couple of weeks of living ashore, reflexes one might believe have been etched in the backbone disappear. Once out at sea again, we must retrain all our handholds and movements.

The first three days are seldom enjoyable. Even if we don't get so seasick that we vomit, Deborah and I are usually listless and apathetic. We take care of what we have to, but nothing more. Lack of proper and contiguous sleep generates further discomfort during the first days. Usually a week passes before we adjust to short sleeps and feel energetic again. But after what Deborah just told me, I understand that this time the situation is more critical than that. It isn't just tiredness and discomfort we have to wrestle with; the concern is Deborah's health.

The question is, What do we do? Perhaps we will have to change our plans completely and set a course south to the Azores, thereby taking a warmer and less windy route and sailing with the wind to the United States. But that would mean not getting the answers to all our questions about the boat. Reason tells me that we have to push on; we simply can't give up. But right now, that decision weighs heavily. I would prefer to focus on Deborah's comfort. It doesn't feel right to expose her to the ardors of the northern route when she's injured. I feel so dejected. For the first time in my life at sea, I sit and cry.

So that Deborah will not see how low I feel, I let her sleep well past the watch shift. When I finally feel a little better and wake her, it is already dark. We chat about how strange it feels that although autumn is approaching, our nights are actually getting shorter because we are sailing north. This will hold true until the equinox.

I report that the visibility isn't all that good. Although I'd seen some stars on my watch, a little while ago when a ship passed, its stern lantern disappeared very suddenly. Perhaps there will be fog farther ahead; it's difficult to judge. While handing Deborah her foul weather jacket, I notice that her forehead has wrinkles I've never seen before. Gently, I caress her brow. In return, I get a hug, and then she makes her way to the cockpit.

When I put myself in the seaberth, there is still a little of Deborah's warmth left. I hear her voice coming from the cockpit, as I often do right after I put myself down for a rest. Today she's having a short chat with a bird, but it could just as well have been a porpoise or dolphin. And I always know when the temporary visitor turns away. Then she calls out: "Hey, don't go so soon!"

Deborah loves being out in the fresh air. When the wind makes the boat's speed increase so that the bow cuts through the sea with increasing force, I can hear how she, out there in the dark, tries to overpower the waves. "Go for it. Bring me to the midnight sun!" she cries. I understand that it's *Northern Light* she's talking to. What an amazing person. Even when injured, she has more spirit than most people.

It takes me a long time to unwind. Over and over, a thought bothers me: our old charts don't show the position of the offshore oil platforms east of the Shetland Islands. The self-criticism that we have put out to sea without knowing the platforms' exact positions makes me squirm in the seaberth, unable to really sleep.

We had planned to buy new charts in Norway, but never managed to. In Mandal, the bookstore only had chart kits for nearby coastal waters. Because it was Saturday, the harbor captain's office was closed, and when we phoned the closest Coast Guard station, we reached an answering machine. We had to choose between staying until Monday and maybe finding a chart or leaving to take advantage of the good weather. We chose the latter.

We have no radar on board; we never have. We accept the uncertainty it means to not always know what can be hidden beyond our view. That is not to imply we are reckless. Whenever the visibility becomes too poor to continue safely, our procedure is simply to heave to and wait.

I do not mean to say it's wrong to have radar; there are occasions when radar is the best aid there is. In fact, at times we've wished we had it. But we have also realized how far too many of those with watch responsibility on other boats have become victims of the myth of "radar's magic capacity to see everything." If we had radar, perhaps we would also take the comfortable way out one day: remaining inside when it's raining and cold on deck, trusting what we see on the radar, or waiting to be alerted by its alarm.

In poor visibility, we remain on deck to see and (not the least) listen so as to be warned in time of any other ships in the vicinity. And because we have been outside, we have even smelled fishing boats or the exhaust from the smoke-stack of larger ships while they were still a long distance away. Other times, we have been able to take bearings to shore and determine our position by using wind-borne smells. Our senses give us the information we need. The more they are used, the sharper they become and therefore the less we need to rely on instruments.

But even in good visibility, the person on watch is only allowed to remain below deck for a maximum of five minutes. At least that often, the watchkeeper looks out and scans all the way to the horizon, 360 degrees. Depending on the wave height, the procedure may take a few minutes. In bad weather, it can be accomplished in the shelter of the cupola.

This rule must be strictly adhered to. It's a fundamental duty at sea based on respect for human life, and not just our own. In addition, the knowledge that there is always a vigilant eye on one's own boat gives the person off watch the necessary security to relax or benefit fully from sleep. Without that security, life at sea would be a nightmare.

After what feels like two to three hours' hazy rest, I suddenly come to again with the same feeling of uneasiness. What concerns me is our decision-making ability when we are so tired. Will we neglect to heave to in decreasing visibility, influenced by our anxiety to get across the Atlantic as quickly as possible? One thing I do know is that we must soon be in the vicinity of the platforms. I feel the boat setting heavier in the sea than it did earlier. The wind must have increased. Instinctively, I listen for Deborah.

The person off watch is always on standby. Even if sleeping or doing something else, he or she reacts immediately to a signal of three thunks, which means: "I've got problems. Come and give me a hand." But I haven't heard any thunks.

Perhaps it was instead the *lack* of sound that woke me? I sit up immediately. But just as I throw the coverlet off, the genoa winch snaps a few times. Deborah is still on deck. Relief surges through me as I lie back down again. A steering block squeaks. Probably that sound broke into my rest. It must have gotten drier outside. Had it been foggy or raining, the block would have worked without much noise. At most, there would have been a light creaking sound in the lines while the windvane compensated for a wind shift.

The way the boat is moving tells me that Deborah has *Northern Light* performing to its potential and in proper trim. The previously choppy sea has flattened out, and is now riding on top of a well-defined, dominant swell. It's not very high, but it's enough to make me rise off the mattress each time the boat has been lifted by a swell and starts its descent into a valley. For a couple of seconds, I am almost completely weightless. Then I'm slowly pushed down into the mattress for four to five seconds while the boat climbs over the next rise. Then I'm almost weightless again.

I don't have to ask Deborah how far we've come. We must have already passed the Shetland Islands. It is the swell from the Atlantic Ocean I feel. And that means the oil rigs are behind us.

The sea slams against the hull, and to block out the noise, I pull the blanket over my head. Even so, I can hear water rushing along the topsides, as it does when the boat is sailed effectively. I hear a breaking sea coming. I can feel how the bow lifts a little when it comes out on the other side of the wave, and for a moment it's absolutely quiet. Then there is a light jolt through the hull. The boat sets in the sea, taking some over the bow. From all the water I hear swishing through the scuppers, I understand that it was an unusually heavy sea we just met.

Down below, I experience the boat's motion differently than on deck, where I have visual contact with the sea. That thought reminds me that it will still take some days before we are so attuned to the boat that we will pick up the "warning" that something is about to happen, especially while below deck. But in time, we won't even notice that we pause, for example, in the middle of serving a bowl of soup, just before the boat is hit by an odd wave, only to continue as if nothing had happened.

It's exciting at the voyage's start, and particularly after three years on shore, to analyze every little sound I hear. I know I will eventually live with the sum of all the sounds without really thinking about them, yet they will register in the subconscious. And if they change or disappear, the body's sensors will signal an alarm. Out at sea it's very important that we function like this. After all, there is nobody here to lend a hand when something goes wrong. Here we must discover every problem in time and effect any necessary measures before it leads to serious consequences. As the saying goes, it only takes a tenth of the time or energy to prevent a problem than repair one.

Because of a light "hooing" sound from the rigging in the gusts, I understand that the wind must be blowing around 25 knots. Because I still lie comfortably in the seaberth, I draw the conclusion that Deborah must have reduced sail by reefing both the main and the genoa. Most likely, she has also hoisted the staysail. I can picture how she must have been smiling when she did what had to be done, without having to call me up on deck to take care of the heavy work. With the new rigging she manages by herself.

With the old rig, the boat lost a lot of speed during reefing maneuvers and therefore did not move in harmony with the sea until the job was completed. Via the change in the boat's motions I always knew what was going on, even while resting below. But with the new reefing system—with which the genoa, mainsail, and mizzen are reefed just by rolling them in—it's now possible to maintain speed throughout the procedure. That means I'm no longer disturbed. In a way, it's an improvement, but it is also strange after all these years to suddenly lose cues about what's happening on deck. On the other hand, the advantages gained are invaluable. The boat no longer sails with a jerky motion during reefing, which not only decreases wear and tear on the rigging and fittings but also saves the sails, since they can now be reefed without undue flogging.

After the rebuild, almost every sound on board is different than before, especially on a beat. The new, thicker insulation, which we mounted right against the hull, makes it a lot quieter inside than before, when we had left an airspace. Since the halyards now run inside the masts, they no longer clang and bang. And furling sails don't have any slides to make noise or to transfer sound to the masts when they occasionally luff.

Another gain from the rebuild is that the boat's performance has increased remarkably. The delta wingkeel has cut leeway in half, and the entire keel now has a lot less drag. Reduced resistance means that our forward motion is not impeded; in other words, the driving forces are not restricted as they were earlier. And furling sails, although they have less area than battened ones, have a lot more power than I thought they would. The net result is that the boat sails faster, even when reefed—of that there is no question.

A final, unanticipated result of the new keel is that the boat's motion is a lot gentler than before. The wings of the keel dampen the setting motion of the stern. It's wonderful. *Northern Light* no longer has as much tendency to set or pitch. We have almost entirely stopped the hobbyhorse motion that double-ended boats typically have. In fact, as comfortable as it is in the seaberth, it's almost impossible to feel that we are sailing hard-sheeted.

Our watch system is based on a four-hour rotation. To alternate the schedule so that one of us doesn't always have two night watches and the other the dreaded midnight watch, we split an afternoon watch into two two-hour stints, thus changing the rotation pattern each day. In two days, my watches are:

24-HOUR CLOCK	A.M./P.M.
1000–1400	10 A.M.–2 P.M. (lunch chef)
1600–1800	4 P.M.–6 P.M. (dinner chef)
2200–0200	10 P.M.– 2 A.M.
0600–1000	6 A.M.–10 A.M. (breakfast chef)
1400–1600	2 P.M– 4 P.M.
1800–2200	6 P.M.–10 P.M.
0200–0600	2 A.M.–6 A.M. (da capo)

To decrease the discomfort of being awakened for watch after what often feels like too little sleep, one wakes the other to give enough time to get up and dress at a pace that feels peaceful. For me, a little more than five minutes is enough, whereas Deborah prefers ten. The same routine applies when the watchkeeper needs an extra hand. But the more difficult conditions are, the more we both appreciate a little extra time and something warm to drink before going on deck. So as soon as I smell alcohol burning and understand that Deborah is preheating a burner on the kerosene stove, I realize that it must be a cold morning and soon my time to get up.

If something requiring teamwork needs to be done in the watch shift, Deborah will inform me before we go on deck. Outside, because of the wind and the fact that we often have the hoods of our jackets up, it is difficult to hear each other. Out there, she'll take charge of the work on deck and its organization, while I—still likely to be a little sleepy—will take care of everything that has to be handled from the cockpit. This morning, however, there is nothing special to be done. While I dress, Deborah just gives me the routine information about our position according to dead reckoning, which sail changes she's made during her watch, and what she thinks about the weather, and then she takes over the seaberth.

When I come up into the cockpit it's very windy. The ocean is gray. The clouds are dark and heavy, and their smooth undersides signal that the wind will continue to increase. It's a raw morning. The season is clearly turning to autumn. Even so, I feel how important it was for us to get underway. No matter how severe natural forces may be, they are predictable. They play no tricks. Out here, whether we feel good or not is up to us and us alone. For that reason and despite the weather, it's starting to feel like spring to me.

Six days in a row, we are hard-sheeted on port tack and have more wind than desired. Then it disappears. Then it puffs for a little while out of the northeast. The new wind manages to stabilize the Windex at the top of the mast, but it is not enough to fill the sails. Then a little stronger breeze picks up from the southeast, enabling us to slack the sheets for the first time during this trip. A minute after everything is trimmed properly, the wind turns to a very light easterly breeze. When it seems like it will indeed hold, we hoist the spinnaker.

When the spinnaker fills, the sail becomes a huge sound reflector, magnifying the noise around the bow. It makes it sound as if we are sailing a lot faster than our 2 to 3 knots. A few minutes later, there's a light rustling and the spinnaker collapses. But the wind doesn't disappear completely. For a little while, I manage to luff and fill the sail again. Slowly, as if it inhaled deeply, all the wrinkles disappear and the sail takes back its smooth driving shape.

But the boat never gains any real speed. It only moves fast enough for me to not lose steerage, and then the sail withers again. With hypnotic motions, the spinnaker billows back and forth until I steer up a little. There is a wave action through the sail, as if a hand were caressing each panel, and the sail lifts. Suddenly the wind shifts faster than I can respond with the rudder and disappears altogether. The sail shudders, as if it doesn't want to let go of the little wind that barely exists, but it finally glides along the furled genoa and rests there.

I have been so intent on trying to keep *Northern Light* sailing that I have not paid direct attention to a noise mixing in with all the other sounds. But now it occurs to me that there has been a whale close by. I spot it the next time it blows. When it dives, it heads straight for us.

Deborah is off watch another two hours, but even so I can't resist waking her. She would never forgive me if I didn't tell her when something exciting happens. And just as she comes out into the cockpit, the whale blows again. When it blows the third time, it's only a couple of boat lengths away. For a moment, I think that it will dive and disappear. Instead, it continues at the surface and with only a couple of yards to spare, passes our port side. The whale continues to move slowly away from us, and before we lose sight of it, it is joined by another. They blow simultaneously, dive, and are gone.

Deborah stands entranced. Her smile is radiant. It was not wrong to wake her. And even though not a word has passed between us, I believe we are thinking the same thing: we both love being in the high latitudes. I ask Deborah how she feels. Even though she still can't sit down, she answers: "I'll make it. We can stay on the northerly route." For awhile we hold each other lightly around the waist, and then she returns below to lie down again.

The wind remains light the entire day. Nevertheless, with the help of the current, we make about three knots over ground and eventually, three very sharp and dark silhouettes rise out of the sea. It's Iceland. The high mountain peaks are 60 nautical miles away. Nevertheless, in the clear, pure air they stand out dramatically against the turquoise sky in the northwest.

Around sunset we have come so close that I can see Vattnajokul, Scandinavia's largest glacier. This huge, snow-covered ice mass is relatively free from crevasses and icefalls. Apparently, it is a resting glacier. But when the sun slowly sinks behind the island and the air closest to the huge dome starts to shimmer, it suddenly looks as if the glacier is moving. The whole ice cover seems to vibrate. I shudder to think how the Vikings must have perceived such strange and inexplicable phenomena from their small boats. To explain it, perhaps they would have invented a tale about a giant who has been roused from his long sleep under the vast white blanket.

As the light fades, I daydream myself back in time, onto a graceful, high-bowed Viking ship. The warriors explain to me that it is most important that they die during an act of heroism. If they do, they will forever enjoy a joyful life in Valhalla, in the company of their equals. I say nothing to them but think to myself, *Isn't it* this *life that we should take good care of and enrich for one another?* Really, what is it that makes us happy? Positive expectations? To be able to have control over our own lives? Certainly those are two components. But I also think that people have an inner need to know someone cares for them. Imagine then, if there could be a down-to-earth creed that would encourage people to build from these inner needs an outward solidarity, fostering understanding and empathy with others around the world.

Close to midnight, where the sky and Earth meet in the north, there still remains a band of light that is on its way east toward a new day. To the south, the day disappears into night. There, in the darkness, no border between sky and sea exists. The sea mirrors the cosmos. The stars glitter in the last ripples of the day, and each time the swell rolls by, the reflections stretch to long, shiny, silvery strands, waving rhythmically in pace with the ocean's pulse.

I turn the watch over to Deborah, and before I fall asleep, I can feel how the boat slowly starts rolling back and forth. In time with the swell, Deborah furls all the sails. We always do when the wind takes a pause.

During the next watch shift, the wind comes back from southeast. We hoist the mizzen-staysail and the staysail, and the boat's speed increases. In the gusts, we make less than half a knot under the boat's theoretical maximum speed. With the mizzen-staysail up, we don't want to drive the boat harder. But we don't want less wind either—it's just right.

There's a special feeling of smooth sailing at this stage of a wind increase. Before the sea has time to build, we experience stillness and speed simultaneously. Especially now, due to the magic of twilight, it seems as if we are rushing through water far faster than the boat has the capacity to sail. It is an exhilarating beginning to a new day.

After more than forty-eight hours of favorable wind, a depression in the Denmark Strait deepens. The effect for us is gale-force wind from the southwest: a headwind. Being on a beat in open ocean is never enjoyable. Nonetheless, it feels good to finally be able to take the bull by the horns. After all, this leg is meant to be a test. Now it looks as if we'll get the weather we need to ferret out any weaknesses in the new systems.

Using a laptop computer linked to a short-wave radio, we can get weather-fax charts. Each day we take in a weather synopsis and a seventy-two-hour prognosis. This is the first time we have such an aid on board. During earlier passages, we have mainly made our own observations and judgments and sporadically received WWV, an American radio station that broadcasts information of interest to mariners, including a North Atlantic weather prognosis and forecast. WWV gives the information in a useful format: the position of each depression's center, the speed and direction it's moving, and the wind speed it packs.

So far, we have been spared really bad weather. But according to the latest prognosis, it seems that the coming depression heralds an unusually windy period for this time of the year. The center goes north of us. We respond by putting the boat on port tack in the southwesterly wind that comes with the warm front. It gives us the best height toward the entrance of Belle Isle Strait. The idea is to remain on this tack until we meet the cold front, and as soon as the wind shifts to west, or, we hope, northwest, tack. If the wind then backs toward south, we will tack again. The tactics are simple. But the farther south we go, the longer and darker the nights become. In addition, it is getting a lot colder. Each passing day we use up more of our almost depleted physical and mental reserves.

Day after day we keep a lookout through the cupola. To be out in the cockpit would be meaningless. The saltwater spray flying continuously over deck stings and makes our eyes ache. And especially in the afternoon if the sun breaks through, it's better to remain inside the boat, where it's dry. There, we can wear sunglasses to block out some of the strong light, and maintain a perfect lookout, regardless of sun or wind or spray.

Before the largest waves collapse, the foam is suspended for a few seconds in front of them, generating 20- to 30-yard-long turquoise tunnels. With the light against us, the upper part of the wave looks like crystal. I can see right through it until the wave collapses with a rolling, thundering accompaniment.

As the wind increases, I am reminded of one challenge of this voyage: to sail effectively without ever changing sails. Formerly, we changed headsails every time the wind increased or diminished; it was the way we kept headsail size matched to wind strength. Once, during a twenty-four hour period, we had to alter sail combinations not less than sixteen times. Without doubt, changing foresails is the most tiring work on board, which is why we now have a foresail we can reef just by rolling it in.

But the system is not yet fully refined. To reef and unreef the genoa (as well as the main and mizzen, for that matter) is no problem. But to keep the genoa's sheeting point correct, the block on the lee rail has to be moved each time we change the size of the sail; this principle holds true for every boat. As soon as we reef in a yard of the sail, we have to move the block forward approximately half a yard (45 cm). And because we don't want the sail to flog while we are moving the block, we use a taut-line, a line temporarily employed to take the load of the released sheet.

First the line has to be wrapped a turn around the free genoa winch on the windward side. Then it is led down to the lee staysail winch, which now acts as a turning block, and from there through an extra block placed specially for it just aft of the genoa sheet block. Working on the lee deck, it is typical to be up to one's knees in water rushing past at 6 to 7 knots. At this point, I consider myself lucky if I still have dry socks in both boots. And because any shirt or sweater would probably already be wet far above the elbows, I usually wear just a T-shirt under my foul weather gear for this job, however cold it may be. It's the only way to avoid generating too much wet clothing and therefore dampness inside the boat on long passages.

Once the taut-line is in position, we work our way back up into the cockpit and crank the line in until it takes over all the load from the genoa sheet. Then we work our way down to the lee deck again. Passing by the genoa winch, we ease the sheet a couple of feet to generate slack in it. Once down in the rushing water again, we move the genoa block to its new position. That accomplished, we work our way back up to the cockpit and winch in the slack on the genoa sheet until it once again bears the load. Then we have to step down on the lee side for the third time to release the taut-line so that we can coil and hang it back in its storage place, jammed between the handrail and the compass.

During this entire procedure, we are wearing safety harnesses and are attached to the boat with a line. As a general rule, that tether gets wound around some winch in the cockpit so that we can't quite reach our destination. Then, we have to turn around, work our way back again to loosen it, and then return to the rushing water on the lee side. One can both love and hate a tether.

In the beginning, we thought that we should be able to leave the taut-line attached to the genoa sheet so it would be ever ready. But we gave that thought up as soon as we realized what it could lead to. If for any reason we would be forced to tack and not have the time to free the line from the sheet, the line could, when the sail is flogging during the tack, all too easily get wrapped around a stay or some piece of deck gear. That would make it impossible to sheet in the sail on the new tack quickly. If the tack is forced on us by another boat that suddenly makes an unexpected move—which fishing boats often do—the situation could be critical. We decided to forget shortcuts and always keep things shipshape. After all, it only means a little extra work. "It's still better than stealing hubcaps," Deborah has been heard to remark when conditions have been at their worst.

The weather is more like what could be expected in October. During the past week, we have experienced three depressions, each of which gave us winds of 47 to 58 knots in the gusts. Even so, day after day, we manage to drive *Northern Light* against the wind faster than anticipated. We are logging 145 to 160 nautical miles per day, and in the last week we have made good more than 700 miles to the next waypoint. Sooner than anticipated, on September 6, we pass Cape Farewell.

The sea is enormous. The average wave rolling under us is 20 feet high (6m) and the odd one as much as thirty. It doesn't help that *Northern Light* is a long-keeled, seaworthy boat. Unavoidably, she sometimes sets hard in seas like this. After seeming to hang suspended in air for a few seconds, she falls into a valley.

Suddenly the boat takes a real pounding. I can't remember ever hearing a more deafening boom. The severity of the crash makes me believe that *Northern Light* could have sprung a leak. I trust the hull's strength, but still. . . . Only after lifting the floorboards and seeing that the bilge is dry can I calm down again.

The next day, I see just how heavily the boat had indeed set in that sea. The impossible has happened. Upon impact, the hull had flexed so much that the saltwater intake, a steel pipe in the head, shattered the sink. The plastic shards lie spread around as if the sink had been smashed by a sledgehammer. Piece by piece I pick them up. Obviously there should be a larger distance between the pipe and the sink. I work my way back to the navigation desk to add another item to the work list.

Later that day, WWV reports that a tropical disturbance has deepened in the vicinity of Haiti. We have about one more week to go to Belle Isle, and according to the prediction, the area of bad weather will move in a northeasterly direction. If WWV is right, it will never come close to us. Nonetheless, we start to plot the storm center's position.

That we have chosen not to pass over the Grand Banks isn't just due to the gathering of icebergs there. There is also fog around the banks an average of twelve days per month. To be hit by a real storm in such a region would be unforgivable. That's why we decided to go through Belle Isle Strait and west of Newfoundland instead. Even so, we have to cross a narrow iceberg-risk zone approaching Belle Isle. If we arrive there at night, we'll have to heave to until daylight.

Once a day we plot the storm center's position. When we have two days to go to Belle Isle, WWV reports that the storm has developed into a hurricane named Gabrielle. They still maintain that the direction of the hurricane's movement is to the northeast, but the longitude in the position report has yet to change. Both can't be true. Unfortunately, since we are unable to pull in any weatherfax station covering the area, we have no way to check whether or not the positions in the WWV reports are correct.

Had we been able to leave as planned at the end of June, we would have made this crossing in the very beginning of the hurricane season, when hurricanes usually disappear into the Gulf of Mexico. Not before this time of year do they start to move north along the American east coast. Typically, in an early stage, they "should" disappear out into the Atlantic Ocean, just as WWV is predicting for Gabrielle. For that reason we were not too worried when we left behind schedule. Still, all the calculated statistical probabilities don't change the facts.

We start to plot the position of the eye of the hurricane four times per day. The more time that passes, the more worrisome is WWV's contradictory information. Gabrielle is all we talk about. Every hour brings the hurricane that much closer. At present courses and speeds, we will meet Gabrielle the day before we get to Belle Isle Strait. Obviously, we have to do something; if Gabrielle is stubborn, we can't be. We reckon that our only possibility of avoiding it will be to turn northwest or maybe even due north. Eventually, we mark a checkpoint on the chart to indicate our turning point.

When we have twelve hours left to the checkpoint, it seems as if Gabrielle is still heading due north. I can't keep quiet any longer. "It is absolutely unbelievable that WWV doesn't realize their error yet. They have updated the position every four hours. The track has been due north, yet they say that the hurricane is heading northeast and out into the Atlantic. Which is it?"

When we have only six hours left, we get a new report. There's still no deviation to the east in the position report. Now it's Deborah's turn to get angry. "Talk about being between a rock and a hard place! If Gabrielle is on its way here, we should turn north to be on the safe side, but we don't want to end up far north of Belle Isle where it's jammed with icebergs for no reason." She shakes her head.

For some hours, the wind slowly shifts toward southerly and seems to be dying out. That's a bad sign. I don't want to miss the next weather report, but I can't see the clock. Instead of getting up to look, I ask Deborah—who is in a better position—to check the time.

After a long silence, I learn that I must have listened to ABBA too much. I understand nothing. What does my question have to do with a pop group? Finally it dawns on me: Deborah never likes it when the same lyrics are repeated five or six times in a space of three minutes. I stand up and walk to the clock. It is still a whole hour until the next transmission. Every minute seems to last an eternity.

Finally, a new report is broadcast. The radio reception is not the greatest, but we manage to interpret the most important parts. Gabrielle is losing her hurricane status, degenerating into a storm with frontal systems. But the wind has not decreased much yet. Three hundred nautical miles from its center it's blowing 62 knots. And the southwest sector is worst. There WWV warns of gusts reaching 95 knots.

There are some exciting minutes before we've plotted the storm's precise position. We are a mere 400 nautical miles north-northeast of Gabrielle. And what irony! When the position report finally does indicate that the hurricane really has started to veer off to the northeast, we can no longer escape. Gabrielle has totally killed the airstream. The boat just rolls in what's left of the old sea. All we can do now is to wait and hope that WWV is indeed correct. If so, the wind will gradually increase from southeast and then change to northeast and we will be fine. For the moment, we cross our fingers and hope that it will remain calm through the night. We are already into the iceberg-risk area. Just eight hours to go.

Around daybreak, the wind picks up, as expected. With one reef in the main, one in the mizzen, full genoa, and slack in the sheets, we fly past the Belle Isle lighthouse around noon. The Atlantic Ocean lies behind us. The stretch from Norway to Canada has taken twenty-two days instead of an estimated thirty. The boat seems to join our celebration. The rigging whistles and the hull hums whenever *Northern Light* rushes faster than the waves. All day long Deborah and I sit on deck and enjoy watching the tundralike and sometimes lightly forested hills rushing by.

Only two to three days from Boston, a depression to the west of us deepens faster than any other during the whole trip. Hard-sheeted, with a barometer that's been falling 3 millibars per hour but has started to flatten out, we are on port tack toward Nova Scotia's coast. The wind is southwesterly, and during the last two hours, it has gradually increased to 30 knots, gusting up to 44. Rain pours down. The visibility is occasionally below 100 yards.

Approximately 7 nautical miles from land, we decide to tack. During the tack I have no time to look at the compass, but when we have all the sails sheeted properly and I check the course, it shows that we are sailing in exactly the same direction as before. My immediate assumption is that the compass must have jammed. The sea is breaking from every possible direction, so from looking at it, it is impossible to determine if we changed course or not. It takes many seconds before I realize that we tacked just as the wind changed a quarter circle in the other direction. As I turn the wheel and ease the sheets, the wind continues to change. As it passes through northwest, the sky clears.

Suddenly the wind is northerly. To keep the boat on course, we have to slacken all the sails fully. The sea is still breaking violently from the earlier wind direction. Each time the boat sails into a wave, it almost comes to a dead stop. That puts tremendous strain on the boat and rigging. To lessen the stress on all the equipment, we have to slow down. Deborah starts to furl the mizzen while I take care of the genoa. But our speed doesn't diminish. The wind has increased to the point that it is blowing the tops off the waves, and it continues increasing faster than we manage to reef. It doesn't help that we only have a fleck of the genoa left and no mizzen; *Northern Light* still sails herself at full speed straight into the breakers. To put the brakes on, we furl everything but the staysail. Even so, we sail with such force into a green breaker that the whole foredeck gets buried under water. Deborah sees it coming, calls out a warning, and dashes down the companionway into the boat. I happen to be on the aft deck. To make the boat balance better in the increased wind, I am in the process of moving a link on the chain that connects the windvane's lines to the tiller. That far aft I escape the worst of it.

Just before the boat jams into the next breaking sea, I also manage to make it down inside the boat. As I am cleating the cupola shut, a roaring mass of water blocks out all the light from outside. Everything around us is in complete chaos, and I feel the blood rush from my face. It's a terrible thought, but had we not made it below, I'm sure that at least one of us would have been washed overboard. Right now, we could have been out there, somewhere.

It takes almost an hour before the old sea dies and the wave action resembles what it should, considering the present wind speed and direction. During the night, the wind slowly decreases. We finally manage to receive a new weatherfax station and can follow the depression's further development. It deepens even more until it reaches its deepest pressure of 955 millibars. It's become the first real fall storm in the North Atlantic. We were lucky to have slid in under the wire. Considering that, our crossing suddenly seems quite uneventful.

Twenty-nine days and twenty-one hours after leaving Norway, we sail into Gloucester, a fishing harbor north of Boston. Via amateur radio Deborah has stayed in touch with our friend Andy, and in the dark of the night, we see how he blinks "welcome" with the headlights of his jeep. His parents, Gerry and Frank, are waiting for us at their home. We look forward to many pleasant hours in front of their fireplace. There's nothing more wonderful than the feeling of sailing to a place where one has friends. And certainly they must have a lot to tell us; it's been more than a year since we last saw each other.

People have asked us many times if we miss friends when we're sailing. I wonder if they really mean *miss*. How can I miss something I actually have? Probably they mean long for. Yes, I can long for friends, but I don't think that's bad or painful. That type of yearning is due to an appreciation for someone or something and is a catalyst for feeling thankful. Ashore, on the other hand, where it appears as though everything is available all the time, I often miss the feeling of longing.

3

GOOD
LUCK

ROLF

■ ■ ■

Our friendship with Andy's family, the Morrisons, actually goes back more than 200 years. More precisely, to the early part of 1790. For in January of that year, Fletcher Christian and the other mutineers set fire to their ship at Pitcairn Island, off a little indentation in the coastline that ever since has been known as Bounty Bay.

Somewhat later, in 1935 to be exact, Andy's great-uncle Charles Nordhoff and coauthor James Norman Hall published their trilogy *Mutiny on the Bounty*. The series sparked the Morrison family's interest in Pitcairn. Then, in 1980, after she returned from visiting that isolated spit of land in the South Pacific and wanted to find a way to stay in touch with the fifty-two people who lived there, Deborah was introduced to Andy. He was an amateur radio operator and had for many years been in contact with Tom Christian (Fletcher's great-great-great-great grandson). But we consider the historical flames two hundred years earlier to be the origin of our friendship.

Andy inspired Deborah to learn Morse code and get her amateur license so that we could communicate with him from *Northern Light*. He also designed our antenna, a wire rising almost vertically from the aft deck to connect to another wire that stretches between the highest points on each mast. Seen from the side the antenna looks like a big T.

To make the antenna's passage through deck absolutely watertight and also to improve its ground, Andy has just made a new "magic box." While installing it, he explains the importance of running coaxial cable all the way from the radio to the box on deck. There, the coaxial cable's center lead is to be attached to the antenna and its shield to ground; in our case, that's to the outside of the steel hull. Andy explains: "If you were to run an unshielded antenna straight out of the radio, the transmitted radio waves would radiate *inside* the boat. That can adversely affect the performance of your radio as well as other electronic instruments."

Andy has brought his good friend Bob Flumere aboard. Bob's an amateur radio operator too, but the first thing I notice about him is that his hands are very large. To me, they reveal that he works outdoors. When I ask what he does for a living, he tells me that he keeps parks and gardens in trim. Mostly, his job consists of cutting down trees.

Although he's not a sailor, Bob seems interested in the boat, so while Andy and I straighten up after the black box's installation, I let him look around. On and off, he shouts out questions that I answer. I hear when he opens the cover to our old Perkins diesel engine, and I expect he'll have some questions about it too. Instead, Bob's absolutely quiet for a few seconds. Then, as if he just discovered a corpse in the engine room, he roars: "LUUUCAS ... ?! Are you absolutely insane? Andy has told me that you hope to go as far as Antarctica. How about I fix this for you?"

It comes as a total surprise that someone who, as he put it, "messes around with trees" should offer to fix a marine electric system. In jest, I give my consent. After all, Bob knows we're leaving tomorrow and it's already five o'clock in the afternoon, so he couldn't possibly think it worth starting a project like that now.

But Bob turns to. And even though I don't have any wiring diagram that shows the factory-mounted electric installation on the engine itself, Bob figures to improve the charging capacity. I try to dissuade him by explaining that we don't use all that much electricity ... , but of course, he already knows that. His half-smile and knitted brow as good as says, How could you, when the generator hardly charges?

"Lucas!" Bob bellows again in disbelief and hits himself on the forehead. "Why do you think we started the War of Independence with the Brits?" Clearly, Bob is not the "forgive and forget" type. I sure don't want to tramp on his toes. When my gaze fastens on his huge hands again, I don't even dare ask if he really knows anything at all about electricity. Bob tells me to join him in the engine room. He points to one cable after another. Any cable I can't defend within two seconds—by telling him what it's good for—is cut away.

I have never seen Bob before today, and now I really worry that it was a mistake to even let him have a look at the engine. I call a stop to the process and explain to Bob that just because I don't know exactly what function each cable has doesn't mean it should be clipped. But he is perfectly untouched by my comments. "You shouldn't have things on board if you don't know what they're good for," he says with a reproachful tone and continues trimming. His implication that I should know more about the engine is something I've long been painfully aware of.

I've always managed to repair problems that have developed during our voyages; it's not like I'm totally unknowledgeable. But now I really feel left out. Our entire future rests in Bob's hands. If we have to hire someone to repair this mess, it'll cost a fortune. Regardless, we'll never be underway tomorrow, that's for sure. Deborah and I are about to be delayed again, this time by an overly enthusiastic fixer who is just now in the process of doing us a devastating disservice.

On top of everything, Deborah pokes her head into the engine room and invites Bob to join us for dinner. Inside, I wonder what possesses her, but I keep my feelings to myself. Dinner is to be pasta with a sauce she calls garlic con carne. As we have neither garlic nor meat on board, she tells us she's leaving now. But I can't stand watching this operation any longer, so I volunteer to do the shopping. Bob accompanies me ashore, and I can't even speak to him.

We part company at his car, where he picks up some gear he needs to "finish" the job. The store's quite a hike away, and I'm gone almost an hour. As soon as I come back, Bob wants me to start the engine. I can see that he's been working hard. Not only is his face sweaty, but there are wires strewn all over the place. The best I can come up with to gain a stay of execution is to suggest lamely, "Maybe we should wait until you have everything in order." But Bob insists. And when I turn the start key and the engine turns over, the meter jumps right up to 14.3 volts. I can't believe my eyes! It's never charged that much before! I look into the engine room. The number of cables has been reduced to a mere fraction of what they were. And when I ask Bob how it's possible that the system even functions with so few cables, his only answer is nonchalant: "That's exactly why it *does* work," he says. I don't bother with further questions.

We eat a colossal dinner together. Bob eats more than anyone, but then he excuses himself to meet his girlfriend. And all he wants as thanks for the work he did is another spaghetti dinner someday and, if possible, a postcard with some penguins on it.

After Bob has left, I ask Andy how he could be so sure that a "fixer" like Bob could manage to solve the problem we had with the alternator. Andy just laughs and says that Bob's a pro! Apparently, my expression reveals a question mark, because Andy continues and tells us, "For many years Bob taught auto mechanics in a technical school. He changed jobs to be able to be outdoors. When he heard about your electrical problems, he thought it'd be fun to help you out. And as you now know, Bob is a joker. He *meant* to confuse you a bit."

During the evening we continue to talk about what it means to be a professional. I like Andy's definition: a person who does a job well is a pro, whether or not the job is a means of earning a living. And, conversely, someone who does a lousy job is an amateur, even if it is his or her profession.

Andy doesn't have to rush away. He's taken a couple of weeks off from work to join us on our way south, and during that time he plans to help us install a VHF radio. We have never had one on board before. Andy is as curious as we are to see how the unit will function.

With the wind blowing out of the northwest at 21 to 25 knots, the broad reach to the Cape Cod Canal is a wet but fast sail. We continue to Onset Bay, where we drop the hook for the night. The next day we reach Cuttyhunk, where all three of us vote in favor of taking the next day off to go ashore and stretch our legs.

Andy is interested in the new masts, and because it has been difficult to explain everything in detail while sailing, I do so before we go on our walk. First, we look at the furling mechanisms. Andy is duly impressed by the engineering. Then, as I explain how the masts are stayed, Andy tests the tension on the mizzen shrouds by pulling on one after another. Suddenly, I see a small glint just above a swage fitting. My first thought is that the shine must be a reflection from a salt crystal. Indeed, I have previously discovered broken strands in shrouds by investigating the cause of a little reflection or color change, just where the wire enters the swage. But these shrouds are brand new. Nothing can be wrong with them. Nonetheless, a cold sweat breaks out on my forehead.

Andy, Deborah, and I check each and every shroud and stay. Three of the mizzen shrouds are about to break. Altogether, eight strands in the 1×19 wires have snapped. For a time I refuse to believe my eyes. We have been underway only a little more than a month and sailed this rigging a mere 4,500 miles. The mainmast's stays and shrouds are intact, but for how long? The discovery and consequences of the broken strands are overwhelming.

To make things worse, the American east coast has already had an exceptionally early outbreak of cold air from Canada that brought freezing temperatures. During one single night some Floridian growers lost 85 percent of all their citrus fruits and their entire tomato crop. If we are now forced to stay north of Chesapeake Bay to replace all the shrouds, we may not get further this year. Thoughts, options, and plans swirl in my head.

Via the newly installed VHF radio, we place a telephone call to Seldén Mast in Sweden. They are upset by the news. They decide to airfreight new mizzen shrouds immediately and insist on replacing even those that have not as yet shown any weakness. I don't have to send measurements; they have all the specs in their computer. Because it will take about ten days for the shrouds to arrive, I ask that they be sent to Annapolis, 250 miles farther south. "We'll stop in Newport to replace the three shrouds that have broken strands and then continue there to pick the new set up," I tell them.

During the call I can feel the knot in my chest ease. Through the way the people at Seldén act, I get proof that some businesses that stand behind their products and really help their customers—some businesses built of individuals like Bob and Andy—do actually exist.

But when I hang up, the truth of the situation creeps back up on me. I remember the last words said. Seldén believes that there must have been a production error in the stainless wire. As they explained to me: When the individual strands of wire are manufactured, they must be heated red hot at fixed intervals; otherwise, the wire becomes brittle. Most likely something went wrong at that stage.

I was also told that, unfortunately, there is no guarantee the new shrouds they send will be any better. The truth is that no one can determine if a wire has been produced properly, not even with ultrasound or X-ray examinations. One must trust the producer. In that respect, Seldén is as pushed against the wall as we are. They will start an investigation immediately, but it can take months before any answer is available. All they can do to help us now is to use wire from a different roll and hope for the best.

After I finish relating all the information to Deborah, we just look at each other. We soon agree that to be safe, we'll have to test sail again, back across the Atlantic toward Europe. We see no alternative. But how much farther we must then sail before discovering any other hidden problems is unknown. There is no way to see into the future. The concern that either of the masts may suddenly collapse is something we will have to live with. Our lifestyle, and indeed our lives, lie in the balance.

The mere idea of putting out for sea trials again gives me pause about other new gear. I consider the keel bolts, for example, that hold the delta-winged keel's total weight of 5,720 pounds (2,600 kg): do they have the promised quality? Spontaneously, I start to tell Andy about some of the problems we've had with gear bought for this voyage.

First comes the story about the keel that I knew would not be easy to form in steel. The welder therefore agreed to give me a buzz after each phase of the production so that I could inspect and approve each stage, but he didn't. Instead, when I called him one day to hear if he had started yet, his response was that he was just about to call me. The keel was already finished!

When we got to his workshop, we learned why he'd worked so fast. The following day, his taxes were due, and he was short of money. Because the balance we owed him would bring him back into the black, he had decided to finish the keel in "record time." The first time we showed him the drawings and questioned if he would be able to build it, his immediate answer was: "No problem! I will fix this." But not until we saw the worthless twisted result he called a keel did we understand that what he'd been looking forward to fixing most were his finances. Although he didn't have the skill necessary to build the keel, he had accepted the job. That he had an obligation to keep his promise and live up to our expectations was of no concern; he only wanted the money.

The three newly installed Italian skylights leak so terribly that Deborah wondered if the word for skylight in Italian might also mean sieve. In the galley, the nonstop drips fall mostly into the sink. It's worse in the aft cabin, however, where the new cushions she upholstered have been repeatedly soaked with salt water. The presence of salt means the cushions will never dry out completely. And the resulting dampness has already affected the new varnish; it's yellowing and will soon start to flake off.

We noticed recently that the nickel-plated brass screws we used to fasten the ceiling throughout the boat have started to corrode! When we tested the leftover screws with a magnet a few days ago, we found that about 10 percent of the screws in the box were nickel-plated iron, not brass.

The first time we used the oven in our new kerosene stove, we found out that the glue in the insulation wasn't heat resistant enough. We had to tear out the blackened mess and reinsulate it ourselves.

The 14 mm ropes we bought were a bluff. They were "puffed up" on the reels in the store to make customers believe they were buying the dimension listed. But as soon as the sheet came under load, the ropes shrank to only 11 mm. Most winches today are self-tailing, and that mechanism works only on the proper diameter of rope. The consequence? Sheets slid in the self-tailing "jaws." That neither Deborah nor I was hurt was pure luck. Had there been a standard stipulating that the diameter marked on the reel must equal the diameter when the sheet is put under a load equal to 50 percent of its breaking strength, such a swindle would never have been possible, but sadly, no such standard exists.

The fluxgate compass we bought a few years ago was supposedly manufactured specifically for high-latitude sailing—where, close to the magnetic pole, an ordinary magnetic compass is unreliable—but we quickly realized that as soon as the temperature fell below 46°F (8°C), the unit got the shivers. The compass needle started to swing frenetically, more than 40 degrees in either direction. It was completely useless in the cold. Fortunately, we discovered the compass's problem as we were swinging it and had the time to request the lowest operational temperature and other particulars. The manufacturer eventually admitted that the compass had been designed, built, and tested indoors and they hadn't considered that it tends to be cold in the polar regions.

The second time I turned on the new fluorescent light in the galley the switch broke off; it had only been melted into place. I couldn't repair it; it could not be mounted with screws. In my naiveté, I thought the switch had broken because of error or sloppiness in the assembly. Fortunately, we had one more reserve fixture, which I put in place. But the first time I switched it on, the switch came loose on that one, too. Where the fixture itself was manufactured is a mystery. There was no name on it, no one to take responsibility for the poorly manufactured product. For the time being, we taped the switch to the fixture.

The day before we left Fiskebäckskil, we cleaned up our work areas in the marina. In the process, I found a piece of plywood on the ground beside the garbage container. I recognized the plywood by its shape and understood that it must have ended up there three weeks earlier while we were building the seat into our new cockpit. The plywood was damp from the last rain, and when I picked it up, I saw that it was delaminating. The sheet of "marine plywood"— supposedly waterproof—couldn't take the outdoor climate. We'd been sold falsely labeled indoor-quality plywood. The grayish piece of wood screamed its message in my face: The new cockpit can't take water, can't take water, can't take water.

Who is responsible for mislabeling the plywood is unknown. It could be the manufacturer, the importer, or the distributor. What we do know is that someone has directed a staggering blow to our project, not to mention our lives. If, in the Antarctic Ocean, the boat is taken by a wave and rolls 360 degrees or is flipped end over end, a hatch or porthole could very well break. As water rushes in, tremendous pressure builds inside the boat. If the cockpit plywood is already weakened by delamination, the cockpit benches could pop loose, and there we will be, with a gaping hole in the boat.

We had neither the time nor strength to build the cockpit over again before we left. We had no choice but to leave Sweden with the hope that the teak dressing on the plywood would protect it enough to prevent the layers from separating—for a while, at least. And some day, before it's too late, we hope to be able to rip it all out and do it again. Until then, we have to live with the worry.

I decide not to bother Andy with the myriad other petty things, because the more I tell him, the more bitter I feel. It seems as if nothing, no matter what it costs, can be trusted today. Andy doesn't say anything. We just stand there, looking at each other.

A couple of days later, when we reach New York City, Andy has to leave us. As usual, we get big hugs and good wishes. But halfway to shore on the long dock, Andy turns and calls out "good luck" before disappearing. Deborah turns to me and wonders if I also thought the tone of Andy's voice made his wish sound like a sad commentary.

After we install the new shrouds in Annapolis, Deborah and I start to discuss our next step. Because the winter storms don't lose their punch until April and it would not be wise to head out into them with wire that we already know *not* to trust, we decide to change our plans. We'll take the Intracoastal Waterway to Florida and winter there. Doing so will give us a chance to see a lot more of the American east coast. It also gives us a chance to spend some more time with people we like and, we hope, to think about more than just our problems.

The morning of December 4, the temperature in the northwesterly wind sinks to 14°F (−10°C). Until late afternoon the deck is as slippery as a newly watered ice-skating rink, and the icicles on the windward lifelines grow into longer and longer spikes. When the bow slices the water, the resulting spray turns into a haze; to leeward, the sea looks like it's steaming. From that, water particles are sucked up onto the lee side of the genoa, freezing to the sail so it becomes covered with a thin layer of ice. Sometimes when the boat sets a little harder than usual, the whole sheet of ice comes loose, creating amazing visuals as it splinters into frozen rainbows glimmering in the light.

Passing the Alligator River bridge, the wind shifts a little more to the north. I ease the mizzen and Deborah also turns aft to take up the slack on the preventer. Astern we both see something very bizarre. . . .

4

AHHH, CRUISING

DEBORAH

■ ■ ■

Fire streaking across the sky pulls our eyes away from the mizzen and rivets our attention. My spine tingles. I think out loud: "What's that? A flare? Nyah, it's moving horizontally." Rolf, saying nothing, watches it moving westward. Whatever it is, the ball of flame is only a few miles away and about 1,300 feet (400 m) above ground.

Suddenly, it changes course and heads straight at us. Rolf requests the binoculars. As I pass them, I tell him that I'm getting a camera. It's difficult to break my gaze, but I dive below. Rolf reports that the fireball is finally turning. When it crosses our wake, it's on a course opposite its original path.

"It's probably a plane," he tells me. I shoot the first frame. With a little uncertainty in his voice he says: "Someone has ejected. Yes, true! A parachute is opening."

I see no chute through the camera's 70 mm lens and ask where it is in relation to the flame. "At the tail end of the smoke," he answers. I see the entire smoke trail in the frame and continue shooting, figuring that I'll get to see the chute when the pictures are printed.

Rolf declares hoarsely: "Another has ejected! His chute is opening. And the first one will land in the water."

I keep expecting to see the fireball explode, but it doesn't. The plane crashes on the island to the east of Alligator River.

"I'll radio for help," I tell Rolf, and he responds: "Fine. I'll watch where the parachutes land." On channel 16 I say, "Coast Guard, this is sailboat *Northern Light*."

Immediately comes the reply: "*Northern Light*, this is Coast Guard Station Coinjock. Can you switch to channel 22?"

My knees start shaking. "Switching 22," I respond.

On channel 22 I hear: "*Northern Light*, this is Coast Guard Station Coinjock. Go ahead."

"Coinjock, *Northern Light*. We have just seen an airborne plane in flames and before it crashed, two people ejected. Their parachutes have opened, but they have not landed yet."

"Coast Guard Station Coinjock. Roger, *Northern Light*, what is your position?"

"We are southbound in the Alligator River, south of the bridge and have just passed marker number 24. The plane was approximately"—I turn to Rolf and raise my eyebrows questioningly, and he extends three fingers—"three miles north of us and . . . "

I pause. A powerboat is approaching us fast from astern. "Standby Coast Guard, I want to contact a powerboat about to overtake us. We'll send it to the scene. It can move faster and leave the dredged channel if necessary."

Rolf is waving at the boat, circling his hands overhead. In international sign language that gesture means "come here." The boat makes a drastic turn toward us and simultaneously comes up on channel 22!

"*Northern Light*, this is motorboat *Mary Ann*. We did not see the plane or chutes. What heading do we take to get to them?"

I reply: "They are on this side of the bridge, east of the channel . . . " Rolf has unfolded the previous page of the chartbook, which is whipping around in the breeze, and points to the relevant information, which I relay "around marker number 18. Head toward the most distant peninsula you see on the eastern side of the river."

Starting into a 180-degree turn, the helmsman guns it, and by the time he's on course, the boat is up on a full plane. I return to the Coast Guard. Coinjock asks for positions: ours, the motorboat's, the plane's, and the chutes'. It's a struggle to find longitude and latitude figures on the chart segments; we are navigating from a waterway chartbook where each chart is made from the appropriate segments taken from "real" charts, and the information is frustratingly difficult to find. With that finally accomplished, the Coast Guard asks for descriptions of the boats, how many there are on board, and a description of the plane.

"*Northern Light* is a red two-masted sailboat, two aboard. *Mary Ann* is a white cabin cruiser, I don't know how many aboard. The plane was engulfed in flames. We don't have any idea what type it was. The plane has crashed on the island that borders Alligator River to the east, but the island has no name on our chart. We saw two people eject and two chutes open. One person definitely landed in the water, but we aren't sure about the other. He disappeared beyond our visible horizon before landing."

The Coast Guard then calls *Mary Ann,* and I hear him answer, but Coinjock doesn't. *Mary Ann* comes back to me. "*Northern Light,* will you relay for me? And am I on the correct heading?" We tell him that he needs to change course a bit more toward the dredged channel.

I relay to the Coast Guard that there are two people aboard *Mary Ann.* Coinjock tells us that it is a civilian plane that has gone down. How he knows and why he says so is a mystery to me. Rolf worries aloud; civilians most likely won't be wearing survival suits, and the water temperature is approximately 45°F (7°C). Our understanding of hypothermia suggests that the people have a 50 percent chance of survival if they are wearing some kind of flotation device, know that they should assume a fetal position to conserve body heat, and are rescued within 55 minutes. This had better go fast and without a hitch.

Coast Guard Group Cape Hatteras now joins the fray, and we repeat most of the information to them, including *Mary Ann*'s approximate present position. I continuously scan the sky, hoping that a helicopter that passed us southbound some fifteen minutes before the crash will reappear.

Mary Ann comes up again and asks: "*Northern Light,* how's my heading now? Hang on! I see a smoke flare less than a mile off my port bow. Standby." I relay the news to the Coast Guard.

The chopper's unmistakable pulsating sound reaches our ears. "*Northern Light,* this is Coast Guard Helicopter 1489. How copy?"

"Fine, go ahead," I reply, figuring that as the only female voice in the group I can save time by not identifying myself with each transmission.

"*Northern Light,* this is Coast Guard Helicopter 1489. We see smoke off our starboard bow. Do we head there to search?"

"Negative," I respond. "That smoke is from the crashed plane. The two chutes landed off your port bow. Look for a white cabin cruiser. He has spotted a smoke flare in the water and is proceeding toward it. The other person may have landed in the water, or on shore nearby." The chopper veers off.

"This is *Mary Ann.* We have picked up the pilot. He is near shock, shivering badly, has lost feeling in his arms and legs, but is otherwise all right. He says that his navigator also landed in the water."

The chopper answers: "This is Coast Guard Helicopter 1489. We see the other man. We will pick him up. Stand by, *Mary Ann.*"

Coinjock asks me to confirm that there were only two people on the plane. I can't. I tell him I can only confirm that we saw two people eject and two chutes. Coinjock politely prompts me to ask *Mary Ann* to ask the man they picked up. Indeed, we find out that there *were* only two aboard the Navy A-6.

Aboard *Mary Ann,* they warm up the pilot. He strips out of his wet flight suit, chiding himself for not having worn a survival suit on a run that included flight over water. They wrap him in blankets and give him hot tea, but he is still shivering wildly. Yet they can do no more for him. Trying to warm him up quickly—by putting him into a warm bath or shower, for example—without being able to determine that his body's core temperature is indeed above the critical 95°F (35°C) could be life threatening. A hypothermic person's body stops circulating blood to the extremities so as to retain heat at the core organs. Warming the skin tricks the body into resuming that circulation and cools the blood, transporting killing cold to the core.

With our naked eyes we can see the spray of water churned up by the helicopter as it drops down to pick up the other man. We wait and wait. Finally, the helicopter reports that they have the navigator on board. He is mildly hypothermic and has injured one hand, but will be fine. Both men are accounted for, thirty-five minutes after ejecting. Rolf and I heave great sighs of relief.

There's no way around it. Our lifestyle makes it tough to maintain a normal social life. Both Rolf and I keep in touch with our families via letters, but we don't get much time with them. Now, however, because we have delayed the departure for the Southern Hemisphere, we can. Taking advantage of a northerly breeze, we go offshore to the Florida Keys, and then up the west coast of Florida as quickly as possible to my folks' place.

Ah, winter in the sun. The relaxed lifestyle will be jolly good for us. Thankfully, Florida's west coast isn't too commercialized, yet we find nearly everything we need within bicycling distance. Hardware store, lumber yard, and upholstery shop are all handy, aiding the completion of the work not finished in Sweden as well as a refurbishing of the aft cabin and touch-up painting on deck.

Rolf decides to have an expert check our fifteen-year-old engine. When the serviceman comes aboard, Rolf explains that we will soon be cruising in areas where we will have no possibility of getting to a workshop or anyplace to buy parts. We want the engine checked thoroughly, then we will listen to his recommendations.

The man is curious just where it is we are going. When Rolf tells him the plan is Antarctica, his eyes light up. "Aha. I understand what you mean. I spent my first years as a diesel mechanic in the Navy stationed in the Antarctic, at McMurdo. The less that goes wrong on The Ice, the better." Seems like lady luck is with us this time.

The first, obvious problem is a leaky saltwater pump, which we couldn't repair on board. But the repairman also decides that the injectors need an overhaul and sends them off to a specialist. When he reinstalls them, the engine sounds great. He listens and listens. No, one injector is not quite right. Off it goes again. Indeed, there *was* something stuck in it and it therefore did not close properly. When the serviceman finishes, a very satisfied Rolf compliments him: "Best trim it's ever had, better even than when it was new! That typical harsh, knocking, diesel engine sound is gone." True, the old Perkins purrs.

The only thing we can't find in shopper's paradise is the highly refined kerosene we usually use in our galley stove. It is important that kerosene for Primus burners has a lot of oomph; it should burn hot and it must burn clean. Lousy kerosene tends to clog and shorten the lifetime of the expensive burners. We have heard somewhere that jet fuel is also a highly refined kerosene and can be used instead. Whenever we have discussed a trial, I have envisioned *Northern Light* taking off like a rocket, and I'm skeptical of a few too many Btus. But now, as we are running low, we decide to try it.

Pedaling to the beach every day, we have been passing a small airport. Today, with a jerry can on the back rack of one bike, we cycle right on in and wheel as close as we consider proper to a fuel truck servicing a private jet.

I guess most of his customers make a lot more noise in their approach, because Rolf succeeds in startling the guy at the truck so badly I doubt he'll have an old age. As soon as he stops hopping around, Rolf asks him if we can please buy "this much" jet fuel and holds up 5-liter can.

"Where's your vehicle?" he asks Rolf suspiciously.

"Over there," responds Rolf matter of factly, pointing to his bike lying in the grass.

"C'mon man. What you plan on using this stuff for?"

Rolf doesn't let a chance like this slip by. With a straight face, he says to the guy, as they both stand sweating on the shimmering Florida tarmac: "It's for the heater." Only after a few seconds elapse does he allow his half-smile to crack and crinkle around his baby blues. "No, no, no. Just joking. Don't worry. No terrorist activities planned either. I just want to test it on my boat, to see if it'll work as fuel for the Primus stove burners."

A few seconds' worth of obvious assessment pass before the guy reaches for the can. "Yeah, OK, man," he says as he squirts some liquid into the container. "You can have some, no charge. But take my word for it. This stuff works better with an afterburner."

We test it. Jet fuel works just the way we had hoped. It also costs a mere seventh of the price of the blue kerosene released to the boat market in Sweden. The only drawback is that it makes the galley smell like an airport. I don't mind it too much, and Rolf says it's acceptable to him just as long as our coffee doesn't start to taste like an airline's.

For months now I have been practicing Morse code, ad nauseam. Before we leave the United States, I plan to be tested on receiving code at thirteen words per minute. If I pass, my amateur radio license will be upgraded to general class, the third level of five in the American amateur radio licensing structure. It's the level at which an operator is allowed to begin voice communications. Voice privileges would sure be nice; when atmospheric conditions allow, information can be passed faster speaking than by tapping. In addition, voice can be "patched" by a land-based amateur into the phone system, so I could even stay in touch with nonamateurs! Last but not least, people who don't know code (like most everybody I know) can listen in on voice communications. For years, poor Rolf has had to wait until contacts were finished before he could get the news, including just whatever it was in that mile-long strings of dits and dahs that had made me laugh.

On top of all those plusses, Andy never lets me forget that he has been enduring my terrible "fist" (slang for a person's individual style of sending Morse code) for long enough. I have often envisioned Andy, Frank, and the other regulars sitting in their ham shacks, headphones on, listening at the appointed time, straining to pick out my thin, reedy, low-power signal from all the others on nearby frequencies, while I sit in my ocean-going shack trying to pound out code while the boat pounds its way through waves and swell.

The worst case scenario for me (and them) is when *Northern Light* is on a beat. Then I sit kitty-corner at the nav desk seat, which slants 25 degrees uphill on port tack and 25 down on starboard. In a contorted position, with legs ramrod straight and feet jammed against the main ladder, I do my best to keep my tapping wrist and hand relaxed. Suddenly the boat pounds, and a dit becomes a dah or even a daaah. And often, concentrating on the high-pitched noise of their code has made me seasick. Yes, I just have to pass this test.

"You can call me *General*," I shout merrily from shore to Rolf. Yahoo! I did it, I passed. I feel a great sense of accomplishment and can hardly wait to meet Frank later on our normal frequency and tell him in code to switch and meet me on a frequency where only voice is allowed. Frank is pleased and congratulatory. A whole new world is opening up for us all.

After a three-month hiatus in Florida, both Rolf and I feel great. Even the crack in my pelvic bone has finally healed. It's time to be on our way. My father would like to come sailing with us for a few days. "What about you, Mom? Wouldn't you come too?" I ask.

"My dear," says my mother, stretching to what's always been, at least to me, her imposing full 6 feet, "I am not the slightest interested in sailing on anything smaller than the *Queen Mary*." She kisses me on the cheek and gives me a long hug and an even longer teary-eyed gaze. We won't be seeing each other for some years.

5

A NEW AND DIFFERENT KIND OF CHALLENGE

ROLF

■ ■ ■

More often than not, while sailing along coastlines we spend our nights at anchor in a bay, bight, cove, nook, or cranny . . . wherever we find undisturbed beauty. But for our last night in Florida, we tie up to a floating dock in a marina. We are as far south as one can go on the 300-mile-long (500 km) peninsula. Our last stop is the southernmost point of the continental United States and Ernest Hemingway's favorite place: Key West.

Deborah and I have just finished our dinner when we hear someone calling. "Ahoy, *Northern Liiight* . . . Hellooow . . . " Then there is silence again. It must be our friend David. He'd never just jump on board. He has style.

Except when we are day-sailing, Deborah and I have seldom had other people with us. But for each of the upcoming legs—Florida–Bermuda–Azores–Madeira–Canary Islands—we decided to have one or two people with us. Who knows? Perhaps this will be the last social contact we have for some time.

By the time David has stowed his gear, it's dark. I suggest we save looking over practical details on deck for the morning. Instead, we sit in the main cabin and I explain some of our philosophy of operational safety on board. I start by telling David that we don't have any "man overboard" gear among our safety equipment.

"After all," I tell him, "it's a little late to think about safety when someone is in the water. I want you to think about what safety really is. It's crucial to settle this issue before we leave, because each of us creates a safe environment through planning."

David nods, and I continue. "To me, safety is keeping ourselves from harm's way by preventing undesirable events. For example, once and forever, Deborah and I decided to remain on board *Northern Light*. We put ourselves in the center of what we call our Stay Onboard System. And it's the same for you. Your own attitude will determine whether or not you are still on board when we arrive in Bermuda!"

David responds that he knows sailing can be physically demanding, and so that I shouldn't think him unprepared for the task, he relates his recent training regimen. "I started running months ago and added hard-tempo bicycling for the last two months. Besides generally good condition, cycling has given me strong leg muscles and good balance, which I assume will be useful in heavy weather, both on deck and below. Cycling also strengthened my wrists and hands, so I'll be able to hang on whenever necessary and handle sheets and winches during different maneuvers."

When I learn that David has done all he could to prepare himself physically, I tell him we do actually have a Lifesling aboard, but to remember that it belongs in a category called lifesaving equipment. And we charge for using it!

David cracks a smile and asks when I plan to leave. I suggest eight o'clock. "The weather prognosis for tomorrow morning is promising, and that's why I want to leave immediately after breakfast. Toward evening they promise increasing northeasterly wind."

These are David's home waters, and I know what he is thinking: wind against the Gulf Stream. He asks, "How much?"

I tell him: "They predict 30 knots. My suggestion is that for the first few days you share watches with either Deborah or me, until you're comfortable operating the systems on deck. Then we can split off into three-hour watches, so each of us can get six hours' sleep.

"And David," I continue, "just one more thing about watch. Keeping watch is actually called 'standing watch.' And there's a good reason: remaining active is crucial and basic to good seamanship. You shouldn't spend your watches sitting in the cockpit. Move around on deck. One benefit is that you will see the sails from different angles and therefore learn more quickly how they have to be trimmed. Another important thing to do while you walk around is to keep a running check on gear. You'll certainly discover any problems in an earlier stage than if you remain in the cockpit.

"You will notice that we haven't led the main or mizzen's furling lines to the cockpit. We don't have furling sails because it's dangerous to be up on deck. In fact, the opposite is true: it's dangerous not to feel at home on deck. Walk around, learn where the handholds are. Get used to *Northern Light*'s motions and reacting to them. The more in sync with the boat you are, the less likely you are to get hurt, especially at night. Another benefit is that as your confidence increases, fear decreases, and therefore so does the likelihood of seasickness. In its initial stage, seasickness can be powered by uncertainties and worries. Doing something, being active, counteracts that.

"And when you have walked around on deck many times earlier, you won't even think about it when you have to run to the foredeck to free a sheet that's gotten hung up somewhere in a tack, or, well, just believe me, there's always something that needs to be fixed on deck."

I also tell David about the problem we had with the shrouds and ask him to help keep an eye on them. And I finish with telling him that this is a test sail, "So we will not slow down for comfort's sake."

David looks perfectly satisfied.

The next morning the weather is as wonderful as it almost always is in the so-called lazy latitudes. The sun shines from a cloud-free sky. The sea barely ripples, and there's only a ghosting northeasterly breeze. When we let the shore lines go, *Northern Light* creeps; our old sumlog barely registers any speed at all. It takes the better part of ten minutes before the first cable nudges the zero away. The total distance now covered is 110,916.7 nautical miles. That's five times around the world, following the equator. So far, *Northern Light* has always brought us to our planned destination, even if it has been difficult sometimes. And at the last channel marker, when I set the trip log to zero, I hope she'll show us now that she has indeed left the trials of puberty behind: she has just turned fifteen.

As a contrast to the fine weather, Deborah cannot resist telling David how it feels when it is really blowing. Although it may not be the best tactic, considering that it's David's first major offshore voyage, she even starts joking about it. She asks him: "David, how is sailing *Northern Light* in a gale like being inside a washing machine?"

David says, "I can imagine, but please tell me."

Deborah answers, "Well, sailing this boat in a gale is like being in a washing machine because we get thrashed around like a pair of jeans in the spin cycle. The only difference is that a washing machine has the water inside." And after a few seconds she adds: "Don't worry. It just *sounds* like we're sinking when it's bubbling and hissing."

David laughs, but I'm not so sure he thought it was very funny. He has probably also noticed the cirrus clouds streaming up from the southeast and therefore knows that Deborah's washing machine humor can soon be our reality.

To change the subject, I suggest we set the schedule for the watch rotation by drawing straws to see who gets the 1600 to 1800 watch. Today I'm the "winner," which means I'll be cooking dinner.

Around sunset, when I start preparing our meal, the wind has increased to

20 plus knots, and exactly as the weatherman promised, it's on the nose, blowing against the current. The sea quickly becomes as steep as one could ever imagine. *Northern Light* barely fits between the waves. The result is that, more often than not, she plows her bow straight into the steep walls of water. Each third or fourth wave she shudders as if to shake off the burdensome weight.

But there always comes a moment of near-total stillness. I kneel in the main cabin, waiting for just such a pause, to take the opportunity to lift one of the floorboards and reach the supply of canned tomatoes. I just manage to get a can up and put the floorboard down again before the boat meets the next steep wave. We meet one more, and one more, and one more wave. It doesn't take long before one feels as if there will never be an end to the terrible pounding.

To lessen the weight on the bow, we have left only one anchor on deck, the one permanently attached to the anchor chain. Before we left the marina I secured it so tightly to the bollard on the foredeck that it wasn't possible to budge it the slightest. Even so, the dastardly thing still moves a bit each time the bow hits an unusually steep wave. Over and over, a thunk travels through the boat. Each time it sounds like we're crashing into one of the steel buoys that mark separation lines between north- and southbound traffic.

It's too wet to be on deck, so while I prepare dinner, David sits on the windward settee in the main cabin. Now and then he goes to the ladder to keep a lookout through the cupola, opening it a couple of seconds at a time to get some fresh air. But whatever he does, and no matter how much he would like to he can't escape the smell of the food.

For dinner, we are having a stew of tomatoes, onions, cabbage, potatoes, and a few other things. To make it easy to eat with just a spoon, everything is chopped into small pieces. I sauté the onions, then add the other ingredients and let it cook. Smells waft throughout the closed boat, with fish and cabbage competing for first prize.

I serve the meal in deep dishes. Deborah, who is sitting farthest in, gets her portion first. I hand a bowl to David, but he doesn't take it. He stiffens, then burrows as far as physically possible into the sofa. He looks at me, then to the stew, and then to me again. His eyes widen as if he had been asked to eat a live poisonous snake. And then he asks, "What is that?"

I answer, "It's a variation of fish stew, and among other things contains Norwegian fishballs. Deborah and I bought them last fall when we sailed there. They don't taste like Swedish fishballs—which just taste like they were made of potato and flour—these have a lot of fish in them. In fact, they almost taste homemade!"

When I've finished, it hits me what a stupid thing that was to say. Of course, David has never even heard of fishballs, let alone tasted them. I try again, saying, "Fishballs are like meatballs, only . . . " when David's eyes start to stare outward, independent of one another. They roll an entire circle in their sockets. One of David's eyes becomes glassed over, the other completely empty, lifeless. I am afraid that David is about to collapse. But he doesn't. Instead he stands up.

Absolutely convinced that we are about to have someone die on board, I find myself waiting for the thud when David falls. What should I do? *David simply cannot die.* If he does, it will completely ruin my reputation as a skipper. And, blast it, I have totally forgotten to bring a large Swedish flag. Or should it be American? For a couple of moments my thinking swirls. I am completely bewildered.

David gathers up strength and for some unfathomable reason takes his portion from me and staggers to the sink. He puts his bowl there, then continues to the aft cabin to his seaberth. Before I turn the watch over to Deborah, I make sure that David is still alive but don't bother to wake him up. Deborah takes her watch, alone as usual.

When she eventually wakes me up, the moon has come up. Soon some of the clouds start to resemble gray ghosts, dancing and cackling across the sky. Other clouds appear as giant bats screeching straight at me. Everytime I see them, I shudder. David was right. Fishball stew wasn't a good idea for the first meal in a jumpy sea. Then again, perhaps it would not have made any difference what I had to eat.

It takes two days before we can steer as high as Bermuda. The sky gets heavier and heavier. We can finally slacken the sheets a bit, but just as the boat straightens up enough to allow us to open the hatches for a little fresh air, the sky opens and rain pours down. The air in the boat couldn't be more stale. When the rain passes, the wind shifts back to northeast, and we are back on a beat. It is as if nothing will ever be in our favor this time.

For the first seven days, the wind is never below 25 knots. Inside, the boat is as hot as a steambath. What a miserable introduction to life at sea. About all David has gotten out of this trip is rough weather. Since the third day out, he's been standing solo watches and pitching in as much as he can cooking. But he hasn't started to feel energetic yet, and there's still no opportunity for him to practice celestial navigation. We haven't even seen the sun.

The last day at sea of this leg, the weather changes, becoming as warm and pleasant as when we left Florida. Deborah decides this is our chance to let David feel the vacation sailors' golden existence. As dinnertime approaches, she puts cushions out in the cockpit then invites David and me to take our places. "For today's first course, we are serving linguine alle vongole," she says. It happens to be a favorite of David's.

Our smiling guest sits to the windward side of me. Deborah, using our finest dishes, serves David first, then me. A second later, the boat disappears down in a valley behind an odd wave, a leftover from the blow. The boat jerks suddenly, and without as much as leaving a trace behind, all the food glides off my plate and into my lap. I feel the long noodles and clam sauce slowly slither along my thighs. Looking down at the disaster, I flash back on a fall day in a Swedish forest many years ago, when I saw thousands of disgusting long, white worms eating their way through a decaying fox carcass.

David stares at my grievous mess. He has managed to keep the food on his plate, but instead of digging in, he offers to share. *What a nice guy David is,* I think to myself. And while I'm eating, I wonder if perhaps the noodles also reminded David of worms, but I say nothing.

A little less than nine days after leaving Key West, we arrive in Bermuda. When David walks out to his plane, I feel a big empty space. It didn't matter how difficult it was, he never complained. He'll make a fine sailor.

Two days later our new guest arrives. Because the weather is still dominated by intense low-pressure activity in the North Atlantic, the next leg will likely be another unpleasant trip. That's fine as far as Deborah and I are concerned because we need to test the new shrouds further. Sailing to the Azores is an investment for our future. But it could be worse for our acquaintance Jim, who is already tired when he arrives.

Yet because Jim is a lifelong outdoorsman and has sailed a lot, including ocean passages in his own boat, I conclude that he must be able to judge for himself whether he can manage the trip without too much suffering. The next day, Jim already looks a lot more rested. He tells us he slept like a log all night.

At one thirty the next afternoon, we depart St. George's Town. The weather has improved and the sky is almost cloud-free. The wind comes from the north at about 8 knots, and when we put our bow on course for the Azores, it meets us just a little forward of abeam, *Northern Light*'s best point of sail. We set the mizzen-staysail, let the boat steer herself with the help of the self-steering, and put out the fishing line. Life couldn't be better. Our three faces all sport smiles.

As usually happens close to land, before long a fish bites. Pulling in the line, I can feel that the catch is a yellowfin tuna. They don't resist as much as bonito or gold mackerel do. Without even having to use the gaff, I lift the fish on deck. It weighs about 6 pounds. Suggesting that we eat it while it still tastes the best, I turn to Jim and say: "If I clean it now, we can eat in half an hour. In the meantime, you take the watch and continue until it starts to get dark. OK?"

Jim nods and takes over, and after our early dinner, I give him all the information I had planned to pass along. To finish I say, "Deborah and I will take tonight's watches, so you'll get one more good long rest while the sea is flat."

By morning the wind has changed to westerly. Deborah and I pole out the genoa and put the boat on a course that brings the wind in 30 degrees from the stern on the port side. The wind has also increased to well over 18 knots, so we drop the mizzen-staysail. In that wind strength and above, *Northern Light* maintains the same speed anyway, but with less tendency to luff in the gusts. It also becomes more comfortable on board. *Northern Light* carries us over the ocean as if we were cloud-riding.

By the fourth day at sea, everything is going well enough for Jim that we change to an around-the-clock three-hour watch rotation. Deborah is to turn her watch over to Jim, and Jim to me. If he has any questions on his watch he is to ask me, because it's better to wake the person who has been off watch longest.

When Deborah takes over the watch at six o'clock in the evening, the wind's direction has become very unstable. In fact, it has already taken the genoa from the wrong direction, backing the sail a couple of times. It's also gusty, varying between 13 and 22 knots. To keep the boat from rounding up too often, we take down the spinnaker pole and gybe the genoa. Now I know that Deborah won't need me on deck during her watch. I sleep soundly until the watch change. I hear Deborah telling Jim about having seen squalls on the horizon and saying, "If any come our way, wake Rolf." Then I disappear into deep slumber again.

Suddenly Jim calls out, "A squall's coming!" I am startled by a terribly intense light. Even though it flashed while my eyes were closed, I am so blinded that I can see nothing but a gray shimmer. Simultaneously I hear a strange hissing. It sounds as if all the sails are being torn to shreds. A deafening boom makes the boat shake, and I feel how *Northern Light* is thrown on its side.

I had been sleeping without using the safety belt. In no time, I am hanging halfway outside the sea berth. As my feet touch the floorboard, the next lightning hits. The boat heels more and more until the cupboards become the floor, which I crawl over to get to the ladder. As always, I was sleeping nude, but there's no time to dress. On my way past the nav desk, I flick on the spreader lights. I make it into the cockpit just as the next lightning bolt hits the water some 10 yards away. In the intense light I see that the boat is beam to the sea, knocked over so hard the toerail is buried under water. The sails are flying with the wind, flogging violently.

Between bolts of lightning I see nothing. My night vision is so completely destroyed I can't even tell if the deck lights are on. There's no chance to see how the windvane is facing, so to bring the boat back on course, I pull the control lines to the windvane the amount I figure *should* be right and hope the windvane will indeed end up facing the correct direction. I do so knowing fully well that it may end up facing the wrong way, so on top of everything else, we could gybe. In this situation, that would be one of the most devastating things that could happen, but I see no other choice. In the light of the next strike I can see that the boat doesn't want to turn. It makes no speed through the water whatsoever, but just lies there, disabled, drifting sideways to the wind.

As long as the boat lies still, the rudder has no effect. To gain speed, the sails have to start to pull. I manage to get a handle into the genoa winch and start to crank. It's heavy work and slow going, but eventually I manage to crank in enough sheet for the genoa to fill. Very slowly the boat starts to move forward, but it still won't turn. As soon as I see that, I decide to furl the mizzen so that the boat will fall off with the wind more easily.

Suddenly conscious of rain whipping my bare skin, I realize I don't have a tether on. I decide not to stop to get it. To save the sails from being completely destroyed, I have to work as fast as I can. To be strong enough to hang on, I crawl on all fours to the mizzen. Even on the windward side, the waves wash over the deck. It must be blowing 50 knots and gusting far more. I wonder if it will even be possible to reduce sail. I'm particularly uncertain about the main and the genoa because there will be full drive in those sails as soon as she falls off.

When we installed the furling masts, our hope was that it would be possible to reef from full sail, on any point of sail and even in storm-strength wind, without having to change course first. What the engineers could tell us was that every mechanism and part was dimensioned to withstand more load than could be expected in such weather. But no one had been willing to go out in storm conditions to test it. I am therefore about to be the first to discover whether or not it really works.

The mizzen is so small that I manage furling it without even paying attention to the boat's point of sail. While I work my way to the mainmast, the boat starts to fall off and sail with the wind. She seems to stay on course, which means I got the windvane right. Good.

I get the winch handle into the furling winch on the mainmast but only manage half a turn. The boat is on the back side of a wave, where the wind pressure is strongest. I pause while *Northern Light* is in the valley, waiting until she accelerates, pushed by the approaching wave. Then the pressure in the sail eases enough for me to take a couple of turns. I continue in this manner until only a third of the mainsail is left.

I work my way to the cockpit to reef the genoa. The furling technique here will be the same as with the main. It doesn't matter that I can't see the genoa; I know by feel when I have the right load on the winch. During the hard sailing through Belle Isle Strait, we learned that when running downwind with full pull in the genoa, it is easiest to reef when we first pretension the line around the furling winch and then wait either until the boat lies on the front side of a wave or until the wind momentarily decreases. Then the genoa practically furls itself half a turn. We also found that it is important to take it easy the first three turns and not crank so hard as to use the full power of the winch. The smaller the sail gets, however, the less consideration we have to give to the power we use.

Because I can't detect the reef markings on the genoa, I judge by the force it takes to furl how much sail is left. Eventually, the boat has a tendency to round up into the wind, which tells me I have reefed too much. I let out a little, and she stays on course.

The discovery that the furling system works exactly as we had hoped, even though the wind pressure on the sail was five times what it normally is when we start to reef, has so totally captured my interest that I only once wondered where Deborah might be. But when the spacing between lightning bolts increases and my night vision improves, I suddenly see that she's standing only a few feet away from me in the cupola, ready to give me a hand if necessary. She gives me a thumb's up sign.

In less than half an hour, the squall is far away. The cold front and its thunder and lightning have moved east, and it is no longer necessary for Jim to remain on deck. He goes below for some sleep, and Deborah stays up with me. As the squall reaches the horizon, we shake out the reefs and then spend the rest of the night sitting in the cockpit, mostly silent. A meteorite enters Earth's atmosphere, and both our gazes are drawn to its long, glimmering tail. But it's not necessary to divulge our wishes; each well knows what the other is thinking.

The clearing doesn't last long. By first light, it's cloudy and the wind has increased. It's time to reef the mainsail and the mizzen. But because the wind still comes in a little aft of abeam, we can keep sailing with a full genoa. So trimmed, the boat almost sails itself, remaining on course so well that the windvane only has to compensate for the odd wave. Even in the afternoon, when the wind increases to full gale, we keep flying as much sail as we can.

The feeling of power that the sails generate is almost dizzying. At night, the phosphorescent trail behind the boat is so long it appears to have no end. Four noon sights in a row show that we have logged close to 200 miles each day. The best run is 102 miles in twelve hours. It makes it physically uncomfortable on board, yet we enjoy it. Sailing in heavy weather really shows whether or not a boat is being handled correctly. And having proof that one is doing it correctly builds the self-confidence necessary to appreciate sailing as an enriching experience, in all weather.

After thirteen days at sea we round up behind the breakwater in Faial on the island of Horta. Jim and I walk together to the immigration office, where he is signed off the crew list, and he leaves to fly home.

When I come back alone, Deborah takes me lightly by the hand. She can barely hold back her tears. I understand that although she is having as difficult a time as I am, she wants to give me all the support she's able. But there isn't much she can do, and I can't do much for her either, really. For a while we just stand there.

It's been nine months since we left Sweden. Even so, we are not more than ten days' sailing from Fiskebäckskil. That is as far as we have come. And just before our approach to Faial's harbor, while making a routine check of the engine, I had found that there wasn't a trace of oil to be found on the dipstick. My first thought was that the engine must have cracked. I looked in the bilge for the oil, but it was completely dry. Confused, I tried to pump some oil out of the engine the normal way, but I didn't find oil there either, just water! Unbelievable. Only after pumping out 3 liters of salt water, did I find oil. I checked the dipstick again. Now it indicated that the oil level was correct. There must have been so much water in the engine that the stick couldn't register the oil level until the water had been removed. At sea, all we could do was to pump all the oil out and replace it with new. As we motored slowly into the harbor, it dawned on me what must have happened.

During the three days when we continuously logged the boat's maximum speed, we had been between a beam reach and a broad reach. But at the same time there was a high swell coming from the northeast; in other words, it was almost dead against us. Each time the boat met that swell, the deceleration forces were so phenomenal that the water left in the exhaust hose and muffler (located aft of the engine and below its level) had been hurled forward and upward so violently it forced its way back past the exhaust system and into the engine, probably through a valve that stood open.

A man on a neighboring boat tells us that after he experienced the same problem, Perkins recommended a succession of oil and filter changes, running the engine hot each time. Doing so should take out any water that may be left. It sounds logical to us.

After the first change and half an hour's engine run, we take off the rocker cover. Steam rises from inside the engine, and there is condensation on the inside of the oil spout's cap. We change the oil and filter and then run the engine six hours, but there is still moisture left. We change the oil and filter again and then repeat the process until we've run the engine a total of twenty-four hours, until finally no condensation is seen. Nevertheless, we run the engine two more deafening hours.

We've done all we can. We haven't had proper sleep for three days, and before that, we had two draining passages. Our energy is so low we don't have the strength to talk about the engine, or anything else for that matter, anymore. Worries about the future break into my sleep. I wake at first light and decide to get up. I climb each mast and check the rigging, inspecting everything from the top of the mast to the chainplates in the rail. I pay special attention to the shrouds. As critically as I look, I don't find one weakness anywhere.

That means we have finally come to our next checkpoint. It's hard to believe, but from now and on we are on our way south. Madeira, Canary Islands, Rio . . . just the thought of heading in the right direction is music to my ears.

Later the same day Kristin shows up. The daughter of a friend, she's our next guest. But she has arrived some days earlier than expected. Deborah and I don't have a chance to let our recent decisions sink in. Now the short time we had planned on using for ourselves will be devoted instead to getting a new person settled on board.

Kristin is a little more than twenty years old and has never sailed any real distance in the open ocean. She has a lot to learn, both before we leave port and en route to Madeira. We were aware of that when we invited her, but now we are mentally exhausted—more perhaps than we ourselves realize—and we act it. Poor Kristin. Our bad mood is not directed toward her. It's more as if Deborah and I no longer share an opinion about anything.

When our relationship remains stressful and unpleasant, I ask Kristin to reconsider whether she really wants to sail with us. "You shouldn't feel forced to, just because of a decision made long ago. Take a walk, think it over, and then decide. It's for your own good."

But Kristin says she doesn't need any time to think about it. She says: "As long as you and Deborah are doing your best to not get on each other's nerves, I can't ask for more. I'm comfortable on board."

For ten days we vacation sail among the islands of the Azores. Kristin's ever-positive attitude helps us unwind. The three of us are met by islanders who are proud of what they have and who show old-fashioned, undisturbed hospitality, friendliness, generosity, and contentedness. They illustrate how much human warmth means to one's well-being and how easily it can be transferred to others. I don't think it's an exaggeration to say that the people of the Azores, and Kristin too, helped *Northern Light* sail away as a happy ship. I feel badly that we can offer so little in return, but that's a drawback to the cruising life.

The first evening on our way toward Madeira, as we three sit together in the cockpit and start our dinner, the moon comes up a little to starboard. It rises just under the genoa, which is poled-out on that side. The main and mizzen are eased out fully to port. The wind is very light and from dead astern. It blows just enough to make ripples on the water. Nevertheless, *Northern Light* occasionally trips over a little wave coming from another direction, rolls, and then continues in a manner that makes it look as if she also may be in need of rest.

The next evening, just as we start our dessert, the moon comes up. This time it is dead ahead. The moon is full and rises so fast that the man in the moon hits his head on the spinnaker pole. "Oh, excuse me, sir," says Kristin, who has the watch responsibility. We all laugh. The night is from the pages of a fairy tale. No one wants to sleep.

The third night, *Northern Light* balances on the rays from the silvery moon until the moon disappears behind the top of the mizzen-staysail. When the moon is in zenith, the silver streaks disappear and we know that the last hour of the day has passed.

The whole way to Madeira, the nights are almost as bright as the days. Six days in a row the wind comes from astern. The spinnaker and mizzen-staysail become around-the-clock sails, and if it wasn't that two new friends are joining us in Funchal, we could have continued along on the moon's silver trail to never-never-land. At least Kristin thinks so.

Jean and Charles are not sailors. But they were aboard once for a weekend when we were on our way south along the American east coast. Our long-time friends were so easygoing and pleasant to be with that it occurred to me they should sail with us a longer time. Why not from Madeira to the Canary Islands?

We have a lot planned for their stay. The first event will be a tour around Madeira to take in the alpine landscape, sheer-sided ravines, jungles, abundance of flowers, and turquoise water. What a fantastic island!

They go to bed late the night of their arrival, but long before the sun is up and a lot earlier than any bus starts moving, we wake them. What we have in mind is to take a taxi as far as the road goes and then walk up to one of the highest peaks, 4,400 feet (1,347 m) above sea level. The idea—which becomes reality—is to give them a sunrise and a welcoming they will never forget.

What we don't know, but realize as soon as the taxi starts to climb the narrow winding road, is that Jean suffers from vertigo. She knows that her only escape is to close her eyes. We feel so badly for her. All the beautiful scenery of her vacation destination passes by without her seeing any of it. She tells us she can't possibly consider the walk we'd planned. All she dares do, once we're on the way down again, is to look into the inner curves of the road at some of the waterfalls.

The day we plan to put out to sea, Jean doesn't feel well. She's caught something and has a slight fever. Yet, trouper that she is, she still wants us to depart. She insists she'll be comfortable in the aft cabin, where she can rest. Charles puts himself on deck, with his back against the skylight, while Deborah and I take care of the sailing. The plan is to sail only as far as Islas Desertas, 20 nautical miles southeast of Madeira, and anchor there for the night. We want our guests to settle into a sea routine gently before we continue toward the Canary Islands.

The wind is light until we come to the place where it accelerates around Madeira's southeast corner. Then, within just a couple of seconds, *Northern Light* is beam reaching at hull speed. The result is that Charles, sitting where the sea now rushes over the boat, gets immediately soaked. Long before we were caught by the wind, I had told him he should put on foul weather gear and move to the stern, but he waited too long, and now he doesn't dare let his handhold go. When I again suggest that he move, he answers, "I'd go overboard!" Charles is a high school science teacher, and he understands how centrifugal forces work. He stays put, continuously washed by spray, probably wishing to reach that little dot on the horizon a lot faster than is actually possible under sail.

After three hours, we are finally outside the bay where we intend to anchor. As we furl all the sails and start the engine, Charles moves for the first time. He doesn't actually let his cramplike grip go, but he does compensate for the lesser heel.

Even though we are on the lee side of the island, the wind howls down the mountain ridge with such force that *Northern Light* heels until the chainplates drag in the water. Charles doesn't say a word. He lets us make all the decisions. The closer we get to land, the more obvious it becomes that we cannot spend the night where planned. When I quit the search for an alternative anchorage, Charles's face shows that he has entered a calm stage, one only open to those who realize how transitory life is.

The last time we look at our planned night harbor, the swell sweeps over the reef with such force that the entire lagoon becomes one solid white blanket of foam. Charles starts to stand up. Afraid that he could get hurt while we set sail, I call out to him: "Wait, it's too jumpy."

Charles nods and replies, "I'll join you." I am not sure I understood him correctly, but he sits down again just as another blast hits us, and I am suddenly too busy to reflect further over what it was he actually said. Not until we are almost halfway back to Madeira when Charles asks through chattering teeth, "When will it happen?" do I realize that he must have thought I said "Wait, we shall jump." He must have assumed I too had reached the conclusion that drowning ourselves would be the best way to bring this painful event to an end.

At nine in the evening we round the corner of the high concrete pier that protects the yacht harbor in Funchal. With a little more than a yard left to the jetty, I see to my infinite surprise how Charles, who isn't very athletic, without even winding up, leaps shoreward.

For a moment I am convinced that he's about to fly straight into the side of the pier, but to my relief he ends up where he planned. On his hands and knees, he moves his palms slowly back and forth, touching the ground, mumbling, "Land, oh, land." Then he jumps up, turns toward us, and calls out, "Come, you must let me treat you to dinner."

And oh, what a meal! Between ordering appetizers, salads, main courses, two wines, and an ancient Madeira, Charles tells the waiter the story of his miraculous survival. When all the other guests have left, the lights dim and in marches the restaurant's owner, proudly carrying a Baked Alaska. The flaming dessert is a gift to Charles. "It's my pleasure," he says. "This is the first time I've ever had the chance to wish someone 'welcome back to life.' "

The next day, we set sail for Lanzarote. It's a wild, wet, three-day ride, but both our guests stand their watches. Once there, we are hit by a two-day sandstorm. Because of the roar in the rigging, neither Charles nor Jean can sleep, and they move to a hotel. When they feel ready, we sail onward to Fuerte Ventura. There, not a green blade can be seen, only lava, and the fascinating island looks like a moonscape. From there we sail to Las Palmas on Grand Canaria, but finding the place dreary, we head for Puerto Mogan. There the ocean is sapphire blue and the water so clear one can see the sandy bottom 50 feet (15 m) down; it's a picture postcard vacation paradise.

This is the end of the line for Charles and Jean. For their last dip, we dinghy to a spot where we see people sunning themselves on the cliffs and playing in the water. After we all have jumped in the water, we are dismayed to see that the surface is dotted with clumps of raw sewage. The hotel, located higher up on the cliff, advertises swimming for their guests: in a pool. Not until later do we learn that the ocean is considered suitable "for locals only."

After Charles and Jean leave, we rush to see what they have written in our guestbook. Just as we had hoped, we read that they "had a marvelous time." The only thing that confuses us a bit is the last line. "If you ever think about starting a charter business, we have the perfect slogan for it: Cruising for a Bruising." Whatever could they mean?

6

THE
NEVER-ENDING
OCEAN

DEBORAH

■ ■ ■

When I take over the watch at 0600, an envelope—addressed to me, no less—is lying on the nav desk. It contains an invitation:

CELEBRATION TODAY!
To be held when Sally says
we've crossed the equator
Dress: optional
RSVP

Sally is the name of our GPS—global positioning system—a navigation instrument that fixes a position based on one's distance from numerous satellites. The predecessor to GPS was called satnav, and when we bought a second-hand unit from another sailboat, the owner informed us that "her" name was Sally Satnav. The name stuck and then transferred to the GPS generation.

The next watch change finds us both glued to the GPS display, watching as the northern latitude approaches zero. I fill the time with a story, telling Rolf about my first equator crossing on board a brigantine in the Pacific in 1979, when with much pomp, Neptune granted me the title "shellback." That day, the skipper had a good laugh at the expense of the guests. He told them they would be able to tell when we crossed the line if they kept a good eye on the water in the toilet: it would change from going down counterclockwise to clockwise. Oh, they pumped and pumped, and I found out that he was master of maintaining a straight face.

On August 30, twenty minutes into Rolf's watch, as the wind begins to shift from south to (yahoo!) the southeast of the tradewind: three, two, one, bingo! Over the line! Sally displays southern latitude at west 24°38′.

Now that I know where we are, I need to know just where we stand. To that end, after we exchange silly gifts in a little crossing celebration, I hand out paper and pencils and tell Rolf it's time to write down the three possible projects we have long ago delineated, in today's order of preference. No talking is allowed. We each write our own list. I am surprised at first that Rolf doesn't even pause before he begins writing. When we've each finished, we exchange lists. With nervous anticipation I unfold Rolf's. It reads:

1. Antarctic overwinter
2. The sub-Antarctic Islands
3. The two Patagonias

His list is identical to mine. Aahhh, we're in sync.

The heat of the midday sun is appalling, and as high as that fiery disc sits in our sky, it's hard to find shelter from it on deck. Shadows are nearly nonexistent. Luckily for us, before leaving the Canary Islands we changed from undercut furling sails to fully battened sails. The very full roach of the bigger sail at least gives us a better chance to sit in shade. "I am sure," Rolf says, "that you are the only person in the world who changes sail wardrobes like a hat."

One of the fine features of Seldén furling masts is that next to the slot for the furling sail is a track where you can hoist sails in the normal fashion. The manufacturer added that track for a storm trysail. When we left Sweden, we didn't know if we would be able to trust the furling mast mechanism or like the undercut sails, so we brought along conventional sails as spares and a set of fully battened sails, which we've never had before, to test and compare against in-mast furling. Either type can be set in the trysail track.

Rolf has sailed *Northern Light* so long he instinctively knows her every motion and tendency. When any one component is changed, he immediately and clearly understands if there is a difference and if so, what it is. That's why we chose, for example, to add furling masts one year and the wingkeel the next, rather than do both at once.

On this passage we've experimented by putting in reefs, shaking them out, overreefing, underreefing . . . all to see how the boat responds and how it is to work with fully battened sails. For me, the biggest drawback is the mere weight of the extra sailcloth and battens. In heavy weather, I'll be back to waking Rolf to take in reefs. As for trimming, the hardest part is getting used to the big roach. It's easy to think that the positive roach has too little twist, so we put telltales on as reference points.

Now, on what has been a light air trip, I can confirm that fully battened sails do indeed pull. And an interesting phenomenon happens in light air: they get a wave undulating in them that seems to create forward motion. We've often watched them undulate during the last 600 miles, as we worked our way through the doldrums.

To cross the Atlantic from the Canary Islands toward Rio, we first headed south, parallel to Africa's coast, and enjoyed a nice downwind run in north-northeast wind for the first eight days. At 9°50′ N a squall announced that we had reached the border of the doldrums, an area of unstable air where the opposing winds of the two hemispheres meet. The doldrums, a composite of the words *dull* and *tantrum,* are rather tiring for sailors. Wind either comes in puffs, where you trim, trim, trim and creep forward, or in short-lived squalls, when you have to reef. In the squalls is more wind than you need for ten to thirty minutes, then calm, then repeat. The Pilot Chart, which depicts statistical averages of information of interest to mariners for each month in each ocean, shows that the belt of doldrums should be much narrower on the South American side, but pity the person who doesn't study all the facts and realize that the current is northbound there at about 1.5 to 2 knots.

At the beginning of the doldrums we had southwest wind and put *Northern Light* on starboard tack, heading approximately south-southeast. At 6°02′ N we got southerly wind and went over to port tack. If the wind remains southerly, you don't make it around the bulge of South America at Cabo Frio, so you hope the wind continues shifting over to southeast for your course to bend south nicely, just as ours did as we crossed the equator, with 1,500 nautical miles to go.

Today is also a "sked" day: I have a scheduled meeting on the amateur radio, with the time and frequency prearranged. Some minutes before I expect Andy to call, I listen around on the band. It's positively jam-packed with voices. For a change, propagation (atmospheric conditions affecting radio signals) is decent. Because the band is crowded, Andy may find "our" frequency already in use. So I scan up and down 10 kilohertz each side of it, listening for his call.

Skeds at sea are always set to take place when Rolf and I normally change watch, so that we can overlap. While I am on the radio, Rolf keeps watch. Tonight he's sitting in moonlight on the bench just outside the companionway, where he can hear what's happening.

"Rolf c'm here. I think I hear Dennis!" Sure enough, just a bit down from the sked frequency, with a nice clear signal, is Dennis Kleén, the only amateur operator in Fiskebäckskil! "N1CCA Maritime Mobile, this is SM6OOI calling. Are you there Deborah?"

What a pleasant surprise. We haven't heard any signals out of Scandinavia for some time and had actually given up hope of any more contact. I give Dennis our position and tell him that all's fine here in the Southern Hemisphere. He also has good news. "I've been accepted to Chalmers Institute of Technology. It means I'll be moving next week. I can't take my radio gear with me, so I doubt you'll be hearing much from my side these next few years."

"Oh, we'll miss you, Dennis," I reply, "but it's great to hear about Chalmers. Rolf wants me to pass you his congratulations too!" Indeed, we both get a wave of good feelings from his unexpected news.

There's more to this surprise. Also in his "ham shack" are Bengt and Cilla: Bengt, an original Mickey Mouse coffee klatch member from the marina, and his girlfriend, Cilla, who painted NO TIME TO TALK on my shirt. This sure is an unexpected blast of contact. Bengt tells about life in a country with a tailspin economy and gives news and greetings from our mutual friends. Sailing along, under a starry canopy, in the warmth of the tropical night, talking to Sweden. . . . Poor Rolf. After an energizing chat like this, with so much news, it'll be hard for him to sleep when it's over.

Andy finds us. He hears me, but not Dennis, and waits patiently until the contact with Sweden ends. Then he (N1BHI) takes over. Andy always starts our contact by asking for our position. Then he asks if all's well, takes any messages we may want him to pass along, and passes messages to us. Often, Frank (KB1FZ) comes up to say hi and will chat if propagation is good, as will "Lucas-Bob" (N1CTY), who has the self-appointed job of keeping track that Rolf is rationing the supply of peanut butter properly.

Propagation remains fantastic for the next few weeks, and I decide to put it to good use and make phone patches (linking me to a nonamateur via the telephone). Patching is most easily accomplished using a net (a group of amateurs who meet at a fixed time on a fixed frequency with the express purpose of facilitating contact). Each of many nets helps a different group of hams, such as those of us on board boats.

A maritime net may have hundreds of land-based operators listening or actively involved. One is designated the net controller. Some minutes before the net opens, the controller checks propagation to the other kingpin land-based operators, each in a different geographic area. Then the net is opened by asking if anyone has emergency traffic (messages). The controller either responds to the emergency or announces that he or she heard nothing, then asks the other regulars if any one of them heard anything.

Therein lies the beauty of a net. As conditions for radio signals are never 100 percent predictable, no one ever knows who they will hear at any given moment. Because the maritime net I use for patches (14300 kHz at 0130–0230 UTC) is composed of operators from all over North and Central America and from boats all over the world, the likelihood is that a call, no matter where it originates or its strength, will be heard by somebody. Ergo, we are "caught in the net."

If no one hears any emergency transmissions—be it an SOS, medical problem, or priority traffic—then the normal business of the net proceeds. The net controller puts out a general call to a specific geographic area: "Any maritime mobile amateur operator in the South Atlantic who wants to join the net, come now." Cacophony ensues as everyone from this area sings out the last three letters of their call signs. The net controller repeats the ones he hears best. He says, "I heard XXX and YYY and a YL (young lady) whose call sign ends with CA."

That's my cue. I jump in and repeat my call. "OK, I got you, CCA." He continues making a list of everyone he hears, and his helpers add in the others they heard.

The net control then starts from the top of the list. "OK, XXX, what's your business?" Generally, it will be one of two things. The amateur wants to meet someone, and if that someone is also on frequency, they connect and go off to another frequency to talk, taking another net participator with them if they can't hear each other directly and need a relay (a person who hears each party and can relay between them). Or, like me, the amateur wants to make a phone call. When my turn comes, I say, "If anyone on the net has copy [finds my signal strong enough] for a patch, please call N1CCA." If someone answers, we move to another frequency, along with all the silent others who are interested in listening to my conversation.

Working a net can be quite exciting, especially in the beginning. Trying to be heard, saying the right thing at the right time, getting the lingo down, and not making a fool of yourself to the thousands of people listening can make a person apprehensive. I listened many times before I felt confident enough to try, but once I had the pleasure of suddenly hearing the phone ring on the other end I was ready for more.

It also took my family time to get used to communicating this way. My sister Lisa nearly aborted her first patch when the telephone operator asked if she would accept a collect call from "Duane, in South Dakota." She doesn't know anyone named Duane and said so, adding that it must be a mistake. Luckily, Duane then offered the pertinent information that he was an amateur radio operator calling collect on my behalf.

Everyone in the family also had to start learning radio jargon and technique. They said it feels somewhat phony to use the new terms in the beginning, and my niece said she felt silly having to say "over" when she finished talking, but that cues the patch operator to throw a switch each time the speaker changes. Of course, I also understand that it takes a while to get used to perfect strangers being involved in what normally would be a private conversation.

I soon realized that it wasn't worth trying a phone patch unless propagation was really good. It takes practice to hear through the extra noise bad propagation carries, and untrained folks have a hard time. I got a letter from my mom after a dismal patch where she wrote: "That was the most unenlightening conversation last night, to say nothing of frustrating. Have you ever seen pictures on TV of a victim or criminal whose identity cannot be revealed, so their faces are made unrecognizable by moving squares? Well, that's what you *sounded* like. The ham that got us together kept telling me I'd get used to it. Then he said I should try harder, which made it even more frustrating. It sounded like you were talking under water, and I found myself hoping that you were at the surface, in your comfy little boat. If the radio operator hadn't translated parts of the call, I wouldn't have gotten anything out of it at all."

To avoid putting people through that, I now listen and wait until I hear a net participant who has a tiptop signal; chances are that the reciprocal signal will also be good, although it can never be quite as good. Land-based operators have more efficient antennas and can use a lot more power (up to 1,000 watts) than I can on the boat, where I can generate a maximum output of 100 watts. But someone with a sophisticated patch setup can also enhance and amplify my signal. A good signal plus the skill and experience—to say nothing of patience—of the patch operator make it easier for the person I am phoning.

Phone patches now enhance an onboard tradition. Each year, Rolf and I celebrate the birthdays of each and every person in both our immediate families plus those of our good friends. We have always devoted the day to the birthday child. We talk about them, wonder about them, bake them a cake, sing *Happy Birthday,* blow out their candles, and (finally, what we're best at) eat their cake. All the above-mentioned people know us well enough to trust that we do indeed celebrate, especially because of the cake-eating part. But patching lets us prove that we remembered them, so each birthday I listen to propagation and, if it's good, we phone. A week after our equator crossing, we called Lisa's husband, Guenter. Not only did we surprise him, but he got a kick out of the idea that he was talking to someone at sea. A lot happened in those few minutes, just by being in touch. The conversation soon disappeared into nothingness, but the good feeling of sending an impromptu gift remains.

Every day at sunset we wind up our fishing line and stow it below. We do this not because we wouldn't catch fish at night, but for safety. If something goes wrong at night or if we have to make a fast maneuver, we don't want the first order of business to be winding up the fishing line or tripping over it.

Since leaving the Canary Islands, we have only caught two fish. Both were small dorado, caught north of the equator. Day after fishless day we continue our false assumption that the major problem has something to do with the design of the lure. I pull it in once more to have a look. There is a plastic bag caught on the hook. Half an hour later, trash again: some polypropylene fishing net. Twenty minutes later, a six-pack ring. "You know what Rolf?" I say. "Now that I think about it, there has nearly always been some kind of plastic garbage on the hook when I wind it up at sunset."

We can hardly believe that trash is *the* problem and the reason no fish bites, but we decide it's worth checking. We agree that the watchkeeper should check the line every twenty minutes. Two times out of three, there is trash on the hook. Granted, the hook is large—the size of a circle formed by touching your thumb to forefinger—but it's not more than an eighth of an inch (3 mm) wide. Isn't it absolutely staggering to think that such a skinny thing being dragged through an ocean should meet trash so often?

During passages, whenever it's calm and sunny, we can look down through the water as far as 30 to 40 yards. Following rays of sunlight into the azure blue depth can be hypnotizing. Our gazes usually find plankton undulating in subsurface currents. Sometimes we are rewarded by the sight of a fish, a ray, or a shark. But on this crossing, it is the trash that allows us to note the layers of different temperature and salinity in the water. Looking down, we see four and sometimes five layers . . . of plastic garbage. Day after day, whenever we look, we see plastic. The calmer it is, the more we see.

Because plastic poses a threat to the lives of fish, marine animals, and birds, we never toss any overboard from *Northern Light*. We do, however, allow biodegradable trash to be disposed of at sea. "Don't panic, it's organic" has been our motto, with some guidelines. In consideration of others, we never dispose of trash near shorelines or when day-sailing. It's dropped only in deep water, off the continental shelf. On ocean crossings we have also allowed overboard disposal of cans opened at both ends and bottles filled with water so that they sink. In light of our recent observation, I broach the subject with Rolf; it's my opinion that the time has come for us to reconsider the practice of what amounts to littering the ocean floor.

By human standards, oceans are vast. It's easy to understand that over the years, man has believed he could dump as much trash as he wanted at sea. It took nothing less than a U.S. Supreme Court ruling to stop New York City from dumping its community garbage in the Atlantic Ocean. But it's still legal to dump other types of garbage, such as industrial and building materials, and many other countries still dump all their garbage into the oceans and seas. We have often dreaded the thought that the plastic waste we save on passages and dispose of ashore may then be dealt with by our host country by throwing it in the ocean. Sadly, we recently witnessed just that. From the island of Terciera in the Azores we saw garbage trucks backing to the edge of a cliff to dump their entire loads into the ocean. The plastic never disappears, it doesn't disintegrate; it just circulates in ocean currents round and round.

In a phone patch I relate to my father what we have experienced. Dad, professor emeritus of environmental health engineering, is surprised by the amount of plastic we have seen but tells us: "Besides the solid-waste problem you are seeing, there are other pressing problems whose effects are becoming great enough to pollute entire oceans. For example, crude oil from ships, wells, spills, and other accidents; lead from the exhaust of internal combustion engines that precipitates into the oceans from the atmosphere; and another highly toxic substance, mercury, which is being found in ever-higher concentrations in fish."

I respond that in my opinion, waste management has to be addressed globally, because spot cleanup doesn't work. I offer him an example. In the mid 1950s, Sweden decided to stop releasing raw sewage, garbage, and industrial pollutants into the sea. Nonetheless, every nook and cranny on its west coast is today filled with trash. The language on each piece gives away the jetsam's source country, and they are all upwind, as far away as Spain. As we have sailed from Sweden's west coast to Denmark, we have crossed pink to green to yellow water. Each is due to a different chemical or industrial pollutant released from countries upstream: Poland, the Baltic States, and Russia. Scandinavian fishing boats drag their nets through that multicolored water, catching poisoned fish for us to eat. Yum. Isn't it time for all nations to reconsider the practice of using oceans, or any water, for waste disposal?

My father replies: "Mankind has always put himself first. By that I mean that his immediate material comfort and wealth is more important to him than considerations of the environment or future generations. I think you are on the right track when you call for global management. So do others. The United Nations is drawing up guidelines for the regulation of refuse disposal in the oceans. And today, worldwide, the thrust is for pollution prevention inside what is called 'total quality management.' For your and future generations' sake I hope for its success. It can happen if people insist on it en masse. You see, the U.N., although a workable forum for developing recommendations, will ultimately fail if it doesn't gain worldwide legal clout. But since we have seen that much of the environmental movement has started from the grass roots, it is my hope that people will call for their countries to empower the U.N. to be able to enforce the recommendations."

I have a lot to think about after the patch. Each of us—personally, each producer or manufacturer, and each country—plays a part. But assuming that the balancing act is ultimately controlled by natural forces, we have to realize that if we don't clean up our act, many "solutions" those forces will present for us—diseases, shortages of water and food, fights for survival—will be painful.

We've got to turn our thinking around. Although economic and political leaders repeat it broken-record style, unabated industrial growth is not the type of progress we need. A change in direction doesn't mean there must be fewer jobs or business opportunities. The cleanup industry will be huge, and we need a lot of design work, to determine a level we can afford to maintain, one with as little impact as possible. I remember the goal my father stated, *total quality management*, and I conclude that the ultimate test of how well we accomplish just that will be measured in terms of the span of our survival, as is any species' fitness.

I hope we choose not to push this problem to the next generation. As Gandhi expressed so eloquently, "Simplify your needs."

7

DIRTY
DANCING
IN RIO

Deborah

■ ■ ■

According to sailing lore, the three cities topping the list of most beautiful to approach from seaside are Cape Town, San Francisco, and Rio de Janeiro. Earlier today we thought we would conclude this passage with a view of the celebrated Brazilian city backlit by sunset colors. But closing the coastline the wind drops and dies, and there's no way we can make it in to the harbor before dark. Luckily for us, we don't have to heave to in the highly trafficked path to the city. Instead, *Northern Light*'s anchor can be lowered in a small nook on the coast.

Our yellow signal flag is already flying. Hoisted some hours ago, it declares that we have not yet cleared into the country. Seeking shelter for extenuating circumstances before being cleared is a rare occurrence. It is allowed, but then going ashore is not; with the exception of medical emergencies, the first steps ashore must have the express purpose of presenting oneself to the authorities to begin clearing-in procedures.

In place of the archetypical landfall—suddenly arriving and having to take care of business while our heads spin from new images, culture, and language—this slow-paced landfall becomes an experience in itself, its essence leisurely, romantic. It seems like a prize at the journey's end to be able to absorb the sights and sounds and smells of land and a new place in a gentle way. I especially like being able to wind out of the watch routine by doing what we can't do at sea: both of us relaxing at the same time, sharing an entire evening. And lying at anchor will take on the feel of a minivacation when the passage's four-hour sleep routine is superseded with a glorious rest through the entire night, my husband beside me once again. If that weren't enough, the boat will sway almost imperceptibly at anchor in a peaceful, protected place, as the movement and noise of ocean sailing fades to memory. Ah, arrival! Tomorrow I will awaken refreshed and ready to brave the city.

We watch the anchor reach the bottom and nestle into the sand, and then we each slowly turn full circle to see just what the ocean scenery has been traded for and to drink in our new surroundings. We are just off a dusty pastel-painted village. Even its parched colors are dramatic to our eyes, so used to a limited palette of blue and white. Fishing boats, attended by flocks of screaming gulls, come and go; kids play, scampering on the beach. Lights twinkle welcomingly in the windows of the local café. The smell of tropical greenery wafts around us; the indescribably refreshing fragrance stands out as the strongest voice in the chorus of changes. As we watch the sun set between knobby hills and begin preparing dinner, a front passes through. The wind shift makes our anchorage untenable and we are forced to leave. Ah, "the best laid schemes of mice and men."

We opt not to put back out to sea to ride it out and instead begin motoring toward Rio against the wind. It builds to gale force. The water of the bay splashing over deck is warm and builds quickly to the type of chop that is just wrong for *Northern Light*'s full bow. Then it builds even further until she slams into each wave marching against her. The bucking bronco ride becomes nightmarish as we head toward landfall in the dark. The severe pitching makes it hard to keep track of lights, and the stinging spray doesn't exactly help our concentration.

When entering an unfamiliar port at night, it's always difficult to judge distances and find landmarks and contours with which to match the surroundings to the chart. And if the port is a huge city, the search for navigational lights is made all but impossible by the overabundance of other ones. Try to find a buoy or lighthouse blinking its white or red against a backdrop of ever-changing car headlights and taillights and blinking brake lights, to say nothing of streetlights and flashing signs, when you've got to find the navigation light in time. And don't forget, oops, I mean *remember* all the while to look around in the immediate neighborhood for moving ships. The experience can be nerve-wracking. Tonight it feels exceedingly so because instead of breaking the four-hour rhythm my body's used to with anticipated extra rest, I'm breaking it with extra work.

There is a marina in the city, but in this wind strength we don't want to attempt an unknown place only to find out too late that it's too shallow, too small, or full. Instead, we turn into the bay before the marina where Rolf has anchored on previous visits. He tells me there's a yacht club in the foot of the little bay, and we anchor outside their buoys. The holding in the oozy bottom is terrible, so we alternate anchor watch through the night. Off watch, my sleep is constantly disturbed by the city's noise.

The wind finally dies enough for us to head into the marina. It's Friday afternoon and we are determined to announce our arrival to the authorities so that even if the entire clearance procedure is not completed, we may be allowed ashore over the weekend. Because the tropical rain continues unabated, we keep our foul weather gear on and head for the bus.

A Brazilian yachtie intercepts us at the gate. "Never," he says, "I repeat, *never* leave the marina with those clothes on. They mark you as rich. You won't make it across the park to the bus stop without being attacked. You must understand these homeless people here are desperate," he continues in a low but emphatic tone, "and *kill* for as little as a pair of shoes or a person's bus fare . . . yes, bus fare. There are gangs living in the entirety of this park." He points left with his left hand and our eyes follow. As he fully extends his right arm we understand: the battle zone rims not only the marina but the entire shorefront. "Never cross this park alone or at night. Never wear jewelry or carry a purse. And if you go shopping and are bringing things back to the boat, take a taxi from town or from the bus stop and have the driver deliver you through the gate. Once inside, you are safe," he says, his voice trailing off as he points to armed guards patrolling the high chain-link fence.

We turn back, so deflated that we decide to have the marina manager phone the authorities to announce our arrival. We secure their approval to delay the start of clearance procedures until Monday, under the proviso that we remain inside the marina until then. Confinement over a weekend presents no problem. After all, we aren't kids champing at the bit to get off the boat to explore an exciting new city. But by Sunday's final hour, looking at that fence and the guards' automatic weapons has made me feel like I am serving time. *So this is what it's like to be rich?* I wonder.

Over the weekend we make the acquaintance of our single-handing neighbor, who kindly volunteers to help us through the multiphased maze of clearance procedures. He's been through it himself and knows where all the buildings are; as an added bonus, he speaks pretty good Portuguese and can translate for us! On Monday morning, the three of us walk out of the cage to brave our way into town. We negotiate the park, which looks as peaceful as can be, listening to his advice on safe routes, and then jump on a full-to-overflowing multicolored bus. My eyes scan the faces of one person after another, seeing much history in the people's varied skin tones and features. During the ride, Rolf points out that people on the streets are crowding around the newsstands, reading the posted front pages. We wonder what has happened. After disembarking, we jostle our way through a crowd to look. Gory pictures of the weekend's typical street "casualties," all butchered and bloody, is the news that draws everyone. I wonder more about this place.

Upon entering the official glass and steel building, our guide leads us to an empty office where we wait until the maritime immigration officer arrives. A rather morose man, he doesn't greet us, at least not in the normal verbal sense. Instead, he removes his gun from his holster and waves it, motioning us to sit down on the other side of his desk, before laying it on the desktop. Passports are passed to him. He looks through Rolf's, then mine. He pages forth and back and forth again, then speaks his first words to our interpreter. "Shapiro, Deborah, has no visa."

"That's correct," I respond. "When we checked in Madeira, we were told neither Swedes nor Americans need one."

"Ah, yes," the immigration official continues. "But just recently the U.S.A. put a visa requirement on Brazilian tourists and Brazil countered. American citizens now need a visa."

What are we to do? The official, working for what's called the Federal Police, explains something we already know: tourists needing a visa must obtain it before coming to the country. Anyone arriving by plane without a visa, he intones, is turned away on the next flight. My circumstances are different. I'll have to leave the country within three days and obtain a visa before coming back. While he and our translator continue conversing in Portuguese, we consider another alternative: sailing away from Brazil. But it's too early in the season to head south to Argentina, and the island of St. Helena is halfway back across the Atlantic. Either is possible, but neither desirable.

We ask our translator what they have been talking about. As his "answer" he waves his hands in exasperation. The policeman is the next to speak. The closest, easiest place for me to go to get a visa is Paraguay, 900 miles (1450 km) away. Just over the border from Iguacu Falls is a Brazilian consulate. Since the tourist buses going there from Rio don't leave every day, he will increase my free time from three days to a week. If I get my visa while the tourists are viewing the falls, then I can come back with the same bus. The most time it can take is a few days. A lot of questions and answers are flying between our translator and the policeman. We keep trying to pry out a translation but are ignored. We wonder what is going on and hope our translator isn't taking it upon himself to answer questions on our behalf. The final statement is clear, however: when I leave the maritime sector office I am to proceed directly to the Federal Police's main building and get my passport stamped. He stamps Rolf's and away we go.

At the main office I do indeed get an entry stamp, valid for seven days, but the man there says I have to pay the equivalent of $150 for it. There's a bank in the lobby of the building where I can pay. "Baloney," says our translator as we leave the office. "The maritime official said your week is free. I've been here a long time and I know that these people are always trying to cheat foreigners out of whatever they can. You don't have to pay. Let's go."

In fact, paying now would be impossible anyway. After the lectures about the dangers of the park, the last thing I have on me is $150 cash. On we trod to customs, the next step in our check-in procedure.

That evening, our translator neighbor has two dinner guests, and one is a lawyer. When the lawyer hears what has transpired during the day he knocks on our boat and asks to chat. He is on vacation and offers to take me to a friend the next day to take care of my problem.

But when the friend looks at my passport, he says there's nothing he can do to help. I understand that it was bad to have left the Federal Police building without paying the "tax." The lawyer decides to investigate. We get a taxi to the maritime policeman, who shakes his head and tells the lawyer that I am damned lucky. The police had arrived at the marina just after we left that morning, planning to arrest me for not paying the $150! I feel lost. I have just delivered myself for arrest. "No, no," says the lawyer. "I can take responsibility for you, sort of like what you Americans would call bail." Oh, brother. My stomach churns.

"It is time," the lawyer declares, "to pay a visit to the main man." We march over to the Federal Police's main building. The lawyer leads us past the front desk and right up to the man who stamped my passport the day before. He is busy. There are lots of people ahead of us. Some heated words pass between him and the lawyer, none of which we understand. Follow me, the lawyer gestures. Through a swinging gate we go as a three-man parade, passing umpteen desks of armed police, and without even knocking, we barge right into the back office, the boss's office.

The boss is very big and doesn't look like he was friendly even as a child. He's scowling; we have interrupted a meeting in progress. Alone, I would never, *could* never, have done this. But "my" lawyer, a criminal lawyer by trade, possesses a well-honed sense of the theatrical and lays right into the mountainous man. I expect at any second to be grabbed and handcuffed. I keep wondering how this can ever turn out anything but bad, or worse. I wonder if Rolf should leave and hightail it to the American Embassy. If I am arrested—ooo, I don't want to think about it—but as captain, Rolf can be held responsible. . . . And if we are both arrested, then anything can happen.

I can't help but worry for the boat's safety. In 1977, the first time Rolf was here, he and his two crew were placed under house arrest for a week because *Northern Light* is red. Evidently, someone on a red sailboat had robbed a woman on Ascension Island, a spit of land rising out of the mid-Atlantic, and Interpol had issued a warrant for arrest. The police in Rio questioned all three on *Northern Light,* but they had not even been to Ascension. Charts with daily positions and the ship's log were produced as evidence, but a week passed before Interpol confirmed that *Northern Light* was not the boat they were after.

During that time there was another foreign yacht at the club plundered of electronic equipment, its owner in jail until he could prove the boat was his. The yacht club was watching over the boat because a previous foreign single-hander suspected of having committed some crime had gone to jail for a week and came out only to find his boat gone. It had disappeared without a trace, the police said. Anything, it seems, can happen here.

The lawyer gets nowhere with the boss, who says I should have paid the tax. Paying the tax now is not permitted. Leaving the country is also not permitted. Well then, what alternative is there? Is this the cue that resolution can only be accomplished by a payoff? I ask the lawyer if my hunch is correct, but whether it is or isn't is not of issue, he says; he is adamantly opposed to the practice. Historically, there has been so much corruption in Brazil that the newly elected president's campaign was based on the promise that corruption was now going to end. The lawyer has long been hoping that Brazil could turn itself around and feels morally bound to participate in making the promise real; therefore, he will untangle this mess without payoffs. Yet it doesn't seem that even he thinks the process will be free of risks. When putting us back into our high-fenced cage for the night he gives me his ID card, as if it holds some magical power. "If anyone comes here, wave this in his face. I promise they will not dare arrest you or harm you." *Oh, really?* I think. Could it get more bizarre?

The next morning, the lawyer has a new idea. We pile into a taxi and head for a new destination. "Itamarati," he instructs the driver. The car winds for what seems forever through a worn-out commercial section of Rio, finally stopping in front of a very inauspicious building. But once through the arched portal we are suddenly in another climate, another century. The pink two-story palace is built around a center courtyard and a shallow pool. Ibis stroll among the lily pads. Not a person is to be seen. The lawyer leads us, wide-eyed, to an ornately carved door sporting a brass name-plate engraved "Consulate of Brazil." And I must be Alice in Wonderland.

The palace was just that at one time, and just because the royals are gone doesn't mean it is no longer a special place. Today, though it sits undeniably in Brazil, it is simply declared non-Brazilian territory. Therefore, consular activities can be transacted on the premises on behalf of Brazil. Man is amazing, is he not? He creates his own rules, then creates ways to legally circumvent them. Poof! "You can apply for your visa here, Deborah," the lawyer calmly tells me. Cautious smiles, but smiles nonetheless, are exchanged.

The lawyer has done his research and found the key the police hid from us. The drawbridge to the palace does not lower for everyone. I have the right to apply for my visa here because of the international maritime convention that states that people arriving by sea who cannot have applied for a visa within the last three months because they were either at sea or haven't during that time visited any country with an appropriate consulate may be granted a visa upon arrival. It is not as strange as it sounds; the convention exists to facilitate world commerce. In many instances a vessel at sea receives rerouting instructions via radio or telex and arrives in port with visaless personnel. In Brazil their visa applications are filled in on the palace grounds; as mine is to be. I finally start to relax.

"Not so fast," the woman behind the desk says. "You can't start a visa application while this tax stamp is in effect. It has to be voided first." Oh, no. Rolf and I frown. But the lawyer smiles; he actually seems to be enjoying himself. Why not? He's on vacation, after all.

We zip back to the Federal Police's main office. I must admit that I'm sweating. And what a commotion the lawyer starts, screaming all the way down the corridor—so the guy can't help but know who it is who's coming—and taking the office by storm, where he verbally corrals the guy who originally stamped my passport and hauls him back out into the main lobby, ranting and raving at him in public. After a few minutes the policeman walks over to a clerk's window, where he borrows a big red VOID stamp, and in one fell swoop he obliterates the only obstacle between me and our freedom. I am fingerprinted and then, albeit more confused, back we taxi to the peace of the palace.

My finished application will be telexed to Brasilia, the capital, for processing. "Could you please come back tomorrow?" the clerk asks. Looking at the residue of ink on my fingertips, I consider refusing to leave this safe sanctuary. But instead we go to buy dinner for our friend and hero at his favorite steak restaurant. He digs in with gusto, but even though the dinner is probably very good, my appetite seems to have disappeared.

The next day, the answer to my application hasn't arrived. The lawyer checks to be sure I am still in possession of his ID card and reminds me to carry it at all times, especially since my passport now sits with the application in the consulate. "It's very bad to be stopped in Brazil and not have an ID," he cautions. It says a lot about the system that it's not just OK but actually good for me to carry *his* ID. But, as I explain to him, it's a moot point: I won't be stopped because I won't be out. Whenever we get back to the boat these days I just don't feel like leaving. For some reason, neither samba school, the beach at Copacabana, nor the statue of an open-armed Christ holds any attraction.

The next day is Friday. It's an anniversary: this crazy dance has been going on for a whole week. The telex is not there in the morning, and no, the telex has not arrived in the afternoon, but we can sit and wait for it. I don't like the slight sneer that creeps into this woman's pasted-on smile, or am I imagining things? We three sit a long time without speaking on a bench outside her office, under a covered walkway that continues around the entire courtyard, meditating on the shafts of sunlight hitting the pool and the birds gracefully drifting freely in and out of shadow. The lawyer tells me the name of the birds in Portuguese. It doesn't stick.

The consul himself occasionally comes and goes from his office, which adjoins that of his underlings. Late Friday afternoon, as it's getting uncomfortably close to quitting time, he pads by us, his slippers making a lovely, soft sound on the marble walk. The homey feeling, antithetic to recent events, gives me courage. "Excuse me, sir. Do you speak English?"

"I do indeed, Miss Shapiro. And I have spent many lovely times in your country."

I venture, "May I speak with you a moment?" He nods and we three traipse into his office.

"I am already aware of your situation," the consul informs us, although by his first words we have all surmised as much, I am sure.

My voice is smaller than usual as I say: "As you probably know my passport is—rather has been—here for three days. Could you please issue a notice on your stationary to the effect that my passport is in the consulate, pending an answer from Brasilia about my visa? I would like to be able to move around the city over the weekend without being scared of not being able to produce any papers."

Before I finish he is already on his way out of his chair. "Your passport has been here? Just a moment, I must check," he says. Visibly flustered, he disappears through the door to the adjoining office. Within moments, he returns with the blue-covered pages, property of the U.S. government, in his hand. Sitting down again behind his massive carved desk, he opens it to my new visa, signs it with great flourish, and says without further ado: "Now, you don't need any letter. On Monday, show this to the Maritime Federal Police and continue the check-in procedure for your yacht. Welcome to Brazil."

Early Saturday morning our Portuguese-speaking neighbor sails away, taking the lawyer with him for what remains of his vacation. Rolf and I do very little all day, but we do brave the park once to shop for fresh fruits and vegetables, in the hope that eating light will help us decompress. After all, we have to be able to face the rest of the authorities the following week.

As always, it takes the time it takes: filling out forms, making copies, going from office to office. Customs wants a list of *everything* we have on board, but it has to be deposited at a different office, and the navy has to double check both immigration's and customs' work. Then last comes what should logically be first: the health authorities have to give us and the boat a clean bill of health. By Thursday we are finally cleared in. We sail away from Rio without looking back. Its beauty isn't even skin deep.

Of course, we aren't the only people with a negative impression of Rio. Once a very popular sight for conventions, the city has been boycotted for some time now. Copacabana's hotel-lined beach is so polluted with raw sewage that people can no longer swim there. More important, conventioneers got fed up with being robbed, mugged, or witnessing crime. Evidently they have found a place where they can have a better time, perhaps a city where the gap between rich and poor is not as great as in Rio. In my opinion, nowhere are moneyless people as poor as they are in big cities.

Whenever we went out of the marina during our twelve days in Rio, we followed all the advice about the park and we were never as much as hassled by anyone. But during one crossing, we had to skirt a pile of cardboard boxes and plastic trash bags on the sidewalk that had lifeless arms and legs sticking out of it. I couldn't begin to bring myself to stop and check. On average, a dozen murders are committed each day in Rio, and that doesn't include the police's killing of street children. We never visited anyone's home in Rio, but we know that many people with money live in guarded compounds. Those without money live in *favelas*. I doubt if any of us can imagine the stench or the despair of those cardboard slums.

Open water has never felt or smelled as good. We continue along the coastline and into the pearl necklace of islands off the Brazilian coast, anchoring every day, swimming in crystal clear water, walking on sandy beaches, and relaxing under palms. People we meet are healthy and happy. The dizzying dance starts to lose its effect on us. When we cross paths with our interpreter and lawyer, it is time for celebration. We barbecue on the beach, feasting on Brazilian delicacies, enjoying the result of the persistence and sharp faculties of a man who gave of himself and took risks on our behalf and for the future of his country. We wish him well.

8

DO YOU RECOGNIZE ME?

DEBORAH

■ ■ ■

I am certainly not the first person, nor will I be the last, to stand under a star-pierced night sky and ponder the myriad twinkling lights and the sheer distances of space. Sometimes, for comfort's sake, I pull back and away from the enveloping vastness and the feeling of imminent annihilation by picking out constellations or individual stars whose names I know. Tonight, for the sake of rapture, I let my thoughts wander to infinity.

Infinity: nonending. What an enthralling concept. It has been said that we humans can't have a conceptual understanding unless we have a word for it. But does it follow that just because we have a word, the something it represents actually exists?

As far as I can tell, there is no thing that numbers infinitely, except numbers themselves, and numbers are our own invention. We accept the mathematical concept that infinity is greater than any assignable quantity—although truthfully, it (the biggest number we can fix plus one) is as incomprehensible as any other devised concept we accept on faith. As far as I am concerned, that type of acceptance, and not ignorance, is true bliss.

But space then, is space infinite? If it is, that means it is boundless. If it goes on forever, that must mean in all directions. If I am to accept that it never ends in *any* direction, pray tell, where or how does it begin? A thing that exists without beginning is difficult to comprehend or even accept for that matter.

Well, what if we consider that if it never ends, it never begins either. It, ergo, doesn't exist. Oops, I don't like that scenario. It puts my existence in big trouble. So just maybe it starts right here instead and radiates away from me in all directions. That makes me the center of the universe. Ha! I always knew it!

Personal entertainment aside, we humans can go only so far. The chance of us ever fixing our place and role in the universe is one divided by infinity, that is to say infinitesimally small. Well, I can be just as happy imagining our solar system as a decorative trinket in some monstrously huge being's aquarium as I can be with no answer at all. Based on all I perceive, we humans don't really get farther than the sorry, shallow, and distinctly limited finite. Maybe for all our creative wishful thinking, nothing more exists.

Probably not dinner even, unless I come back down to earth soon. Hmm. Bring infinity to bear on woman's work and maybe I can accept it after all.

No more time to kill under space's canopy. My anchorage reverie is broken by the buzz of an outboard motor and, above that, the sound of voices. First Rolf's, then Rubens'! For our last night in Brazil, we have the pleasure of a visit of our friend and honored guest, Rubens J. Villela. A meteorologist and professor at the University of São Paulo, he is an expert in Antarctic meteorology and has gathered data since his first visit during the International Geophysical Year of 1957–58. We met Rubens in 1984 in Ushuaia. He, too, was on his way to Antarctica then, but his transportation was a Brazilian research vessel.

Very special friendships always start intensely, I think, as between us and Rubens. We had many shared interests, but our different fields of expertise allowed all three of us to give and get. Over the years, we have secretly planned on "kidnapping" Rubens, to have him with us for an extended period of time, to be able to truly get to know him and learn from him. An evening's chat is so short that it's almost painful.

We exchange all the news since our last letter volley and then future plans are spread like cards on the table. After Rolf outlines the three expeditions we have in mind, Rubens informs that the two previous winters (1988 and 1989) along the peninsula were both very mild. In addition, he just recently received an eyewitness report that right now, at the onset of spring, there is very little ice to be seen. I can feel a smile building deep within me.

For the rest of the visit Rolf can hardly sit still and has a hard time keeping track of the conversation, to say nothing of his duties as host. I certainly understand. The key puzzle piece to our years of planning and work has just fallen into place. Our elasticity, nearly spent, may just be on the rebound.

At about the witching hour, with the dinghy secured on deck after ferrying Rubens ashore, Rolf stands near the mainmast, each hand gripping a shroud, gazing out into the cozy tropical darkness and looking at nothing. I tap his arm gently. As he turns toward me, a relaxed face starts to open, to blossom, until both eyebrows are up to his hairline in anticipation. There's no need to say anything; I simply smile. I am grabbed in his arms, whirled around so many times I become dizzy. We are both giggling, smiling, a little breathless. Overwintering has always been the project we each favored, and now it's on. Tomorrow we'll set sail for Mar del Plata, Argentina, where we'll provision for Antarctica. We'll be sure to have all we need aboard so that if we find a suitable anchorage and the conditions are favorable, we can stay the time it takes for Earth to complete an entire orbit around the Sun.

A mere 12 miles of our 1,000 nautical miles to Argentina have ticked on the log when its wire snaps, rendering it useless. As a backup, we have a tow-log we can trail behind us if necessary, while closing the coast, for example. In actuality, the loss of the log is not perceived as a problem in these latitudes, where we can almost always get at least one sight a day and fix our position. In fact, we both think that without it, we can have some fun testing ourselves.

For us, the worst instrument to lose would be the compass; estimating steered course is exceedingly difficult. Estimating wind speed is next most difficult, Rolf tells me, although because we have no instrument for it, I wouldn't know. Easiest of all to estimate is speed through water. In my early sailing days, with the help of the log, I soon got to know the sounds and feelings of different speeds. On *Northern Light*, the magic breaking point that is the easiest increase to feel is around 3.6 knots. Then the fresh sound of water frothing along the hull is first apparent.

With a functioning log, it's only a matter of reading it at the end of each watch and adjusting the miles logged for known instrument error to record how much distance has been covered. Without a log, we must instead record each time the speed changes, what the time is, and the speed we estimate the boat's had since the previous entry and then compute the distance. By coupling each distance with the true course steered and adjusting for current, we can keep track of our estimated position, a necessary starting point when working out a celestial sight.

During this passage we check our estimations at the end of each watch with the GPS. It turns out that neither of us is ever more than half of a knot wrong in our speed estimation. Sally says so. It's great fun, with a great payback: the process of guesstimation, simple arithmetic, and navigation, like any other form of mental gymnastics performed at sea, helps keep the gray matter from addling.

I once met a man who had made a passage from the Canary Islands to the Caribbean and who told me he was bored to death the whole way. He had nothing to *do*. There was nowhere to go and nowhere to get stimulation. When I said I enjoyed long passages, his conclusion was that my tolerance for boredom was much higher than his. Perhaps he was right. On the other hand, if he had been out longer or tried again, perhaps he would have found the key: whereas solutions for boredom on shore can be bought, at sea they must be created.

Sailing in itself is an active endeavor. Where there's already momentum it's easier to be drawn to or move into any other activity. Opposing this human trait is a natural law that says that every organism seeks its lowest energy expenditure. This seems to divide us into two teams: the A team, where A stands for active, and the C team for the couch potatoes (previously known as the T team "tubers," for those of you interested in phylogeny).

What happens to people when there really is no stimulation? I don't mean at sea, or when there's nothing good to watch on TV, or even when frozen in for the winter in Antarctica. I mean when a person, for the sake of experiment, is suspended in an isolation tank. The water is supersaturated with salt, so the subject is weightless. The water is heated to exact body temperature, so one feels neither warm nor cold. The tank is totally sealed, so there's no sound, no light.

After only a few hours without stimulation the brain starts to compensate. The subject hallucinates. In the absence of outside stimulation, the brain creates its own. From that I deduce that we actually *need* to be mentally stimulated, i.e., active. I daresay it's the simplest answer to the question, What's life all about? and therefore a key to a healthy life.

Out at sea, a bored person first looks for known avenues of stimulation. He or she listens to music, reads a book, watches a video, or talks on the radio. There's nothing wrong with that; we are all creatures of habit. But healthy people can accept change. They can become involved in what it takes to sail a boat from point A to B. Sure, there's the obvious boat handling and sail trim to learn, and there are often fellow crew to take care of and socialize with. And there's navigation. I don't mean the "tubers" electronic type. Although it's fast and often convenient, there's nothing fascinating in getting the answer from a black box.

Celestial navigation not only puts your position on a chart; in the process it places Earth in perspective with its moon and sun and in the solar system! Now that's a benefit. Beyond pure learning and skill building, you also gain a new vantage point on perspective itself. Ironically, your new position reinforces the idea of the starting point, the importance of activity. Because not only is it fulfilling to have learned how to fix your position from celestial bodies, you have the security of knowing that when the electricity fails (for fail it will), you will not be thrown off course. Yes, it's hard to stop a person with momentum.

And then, just maybe, suddenly, as if from nowhere, creativity starts to flow. Other projects and possibilities appear. Small things bud and blossom. A person writes, paints, plays, designs, or thinks.

I don't find that there is much time on shore to think. There we spend most of our nonworking thinking time being informed: listening, watching, reading. When we cut the shore lines, that source evaporates. One starts to think about "old news," dissecting, cataloging, and judging it along with old thought patterns and habits. Instead of always taking in what others are doing and therefore moving laterally, one can go deep.

It's like the white man we've seen following an Indian scout in so many movies. The white man sees the forest like a painting, in two dimensions. The Indian scout also sees its depth, with overlays. Animal tracks speak to him, adding historical perspective and providing him with clues necessary for survival. Smells and sounds turn his head, while the as-yet-uninitiated wonders what's going on.

A city person's senses are shut down; they have to be. Imagine what would happen if you really took in every sight, sound, and smell on a subway. You'd go whirlwind crazy in mere minutes. To protect yourself there, you have to be able to block things out. It therefore follows that it takes an adjustment period for us to see and hear and smell in the wild, just as it takes time to get used to not living in heated spaces. But the capabilities are there in us all, waiting to be opened like the birthday presents they are. Observe and you will find infinite variety inside the infinitesimal as easily as within the infinite. Listen, and whispers will become shouts.

Watching TV is simple and doesn't take much energy. Turn on the tube and we have instant *something*. But there is real and tangible danger from taking the easy route. While watching TV, we are in a passive-absorption mode. We tend not to question the information in programs or advertising. Why would it be false, why should it be? Nor do we question the news or even the selection of subjects presented there. Maybe, when angered, we yell aloud, or perhaps we groan at someone else's pain. But what do we do about it? We can't do anything for or against anyone in a TV program. What do we do about what we see on the news? I find it worrisome not just that watching TV is a passive pastime but that TV trains people to be generally passive, to watch without ever thinking to react, respond, or do anything about the information.

What's the result of packing in 100 channels' worth of information? What about the "bombardment" presentation style that's prevalent now on TV and getting worse each year? What does mental indigestion do to us? What is the result of knowing about all the bad things people are doing to each other? Why do we accept violence as entertainment, when it's the last thing we want in our real life? Where does all this lead? Does it encourage us to think about the future or provide us with the tools to develop analytical thought or vision?

I think about the word *lead* in the sense of guidance. The strongest powers in our Western world are commercial, and they want to keep us on the path of consumerism. We ought to give a thought to equality, sharing, the responsibility of democracy, and other concepts we try to teach children. We can do it and lead ourselves to better-balanced times if we turn to each other instead of a black box. In China there is a saying, "Look afar and see the end from the beginning." If the beginning is now, based on the shape we're in, we'd better get active.

Statistically expected, the wind remains southwest, against us on a jaw-jarring beat into the long swell. But the sky and water are an azure blue, the same color as the inner peace I feel. The future pleases me. That helps to look past present discomfort and be pleased now as well.

After three days the headwind dies down and we heave to. The old, worn-out genoa we've been using under the harsh sun of the Tropics needs repair. The entire foredeck, an uncluttered space on *Northern Light,* as it should be on any cruising boat, is our biggest workshop. Kneeling, I move the roll of cloth under the arm of the sewing machine, feeding the machine as Rolf cranks, spinning the wheel at a constant medium tempo, the only tempo the persnickety machine accepts.

"I wish I could work faster," Rolf mutters as the needle stitches a zigzag pattern on a panel near the leech. "This machine has got to be below before that headwind picks up again." Luck is with us. Not until the sail has received the attention it craved does the wind pick up again, after veering into a favorable sector astern. We hoist the genoa and take off, enjoying four straight days of positively delicious idyllic sailing, discomfort replaced by cloud-riding. More kinks unwind.

Approaching the broad mouth of Rio de la Plata, with the wide-open space of the pampas to the west, we enter a new weather pattern, directly influenced by Antarctica. Here, the cool southerly wind can meet and mix with warmer air from the Tropics and create tempestuous gales called *pamperos.* We keep a sharp lookout. Crossing the river mouth, there is a front flanking the western horizon, lightning delineating its outer edge. Concerned that our old sail won't withstand a heavy blow, we replace it with a newer, high-cut Yankee. *Pamperos* are often accompanied by heavy rain. We get a day-long torrential downpour, but the front stalls and the wind never reaches gale force.

As we approach the manmade harbor of Mar del Plata, a string of big trawlers is leaving. Without them as a reference point, I would never have realized the immensity of the stones comprising the mile-long breakwaters. The fishing boats favor the north side of the entrance, so we stay to the middle. There are no depth markings on the chart, but we can clearly see from the shifting color that there's a shoaling problem from the southern arm toward the middle of the entrance. The ocean swell rises up, rolls, and breaks over the shallow area, and *Northern Light* surfs in through the harbor entrance. Whoa, Nelly!

Tucked into the very back of the otherwise commercial harbor is a small yacht harbor. The Yacht Club of Argentina, one of three clubs inside, welcomes foreign yachts by extending one month's stay free of charge. We have arrived on a Sunday afternoon in late October, and the onset of summer has everyone in high spirits. People help us tie up at the guest pontoon, alongside visiting yachts from all over Europe and two from Japan! These rather small fiberglass boats are the first Japanese cruising boats we have ever seen. *Shirahae* has a couple on board. On the dock, I cross paths with pretty, petite Akemi, her straight, jet-black hair and bangs framing her alabaster face. While we chat, her husband, Yoshio, sitting out in their dinghy painting pastels, suddenly closes up shop and rows like mad to us. He has something he must tell me.

It seems that after searching a long time, he had finally located a copy of our first book, only to be terribly disappointed. *Oh, no,* I think and look down, studying my toes. Yoshio's voice becomes measured. "I don't care what anyone else says, that book is *not* a book for us cruisers," he says. My eyes close. He rants on, "It's . . . it's too heavy."

Man, oh man. Sometimes, I wish my name were Dorothy and I could just click my heels together and disappear. After an uncomfortable moment passes, while I wonder how anyone could ever think high-latitude sailing is simply fun and games, Yoshio clears his throat. Then he lays into me. "Yes, heavy, by which I mean, it weighs too much. So I tore the hard-back cover off and threw it away." A smile creeps into his face. "And now, everything's OK Deborah. If I go get it, would you and Rolf sign it?" he asks.

When our laughter peters out and I regain my composure, I must still seem a little distracted to my new friends. I am on the lookout for an Argentine man who I hope to recognize even though we have never met. All I have to go on is a photo of him taken thirteen years ago, when he was just a boy.

When Rolf arrived here in 1977, visits from foreign yachts were uncommon. The first person to greet *Northern Light* that day was a twelve-year-old dark-haired boy. He rowed out just after Rolf and his two crew had anchored, to formally welcome them to Mar del Plata and the club and to offer any help they might need. In his school-learned English, the boy said he would be pleased to show the captain where the authorities' offices were the following day. Rolf didn't entirely believe the promise, but sure enough, he showed up on schedule, knew his way around, and was of exemplary help!

During their stay, the boy, named Mariano, invited Rolf and the crew home to introduce them to his entire family. And when *Northern Light* departed for Cape Horn and the Chilean channels, Mariano and his pals stood on the breakwater holding up a bon voyage sign that they had handpainted on a bedsheet! I figure if Mariano still lives in Mar del Plata, chances are he is now a full-fledged member of the club himself, and as it's Sunday, he just may show up today. But no, no Mariano.

Check-in takes nearly all day Monday, and just as the closed sign is being turned streetside, we squeeze through the door of a travel agency to buy me a plane ticket to the United States. I am being sent to do what I least like to do in the whole world: shop. But we are lacking some important pieces of gear: wind generator, carbon monoxide alarm, desalination plant, spare skis, fresh film, and freeze-dried food, which we didn't want to buy until we were sure we were going to overwinter. We figure the fastest, least expensive, and most reliable place to buy everything is in the United States. The ticket is easily arranged. I'll fly in three days.

The next day, as Rolf works on deck, hanging nearly upside-down to service a block at the rail, a fancy speedboat pulls up and idles alongside. "Hello, Rolf," says a handsome, swarthy young man. "Do you recognize me?" he asks. For a few seconds Rolf draws a blank, because he never really had any hope of seeing him. But when Mariano knows he's been recognized, he jumps aboard and gives *El Sueco* a bear hug. "I saw the red boats when I left this morning, but didn't realize until later that one was *Northern Light*," he says. "I had no idea you were coming. How are you? How have you been? Do you have the same crew as last time? How wonderful to see you again. You look just the same," finishes Mariano, as he tugs playfully on Rolf's beard and backs off, hands on hips, to look at his friend once again.

Seeing Mariano again is like giving Rolf the key to the city. They are instantly connected. Mariano promises me an Argentine barbecue when I return. I depart for Pittsburgh, without letting anyone know I am coming. How often does one get to surprise the whole family?

My parents are both curious and concerned about our imminent project, and I detail our overwinter theories and plans for them. One of my father's (and our) major winter concerns is the danger of carbon monoxide poisoning. No one wants to wake up dead, so my shopping list includes a CO detector with an alarm. My father gives it to us as a present. In addition, he arranges a package of dosimeters so that we will be able to measure the amount of carbon monoxide present inside the boat each week. With constant monitoring, we'll be able to check that everything is working as it should and be alerted of any change long before it hits dangerous levels.

In my absence, Rolf has a modicum of peace and quiet and accomplishes job after job listed in the back of our logbook. One time-consuming chore is to sort through all the spare parts and assorted repair materials we have accumulated through the years. Because *Northern Light* will soon be loaded with tons of provisions, it is crucial that it first be lightened as much as possible. Rolf must get rid of everything he can, but he can make no mistakes; today's junk can be tomorrow's gold. One thing after another leaves the boat. Rolf arranges with other sailors that anything he puts on the dock is free for the taking. What isn't snatched up goes to the trash. When he's feeling creative, he designs and builds a "moonlander," at least that's what the other yachties call it. None of them ever figures out its purpose, but it's to be a steplessly adjustable (both fore-aft and port-starboard) video camera support.

When I return, we begin a mammoth provisioning. Because *none* of our food will be taken by hunting, fishing, or gathering in the Antarctic (for the reason that we give it wilderness status), eighteen months of supplies are to be brought aboard. As always when we foodshop in a new country, scouting comes first. Mariano and his family are a big help. His father, Hector, has contacts in the meat business and takes us to a couple of specialty markets. Mariano and his girlfriend, Karina, drive us all over, first to case supermarkets with lists, dictionary, and calculator in hand. We price and buy samples to test, then return and buy basket after basket of food. What a charge the supermarket employees get out of watching us! Not since grade school has the air around me been so saturated with whispers and giggles.

Gradually, we become adept at shopping Argentinian style. It becomes clear that what you see you can buy, and that tomorrow it may have disappeared. If it's not on the shelf, don't ask. Even if it is in the stockroom, you won't get it, and not one store manager is willing to place special orders for us. Another reason not to hesitate purchasing is that it will be more expensive tomorrow than today, both because of runaway inflation in Argentina and because the dollar happens to be lower each time we exchange.

Our wallet may be thin when we leave, but the pantry shelves will be well stocked! Many different food cultures are represented in Argentina, and a wide variety of comestibles are available. Mar del Plata is a fishing port, so the canned fish products are fantastic. Yes! Pasta will be served with my favorite clam sauce made with whole, succulent nuggets, no less. Meat is a number 1 priority in Argentina, and their beef is the best I have ever tasted. But, the canned corned beef and roast beef we buy elsewhere in the world that comes from Argentina is not available here. On the other hand, cured meats are.

The suppliers can't tell us just how long dried, smoked, or salted pork and beef will last. Although we are optimistic and buy as if they will last the entire time, we take on extra beans, lentils, and brown rice as part of the normal extra percentage we always buy as emergency stores. We stock up with wheels of cheese, kilos of aromatic coffee beans and cocoa, and bag after bag of flour ground within the last month. There are also great health food stores where we buy dried vegetables—leeks, carrots, spinach, squash, tomatoes, and potatoes—and dried peaches, pears, apples, raisins, and apricots. And luck of luck, from friendly neighbors we get a piece of a fungus that lives in symbiotic bliss with bacteria. If we feed it milk reconstituted from whole milk powder, we'll end up with fresh kefir and therefore cream cheese. Both will add variety to our diet. We'll also have sprouts. Long may "bush gourmet" reign!

While alongside the fuel dock, filling our diesel and former water tanks and our five 100-liter (26-gal) plastic barrels with the 1,175 liters (310 gal) of diesel we need for the expedition, Tate, the Japanese singlehander from *Red Sun*, stands on the dock watching the pump's meter spin round and round, shaking his head and chuckling. When Tate tells me that he is considering going to the Antarctic Peninsula for the summer, I tell him we've heard there is little ice this year, although going in a fiberglass boat is never to be recommended. His answer is forthright: "I career Japanese paratrooper. I do anything." He says it without conceit, simply stating it as an indisputable fact.

The weather is unfortunately sunny and warm, not at all good for food-storage conditions on board. Canned and dry goods, the foodstuffs least affected by heat, are brought aboard first. Before we hit the hay each night, everything is properly stowed and even though the sheer volumes are incredible, there always seems to be space for more. Experience comes in handy sometimes. Eventually, it's time to shop for the sturdiest fresh fruits and vegetables. Onions, potatoes, squashes, apples, and oranges fill a few carloads. Finally, the day before departure, we scour the *supermercados* within walking distance for delicate fresh vegetables.

Late in the afternoon, the last of our provisions arrive: 500 eggs, fresh from the farm. They are a gift from Don Carlos, a man Rolf met on his previous visit. Back then, Carlos had fishing boats. Today, he sells fish meal to egg farmers. When he read over our shopping list (a "must read" circulating in the marina), Carlos wondered if eggs could last as long as our planned stay in Antarctica. Rolf twisted his question by answering that the eggs would last only if we ration them to one per day! Carlos laughed and replied that when we crack open that 500-day-old egg, he'll be perfectly happy to be as far away as Mar del Plata.

The truth is, the eggs won't be edible that long, but we'll have to learn by experience just where the cutoff point is. As soon as the first rotten egg appears, we will break, beat, and freeze the rest, or start eating a lot of omelets! Carlos said that no matter what happens to them, he would like to provide the eggs and, upon our request, promises that they will never have been refrigerated.

We finally finish shopping! I don't complain; after all, five weeks of concentrated shop shop shop means none at all for the next eighteen months. We are headed to a realm where money is of no use.

I call Rolf up on deck. It's time, I tell him, for a little ceremony. Holding the sheaf of lists we've lived with and from, I put a flame to them. Poof, they go. It is time to move on. I certainly hope we haven't forgotten anything.

That evening is the weekly potluck dinner that cruising folks share in the clubhouse. They declare it a good-bye party for us, but—visions of Fiskebäckskil—we don't have time to attend.

9

PREGNANT
TURTLE

ROLF

■ ■ ■

The night before something special is supposed to happen, I usually sleep fitfully. This time is no exception. My rest is repeatedly broken. Each time I wake, the tension generated by the prospect of our pending departure builds. I toss and turn, mentally reviewing every predeparture checklist. It doesn't seem to matter how well prepared I am; there's still an undercurrent of uncertainty, just as I used to feel on the night before a big exam.

I think about the future and what is at stake. Once in Antarctica we will be directly responsible for every decision we make. The continent is a No Man's Land in its true meaning. There is no other person, group, or governmental agency to judge our level of skill or tell us what to do. We will be answerable only to ourselves, but we are our own toughest critics. If we make even one mistake that leads to environmental damage of some sort, our consciences will haunt us the rest of our lives.

As the pouring rain drums on deck, my thoughts take me to 1984 when Deborah and I first visited the Antarctic Peninsula. We found then that all human activities were undertaken arbitrarily. People's doings were not steered or controlled by international laws; even the few that existed were often ignored. The result was that military, scientific, and tourist groups had already had such an impact on the environment that Antarctica could no longer be called a wilderness. Yet huge areas were still completely undisturbed. We came to believe that guidelines placing the future of Antarctica above human's convenience would offer nature a possibility to recover fully. Its recovery is important, not just for the future of Antarctica itself. The continent influences the weather of the entire planet Earth and thereby steers the global ecological balance.

Deborah and I had always wished to live for a while in a place that had not yet completely lost its primordial nature, yet as time passed, a need grew. We wanted to ascertain whether or not it is possible to live in a fragile ecosystem without any demonstrable impact on the environment. If we can leave a place as we found it, so can others, we reasoned. To understand what measures must be taken for Antarctica's healing to start, we decided to study its present state in situ.

My restless thinking carries me back to when we outfitted *Northern Light* for this voyage. As soon as someone heard we might sail to Antarctica and let the boat freeze into the ice for a winter, we were asked, "How can you possibly take along everything you'll need?" And often that question was followed by one I really came to dislike: "Won't the boat be crushed by the ice?"

I had theories about what happens as a boat freezes into the ice. I took into consideration the possible influence of the tide, current, and violent storms on ice as it builds. I studied all the facts I could find explaining why other boats had sunk or survived. But because I didn't have any actual experience with the winter conditions along the peninsula, that question always reminded me that I didn't have any *real* answer.

Despite that, I explained to people that as the ice forms, there is no pressure generated that would crush the hull as long as there is room for expansion, on the vertical plane, for example. But when the one hundredth person asked the same question, I started to wonder if I was really right. Could there be something I hadn't given thought to? *Can* the boat be damaged and sink?

There was no one around to ask. No other Swedish vessel had ever spent the winter in Antarctica, and of the five foreign sailboats that tried earlier, one was pushed down through the ice by the weight of the snow and filled with water, one got its rudder damaged, one sprung a leak, and one needed the help of an icebreaker to get out. Only one of the five had made it away scot-free.

Before we left Sweden, some people insisted that just the idea of spending the winter in Antarctica was insane. Maybe they were right, I thought. Perhaps Deborah and I had started something that we would not be able to pull off. The more delayed and overworked we became, the more I wondered if the whole project wasn't an unrealistic dream. Maybe dangers I wasn't even aware of would lead to catastrophe, and I don't mean only for us personally. What will happen if we sink and over 400 gallons (1,500 liters) of diesel, kerosene, oil, and other chemicals leak out among seals, penguins, and other birds? How could we be absolutely sure that we weren't actually on our way to *create* an environmental disaster in one of Earth's most fragile areas? What knowledge do we have to judge beforehand what our minimum and maximum effect on the environment can be, either if everything works as we planned or if the worst were to happen?

For more than three years, I have tried to answer the questions as fairly as possible, but I'm still uncertain. Questions loom about responsibility, such as, What gives us the right to personally take such a great responsibility? What does it actually mean to take personal responsibility? Can we as individuals really take the responsibility for the environment?

Certainly we can, many would answer. But can an individual really judge that his or her presence doesn't disturb the balance in a fragile ecosystem? I don't think so. Can one then really say that one can shoulder personal responsibility? Regardless, if the individual cannot guarantee either the physical or monetary capacity to correct the negative effects he or she causes, then that person doesn't have the right to assume this responsibility. How can they?

When it eventually starts to get light, I wake Deborah and we quickly get going. There are some loose ends to tie up before Mariano and Karina show up to help us get away from the dock. *Northern Light* was put in such a cramped back corner of the marina while being loaded with provisions that we can't make it out without a tow. At ten o'clock, just a couple of minutes after Deborah and I have brought aboard the last jerry can of fresh water, they come alongside with Hector's 24-foot powerboat.

We had hoped to get underway before the cold front that gave us last night's downpour passed; while the southwesterly breeze stood, we would have had a broad reach out of the harbor. But we weren't that lucky. The conditions we wanted lasted until just before twilight, when the wind diminished and started to shift to southerly. Now there is a very light southeasterly, on its way to becoming easterly. We are going to have to beat our way out.

Because the barometer is rising, we expect the wind to continue to shift counterclockwise to northeasterly. If it does, we will be able to give some slack in the sheets later in the day. My belief is that the big weather picture portends a nice start for the 1,600 nautical miles we have ahead of us, to our intended landfall on the Antarctic Peninsula.

It is still some time before high water, and the tidal stream is setting into the harbor basin. That means that we will have considerable current against us where it is the narrowest, the opposite of what we would normally wish. But during the present wind condition, the current against us is actually a "must" to be able to make it out.

Because the shoaling we saw in the harbor entrance could create problems or dangers for our departure, I've watched the entrance during our weeks here, checking what happens in different wind directions and wind strengths. When the wind is westerly, blowing offshore, a boat can enter or leave the harbor practically any time. But if the wind is easterly, one must go when the tidal stream and waves are running in the same direction: into the harbor. When the tide shifts to outgoing and instead meets the swell, the sea breaks so violently that it is absolutely impossible to leave. That is why it is important to make it out now. Because I don't want to attempt this tonight when it's dark, this is our only chance until tomorrow. Then, with all certainty, the increasing northeasterly wind will make the conditions even worse.

Leaving the yacht basin and entering the outer harbor, I see that no cars are driving on the southern arm of the breakwater today, nor is anyone fishing from it. The swell breaks and washes continuously over the massive stone mole, although it is considerably higher than our mainmast! The remains of smashed waves are carried by the wind as a curtain of spray and foam, drifting north all the way across the 300-yard-wide harbor entrance. The swell is so high between the breakwater's giant arms that Mariano will clearly not be able to tow us into open water. We let his line go and set sail.

In the shadow of the breakwater, the wind is very light, and it is almost impossible to get the boat moving. The little wind that exists is consistently uneven and often shifts direction. I don't count on cleaner wind or better boat speed before we have passed the most shallow spot. We do what we can. I take the rudder and handle the main and mizzen, while Deborah constantly trims the genoa. It's exceedingly tricky sailing. But besides being exactly the type of practice that's good to get, we have decided not to use the engine for this passage unless an emergency forces us to. Our diesel supply is meant for the heater during the upcoming winter and for times in Antarctica when we must use the engine.

The boat is heavy and accelerates poorly, and the closer we come to the narrowest part of the entrance, the more our speed is slowed by the swell rolling in against us. Each passing minute, I become more uncertain, questioning if it will be possible for us to even make it out. In some places close to the entrance the swell crests and breaks. Sometimes the swell even backs our sails and they lose air completely.

Less than a hundred yards away, just outside the breakwater, are some youngsters on surfboards. When a wave is high enough, they paddle frenetically to gain the speed necessary to stand up. Most lose their balance to the big waves. But we watch those who succeed until their waves collapse with a thundering crash. Then their surfboards shoot high into the air and they disappear in a jumbled confusion of water and foam.

The closer to the shoaling we get, the higher each swell rises. Fully occupied, I don't give a thought to our friends for a long while. The last time I looked, they followed at a safe distance, and Mariano called out that they would eventually come alongside to say farewell. When I turn around to see where they are, it's already too late. The boats heave so much that Mariano can't risk coming close.

I know that they are worried about us. We have made it clear that for philosophical reasons, no rescue action is ever to be set in motion, even during the time of the year when a rescue could indeed be possible. And they know that when the pack ice and the winter storms are at their worst, we will be totally cut off from the rest of the world. Karina has repeatedly wondered if we will ever meet again. Now she can no longer hide her fear for our safety. Her swollen eyes are riveted on us. Mariano waves but then turns his head away and leans against the steering wheel. Karina holds him while his body convulses with sobs. It's a difficult time for us all. I had really wanted to hug them and tell them one last time how thankful we are for all their help. But now all I can do is wave good-bye.

When we eventually pass the shoal and *Northern Light* meets the first long ocean swell, I can feel that she is heavier than ever before. To be totally self-sufficient, we have loaded five tons of gear: 5,500 pounds (2,500 kg) of food, 750 pounds (350 kg) of personal belongings (skis, sledges, tents, sleeping bags, climbing gear, ice axe, snow shovels, and so forth), 550 pounds (250 kg) of books, 110 pounds (50 kg) of charts and pilot books, 550 pounds (250 kg) of spare parts and tools, 80 gallons (300 liters) of kerosene for lamps and cooking, 16 gallons (60 liters) of alcohol for preheating the Primus burners, and all the diesel for heating and engine usage. As a result of the extra weight, the upper part of the waterline now lies 4 inches (10 cm) below the water's surface. Yet we have only three plastic jugs for a total of 30 gallons (110 liters) of drinking water aboard. From experience we know that's enough for twenty-one days. The trip should take sixteen days, and we don't want a smaller margin.

Even when we reach deep water, *Northern Light* moves so strangely that Deborah comments: "This must be what it would be like to ride on the back of a pregnant turtle." Yes, it's odd to ride in a boat that heaves so. Yet in Mar del Plata, we sorted out and left behind more than 1,100 pounds (500 kg) of gear! Every last item we judged unnecessary for this trip we left off. Duplicate pots and pans, dishes, and flatware are in storage. Unnecessary charts and pilot books were left behind. Even the five H.O. 229 volumes that we normally use to work out a line of position from a celestial sight are in storage. The only sight reduction table that we now have is the abbreviated one in the *Nautical Almanac,* but it's a new system for me. If the GPS breaks down before I've learned the new method, then beside dead reckoning, we'll only be able to get our latitude from the meridian passage of celestial bodies, the way of navigation until the early 1700s when John Harrison invented the chronometer.

Indeed, only the most important pieces of gear were allowed to join us. Everything not thrown or given away has been left with Don Carlos. Deborah reminds me about how worried he was by saying: "He, if anyone, really meant what he said when he wished us good luck. Remember how his wife said she would move out if she didn't regain access to her closet at the promised time? Poor Don Carlos. He really has reason to be worried about us!" She laughs lightly. Her mood eases my inner tension a little and I take a deep breath.

The water is chilly, the breeze therefore fresh and pleasant. We are finally underway. It is as wonderful to get away from the dust and bustle of Mar del Plata as it is to be at sea again. But the salt air also saddens me. It reminds me how privileged Deborah and I are and how unjust life can be. We have managed to get away on this voyage, but Mariano is still in the hectic noise. He expressed a wish for a chance to live a richer life, but right now he doesn't know how it would be possible.

When I look around, Deborah is leaning against the doghouse, her eyes closed. I am not at all surprised that she has taken the opportunity to nap. Perhaps she had tried to talk to me but didn't get any response. That's not unusual when I am deep in thought.

Without anyone to talk to, I study in detail how the boat is moving through the sea. It suddenly hits me that maybe it isn't just because she is so heavily loaded that she sails so strangely. Perhaps the bilge is full of water. After all, now that the boat sits so much lower than usual, a siphon could have developed in one of the saltwater intakes. In that case, we are sinking!

I swing down into the boat and lift a floorboard. The bilge is as dry as it was before we cast off. At first that gives me some relief, but the angst soon creeps back: we may have nonetheless overloaded *Northern Light* to the point that she is no longer seaworthy. I may have to live with this feeling for the rest of this passage. At least I will have to live with it until we have ridden out some rough weather. No matter how strange it sounds, I therefore hope that it doesn't take long before we get full gale-force wind. The worst that could happen would be to discover too late that it is not possible to push *Northern Light* on a beat. If it's not until south of Cape Horn that we find out that the boat is too heavily loaded to make it against the sea or that breakers wash over deck with such force that we can't hang on, the result will be catastrophic.

This is my second time sailing south along the Argentine coast. The first time, just after I had met Mariano in 1977, we experienced a bad storm outside the Valdes Peninsula. But, no matter how hard I hope for similar weather, all the way to the latitude of the Strait of Magellan we have moderate westerly winds and a steady barometer. Day after day is sunny. As a matter of fact, for the first eight days there is not a single cloud in the sky.

Yet a cloud of worry still hangs over me. During radio contact with Andy, we learn that the distributor of our GPS still hasn't answered my request for information about the system's lowest usage and storage temperatures. Considering that the predominantly overcast weather in Antarctica most often makes it impossible to get celestial sights, it could become critical if the GPS were to be damaged by cold and stop functioning. The information I requested is therefore essential to our safety at sea. When I first realized in Mar del Plata that the manual was not complete, I wrote to the distributor. When I did not get a reply, Andy called them and found out that the person I had written to hadn't yet looked for the information. Andy asked him to do so and call back, but he hasn't heard from them and will have to phone again.

Andy also filled us in on the news and told us that the United States is preparing to send troops to kick out the Iraqi forces that invaded Kuwait. It is also possible that the Americans will attack Iraq. As usual, the dispute is over the control of natural resources. The same type of friction prevailed in 1984 when Deborah and I were sailing around Tierra del Fuego. We suddenly found ourselves in the middle of a military conflict between Chile and Argentina over ownership of a couple of islands in the eastern entrance of the Beagle Channel. The previous year, Argentina had attacked the Falkland Islands. In both cases, the motivating reason was the control of oil reserves and fishing rights. *Isn't there a saner way of dividing up these resources?* I wonder.

With only one day left until we reach the Strait of Le Maire, rain starts and the wind turns northerly. The barometer starts falling 2 to 3 millibars per hour, indicating that a depression is approaching from the west.

At noon the wind has swung through easterly and stabilizes there for a while. But after a couple of hours, it backs through north to west and increases. We douse the mizzen-staysail, which has been up over the last two days, and stash it in the forepeak, where most likely it and the spinnaker will remain untouched for quite some time.

Because of the rain, the sky stays dusklike the whole day. Not until evening, when the sun manages to break through the cloud cover, does it become a bit more pleasant. But this clearing doesn't fool me; I have experienced similar ones before. There's a saying that originated in the 1800s, when square riggers carried wheat around Cape Horn en route from Australia to Europe. Joshua Slocum passed it along in his book *Sailing Alone Around the World*: "Only a fool doesn't reef when it clears from the southwest."

For now, the wind is no stronger than 17 knots. But for safety's sake, I hoist the cutter staysail and take in the first reefs in the genoa and main. I leave the mizzen full while waiting for the cold front's wind increase.

During that time, I reflect again on my 1977 voyage here. In December, I and two crew, beat south through the Strait of Le Maire. When the wind-induced sea opposed the tide, running south at 3 knots, the waves became monstrous. Every fourth or fifth wave was so steep that the boat was stopped in its track for a fraction of a second. On several occasions, the boat fell uncontrolled into deep valleys.

The strain incurred by the hull and rigging was enormous, so much so that one of the two diesel tanks in the aft cabin—a welded tank, made from $\frac{1}{6}$-inch-thick (4 mm) steel, but lacking sufficient baffling— cracked. By the time we realized what had happened there was already so much diesel in the bilge that hardly a foot of air was left under the engine. Each time the boat leaned, the diesel flowed along the curve of the hull all the way to the cabin's ceiling. We

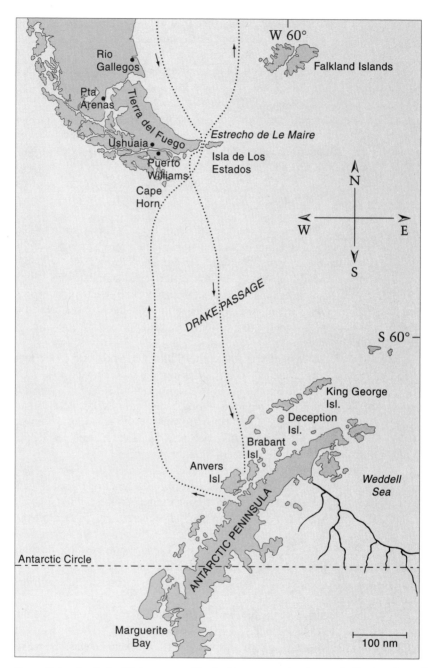

From Estrecho de Le Maire across Drake Passage to the Antarctic Peninsula and return. The distance from Cape Horn to Brabant Island is 475 nautical miles.

had no choice but to demolish woodwork in the aft cabin and saw it up into wedges, which we then hammered in between the hull and the tank to "mend" the crack so that we could pump the diesel back in.

I think about the five diesel barrels we now carry, strapped down and secured to steel floor beams in both the main and aft cabins. If any of them comes loose and bounces around, the interior will be destroyed, and most likely the barrel would crack. If that happens, the fumes will make it almost unbearable to be down below.

We have another "problem," although from a larger perspective it is rather humorous, I guess. It so happens that Argentina only allows visitors a three-month stay on a tourist visa, with a maximum extension to six months. If we stay longer, we have to pay import duty on the boat. One may think that because we left Argentina after six weeks, there shouldn't be any problem. But Argentina claims the Antarctic Peninsula as their territory. Indeed, to maintain peace with other countries that have also signed the Antarctic Treaty, they have agreed to put their claim on the shelf. But as far as their internal policy is concerned, the Antarctic Peninsula *is* their territory. Children learn that at school, educated adults told us it's true, and official maps show it. If we sail directly to Antarctica, spend the winter, and then return to Argentina without stopping in any other country, in their eyes we will not have left Argentina. They can thus demand a tremendous amount in import fees when we come back.

The dilemma is this: When leaving Argentina, we must declare ourselves bound for another country. We cannot declare ourselves bound for Antarctica; because it is not a nation, there are no officials there to stamp us in or out. Our only logical solution was to declare ourselves bound for Chile, for it is not only possible but likely that we will be forced to stop and seek shelter in Chile, or we may want to stop there after the winter to buy fresh provisions. We therefore officially left Argentina for Chile. Meanwhile, we realize that Chile also claims the same exact wedge of Antarctica. If we do indeed go to Chile now and then on the way back want to, or are forced to, stop in Puerto Williams for some reason, we will be caught in *their* bureaucratic web. Time will tell.

When the wind arrives, its strength increases very suddenly, but the blow is short-lived and never reaches storm force. Nevertheless, it builds seas steep and high enough to indicate just how *Northern Light* will behave if we get really difficult sea conditions. The boat heaves in the sea a lot more than usual. When she sets in the waves, she plows down and down until the topsides disappear. Yet as she lifts, she doesn't drag any amount of water up on deck, at least not enough to be considered dangerous.

The bad part is that all the motions we have become used to over the years, and for which we instinctively compensate when we work on deck, have changed. All motions are much more drawn out than usual, probably because most of the boat's reserve buoyancy is gone. Deborah and I discuss it and agree that adjusting routine actions is easier said than done, especially when tired.

But after promising to suspend her expectations each time before going on deck, Deborah peps us both up. "Let's show 'em that salty dogs can learn new tricks," she declares.

During the blow, we concur that, most important, the boat isn't unseaworthy. At our final checkpoint, when we decide to continue out into Drake Passage, there is a great feeling of relief. Now we at least know what we are facing. Even so, a thought that has festered since we started planning this trip to Antarctica returns: What shall we do if we are nevertheless forced to turn around? What shall we do then? I think a long time, but still find no answer.

The wind decreases as quickly as it arrived. Before we're through the Strait of Le Maire, the wind subsides so much that it's difficult to maintain boat speed. When dawn arrives, the sails hang. The boat is still, but only until the tide changes, when we drift back into the strait again. It's too hazy to see land, but according to our dead reckoning, almost two nautical miles of water separate us from Staten Island. While we wait for the wind to come back, we relax and watch five Magellanic penguins look for food in the eddies created by the changing tide. It's possible to get a glimpse of them for only a fraction of a second when they pop up for some air. Then they're on their way to the depths for more to eat.

A pair of sea lions are also drifting north. Unlike the penguins, they seem to have already filled their stomachs, so they only loll about on the water's surface. One of them is so lazy that he barely bothers to half-open one eye to see who we are, and then he folds his huge flippers across his belly and falls asleep again. The other is lying on its side sleeping with one flipper high in the air. In the swell, the animal rolls and its flipper waves back and forth. For fun, we take it as a greeting. But suddenly the sea lion chokes, as if it has taken in water instead of air, coughs a couple of times, and swims away.

At sunrise, the haze turns to fog clouds, draping what we assume must be high mountains, although we can't make out any distinct contours. Slowly the fog clouds slide down the steep sides then suddenly, as if with the wave of a magic wand, rise instead, carried on the updraft generated by the morning sun. The curtain has risen. Sparkles top the highest peak, where sunlight is reflected by ice crystals in a snowfield. Farther down, the mountainsides are a beautiful green. In front of us the most magnificent alpine landscape one can imagine takes our breath away.

We soon sense the most delicate smell from land. There is no aroma in the entire world like that coming from the fir and deciduous forests that wind west through Tierra del Fuego, edging the distant waterways. We absorb the sensation as if it will soon cease to exist. After all, it may be two years before we again experience the air from forest or field that carries the message that spring is becoming summer.

While we breakfast in the cockpit, we are so taken by all the impressions that we discuss sailing to Puerto Williams. We could take the time to enjoy a couple of early summer days in the Beagle Channel, stroll one last time along a colorful field of flowers, and intoxicate our senses. It shouldn't take more than ten, perhaps twelve, hours to sail there. . . .

But when the wind picks up a half hour later, it's from the west. The air immediately chills and shocks us to our senses. Deep inside, we've always known that in these waters it would be foolhardy to not take every advantage to sail toward the ultimate destination. Freedom, not coupled to goals and obligations, is an illusion that exists only in a dreamer.

10

TEMPEST FUGIT

DEBORAH

■ ■ ■

The Japanese trawler *Casula Maru* crosses our wake just south of the Strait of Le Maire. "Shall I give them a shout on the VHF and ask if they have a weather forecast?"

"Sure, go ahead," Rolf replies. "The wind's increasing quickly. If it's a precursor of some really bad weather, we can backtrack to Staten Island and wait there for it to blow over. No reason to stick our heads out into something nasty."

My call to the trawler is answered by an onboard Argentine fisheries observer. He tells us that a new forecast is due in about ten minutes, so we should stand by and wait for their nearby base to come on the air. In due time, a military radio operator on Tierra del Fuego calls us. His conversation doesn't start with the weather, however.

Instead he asks, "What is your vessel's name and registration number?" I supply the information and then other requested descriptive particulars of the hull and rig. But I am still not rewarded with a weather report.

"What was your port of clearance?"

"Mar del Plata," I answer.

"And you are cleared to . . . ?"

"Puerto Williams, Chile."

"How many on board?"

"Two," I reply.

"When did you leave Mar del Plata?"

"The tenth of December."

"When do you expect to arrive at Puerto Williams?"

Here we go. Puerto Williams is only 70 nautical miles away. Even at a snail's pace in head wind, it couldn't take us more than a day. Today's date is December 22, 1990. "We should arrive around the fifth of February 1992," I answer.

"Could you repeat that?"

I do. A long pause follows, during which Rolf and I half smile, half shake our heads. We know exactly what conversation is transpiring in the radio room.

Then, on the voice of authority, comes our weather report. "Today: strong wind, then very strong wind from the southwest sector. Light cloud, good visibility, except in rain showers. Forecast: very strong to storm force wind from the west sector. The Navy recommends that you do not endeavor to cross Drake Passage at this time. I repeat: do not go out into Drake Passage at this time. Furthermore, do not attempt to spend the winter in Antarctica. It is not possible in such a small boat. And during the winter months, we will not be able to help you."

First things first. Rolf wants a translation of their plain language weather report. "Ask him how many knots of wind in very strong and storm-force wind." Their answer: very strong is 27 to 33 knots and storm is 33 to 40 knots. I thank the radio operator for the information and tell him that we will be happy if we can cross without getting more than 40 knots of wind and that we are able and ready to handle at least 60. I also inform him that we will rely on ourselves during the winter and have prepared to need no outside help.

Their recommendation is not unexpected, for we have heard it before. When we requested to be cleared from Chile for Antarctica in the summer of 1984, the commandante of the naval base in Puerto Williams summoned us to his office. It was a snowy, blustery day. Seating us before a roaring fire, bordered by windows through which we couldn't help but watch *Northern Light* straining her anchor chain, the commandante tried to talk us out of sailing for the Antarctic Peninsula. He minced no words. First, he didn't like that we were a crew of only two, especially since I am female. He thought we should never sail in these waters without at least a third crew member—another man—on board. In hindsight, thinking about all the anchor chain I had pumped up in deep Chilean anchorages and all the times I rowed shorelines and set and gybed sails, I wish I had asked him right there to arm wrestle.

But I do not mean to belittle his opinion or his advice. The Chileans are exemplary seamen. Given the heavy weather conditions of the channels, they have to be. During his years of service, the commandante had probably encountered his share of dangerous work involved in the rescues of yachts and yachtsmen who hadn't succeeded in the channels or in rounding Cape Horn. We appreciated that his port clearance was not simply formality.

The commandante also expressed his belief that "even if you *are* tough enough, when you get out into Drake Passage and are hit by a westerly storm—as heavy westerlies are a certainty—your boat simply will not be able to hold enough westing to make the peninsula. Next stop, in that case," he said "is Cape Town."

Rolf reiterated, "We are sailing for the peninsula." But the commandante had the last word, reminding us that the granting of clearance is an implied agreement of intent. "I will not be responsible for granting you clearance for Antarctica," he intoned. "As I write on your papers, I clear you for the High Seas. You may go where you wish." He rose from his armchair, walked to his desk, and signed our papers. We were dismissed.

Had we not felt secure in our preparation, including contingency plans, we could not have taken the responsibility of negating an authority's directive. The same holds true today. We are in no way complacent about crossing Drake Passage or about our wintering plans. In fact, we have serious concerns. We have done our very best to identify and deal with them all, long before now. We've done our homework and preparation. Among a million details, the watertight bulkhead's door is battened for this passage, as are floorboards and cupboard doors, and Rolf's waterproof ventilation system is fully functional, even upside-down. This time, as in 1984, the balance hangs on our competence and, as the commandante said, in the total energy one man and one woman can muster.

The weather information the Navy radio operator has just given us—that the approaching depression is forecast to pack 40 knots—is actually good news to us. Since Mar del Plata we've been constantly trying to take weather charts, but the Argentines make it difficult by not keeping to the schedule. What we do know is that the current slew of depressions have been mild, the upper-level isobars are evenly spread, and the lows are currently taking a track north of us. This forecast continues that pattern. And because the heaviest weather is on the northern side of the low—if we can scoot out into Drake Passage and use these 40 knots of wind to make some hundred miles before the next low—we may be lucky and have it pass north of us also.

Yes, lucky is the right word. Once you leave South America and sail into Drake Passage, the dice are rolled. Gales occur every third day here, and secondary lows can build behind any of them, usually far too quickly for any shore station to predict, and the secondary wave is the one that packs the punch. Superimpose a lightning-fast wind shift on an already high sea and you get furious cross sea and therefore an increased possibility of freak waves. Meeting one can mean turning a boat over or flipping it end over end. One Drake crossing out of ten can be a question of survival. To be properly prepared, sailors must be ready for that storm.

The worst part for us is that we are not as physically adjusted as we would like to be, like we were the last time we crossed. Then, we had come from three months in the Patagonian channels where we had sailed in strong wind, enduring rain, and steadily declining temperatures. Our bodies were used to cold, were hardened. This time, it is a mere two weeks since we enjoyed full summer in Mar del Plata. We will no doubt suffer until our bodies adjust. Our metabolism is already speeding up—a sign that our internal furnaces are dealing with cooler weather and perhaps the excitement and broken sleep—but the skin on our hands hasn't toughened yet nor have our fingers ballooned from increased blood circulation. We've been trying to speed up the acclimatization by not wearing gloves or too-warm clothing, but two weeks is simply too short for the process. The French have a saying: "You either pay for Cape Horn before, or you pay later, but you pay." My fingers and toes tell me I've already anted up.

We don't sight Cape Horn—my diamond in the rough—because all afternoon the wind continues to shift counterclockwise until it reaches southwest, gusting 40 knots plus a little. While still in the shelter of the southern tip of South America, we sheet *Northern Light* up as hard as we can. The ideal course is a little west of south, and although the compass reads exactly that, our course over ground is affected by a 1.6-knot northeast-setting current, resulting in a true heading of only south-southeast. Still, we are pleased. The current runs with the sea, dampening the waves. The mild sea state allows us to keep to 6 knots, *Northern Light*'s maximum speed close-hauled, and that transports us to the latitude of Cape Horn at midnight. We're out, into Drake Passage and the control of the West Wind Drift, so dominant a weather determinator that meteorologists refer to it as the "flywheel of the atmosphere." The concept of power is about to become tangible.

Every minute of heavy weather experience is worth its weight in gold, because for every knot of higher wind managed, there is one less to worry about. When we passed Cape Horn southbound in 1984, I was so intensely worried about the storm we were bound to get in Drake Passage that the blinding-white anxiety made me what I call "emotion sick." We indeed encountered a six-hour blow of 60 knots from the beam. It started halfway through my watch and continued all through Rolf's, and it presented him with the heaviest gusts he had ever experienced at sea. Off watch, I slept through that while *Northern Light,* flying cutter staysail only, made 7 knots toward the next waypoint. *Wow,* I thought to myself when I went back on watch and looked at the turbulent scene. *This boat can obviously withstand a lot more than its crew. Take the hint, Deborah, and steel yourself. You'll be able to think more clearly.*

Yes, with all certainty, a seaworthy boat is a good thing to have under you. A boat, designed to be in harmony with a high wind's sea, rides gently there, comparatively speaking. Seakindliness means not only that crew can rest; it also means that we work more safely on deck. I can't imagine crossing the Drake in a boat not designed for heavy weather.

For the novice sailor, like me when I first signed on *Northern Light,* there is no other option than to take weather one step at a time. I worked on deck in higher and higher wind speeds and sea, learning and becoming accustomed to the different routines needed to match each successive state. Early in the game, Rolf taught me his heavy-weather downwind sailing maxim: Sail fast; speed creates safety. As he explained, in a gale or storm, even if a displacement boat is driven as hard as possible, its speed is very slow compared with the speed of the waves. Waves therefore continuously overtake the boat. As the top of a wave passes, the boat actually "backs" through the breaker. The more one reefs down, the slower the boat sails, and therefore the larger the impact the wave has as it hits.

Based on that, he told me that the rule for sailing with the wind in heavy weather is to always sail the boat as close to its hull speed as possible. To put it to the test, we decided we should sail *Northern Light,* a medium-heavy displacement boat, "too hard." What we wanted to find out was, with the wind aft of abeam, does driving the boat hard lead to loss of steerage and result in a broach?

In the beginning of a very strong gale in the Roaring Forties, when the average wind speed was 45 to 60 knots, we purposely carried 50 percent, 75 percent, and then 100 percent more sail than necessary to keep *Northern Light* at hull speed. The point was to press her so hard that on the back side of each wave, where speed normally decreases, the boat would maintain its theoretical maximum speed of 8.35 knots. Over twelve hours, we covered 103 nautical miles, an average of 8.58 knots. Yet even though we sailed faster than the boat's theoretical maximum speed, there was never any tendency to broach.

The only time Rolf has experienced a knockdown was on his first voyage with *Northern Light.* It happened because they had sailed too slowly. They had overreefed one night specifically to delay an arrival at an atoll until daylight. Hours before dawn, the stern was lifted by a breaking sea, and as one could expect, the boat didn't have enough speed for the rudder to have effect. The boat yawed and broached, and the mast hit the water.

What about other points of sail in heavy weather? To claw off a lee shore in storm-force winds is not exactly accomplished easily; there are tremendous forces involved. The principle to keep in mind in a heavy-weather beat is the same as when on a broad reach: drive the boat as efficiently as possible. Of course, a boat on a beat has to be reefed more than when sailing with the wind, but not so much that it doesn't sail fast.

Beam reaching should be avoided as much as possible when the sea is steep and high, however. And that concept should be kept in mind when reefing for a heavy-weather beat, too. If reefed too much on a heavy-weather beat, a boat won't have the power it needs make it over the waves. Instead, it will get forced beam to, temporarily beam reaching, with the topsides exposed to the sea. That leads to a moment of vulnerability, and if the boat is taken by the wave, there's a big mess onboard.

For a contrast to last time's hurricane-force gusts at this latitude, I am taking advantage of today's light wind to bake chocolate chip cookies and bread. I might as well stock up. As fast as depressions fly through Drake Passage, we'll encounter at least one more blow before we get there and, regardless, we'll soon be to the Antarctic Convergence, where a new job will be added to the list of watch responsibilities.

The convergence is an ever-shifting though well-defined line that marks our zero-altitude, sea-level entrance to the Antarctic. Circumscribing a wavy circle through the southern portions of the Pacific, Atlantic, and Indian Oceans that comprise the Antarctic Ocean, the convergence is the northern border of the southernmost continent's surface cold water. The convergence is not a constant line and does not remain where the dotted line is marked on the charts; instead, it is where it is. The fun way to find it is to watch. Chances are, you will either see seabirds aplenty feeding on the poor krill and other stunned creatures that suddenly find themselves in the wrong temperature water or you will see Cape pigeons and other birds that prefer to be south of the convergence. But if there's nothing to be seen or it's too foggy to bother looking, you can do as we do: measure the water temperature. When it dips below 35.5°F (+2°C), you're at Antarctica's threshold!

The convergence also happens to be the place where we start to have twenty-four-hour light, the gift of high-latitude summer. It's a big aid now, because south of the Antarctic Convergence it's time to keep an extra sharp, constant lookout for every form of ice from little chunks to huge tabular-shaped bergs.

Even in good conditions, it is exceedingly difficult to detect "growlers" that lie at the surface and heave in the swell. A diffuse, almost invisible shadow is the only thing that betrays the presence of these old, smoothened bobbing ice chunks. As far as we are concerned, growlers are floating rocks. We are not allowed to sail into one. When the wind picks up and the sea begins to break, these polished clumps of ice are almost impossible to detect. Oh, why does it have to start snowing, just now when we can't afford bad visibility?

The first iceberg we sight is 100 nautical miles from the Antarctic land mass. It is not a large table-topped piece of the ice shelf but a piece twice as high as our mainmast and a cable in diameter, with a jagged edge and spires on top. Translucent blue, glowing from within, it's an absolutely beautiful ice castle. The biggies have to be described differently. Lacking appropriate figurative descriptors, we usually rely on numbers. Yet the enormous dimensions of icebergs that break away from the Antarctic ice shelf are still difficult to appreciate.

For example, consider one of the biggest bergs to break away from the ice shelf in the Weddell Sea recently. It is understandable that these big bergs are given a number and reported here, where they pose a considerable danger to ships, but this one is so large that its march north toward the South Atlantic is being reported on the news in the United States and Europe. Andy has related to us that iceberg number A-24, measuring 50 by 70 statute miles, is three times the area of the state of Rhode Island. But just how big is that? We take out our calculator and learn that A-24 is so big that not only could everyone on Earth stand side by side on it, but each person would have two square yards! Perhaps even more impressive is that the iceberg could provide drinking water for all 5.5 billion of us for no less than 450 years.

Toward the end of my watch, 60 nautical miles west of the peninsula, I awaken Rolf to share the moment when we sail over the edge of the continental shelf and into a 15-nautical-mile-wide band of bergs, spaced 2 to 3 nautical miles apart. Rolf climbs the mainmast to the second spreader. To the southwest, the visibility is very good and ice glitters as far as he can see. He scans the horizon and reports that a weather change is coming at us from the northeast. We are soon ringed by snow gusts and the visibility drops to near zero. We take turns keeping a lookout on the foredeck and searching for the best path through the labyrinth of ice.

The visibility never drops to the point where it would be prudent to heave to, and the northeasterly wind increases incrementally until it lifts the low cloud a little and affords us a better view. Although it's an exciting time, I am sent to bed to put some hours "in the bank." Landfall is never a certainty here, and safe anchorage are two words we won't combine again until we return to lower, lazier latitudes.

11

JET
SCREAM

ROLF

■ ■ ■

Deborah and I have often discussed how we think it will feel to sight the Antarctic continent again. Last time we were so captivated by what was an unknown for us that the mere sight of it forever changed our lives.

That was seven years ago. Since then we've often wondered if the overwhelming feeling of humility would be equally strong if we ever came back. I expect so. After all, a drama plays continuously around this continent, the likes of which are to be found nowhere else on Earth.

While researching for our first visit, we came across paintings made by artists aboard the first ships to visit Antarctica. They pictured a coastline more frightening than even our imaginations could accept. The same applied to the icebergs, which were depicted as grotesque monsters about to swallow the ships. We chuckled at the painters' fantasies. They painted from their emotional impressions, rather than from reality, or so we thought. But when we arrived and looked with our own eyes, those paintings suddenly came alive. For seven weeks we lived in such breathtakingly scary surroundings that we were ashamed of our own naiveté. After all, the pilot books had warned us to not trust our charts; when the soundings were taken, icebergs could have hidden shoals. In addition, we had difficulty learning to distinguish between snow-covered islands, islets, and skerries and icebergs or find shoals and rocks because they were overrun by ice. Truly safe navigation was impossible. Spots on the chart that looked like promising anchorages turned out to be blocked by ice or rimmed by calving glacier walls and we had to press onward, no matter how cold or tired we were. Good shelter often turned bad in a wind shift or a tidal change. Ice pieces, often as beautiful as a marble sculpture on first view, turned nightmarish as they let loose their captured energy, heaving, cracking, and rolling without warning.

Last time, we made our landfall as far south on the Antarctic Peninsula as that year's ice allowed, trusting that the information on the area's pilot chart was correct. According to the wind roses, we should have had fair winds from the south when we turned around, but that wasn't the case. The prevailing winds along the peninsula proved to come from the opposite direction, resulting in a long and sometimes very demanding beat back north. Therefore, this time we have decided to make our landfall at the Melchior Islands, off the northern part of the peninsula, to be able to sail with the wind as we continue south.

So far, everything is unfolding according to plan. The northeasterly wind that developed during Deborah's watch has remained steady during mine. The sea hasn't grown, however, and is more moderate than what we are used to for this wind strength. There's a reason: cold water is denser than warm water. Therefore, waves here build more slowly and break later. In fact, not until the wind is above gale force do the near-freezing water's waves first start to break. We must always remember that cold water's breaking seas have more punch and are thus more dangerous than their counterparts in warmer climes.

Late morning, the northeasterly wind starts to intensify, and by noon it reaches 23 knots. In response, I roll in the genoa to the second reef marker. I also take in a reef in the main but keep full mizzen for the time being. To be on the safe side, I also set the cutter staysail. Then, if there's a rapid wind increase, I can furl the genoa without losing headway.

I sincerely hope this wind increase is not the beginning of the Antarctic Bellows, a wind condition we named the last time we were here. When we met meteorologist Rubens Villela in Brazil, he explained that our bellows is actually called a low inertial jet. The phenomenon occurs when a cell of high pressure exists in the Weddell Sea east of the Antarctic Peninsula and a depression moves through Drake Passage. North of the high pressure, the air stream is easterly. Usually, that wind's flow is blocked by the mountainous ridge of the peninsula, and the higher altitude's layer of cold air puts a lid on it.

Without an escape valve, the pressure builds. When the approaching depression "lends" some energy, drawing the air out and around the tip of the peninsula, it joins forces with the depressions' northeast air flow to rush west past King George Island. When it reaches Deception Island, it is often a hurricane-force wind. It continues to arc along the peninsula, passing Brabant Island where it starts to diminish.

Around two o'clock in the afternoon, the atmosphere in the cockpit is like the waiting room at the dentist; although there's nothing to worry about, butter-

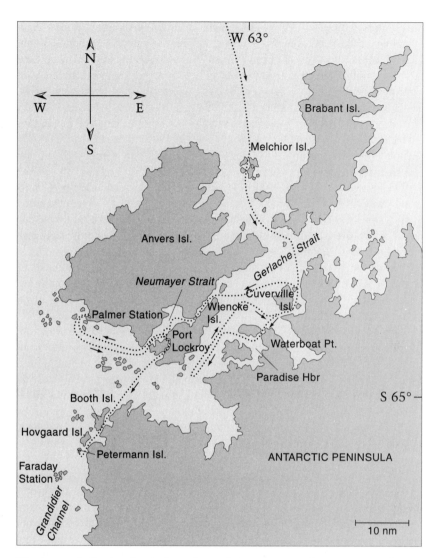

The Antarctic Peninsula. At first glance, it is easy to get the impression that the area between Brabant Island and Faraday Station contains an endless number of fjords, bays, and coves where one can seek shelter from nasty weather. In reality, the majority of potential anchorages are ringed by glaciers and full of ice.

flies flutter nonetheless. I start looking for land. The visibility is at best about 10 nautical miles, and even though we have over forty miles left to landfall and I know looking is senseless, I can't resist. Were the weather clear, I would certainly see both Brabant and Anvers Islands high above the horizon. They are each well above 6,500 feet high (2,000 m), and right in between them lie the Melchior Islands, our designated landfall. Even more than for orientation, I'd like to see land to check for condensation streams trailing off the highest peaks. If so, then soon the ferocious northeasterly will descend to sea level. The tension builds as the hours pass, my feelings churning along with the low clouds and the gray sea.

When we have 30 nautical miles left, a small clearing wipes part of the cloud away. As the sun breaks through, I catch sight of a solitary cluster of high, white mountain peaks 10 degrees to starboard. They must be the highest peaks of Brabant Island. Behind them remains high gray cloud, now brilliantly banded by a light underside, which is the sunlight reflecting from a huge glacier located on the peninsula. I can't see any sign of Anvers Island yet; it must still be too far away. But that's as far as my thoughts get. Suddenly, the boat is laid on its side by a tremendous gust. To keep my balance, I instinctively grab one of the windward winches.

To ensure that we could make it in to the Melchior Islands without any forced tacks, we have gained as much height as we could the past two days, and right now I'm thankful we did. That extra easting enables me to fall off to a beam reach now, easing the genoa so the boat straightens up, and still steer the right course. Before bothering to adjust the mainsheet, I open the cupola and tell Deborah that she should dress in foul weather gear and be ready to give me a hand. "The wind is increasing very rapidly," I tell her. She smiles and looks quizzically at me from her position in the galley. By her compound expression, I understand that she also had difficulty hanging on a few seconds ago.

While the hatch is open, I take the opportunity to lean farther down into the boat and grab my tether. The timing couldn't have been worse. The boat is bashed broadside by a wave, which crests and breaks with its full power on the topsides. The hood on my foul weather gear is not up. As I close the hatch and stand up, ice-cold water pours down my neck and runs down my spine. I look to weather. In a few seconds, the sea has nearly doubled and our safety margin has been crimped. In the steep sea, it has suddenly become more difficult to see if there's any ice ahead. We'll now be lucky to see growlers at a distance of two wavelengths. If we don't spot them until the wave crest just before, then we will only have four boat lengths to avoid them. Considering the speed that we are sailing, that gives us less than ten seconds. It's barely enough.

We can't afford to take any chances. Deborah will have to keep a continuous lookout. But instead of having her come on deck, I decide that she shall remain inside the boat and look out through the cupola. There she can concentrate on her job. On deck, where she can help me, were something not to work as it should and were she to turn her gaze away from her lookout, she could easily miss seeing ice.

As soon as Deborah is positioned on the ladder and understands her job, my mind turns to the question, How much do I dare reef? For the purpose of the lookout, I want to sail slowly, yet speed is essential for steerage in this sea condition. If our speed decreases, we will not be able to steer away from ice as easily, and the impact of breaking waves can be greater, than if we were sailing faster. I don't want to sail below 6 knots.

A swell, barely discernible earlier as a long gentle heave, has taken on enormous proportions since we entered more shallow water. When it meets the waves that the wind is pushing from the opposite direction, the sea stands on edge and explodes like two heavily loaded express trains colliding. When we happen to be in the same place, the sea roils and roars across the deck. There's no established rhythm to these waves, whose vertical breakers are 10 feet (3 m) high. Sometimes the boat is drenched from both leeward and windward simultaneously. At worst, the entire lifeline is buried under masses of water.

I have never seen anything like this in my entire life. And it's never felt so ghastly to have to go on deck. But I have no choice; the sails must be reefed. During the time it takes me to clip on my tether and move to the mainmast, the wind has increased to over 42 knots. I immediately take in the third reef in the main and then the second reef in the mizzen. But to have as much drive as possible in the sails, I don't totally furl the genoa. Instead, I have a 3-square-yard "storm fleck," the purpose of which is to steer the wind in behind the staysail. Doing so practically doubles the staysail's driving force.

I alternate reducing sail with stowing all the lines and sheets leading into the cockpit in their respective cubbyholes so they can't wash overboard and interfere with the windvane's pendulum or, even worse, tangle in the propeller. The more I work with the boat, the more my discomfort dwindles. In its place I start to appreciate the fast and exceedingly dramatic sailing. It is so exhilarating that were I younger, I probably would've wet myself.

When the work is finished, I lean out to the lee to check if the foresails are properly sheeted. I spot a stretch of brash ice a couple hundred yards ahead of the boat. To make sure that Deborah also sees it, I tap on the cupola to get her attention and point forward.

Hand signals are something that we have developed over the years; without them, it would often be impossible to coordinate our work on deck. Deborah answers me by pointing to her eye and then nodding her head. When she signals that she has already adjusted the course to sail closer to the wind and, by moving her forefinger away from her thumb shows me just how far she has pulled the control line to the windvane, I sheet the sails accordingly.

The wind continues to increase. Eventually it's above 50 knots and gusting above 65. At this stage I don't dare drive the boat harder, so I roll in the genoa completely. Then, since I know that in this wind strength *Northern Light* will make above 8 knots with just the mizzen and staysail, I decide to drop the main.

Seas break continuously over deck. When I move toward the mainmast, the water is more often than not up to my knees. As I ease the mainsail halyard, I have to brace my upper body against the mast. The work goes very slowly. Probably six or seven minutes pass before I pull down what's left above the third reef. There's a constant threat of getting my feet washed out from under me, and I maintain "one hand for me, one hand for the ship." I also have to concentrate more on the sea and how it affects the boat's movement than on the work I am trying to accomplish. Even so, I am surprised two times by heavily breaking seas.

When the mainsail is finally secured, I make sure to start back for the cockpit at the right moment. To have something to hang on to the entire way, I creep on the windward side from one stanchion to the next, the upper lifeline running under my armpit and my hand gripping the toe rail. I continuously keep my eyes on the sea, but I do not see much. The air is loaded with spray. The force of each approaching wave is therefore best judged by the speed and angle the boat moves in the valley while rising to meet the next sea.

On my journey aft, the boat takes itself up and over the first and the second waves with no problem. But when the boat is in the third valley, I hear the hissing noise that proceeds each breaker suddenly change to a deep rumble. We hit a momentary vacuum. All motion takes a pause. When I look up I see, just as I could expect, that the coming wave has built tremendously higher than the others. The breaker starts its lionish roar, and instinctively I loosen my grip around the rail and rush for higher ground. To make it up on the main boom seems to be my only possible escape. As quick as I can, I lock my arms around the boom and try to heave myself up on top of it. But halfway there I come to a dead stop. I'm yanked to the side and end up hanging by my arms.

For safety's sake, when I left the cockpit I attached my tether to the jackline, a stainless steel wire that runs on deck from bow to stern. This tether is made to be just so long that there's no way I can possibly ever be washed farther than the rail. That's great, but for the moment the short length of my tether keeps me from being able to reach safety!

I am almost completely exhausted. Pulling down the mainsail used up practically all my energy. And because it would be meaningless to attempt to make it down on deck again, free the tether, and then figure out where to re-hook it before the next breaker hits, I decide on another plan. I throw one leg around the boom and heave myself up just far enough to hang underneath it. Suspended upside-down, I watch how the cockpit, cupola, and Deborah inside it disappear under churning water.

I feel like a cat that's been chased up a tree and is waiting for the appropriate moment to come down again. The entire incident has become very comical. When the wave has rolled by and I spot Deborah again, I grin and wave at her.

She opens the cupola momentarily and calls out to me, but I can't make out what she says; her voice is drowned by the engulfing din. I could, however, see that her look was quite tense, which is enough to tell me that she doesn't exactly share my appreciation of the moment.

It's not always easy for other people to understand my sense of humor, but just why eludes me. But the fact that I, during difficult situations often perceive circumstances as pleasurable whereas onlookers can't see past the life-threatening elements, can be explained medically. During stress, the body produces adrenaline and endorphins. Without these chemical changes, we wouldn't manage the work that we—even with the help of these chemicals—perceive as both physically and mentally difficult. Then comes the good part: when the physical work is over, there's a very pleasurable side effect that I have felt strongly many times. So, it is not strange that I think there's a real kick to rough days. Of course, the one who is not working can't feel it. All I can say to Deborah in this instance is an American saying she taught me: tough luck!

Around six o'clock in the evening, we come in line with the northern point of Brabant Island. In its shelter the wind drops quickly, but the novelty doesn't last long enough for more than a surprised look at each other. The next second we are in the path of an enormous downdraft rushing off the glacier-covered mountainside. There is no remote possibility to parry it by steering into the eye of the wind. Were we to do so, the sails would flog and be torn to pieces. When one of us sees one of these katabatic gusts churning up the surface of the water, we simply warn the other and hang on. For a few seconds, the shriek in the rigging is painful to hear. Three times, with just a couple of minutes in between, the boat is knocked down. We wait for the fourth, but nothing happens.

Northern Light glides forward a bit on its own momentum, then slows to a stop. She doesn't even roll. The sea has died completely, and the absolute, almost stark quiet is broken only by the calls of two penguins in search of each other. The quick transformation from inferno to calm borders on the incomprehensible. Positively dumbstruck, Deborah and I look at each other. After sixteen days of strenuous sailing from Mar del Plata—and before that, years of wonder and worries—we have reached our destination.

We still have to find a place where we can anchor, though. All the reefs are released, but that doesn't help; there's no wind for the sails to catch. The airstream is totally blocked by the islands. Because it seems meaningless to just wait while the current takes us somewhere inside the island group where we *don't* want to go, we start the engine.

While dropping the mainsail, I had noticed that the antenna had snapped at its attachment point on the mainmast. So, while we motor I attach a new temporary antenna—a quarter-wave length of household electrical wire(!)—and climb the mizzen to hang it. Precisely on time, as if we had been waiting the whole day, Deborah tunes the new antenna and contacts the other amateur radio operators in the United States who are always waiting to hear from us. I take the wheel while she gives them all the good news. In this case, *all* isn't exactly a short message. While the *yackety yack yack yack* continues I'm glad to have an engine with which to power the radio!

When Deborah eventually finishes, we look at the detail charts of the Melchior Islands and see an excellent anchorage in a lagoonlike bay on the west side of Eta Island. The depth there is between 23 and 30 feet (7 to 9 m); in other words, it's ideal. At eight o'clock in the evening, we make ready to anchor. So that I know when to put the engine in reverse, Deborah sings out the readings from the depth sounder: "One hundred and sixty-five feet [50 m]. Hundred and fifty [46 m]. Hey, it's getting very deep. . . . Three hundred and twenty-seven feet [100 m]!" We turn around and circle for nearly an hour, but we never find any bottom less than 100 feet (30.5 m) deep.

It remains absolutely calm. Because there's very little ice, eyeball navigation should be easy. Besides, there's no rush. Deborah suggests that we put the charts away and use our imagination to find a place with the desirable depth. I agree. After all, exploration makes life truly exciting. "Imagine that there had been signs marking the anchoring spots. There wouldn't be much wilderness feeling left then, would there?" Deborah asks. I agree with her but wonder if I really should have. "You agree? With *me*? Again?" she asks. For the next few moments, Deborah looks very serious and stands with her hands on her hips, but then I see a spark in her eye as she points toward a cove she thinks is good and protected. "While we're on the same wavelength, let's anchor and fix the double berth," she says.

Around midnight we are still awake and our spirits are too high to consider sleeping. The only thing that doesn't fit the mood is the squeaking and grinding noise of the anchor chain. We have apparently anchored in a "rock garden" and I can only assume that there's no real holding. The thought pulls me out of bed, but when I look through the cupola I see that we're still in exactly the same spot, and there's no danger. It's perfectly bright outside and still calm. The only change since we anchored is that it has become overcast and snowed some. Because it is only a few degrees below freezing, the snow is light and the boat looks like a newly hatched gosling whose down has just dried. I feel as if I too have just been born to the life I love. As Deborah said to our friends over the radio, "What an arrival!"

Standing in the cupola, I reflect upon how much better prepared we are this time compared with our first summer visit. Both of us are in top physical and mental shape. The engine purrs. The rigging hasn't shown any problems whatsoever.

Staring out, my eyes fasten on the fully battened sails, and I reflect on how well they have worked. All that talk I've heard about not being able to reef them downwind without luffing was nonsense. And because of the large roach, the battens have no tendency to get stuck between the spreaders and the shrouds when hoisting the sail after shaking out a reef, which often happens with ordinary sails' short battens. In addition, the boat required a smaller area of fully battened sail to maintain speed. In other words, we could reef down the boat more and still have the same driving force we do with a larger area of conventional sails. The result? With a lower center of effort, the boat heels less, which in turn makes life on board more pleasant. Especially where the mizzen is concerned, we certainly came to appreciate the "lazy jacks" collecting the sail when we reefed or dropped it entirely. They keep the sail from ever hanging down and interfering with or damaging the windvane.

Using fully battened sails was a fun and different experience for us, but nonetheless we will now change back to furling sails; we prefer the advantages furling systems provide, especially in these waters. It takes only eleven seconds to bottom reef and stow the mizzen and approximately eighteen seconds to take care of the main. When sails can be doused that quickly, it's considerably easier to anchor under sail. And tripping the anchor under sail is equally as easy, especially for us with a ketch. Because we determine beforehand by using the preventer to force the mizzen boom out in the direction we want to go, we always know which direction the bow will point when the anchor trips. Then everything takes care of itself, assuming, that is, we will be able to get the anchor up. The tide has swung the boat around so that the bow is pointing in a different direction from when we anchored. But while jumping down from the ladder and crawling back under the blanket I think, *That's tomorrow's problem.*

The next day, everything continues going our way. We get the anchor up without any trouble and move to a place where we find good holding in clay. There we sit for ten days. The first business is to move all the provisions that were stowed in the main cabin while we sailed across Drake Passage. Weight distribution of the cargo inside the boat is no longer of paramount importance; comfortable living is. Everything that has been stowed on the settee, stashed behind support pieces, or roped down is moved elsewhere. Altogether, about 1,100 pounds (500 kg) of food—everything from dried fruit to spaghetti, and cheeses to sacks of potatoes and onions—are stowed in new places.

We also want to move the oil drums off the floorboards in the main cabin. Together, we manage to lift them onto the starboard bunk and resecure them by strapping them to the sea berth's laminated long-ship's supports. We remove the windvane and in its place mount the wind generator on the support frame. Deborah and I then row ashore and fill a sail bag with snow, which I lug over to the dinghy. We row back and hoist the 130-pound (60-kg) bag on board, using the cutter staysail halyard. We let it hang next to the mainmast, with the lower part of the bag just inside a plastic tub. Once the bag is covered with a sheet of black plastic, we break for tea on deck while the sun makes drinking water for us. For the first time in ages, we feel really lazy.

Before we had rowed ashore, we had baked a *tosca,* a Swedish butter cake crowned with a crunchy almond and caramel icing. It is now cool and we each enjoy two pieces with our tea. Sitting on deck, we count eighty-seven Weddell seals lying in the sun on the bay's remaining fast ice. They occasionally lift their heads to check what's happening, and they are especially aware when another seal comes back from the water. But most of the time, they lie perfectly still, sleeping. On a cliff face farther away, a few gulls chatter. One of them has most likely found a mussel or some other morsel that it wants to keep for itself. Antarctic gulls are apparently as willing to squabble as gulls in other parts of the world. Honestly, what do gulls do, besides eat and be jealous of one another?

Before our tea is finished, we hear an engine. The sound becomes stronger and stronger, and finally a helicopter tears over the edge of the glacier covering a neighboring island. The island is only 40 yards high, and the helicopter hugs its contour. We have to cover our ears as it screams right over the top of our masts. The helicopter disappears as quickly as it came. Still, all the gulls take flight. The seals have been woken up and are wriggling toward the ice edge. Although their foe is already gone, they disappear into the safety of the water. The bay is suddenly deserted.

What a rotten thing to do. They weren't even planning on landing here. Was it really necessary to fly so low and scare all the animals, us included, for that matter? Without finishing our tea, we go below.

12

IN AND OUT, BAD AND GOOD NEWS

Deborah

■ ■ ■

The raspy edge to his voice is a dead giveaway that Rolf is not fooling around. I wish he was, especially because he's already unzipped his pants while saying: "Deborah, come here. I have a bulge I want you to examine." What's this? There's an aberrant egg-shaped mound under the skin near his groin. It's a very concrete symptom, easy for even amateurs to diagnose. Oh, no, a hernia.

Sitting in our bookshelf is the *AMA's Encyclopedia of Medicine*. I pull the thick volume out and start to read aloud. It soon becomes clear that Rolf's hernia is type inguinal. According to the encyclopedia, part of his "intestine has bulged through the inguinal canal (the passage through which the testes descend into the scrotum)."

When I read, "The protruding intestine can sometimes be pushed back through the abdominal wall," Rolf tries the described technique. On his back, knees up, he applies slight pressure to the bulge. Sure enough, the intestine disappears back from where it came! Our anxiety level moderates enough to sleep. Before we doze off, Rolf reminds me that he had this bulge before—albeit slighter—in Fiskebäckskil. "But it disappeared. Remember?" he says. "That was two and a half years ago, and it's never shown itself until today. Maybe it will disappear again." I sure hope so, because the AMA book says that hernias don't heal and that repair can only be accomplished by surgery.

But after a few hours of normal exertion the next day, Rolf's intestine pops out again. Have we come this far for naught? Our eyes rarely meet and we move through the day like zombies. What shall we do? The encyclopedia said that a person who could readily push the hernia back in could help keep the intestine in place by wearing a support truss. No picture or diagram was given, but we haul out a belt, some webbing, foam, and leather and whip up one of our own design. Unfortunately, it doesn't help. I don't like this one bit.

We decide to move on, leaving Melchior bound for Cuverville Island. It's a blustery Antarctic summer day. The wind direction is in our favor and is strong enough to churn up whitecaps. Slowly, we sail out between Omega and Eta Islands, then pass Gamma and the rest of the Greek alphabet soup group, sightseeing. Reaching free water, we roll out full sail and gallop off. The big-scale scenery that's been hidden from us for nearly two weeks in that cozy black hole of an anchorage is suddenly available again.

Hey, we're here! The peninsula's backbone stretches for miles north and south, thousands of feet high, glaciated, with dramatic craggy peaks. Natural beauty abounds, with icebergs galore. The air is nice and cold and pure, and some kind of weather is flying through. The clouds boil and scud across mountainsides at different altitudes. Dark gray ones obscure midlevels. White wave clouds form at rounded tops and steam off downwind. Deep violet clouds loom on the horizon.

Penguins swimming to or fro fishing grounds in groups of ten or twenty are momentarily airborne when they "porpoise" out of the water to catch a breath. I can understand where the descriptor comes from, but I think their in-flight body more resembles a bonito's. The penguin takes a rounded fishlike shape when it arcs through the air, looking like the simplified outline of a fish a child might draw. Truly airborne above us, giant petrels wheel and soar. For big birds, this wind is their element, their ultimate place. Now, if we could only see some whales. . . . *Patience, Deborah*, I tell myself.

Cuverville Island is like most Antarctic anchorages in that it provides a modicum of shelter, "if" and "as long as." Cuverville is adequate if the wind is not southerly, because when it is, lots of ice blows in. Yet even if the wind is in our favor, there's shelter only if the ice that comes in with the current isn't too big. Smaller pieces may dent the hull a bit or cause cosmetic damage, but one has to be willing to accept that to sail here. But pressure on the hull from large pieces can uproot the anchor. Aboard or ashore, we always have to be aware, keeping our third eye open for ice.

Although Rolf's concentration level is diminished because of discomfort from and worry about his hernia, we force ourselves to start video filming Cuverville's gentoo penguin rookery. In our approach we come first to a group of skuas congregated at the edge of rookery, like teenagers parked outside a drive-in restaurant. The skua is a predatory bird, here only during the summer season, and the nearby gentoo chicks and eggs can be a mainstay of its diet. The skuas chatter among themselves and hassle one another in a continuous king of the mountain routine, and they alternate flying away for a bite to eat. Rolf films them from a distance using an extreme telephoto setting. Our idea is to film in the same manner as we always shoot still pictures: we stay as far away as possible from our subject so as to not disturb or bother them. In that way we capture as much of normal behavior as possible and not just their aggravated response to interference.

Happy with our documentation of the skua club, we move progressively closer to the edge of the rookery. The gentoos number in the thousands and it seems as if the decibels pulsating from the rookery are in the hundreds of thousands. At least a million units of "oosh" (my name for a measurement of level of smell) emanate from them as well. We cover the last distance to them by creeping on all fours, and when the first penguin response to our presence is noted, we back off a bit. Then we watch.

Individual penguins look cute, indeed they do. But the overall impression from a huge rookery is anything but cute. The general din is continuously perforated by the loud braying individual penguins make, just to strut their stuff or to warn of or ward off skua flybys. They also make other aggressive noises at each other. Poor penguins. Because there isn't much snow-free nesting area in Antarctica, they build their pebble nests with less free area around it than they would probably like. A penguin can barely stand up to readjust itself or its egg without hearing a running commentary from and, being pecked by, its worried neighbors. And I pity each and every penguin, on its way to or from the water, as it is forced to skedaddle quickly through the rookery, sustaining nips and dodging outright attacks from other nesting birds it passes. Worst, however, is the poor chick whose one or both parents fail to return from the water. Any time an unchaperoned chick leaves the confines of its nest, it is immediately attacked by other adult penguins. Thus stressed it flees, gets too close to another nest, is attacked again, runs, and becomes too confused to find its home again. The farther astray this whirlwind takes the chick, the more likely it is to be killed.

On the other hand, the behavior between mates is pleasant to watch. If both are standing, as when they exchange nest-sitting responsibilities, they bow to each other, weaving and dipping their heads. If the food supply is plentiful and both can be at the nest for a while, the standing mate does its best to secure more pebbles for the nest, most often by stealing from a neighbor whose back is turned. Nonetheless, the thief brings the pebble, shows it, bows, and then deposits it before its mate's beak.

I suppose nothing's more adorable than new life, and penguin chicks are no exception. Newly hatched chicks have difficulty supporting their heads, which bob around like the plastic toys some people put in their cars' rear windows. The older a chick gets, the more it resembles a beanbag. I like that dumpling stage best. It carries the implication that all is as it should be. Once the chicks start to molt, with their feathers in weird disarray, they look like they're dressed up for Halloween. Some sport a ridge on their head that looks like a Mohawk haircut, others wear the equivalent of a fluffy boa scarf. Because the rookery already includes chicks at each developmental stage, we can see or watch whichever age we prefer.

We're concentrating so hard on the rookery and our work that we never notice that another sailboat has come into the anchorage. What a shock to suddenly see people walk over the crest of the hill! Rolf is still oblivious to them. My husband's concentration on one subject is all but total, so it is up to me to announce their arrival. I tap him, then point in their direction, saying "Rolf. Quick, look! A new species of bird has joined the rookery: red-jacketed tourists. *Struthio touristicus antarcticus.*"

The charter boat's guests are coming toward us, but not by skirting around the edge of the rookery. No, instead they plow right through as though it's here for their pleasure, paying no attention to the noise and commotion that ensues. We have deduced from watching how nesting penguins usually treat others of their own species waddling by that they'd actually like to have up to a few yards of space around their nests. When people say that nesting penguins seem tame because they can walk right up to a bird on its nest and the penguin doesn't even move, I must counter that the reason the bird remains still and stays put has to do with its instinctive drive to defend its egg or chick. That doesn't mean however that penguins or, for that matter, other nesting birds, are not stressed to the nth degree by these too-close encounters. Here, there are consequences from disrespectful intrusion. Opportunistic skuas follow the tourists, attracted as they are by any disturbance, knowing that therein lies a chance of nabbing a momentarily abandoned egg or chick. We are disappointed by these people's behavior. They obviously haven't given any thought to how they should conduct their visit nor been instructed by their skipper. Even worse, they seem oblivious to the effects of their presence, incapable of assessing that effect and adjusting as they go.

Leaving Cuverville on a windless day, we power south through Gerlache Strait and into Neumayer Channel. There's a sudden flash of light, a reflection from the wet, shiny, black patent-leather back of a behemoth. Humpbacks! Oh, I've been hoping and waiting to meet them again, ever since last time we were here and they approached us and stayed to play for two hours. They swam and dove around *Northern Light*, alternating powerful shows of broaching and bellyflopping with displays of lithe grace. I will never forget how one of them surfaced vertically, sticking its head out of the water until an eye appeared, and then sank down, leaving behind a trail of bubbles aerating the water to a light green color; then it surfaced seconds later and extended a long flipper to me. Yes, deep inside, I have been waiting for this day ever since and hoping, hoping, for an encore.

I dash below for a camera, making a quick instinctive check of the engine instruments in passing. The oil gauge isn't working *again*. I give it a love tap, but I don't have time for finicky instruments. Whales are calling.

Rolf has already climbed the mast steps and is standing on the second spreader. He points to the whales, now off our starboard bow. I engage the engine and move slowly in their direction, staying at least 100 yards away and idling whenever they dive. But this pair is interested in food, not in us. Today we get no contact. Maybe the whales have seen so many sailboats that they've lost interest. When we came to the Antarctic Peninsula in 1984, we were the fourteenth sailboat to have ever come here since Tilman's *Mischief* in 1966. Now there are at least that many each summer season.

Still wearing wraparound smiles from the encounter, we anchor in Dorian Cove, which is formed and nearly walled off by a sandbar that collects all the deep-draft ice pieces. The bar's a great protector, as long as the wind doesn't shift to allow the ice to plug up the entrance, a.k.a. exit.

We are not alone for long. In chugs *Red Sun*. I can hardly believe it. Here comes Tate! When his anchor is down, we row over with some freshly baked cookies. Tate relates to us his experience of crossing Drake Passage and the difficult balance between need of sleep and the need to keep watching for icebergs. Using body movement when common language between us disappears, Tate pushes one palm up while letting the other sink; yes, the balance was like the scales of justice. Now that he's seen the ice, he tells us that he is indeed concerned about being here in a fiberglass boat. He wishes he'd brought some plywood to sheath the bow. Tate points to the ice jam on the sandbar. The back of his hand brushes his brow and he shakes imaginary perspiration from it. But then he smiles and goes below to get an article from a Japanese yachting magazine written by a fellow countryman who had recently cruised the peninsula. Tate shows us the route the other sailor took and explains that he will follow it, as much as ice allows.

As we speak, a 60-foot aluminum yacht enters the cove. We had hoped to cross paths with this Brazilian boat, the *Paratii*, singlehanded by Amyr Klink. Over the years, included in nearly every letter Rubens wrote, had been several paragraphs describing Amyr and his preparations for a winter alone on the peninsula, which he accomplished the previous season.

Amyr is busy for nearly an hour securing his boat with a spiderweb of shore lines. What a job when alone. Forth and back and forth he buzzes, with line after line. But then he knows every possible attachment point in the cove—for this was his winter harbor. When he is satisfied, he ferries himself directly to *Northern Light*. I guess the pipeline has worked two ways. After introducing himself as "Amyr, professional tie-upper," he greets us as though we were long-lost friends.

Although he has just finished a long nonstop sail back up from a sightseeing tour as far south as Marguerite Bay and is extremely tired, the weather is stable and Amyr says we should grab the opportunity to chat. He knows we have arrived prepared to winter and wants to describe his. He progresses methodically and without any modern concept of time, detailing the weather conditions he experienced, his mental stages, and what was good and bad with his choice of anchorage. Good was the abundance of penguins and seals to watch, bad was that Wiencke Island is too crevassed for safe solo skiing and neighboring Anvers Island is so high that it totally blocked the sun through the midwinter months. From what we can deduce, Amyr was very well prepared and handled challenges and problems adroitly. Given that his first solo expedition was a successful *row* over the South Atlantic Ocean from Africa to Brazil, this does not surprise us.

It's encouraging to hear that Amyr considers his winter experience so worthwhile that he hopes to return with his girlfriend for a reprise! He asks for a chart and shows us where he plans to take her. It is just south of Lemaire Channel, the spot I considered the most beautiful last time we were here and that is at the northern edge of the area where we plan to search for our winter anchorage. As the water around the island group he suggests has never been surveyed, Amyr pencils a line showing how to get in and notes the unmarked shoals he knows of. He also marks the spot where he plans to winter and another spot where a French singlehander just spent the winter.

While serious, possessing deep and logical insight into his own endeavors, Amyr is also very entertaining. We find him gregarious and laugh heartily as he describes his favorite penguins' antics. Clearly his solo time did him no harm. In fact, just the opposite seems true: he has a settled and sparkling spirit. Amyr is a hero in Brazil. He has dedicated energy to being a role model for kids there. He teaches them how to set and accomplish goals, to help as his country tries to break away from the concept that their society is corrupt but no one can do anything about it. But as Amyr sees it, from being alone in an icebox to being the center of attention of an entire hot-blooded country requires mental preparation. To have the time to adjust and prepare for the onslaught, he is planning to sail first to Cape Town and Iceland and then home. . . .

Rubens had written to us about Amyr helping an Argentinian military ship when its radio equipment failed. Amyr lent them a radio and installed it and the antenna for them. His only commentary was, "It could have happened the other way around." Amyr now tells us that as thanks for his help, the Argentinians have left 185 gallons (700 liters) of diesel for him at the base in Paradise Harbor. "I don't need it, so you may feel free to take it or tell other sailors. And by the way, the Chileans have jet fuel at Waterboat Point that they can't use. The barrels are rusting away, and they told me that yachties do them a favor to take it."

The conversation has been rewarding in many ways, not the least being that Amyr is the first person who ever says to us, "I know you will have a wonderful winter!" Although we don't like breaking it off, he has a radio sked to keep and is in desperate need of sleep. After accepting an invitation to share dinner with us, he takes his leave for a few hours. Within minutes, the wind picks up from the direction not allowed. We are scheduled to be in another anchorage on the same island in two days for a rendezvous, and as that place is more suitable in the new wind direction, we decide to up anchor and leave. We will meet Amyr another day, we hope.

It isn't more than a few miles to Port Lockroy. In the final turn, we suddenly, shockingly, have a huge white wall ahead of us, blocking the path. It's a cruise ship of Caribbean proportions and without a doubt the biggest ship we have ever seen here. "But Rolf, that's *Ocean Princess*," I say. "Have we made a mistake and gotten the date wrong? I can't tell if it's arriving or leaving. Gotta call them."

"*Ocean Princess,* this is sailboat *Northern Light*," I radio.

Over channel 16 comes an immediate response, laced with a melodic Scandinavian intonation. "Hallo *Northern Light. Ocean Princess* here. Lars-Eric Lindblad speaking. We have a lady passenger who says she's got an appointment with you. Why don't you join us for dinner in an hour?"

Bingo! The ship has arrived ahead of schedule, but here we are and our friend Mary is on the cruise ship. An hour to prepare for dinner sounds fine from the bridge of her ship, but it's tight from our small-team view, so we scurry. The wind speed is 22 to 25 knots, and because we won't have time to check the holding, we anchor and take a stern line ashore. In the process of rowing and climbing over the rocks, I work up good sweat, but there's no time for as much as a sponge bath. But Mary, who at 70-plus years spends her time walking in Nepal and doing Earthwatch projects all over the world, won't care the slightest. Of that I'm sure.

Ocean Princess is too large to anchor inside Port Lockroy and hangs on the hook outside in the bay instead. It's downwind to get there, but nonetheless on top of our best clothes goes the *de rigueur* orange survival suit for the dinghy ride. We are met at the gangway by crew who lead us inside, into the sterile glitz and overpowering heat.

The first passengers to cross our path are a handsome young couple on their way to dinner. I'm American; when we make eye contact, I add a smile. But it is not reciprocated. They are already backpedaling, perhaps riding on one the heat-released waves of "oosh" from our survival suits, which we last used to crawl around a penguin rookery. On the other hand, maybe they are already used to that smell and it's actually the way we look that bothers them? I mean, he is freshly shaved, styled, and suited up, with his creases crisply pressed no less. She is painted all the way to her fingertips, wearing a—wow!—emerald green satin strapless evening gown, jewels sparkling from her cleavage. I know, I know, it's a cruise, and perhaps Lindblad will have some explaining to do if this pair hears that we scraggly wilderness creatures were actually invited aboard. Then the smell of their combined perfumes overlaid with her hairspray hits me and I rebound, catch my composure, and think that even though she may be permanently coifed, that isn't to say I'm not. In fact, I have a cupola-formed hairdo that would make any poodle jealous!

Mary comes skipping down the stairs. "Deborah! Rolf! I can't believe it! The improbability of it all!" We proceed to dinner. Fresh salad is a real treat. Ditto not having to do the dishes. Mary has scads of news for us from Sweden and the United States. She tells of her exciting voyage thus far, but I often lose track of what she is saying. Rolf and I are trained to pay attention to all sounds around us, and there are oh so many conversations within earshot. Bits and pieces break into ours. And it's so hot, I think I will expire.

When dessert is over, Lars-Eric Lindblad appears at our table and suggests that we meet in the lounge in a half hour for a chat. But first, it's his birthday, and the dance troupe on board has prepared a special revue for him, complete with a cancan routine! I don't know how much more culture shock I can handle. And if I know Rolf, he'll soon be complaining about the lack of class entertainment at home.

Mary leads the way to the lounge. The captain, Leif Skoog, suddenly appears. What a pleasant surprise! We've crossed paths with Leif several times, the first in 1984 not many miles from here. He was then captain of *Lindblad Explorer*, alternating trips with the legendary Captain Hasse Nilsson. Polar passengers are very fortunate to have captains of Leif and Hasse's caliber.

Lars-Eric and his wife, Ruriko, join the group. We have never met before today, so we now formally introduce ourselves. After two minutes of small talk, Rolf says that he has a problem he'd like to discuss. The group, professional travelers all, turns every iota of attention directly to him.

Lars-Eric dismisses himself after hearing the word hernia and returns momentarily with a ship's nurse; the doctor is off the ship, sightseeing. Rolf describes his symptoms to the nurse. She concurs that it most likely is exactly what we suspect, but thinks that Rolf should take the doctor's first appointment at 0800 tomorrow.

Innocuously enough, Rolf questions her, "Before you go, may I ask you one thing?" She nods. "Is the hernia repair operation one that Deborah would be able to take care of aboard *Northern Light* at some later date, if the doctor were to give her instructions?"

As if absorbed in watching a tennis match, all heads move in unison from Rolf's direction to the nurse's. In the lounge's dim light I cannot tell if she has a good poker face, but her voice is measured in a way that belies her disbelief in the question itself, as if Rolf were challenging the very existence of the medical profession. She says simply, "It is absolutely out of the question that anyone would be able to perform surgery of this type without proper training or facilities."

Rolf's question is far from flippant or inappropriate and is rooted in years of wilderness experience: backpacking, mountain climbing, skiing, winter camping, sailing. Anyone who spends a good deal of time away from the security net provided by civilization quickly understands the need for advanced first aid training and gets it. The better trained one is, the less fearful and therefore more useful one can be when a companion gets hurt.

Rolf and I agreed on a basic tenet long ago. Out in the wilderness there may come a time when one of us will have to perform medical procedures beyond our training. I may, for example, be injured to an extent that without help I would *surely* die. In that case, Rolf would operate to try to save me even if he actually kills me in the process. Although I assume that anyone who gives thought to this eventuality would get past their initial squeamishness to reach the same conclusion, the only two people I have ever met that had given thought to it were both already medical doctors. But, in a parallel example, one of them had gone beyond the norm and removed his own appendix. Both thought laypeople should be able to do minor and emergency surgery.

Indeed, either of us may have to be an amateur surgeon some day, either at sea or perhaps during the upcoming winter, when ice and winter weather will make it absolutely impossible to get any physical help from the outside. We are prepared to the point that we have a book on board that deals with emergency medicine and procedures, which we have studied and usually reread during long passages, and we have surgical instruments. In addition, propagation permitting, we would try to establish a radio link to a doctor who could talk us through a procedure.

Shortly after the nurse takes her leave, we bid all gathered adieu. It has become dark, and the wind has kicked up to 28 to 32 knots. We have a wild, windy, wet, and unsafe upwind ride in our little dinghy. I hope someone on the bridge is monitoring our progress; Rolf is dismayed that we didn't think to bring our handheld VHF or borrow one from *Ocean Princess* to maintain contact with them on our way back. Then, if anything were to happen to our outboard they could help us. This is far too much wind to row against.

The following morning, the doctor confirms our diagnosis and answers the questions our medical books don't address. He tells us that many men live for years with unrepaired inguinal hernias. Unfortunately, the only risk that poses, although no problem for a man living close to a hospital, could be deadly for Rolf. If the protruding intestine twists, its blood flow is impaired. In medical terms, the hernia has "strangulated." The intestine turns gangrenous and requires urgent treatment: surgery within 24 to 48 hours. In addition, his response to the question about me doing the surgery is the same as the nurse's.

The doctor's opinion is that Rolf should not attempt to overwinter in this condition, to which he gives time-bomb status. He predicts the following scenario: four to six months from now (the latter being midwinter) Rolf may no longer be able to push the intestine back each night. At that point the truss may not be of as much help as it is now and the hernia may even start to spill out around the truss. Simultaneously, the pain level will likely increase, as will the risk of the hernia strangulating. His advice: have the operation. However, if Rolf elects not to have surgery now, he should severely curtail physical activities over the winter. "Too bad," Rolf says despondently, as we walk the narrow corridor away from the doctor's office, "that you never took a night class in surgical procedures."

Lars-Eric offers Rolf a ride on *Ocean Princess* to South America where he can be surgically fixed, but Port Lockroy isn't a secure enough place for me to remain alone at anchor. Rolf and I have some decisions to make, and we move to the ship's dining room to have a cup of coffee and talk.

First, what about having surgery versus taking a chance that nothing happens? Even if the doctor is overstating his case to get Rolf to play it safe, Rolf's present discomfort will continue without surgery. Probably the majority of our planned outdoor activities and certainly our six week ski tour would have to be skipped. And he could die. I admit I don't like the idea of having to live through the polar night with my spouse's body in cold storage in a nearby snowbank. We conclude that if there's a workable way to get him to surgery, spending the winter with a threat of death hanging over us is not worth it.

What about time? If we sail back to South America for the operation and then have to wait six weeks before Rolf is fit enough to cross Drake Passage again, that puts us back here in early March, which is far too late to start looking for a winter anchorage. The best solution is what Lars-Eric suggested: Rolf should ride up and back on cruise ships. If the operation is a success and Rolf heals well, the winter is on. If he doesn't heal well enough, we hope we will at least be able to sail ourselves north toward the end of this summer. Our decision is made.

The first step now is to get *Northern Light* to the safest place possible where I can wait. It has to be a place where we can secure the boat with shore lines rather than lie at anchor, as reanchoring solo is difficult for me in heavy weather. But this place also has to be close to the normal cruise ship route so that Rolf can get out and back without asking any ship to detour on his behalf. Twenty miles away is an American research base, Palmer Station. As it offers tours to cruise ship passengers, it is probably one of the most oft-visited places on the Antarctic Peninsula. Near the station is an inlet where we satisfactorily tied up the boat in 1984. We figure it's our all-around best bet.

While we outline everything for Lars-Eric, he continuously nods in agreement then checks his list of this summer's ships' routes and calls his old ship, now the *Society Explorer*. Its captain agrees to transport Rolf north from Palmer Station in five days. Rolf will hitch a ride to Punta Arenas, Chile, where Lars-Eric knows of a private clinic, have his operation, and then, with the help of the shipping agent there, get on the next possible southbound ship. Lars-Eric also sends a telex to the clinic, requesting an immediate reply, but none comes before it's time for *Ocean Princess* to leave. Mary and the Lindblads give us warm, encouraging hugs. It's both confusing and a little unnerving to continue without confirmation that the telex has even been received, yet merely having a plan, however scant, has started to dispel the dark cloud of the past few weeks. It won't be an easy time for us, but while saying good-bye, we thank Lars-Eric deeply for his help and expediency. He has facilitated the possible continuation of our winter project.

13

HERO U.

DEBORAH

■ ■ ■

Attachment points for mooring ropes are difficult to come by in the rotten-rock sides of the inlet near Palmer Station. But for this purpose we carry an array of pitons, bolts, and rods on board, and eventually eight ropes are secured, one floating rope and one sinking rope off each quarter. The idea is to let the boat hang in the floating ropes while the heavy ones sit on the bottom, out of the way of ice until needed.

Hero Inlet opens to the west-southwest onto a big glacier-rimmed bay. In the other direction it dead ends at a calving glacial tongue, tiny by comparison with the wall in the bay. As the inlet is 33 to 49 feet (10–15 m) deep, ice pieces weighing easily as much as 4,000 tons can move through it. This is not a place we would stay for any length of time by choice.

Ice calving from the glacier will enter the inlet any time the wind blows from the west sector. If a big piece comes in and catches on a floating rope, my tactic will be to take up on the sinking rope temporarily, free the floating one, row it around the ice, and resecure it, then let the sinking one down again. The attachment points for the floating ropes on the south side are high, approximately 33 feet (10 m) above sea level. Most ice should go under them. The north side points are lower. One is at 13 feet (4 m), the other at sea level. But it's steep to on the north side, so if I need to sidestep ice, I can move the boat over quite far in that direction.

"If, if, if, then, then, then," I say after one-too-many hypothetical discussions. "Maybe I'll be lucky and never get to know which of the tactics were right and which were wrong." On the other hand, I dread the thought of the worst-case scenario: when big ice or lots of it bears down on the boat. Rolf counsels, "It'll be OK, if you just do everything right." *Yeah*, I think to myself, *that's some kind of "just."* Oh, how that word can grate.

People have work to accomplish at nearby Palmer Station and officially, other than prearranged tours, visitors are no longer welcome. We understand, especially considering the little of station history we know. By 1984 yachts had already become a burden on the station. Few hesitated to use it as a kind of repair station or mechanical workshop. Some ill-prepared yachtsmen have actually stolen food and others have behaved so badly that they had to be asked to leave. The truth is that a visit to a station is more of a social call than anything else (even if we are curious about the science) and at best an interruption for the ongoing work. Actually, there's no reason sailors should *expect* a welcome, let alone hospitality. Such an idea would never occur to anyone sailing past Woods Hole or Scripps.

Considering that, we make it known to the station manager that as far as we are concerned the station does not exist. Still, there are people we know from our 1984 visit we'd like to see, and as others on station may find a yacht and new faces a welcome diversion, we ask the station manager to put a notice on the bulletin board that anyone who wants to visit us, or the boat, is welcome.

Imagine our surprise when, two days after our arrival, we are invited in for dinner. Meanwhile, *Red Sun* arrives, and the invitation is also extended to Tate. There is quite a hubbub in the dining area, as all 60 people descend to dinner. We are never formally introduced or presented to the group, so we eat and chat with the station manager, Polly, people we know from our previous visit, and the few others who are interested in sailing.

From experience we expected it to be Saharan-hot inside the station and dressed as accordingly as we could, considering that we left our bathing suits in storage in Mar del Plata. Tate, who never took off his sweater or foul weather gear, is beet red halfway through dinner. He is also struggling to converse in English. When he gets really stuck, he turns to me and speaks in Spanish, and I help the few times I can. A woman sitting next to him asks what route he has taken thus far from Japan. With both hands he tries to convey the concept of a globe and then proceeds to "draw" on it, when suddenly, he coughs, stands up, and dashes off. What's wrong? Everyone is concerned; Rolf follows on Tate's heels.

But Tate rushes only as far as the couch at the edge of the dining area where he has left his daypack. He rummages through it and brings out a brightly colored plastic thing, and huffing and puffing starts to inflate . . . a beachball? *So he was prepared to be on station after all, in his way*, I think.

The beachball turns out to be an inflatable globe with his route thus far marked in black ink! I nearly die giggling.

Our fifth morning in the inlet, right on schedule, a ship's horn announces its impending arrival. Minutes later we see the red bow of *Society Explorer* nosing into the bay. I ferry Rolf out. To the crew we meet on board it's a normal day, and they are pleasant and talkative. Their mood contrasts so sharply to mine that the scene takes on a hard-edged feel.

For us this situation is a nightmare. So much can go wrong. To start, we still don't know if the clinic received Lindblad's telex or, for that matter, if it's even in business. Secondly, the operation can be a success but the patient dies. Although not likely, it can happen, and much else could go wrong. We've not had to trust anyone else's work for a long time. In addition, we've been like Siamese twins, joined at the boat for the last few years. My throat is tight. Our embrace is not drawn out. Then I quickly take my leave.

It so happens that one of *Society Explorer*'s passengers is a surgeon who specializes in hernia repair. After talking to Rolf, he radios Palmer Station and asks if he can do the operation there, with their doctor assisting. The answer is that if the surgery were an emergency, maybe, but as it's elective, no. Palmer belongs to the National Science Foundation, which has the express policy of not supporting private expeditions with U.S. taxpayers' money. There is also a question of insurance and problem of possible lawsuits that they would rather avoid. No, Rolf signing a paper obviating Palmer of responsibility wouldn't change their mind. Listening in on the conversation, I suddenly feel like I've bounced back to the United States, where it seems lawsuit fever mutates faster than researchers can discover new cures. I guess it's just like a scientist said to us recently: this frontier has been settled.

But the doctor doesn't give up very easily. He suggests to the captain that he could just as well operate in the ship's surgery with Palmer's doctor assisting and me watching. A telex is fired off to the head office in Germany. The immediate answer is a resounding *no*, also due to insurance (read lawsuit) considerations.

The ship's mournful horn sounds again. Standing on *Northern Light*'s deck, weirdly alone, I can't take my eyes off the red cruise ship. The last glimpse of *Society Explorer* is her aft deck, where a single person stands. I recognize the yellow jacket.

My tears clear as I contemplate my job. This is one hell of a situation for my first time in the captain's seat. I figure that nothing can happen in here that will threaten my life, but the boat can certainly be seriously damaged or sink in this rock-rimmed channel. What makes the responsibility loom extra large for me is that these red steel plates are our home, our life support, and our working platform, and we have no future plans that don't include *Northern Light*. I know that Rolf's heart, indeed his everything, is right here in this boat that he has lived aboard since 1977. "Nothing will happen to you, *Big Red*, not if I can help it," I vow aloud.

By midnight the wind is gale force from the northwest, and the barometer flattens. I assume a low is moving south of us and expect the wind therefore to shift to west, then southwest. It's an anxious wait. At noon the next day the wind turns in my disfavor, blowing right into Hero Inlet. When the ice parade starts, large growlers and small bergs march in, and for the next sixty-three hours I get not one wink of sleep. My job is to dodge big ice (as high as 10 feet off the water) by moving the boat back and forth in the channel, winching and winching. Each time ice gets stuck on a rope, I follow the routine: take up slack on the sinking rope and secure it to keep the boat in position, launch the dinghy, let the tangled rope go, row it around the ice or pull it free, resecure it on board, winch and winch, lift the dinghy back on deck, and let the sinking rope down again. It's tedious work, heavy labor. Sometimes, I luck out and don't have to do anything; either the ice goes under the ropes secured on the high side or it catches but its momentum and instability causes it to rotate and in the process its water-smoothened underbelly glides along and under the rope.

By midafternoon the outgoing tide starts to clear the inlet. The current's 2 knots' pressure to the ice's underwater bulk overpowers the gale-force wind's push above water! The bad part is that I now understand that every piece of ice that comes in is going to have to be dealt with a second time, on its way out, Oh well, at least I can look forward to a lot of free exercise.

One very big ice piece, in the 50-foot-diameter category, goes aground farther in the inlet, and while it blocks the path to *Northern Light*, I get to catch my breath and watch the show. One after another, ice pieces crash into the grounded one, spin off, and float away and out on the south side. But the last piece on its way out is bigger than my guard, and when it crashes into the grounded one, its momentum transfers like a pool ball's to the grounded berg and my guard takes off, right for me! "Luckily" it's taller than the bowsprit is high, so although it hits and sends a shudder through the boat, it does not catch. Had it, I could have been on my way out to sea. Whew, I think, it's only taking a little of us with it; some red paint now adorns the berg. Looking at the fleck, I realize that repairs included, this job is going to last longer than the time Rolf is gone.

Tate, who has *Red Sun* tied up to Palmer's dock, takes advantage of the relatively ice-free period during slack water to row over to visit me and exchange concerns and tactics. As we are talking, *boingg!* My stern starboard rope and piton pull free from the rock and ricochet toward us. Without a moment's hesitation, Tate fishes the rope from the water, rows ashore with it, and climbs the slippery snow-covered rocks, then finds another attachment point and resecures it! I'll just have to wait to see if it will hold. He starts to row back toward me, but I yell and point to his boat. The ice is moving in on the rising tide and he has to hustle to get back to keep little *Red Sun* from being crushed against the dock.

Out past the farthest of *Northern Light*'s attachment points the Argentine Navy has put a 2-inch (51-mm) sinking hawser across the inlet. To it they have tethered a 20-foot (6-m) dive boat with twin outboard engines. This presence is because some years ago an Argentinian ship went aground outside Palmer and sank, and the Argentine Navy, in anticipation of continuing leakage from the wreck, is currently practicing pollution containment techniques. Many birds' and animals' lives, as well as humans' long-term research projects, hang in the balance.

When the new wave of ice starts to jam the neighboring workboat, I radio Palmer to ask them to relay to the Argentinians that their outboards are taking a beating. Some time later, a five-man team arrives, paddling a dinghy through the ice all the way from the ship anchored in the bay. As they prepare to turn the workboat around, they let the hawser go and with it, the extra length that had been coiled in the boat. The hawser sinks toward the bottom of the inlet, and the big, deep-draft ice it had been keeping at bay starts moving in. Oh!

Keeping *Northern Light* from harm is like guarding one's queen in a chess game. I file away a variety of contingency plans for each piece of ice I can see coming, but wait until the last moment before I do anything, because currents and gusts can pull tricks at any time and make the ice change direction or speed. Thinking is time well spent. Suddenly it occurs to me, written in wind-driven snowflakes, what Rolf meant when he said, "Just do everything right." My partner really meant, "Do everything just right." No longer blocked by irritation, energy courses cleanly through me, just in time. . . .

The Argentinians' maneuver has released three very big pieces of ice, and they all bear down on me simultaneously, traveling *along* my high rope, a track that leads directly to *Northern Light*'s stern. I know just what to do. I let the rope go and ease its complement on the port side to move farther in, where the inlet widens a little, in the hope that the three pieces will fan out. We would actually have positioned *Northern Light* much farther in, where the water is shallower, were it not that Palmer has a cable car strung across the inlet there. I move farther and farther in until I dare go no closer to the cable. The ice jam spreads. Whew.

I've been on deck for five hours now, working constantly in snow driven by gale-force wind. Suddenly Polly shouts at me from shore. "Langdon and Maggie [both marine biologists] have finished work for the day and still have their dry suits on. They're bringing you some hot chocolate."

Sure enough, here come two divers, doggy paddling through the brash ice to hand me a thermos! They want to know how I am doing. Well, I haven't thought about myself, and just because they're there doesn't mean I don't have to keep my eyes and mind on what's coming. Looking over the channel, I answer rambling: "I had no idea it was already so late. I've been too busy. I am perfectly warm and comfortable in my survival suit, and considering the constant line handling, happy I don't need gloves. Preparing hot food will be difficult, but I baked bread yesterday after Rolf left, so I can make sandwiches when I get hungry. So how am I? Fine for now, thank you. I'll just have to wait and see how long this lasts."

While Langdon and Maggie alternate treading water and hanging onto our mooring lines, they push and kick on smaller ice pieces, diverting them away from the boat. But I worry for their safety and because as far as dangerous pieces are concerned they can do me no good from the water, I tell them not to bother with the small stuff. Langdon says: "Well, we're done with work for today. Is there some way we *can* help you?"

I know that accepting help can sometimes be a mistake. The help may not outweigh the loss of concentration another's mere presence brings. In normal circumstances it can be difficult to coordinate a newly formed team, but in this already critical situation there's little if no time to spare. I don't know their capabilities, especially as far as boat handling goes, so I'd have to keep an eye on them. The force of ice on mooring ropes is staggering and I certainly don't want them to get hurt.

I do know, however, that as divers and dinghy drivers, both have years of experience in extreme conditions. Those activities crave the same aptitude I can use right now. Their living and working conditions, like mine, must be based on cooperative teamwork. And, with no culture clash or language problems between us, I'll be able to tell them immediately if it doesn't work. At least with them aboard I'll be able to get to the bathroom before I burst and then grab a real dinner. I accept their offer and lower the dinghy, and they climb aboard.

At first they help me winch. What a relief! Because we do not normally have to deal with mooring ropes this way, no system for it has been incorporated into the winch layout, and the temporary system I am forced to use is cumbersome. The major problem is that the only path the mooring rope can take from the bollard arrives at the winch at too perpendicular an angle. The result is that the lowest turn of the rope wants to creep up and jam the upper turns. If you don't see that happening and correct it in time, the only solution left means using a knife. Because that is *never* allowed to happen, I have had to push down on the rope with one foot near the winch's drum, winch with one hand, and tail with the other. Now Maggie stands on the line, Langdon winches, and I tail. It's a picnic by comparison.

I see now that I actually have even more help. Someone, although in the winter getup I can't tell who, is on shore on the Palmer side, and whenever ice approaches, the person whiplashes the rope to try to walk it over the ice.

When I'm sure Langdon and Maggie have the winching system's inherent dangers clear, I suggest we eat, and ten minutes later I reappear with newly boiled ex-freeze-dried food. Actually made for the Swedish Army's winter maneuvers, it's an energy-rich Chinese-style chicken dish with vegetables and rice. Not bad for "heat it 'n' eat it" we concur.

Some hours later, Langdon suggests that I rest. I lie down, but sleep will not come; there's still too much adrenaline in my bloodstream. I get up after a few minutes and Maggie goes off watch. Slack water arrives. Langdon and I take advantage of the "calm" to fish up one of my sinking ropes that I had been forced to let go when "attacked" by the pool ball berg. We free yet another rope that has wrapped around a rock and then reposition the boat back, away from the cable car. Palmer radios to me that their shoreside watch at the rope has been called off as they didn't feel they were doing much, but that five people have volunteered to remain on call.

Langdon and Maggie have to go back to work. But they saved me much energy during the night. The same wind and routine continue the next day. I would like to get ashore to check the attachment points' holding and the ropes for chafe, but there's too much ice for me to work with to leave the boat. I hesitate to bother the people at Palmer Station, but then figuring that an ounce of prevention is worth a pound of cure, I radio to get one of the volunteers to check everything on shore. Out in the driving snow comes Gail, who is responsible for Palmer's fleet of boats, and Rusty, an electrician. They wrap rags and tape in numerous places; calling them out was not a bad idea after all.

A big, tall (and therefore deep) castlelike berg sails in only to catch on the repositioned Argentine hawser, which I now refer to as the submarine net. The berg sits there for hours. I take advantage of the time out to go below to make some tea and eat. Suddenly I hear water churning and bubbling. I rush up to see the big berg still rotating—and it's bringing the hawser up with it—until the berg sits upside-down with the heavy rope on top of it! I sigh. Protection is a concept I may as well suspend. The berg doesn't move far before it goes aground on the south side. I wish an even bigger one would arrive and simply plug up the channel.

That night Rusty comes out and we alternate two-hour watches. I get a chance to relax my weary muscles under my warm cozy winter comforter, but sleep never comes. What an energy elixir recipe: mixing almost twenty-four hours of daylight, adrenaline, and willpower with responsibility born of love in whatever proportions necessary. Off watch, I breathe deeply, stretch, and massage my weary shoulders, biceps, and forearms, but my brain will not be diverted from the task at hand. I review and conclude that I've got the systems down now, at least for what I've experienced so far. But just how long can a person remain effective without sleep?

At the end of the third such day, the wind finally shifts to north. Palmer Station records 52 knots. Yahoo! Icebergs, brash, every piece of white is on its way out, under the high ropes on the south side. When only little harmless stuff remains I have a little party. Rosehip tea is my aperitif while I prepare beef struggle-enough. Dessert is a favorite tape my brother Joel made long ago and far away. I know it by heart, sing along, and even dance a little as I begin to wind down. I feel pretty good. After all, I passed the test. Hey, doesn't everyone in this neighborhood have a Ph.D.? In the spirit of the *Wizard of Oz,* I make myself a diploma from Hero University's School of Hard Knocks and declare myself Dr. Deb, Ph.D. in Ice Management.

Now I can rest on my laurels, albeit for only twenty minute increments, when with the help of alarm clocks and timers I am jarred awake to check around outside. Everything is simply fine until around midnight, when I wake to the sound of deep, crashing booms coming from the glacier. Three hours later, big brash and chunks have totally covered the inlet. Most pieces are about 3 feet (1 m) high. For the paint's sake, I had been pushing this kind of ice out of the way with an aluminum seaberth support pole, but this time there are far too many to deal with simultaneously. A smallish berg plows through the brash, pauses at the Argentine rope, then rotates and slides under, only to shoot out from the deep on a path toward the stern. It moves in too quickly to get the boat out of its way and it is much too big for me to fend off. It pushes on the hull. Mooring ropes squeak and groan under the strain. Two fenders tied to the windvane bracket burst, and one support pipe bends. Aw, there goes my diploma. The berg deflects sideways a bit and grinds along the side of the hull. I push on the berg to move the boat away. Sometimes, like now, I get energy from yelling. "Hey you! Get outta here! You were not invited!" What a circus.

The whole first week I can't ever think of leaving *Northern Light* to go aboard any of the yachts or cruise ships that arrive to visit the station. It's as if we exist in parallel universes. *Polar Circle,* a brand-new beauty of a cruise ship with a sharp clipperlike bow anchors in the bay. While his passengers are ashore, the Norwegian captain hails me on channel 16. "Looks pretty cramped in there. Anything we can do to help?" he asks.

"Perhaps," I respond. "Do you have any dynamite you can spare?" He chuckles and apologizes that he doesn't have any. Well, while I've been alone I haven't bothered to censor my thoughts, and unfortunately, before I even realize what I'm saying, my gallows humor slips out. "Uh, OK," I tell him. "No problem. There are plenty of other ways to kill myself." Whatever the reason, the Norwegian captain doesn't find my joke funny. The reply is uncomfortably empty airspace. I suddenly feel very alone. Tears spring. Where *is* the man who understands me?

14

VOYAGE
TO THE
KNIFE

Rolf

■ ■ ■

At quarter past eight Saturday morning, five days after I boarded *Society Explorer* and only fifteen minutes later than scheduled, the ship docks in Punta Arenas, Chile. An ambulance is parked on the wharf. I let out a sigh of relief. Apparently the hospital got the telex. *So far, so good*, I think.

En route to the hospital the ambulance stops at Comapa, the office of *Ocean Princess*'s shipping agent, so I can meet the man in charge of my "case." He introduces himself as Gonzalo Aviles and shows me a telex from Lars-Eric Lindblad requesting that Gonzalo find me a ride back to Palmer Station.

Gonzalo explains that the doctor at the little private clinic is waiting for me. "If your surgery goes well, then the rest should go like clockwork. You're in luck. There is a cruise ship leaving Ushuaia the day after tomorrow." Then he pauses. When he continues, I understand that he wants the rest to sound as promising as possible. "As you know, Argentina and Chile are still quarreling. Therefore, it isn't possible to fly from here directly to Ushuaia. But a good friend of mine has promised to drive you over the border to Rio Gallegos in Argentina. It's the closest place you can catch a flight to Ushuaia. The car ride takes five to six hours. I've talked to the doctor about it. Of course, he can't promise beforehand that he'll permit you to ride so far so soon, but it'll work out, you'll see. Go now," he directs.

At quarter to nine, I meet the doctor and he examines me. Because I rested most of the way here, the swelling has lessened. I worry that the doctor may think my problem too minor to be willing to take the risk that an operation always includes. But to my relief, he says, "This is nothing to fool around with, especially considering the circumstances of your lifestyle." He asks me when I last ate, drank, and so on. Then he calls for a nurse to ready me for surgery. I can feel my heartbeat pick up. It seems as though I've been put onto an assembly line. Within two days I can be on my way back.

But I can't let this go too far, too quickly. I must first know what the charges will be. After all, I doubt they'll let me work off the bill by washing dishes. I ask the nurse to find out what everything will cost. Asking her feels a little strange. First, there's socialized medicine in my home country, and I'm not used to having to consider the cost of medical treatment. Second, I realize my negotiating position is quite disadvantageous with my pants already down. But the nurse just smiles and says that she will check.

Some nervous minutes pass. After all, a private clinic has to turn a profit. When the nurse returns with an even broader smile, I fear the worst. "I have talked with Gonzalo," she says. "We will send the bill to Comapa, so you will pay them for everything. Including your flight, you will owe a total of $1,200. Will that be OK?" It's half what I'd expected. I consent, and she wheels me to surgery.

The next thing I know, it's just after eleven o'clock, and I am being wakened by the doctor giving me good news. "We have fixed you!" he exclaims. Still a little dizzy from the anesthesia, I tell him that I want to leave the hospital the day after tomorrow at 0500 so that I can make it aboard the ship leaving Ushuaia at 1500. But the doctor won't promise anything. He tells me he must make sure I've recovered enough before he signs the release form the ship's captain requires declaring that I won't need any medical attention on board. "We will see tomorrow," is the only reply I get. Soon after he goes, I fall asleep again.

When I next wake, it's completely dark. Rain is pounding on my window and running in rivulets down the panes. The streetlight outside the window swings violently each time it is hit by a gust of wind. When I come to a little more, I piece together that the nasty weather must be related to a depression passing south of here. South of here . . . My thoughts fly to Deborah. She may be dealing with bad weather right now. I hope she's coping well and doing all right.

I remember the morning we waited for *Society Explorer*. Deborah sighted the ship first, but she took a long time before letting me know. When she did, it was in a manner I could never have expected. Under her breath, she said, "I hate the sight of that ship." Then her eyes brimmed with tears, and she looked away from me.

I didn't understand. After all, the ship's arrival started a chain of events that might allow us to continue our winter as planned. But then I realized it wasn't quite that simple. Beside worrying for me, Deborah was also about to have the solo responsibility for our boat under the most difficult conditions imaginable. Usually, we face problems as a team, with each other's support. Now Deborah would be alone with her fears. I saw that anguish was about to take the upper hand—a dam was about to break—but she was quiet a few moments. Then, all I heard was her laconic question, "Shall I take you over now?"

While *Society Explorer* was tripping anchor I stood on the aft deck. I could see that Deborah had made it back aboard *Northern Light*. The distance was too great for me to really make out any details. But after a while it looked as if Deborah was giving some slack to one of the shore lines! That confounded me. *Northern Light* was so well situated in the inlet that practically nothing could happen.

Then I looked around. From my high vantage point I could see that a collection of brash ice and icebergs that the glacier had recently calved was on its move out of the bay. If the wind shifted slightly more, it could all start to head toward *Northern Light*. Either Deborah had seen the situation as she left the ship and was preparing for the eventuality or some of the ice had already drifted into the inlet. My fist hit the handrail. Damn. That was exactly what was *not* allowed to happen.

I waved to Deborah, hoping she would see me. I wanted to give her my support. When she didn't wave back, I pulled off my yellow windbreaker and waved with it, but there was no response to that either. I was completely beside myself. I needed to be able to say good-bye to her one last time.

In just a few minutes the wind increased to gale force. My last glimpse of Deborah was as she reached outside the rail to do something. I wished I could see what she was doing, but it wasn't possible. And, really, what difference would it have made? Tears started to wet my cheeks. I wondered what Deborah would do if she got hurt or fell overboard.

I remained alone on the ship's aft deck. Even though I was cold, I couldn't possibly bring myself to go inside where I would have to join the tourists. They would ask how I was doing, and I simply wouldn't be able to answer. I couldn't even come up with answers to my own questions. I remember realizing that I must have been an idiot to think that this could ever work.

I stare at the window of my hospital room. As slumber envelops me again, I still wonder what the future has in store for us.

When I next wake up, I have difficulty figuring out where I am. Eventually, it all comes together. I realize that it has stopped raining and gotten light. I must have slept for quite some time.

There are footsteps in the corridor. The doctor arrives on his morning rounds, squeezes my thighs lightly, and asks how I feel. During the night I experienced some cramplike pain in my left leg. It still hurts around the incision, and

I have had difficulty standing up straight. But because I want to leave as soon as possible, I simply tell him, "Everything is fine." The doctor looks at me suspiciously, then comments, "You must be in good shape." He walks out without a word spoken about whether or not I will be allowed to leave tomorrow.

Of course, he must have known I was lying. That was a terrible mistake, and now I will probably not make it to the ship. The freeze-up on the peninsula will start in a mere five weeks. How could I be so dumb as to think I would make it back in time?

At 10 P.M., the doctor makes his night rounds. After a few words, he passes me the release form that the ship's captain requested and wishes me good luck. He informs me that the healing has started but that I nonetheless have to take it easy. He warns, "A second repair to the internal scar—the reinforcement which now holds your intestines in—would never be as strong as this first one will be *if* it indeed gets to heal undisturbed. You'll do yourself a favor to wait six weeks before you jump and run." He smiles, taps me on the shoulder, and is gone.

When the doctor has left the room, I concentrate on my next step. It suddenly occurs to me that Chile and Argentina are not in the same time zone. That means that my flight will be leaving a whole hour earlier than they told me. I ring for the nurse and ask her to try to reach Gonzalo's friend to tell him to come earlier. The nurse never comes back. I interpret that to mean that she didn't manage to reach him. The night is long and full of wondering.

At a quarter to five, Gonzalo's friend arrives to pick me up in his 1966 Chevy. Painted bright yellow, it looks like a giant canary. As I settle into the front seat, the car bounces up and down and sways sideways for a long while, and when Gonzalo's friend puts himself behind the wheel, it sinks down in the way that only an old American car can. Already, I understand that I'm in for some kind of a ride.

I ask if the nurse ever reached him. He nods. And when I ask if he thinks we'll make it to the plane on time, I get the answer. "No problem! That's why I am fifteen minutes early." I wonder aloud, "Fifteen minutes to gain an hour?" But he promises that everything will be all right. As he puts the car in gear, he says, as if to be somehow encouraging, "Only the last 250 kilometers [155 miles] are poorly maintained dirt roads."

For the first hour, everything goes quite well. The road is bumpy but it's paved, and we maintain a fairly even speed. I'm comfortable enough and everything feels all right. But just as we come out of a sharp bend at 62 mph (100 km/hr), I see trouble. Less than ten car lengths ahead of us, the pavement stops, or actually, disappears into thin air. The gravel road it's meant to join is at least 3 feet (1 m) lower.

I have never tried parachuting, but something tells me that the sensation of being suspended in the air must be similar to what I now experience. The difference is that this landing could not be more uncertain. For safety's sake I brought a pillow from the hospital, which I have had behind my back the entire time so far, to dampen the *normal* unevenness in the road. Half-sitting and half-lying in the now airborne car, I place both hands over my incision. As I inhale, I tighten my abdominal and back muscles as hard as I can and hold my breath.

The springs and shock absorbers bottom out. A searing pain pierces my wound. I am scared, but when I don't feel any sensation of warm blood seeping, I don't bother to unzip my pants to check. Instead, I simply ask Gonzalo's friend to take it a little easier. He apologizes sincerely, and we're off again.

Hour after hour on the gravel road he is repeatedly forced to jam on the brakes. The car often comes to a stop just at the brink of a deep sinkhole. Some holes are so huge that they could have swallowed the car. Finally, I can no longer resist asking him why the road isn't better maintained. He answers, "To keep the Argentines from being able to make a blitz attack on Chile." I don't comment, but I can't help wonder what the difference is between a blitz attack and what we are doing. Why should a road that doesn't slow us slow them?

When we get to the airport, I am shaken and weary, but we have arrived in good time. To show my appreciation I try to give the driver a tip, but he just waves me off. He rolls up his window and takes off in the same cloud of dust we brought with us.

At the check-in desk, I'm told that my plane, a DC8 from Buenos Aires, is somewhat delayed. The time it is now scheduled to depart is the same time my ship leaves Ushuaia.

I have no choice but to go to Ushuaia anyway and wait for the next ship. At 1500 Argentine time, we take off. After an hour's flight, as we approach the airport in Ushuaia, I see from my window seat on the port side that there's only one large ship in the harbor. To my surprise, it's a white cruise ship. Tension builds in my chest. My ship! If I'm really lucky I will make it aboard.

The airplane changes course so that I can no longer see the harbor. Instead I look out over Beagle Channel, a couple hundred yards from the runway. It's very windy, and whitecaps are everywhere. When the plane is only 80 feet (25 m) above the tarmac, I see a williwaw rend the water's surface.

I have experienced this wind phenomena while sailing here, so I know to expect a gust of hurricane force, with windspeeds between 80 and 110 knots. It is almost an unfathomable force. Convinced that the wind will hit the plane broadside, I brace myself. There is a tremendous jolt. The plane is slung sideways, and when I look out, I see that although we are only a few feet off the ground, we are already far outside the runway. Simultaneously, the pilot throws the throttle wide open and I am forced back deep into my seat. A hangar rushes by so close that I am amazed that the landing gear doesn't hit its roof. Never have I been so close to death.

An Indian woman in the next seat turns and looks at me, searchingly, her dark eyes panic-stricken. As the plane barely clears the church steeple, she crosses herself. That motion hits me hard. We are flying over a country where missionaries long perpetrated injustice, especially for her Fuegian ancestors. She if anyone should have recoiled when seeing how close we came to hitting that steeple, rising more than symbolically over the settlement.

As the plane continues to gain altitude and arc away from Ushuaia, I wonder how well the history of the area is taught in the schools here and if she even knows what happened. The Fuegians' demise started in 1826, when Captain Fitzroy arrived to map the area from the deck of the *Beagle* and came into contact with the Indians. On his second voyage, he brought a group of Christian missionaries, thinking that he did both the Fuegians and the rest of humanity a favor. But Fitzroy became depressed by what took place. In the end, when he realized that not only had disease decimated the population but that the imported culture had led to the ruin of the Indians' own, his burden of guilt became so strong that he could never return.

Fitzroy then served as governor of New Zealand for two years, but he was dismissed because he supported the Maori people's demand that their claim to land should be as equally respected by the law as settlers' claims. On April 30, 1865, Fitzroy committed suicide, spilling drops of humanitarian blood that the world so desperately needed.

In the early 1900s a premium was still paid in Argentina for each Indian killed. When a chopped-off right hand was presented as proof, a bounty equal to $800 U.S. dollars was paid out. As late as 1978, when I asked a man from Buenos Aires why there are only whites in Argentina when there are both Indians and Africans in Brazil, I got the following answer: "We're a little smarter than the Brazilians. We shot them."

Have today's politicians and lawmakers—our representatives who shoulder the responsibility for developing trends—thought about the past so as to change and improve upon our legacy? Sadly, they have not. Even today, our so-called civilized, democratic world's leaders carry out policies that indirectly make us nothing better than exterminators. To maintain our lifestyle, we are willing to add groups of human beings to the endangered list. Whenever it suits us, we drive native peoples from their rightful ground. We make it impossible for them to live according to their own cultures. It is happening on every continent, and we let it happen for the same reason as always: we benefit from it.

I notice that the Indian woman is looking at me, and my thoughts return to her ancestors. They had been so well adapted to this environment that they lived year round practically without clothes. In winter, even in below-freezing temperatures when snow accumulated, they could survive nearly naked. But the lifestyle forced upon them by spokespersons for the Christian religion—which in this case lacked respect for other cultures' right to exist according to their own terms—killed them. When I think of this, my skin crawls. I turn my face to the window to avoid looking the Indian woman in the eye again. Never before have I felt so ashamed to be European.

I remember the essence of an idea Mark Twain had a hundred years ago.

How can we "civilized people" ever consider ourselves less wild than those people we so degradingly call savages?

The pilot announces that he has decided to not land in Ushuaia. "It's too windy here," he says. No kidding. He informs us that he plans instead to land in Rio de la Grande and wait there for the conditions here to improve. He doesn't know how long we will have to wait but will keep us informed. As his voice disappears, I understand that my last chance to catch the boat has also disappeared.

Three hours later we are over Ushuaia again, about to attempt to land again. As I look out the window, I can't believe my eyes: the white ship is still at the dock! A second later I realize what a fool I am. It can't be the right ship; mine must have left even before we tried to land the first time. Spiritlessly, I brace myself for the jolt I expect when the wheels hit the landing strip, but the landing is as smooth as can be.

When I stand up from my seat, my incision aches. On another day, I would have run the kilometer to the harbor, but today I take a taxi. I know it's pointless, but I want to get to the dock as fast as I can to see which ship is there and find out where it's heading. Before the taxi ever reaches the dock, I see in huge block letters on the stern the name *Illiria*. My head gets light. It *is* my ship!

At the top of the gangplank, I am met by the purser. He has been expecting me. He asks for the medical release form and my passport. He explains that he'll clear me out of Argentina and get my passport stamped along with all the other passengers'. I don't have to be present. When I ask why the ship didn't leave on schedule, the purser responds that they haven't been able to get diesel yet. "Our home office deposited the money into the wrong bank," he says. I shake my head, but he insists that's what has happened and declares, "We leave tomorrow morning." As long as there is actually no other problem and everything goes as planned, I'll be reunited with Deborah within five days. Tired but satisfied, I go down to the cabin I'll be sharing with two other men.

The next morning, when I hear that the ship is leaving the dock, I go to breakfast and then work my way up to the bridge to see the captain and thank him for taking me aboard. "Oh, that's all right. Just a pity," he says, "that we aren't going to Palmer Station this trip."

I can't believe what I just heard! The captain continues: "But you are welcome to stay and join us on the next trip as well. In three weeks we will stop there." He smiles not in an unfriendly way but in such a manner that I understand that it's meaningless to try to explain the consequences. I'm speechless. Why didn't the purser mention anything? I could just as well have stayed ashore and tried for another ship. I'd probably have been able to get to Deborah faster that way. What is it with people? Is is that they just don't think, or is it that they just don't understand? Bewildered and discontent, I go to the aft deck where I can be alone. I don't seem to be able to get any human warmth, so the sun will just have to do.

It's a beautiful morning. The air's clear and the few clouds don't seem to be in a rush. Many times Deborah and I have joked that the Beagle Channel is like looking at Norway through a magnifying glass. It's one of Earth's most magnificent waterways: 150 miles (240 km) of practically undisturbed nature, rimmed with 6,000- to 9,000-foot-high (1,830 to 2,745 m) snow-covered peaks, with glaciers whose blue shimmering tongues wind through verdant valleys and forest-covered mountainsides all the way down to the turquoise-green water.

An albatross is following the boat, its beauty and grace soothing to my eyes. I fasten on it and follow its progress. Whereas albatross usually soar for hours on end, this one has to work its wings to stay aloft in the almost windless channel. Suddenly it dives. Never before have I seen an albatross pick any food out of the sea; from what I understand, they usually feed at night.

Up pops garbage in the ship's propeller stream. They are dumping stuff from the ship. How much they let out, I don't know. I count fourteen heads of white cabbage, a huge number of carrots and onions, and a bunch of other food waste I can't identify. The boat turns, and the wake is perfectly shiny. I suppose it's vegetable oil, but still.

I do not feel capable of doing anything about it. Had I been an ordinary passenger, I should have gone directly to the captain to question him and tell him off. But since I'm riding for free, I can't bring myself to do so.

I want to see the albatross take off again. But as long as I can see it, the bird sits listlessly on the surface. Perhaps it is now the albatross's turn to lose its capability of getting food in its natural way. When the supply of garbage stops, it will die. If that's true, it won't be the first species to suffer from the hand of humans. Disappointed and spiritless, I go below to my cabin.

After two days at sea, we establish radio contact with Deborah and I talk to her for the first time since leaving. She tells me it was tough the first week but that the ice situation isn't too threatening for the moment. She also reports that the windvane was damaged but that we can certainly repair it.

When she hears that the ship is not scheduled to stop at Palmer, Deborah suggests that she take *Northern Light* out of Hero Inlet and intersect *Illiria*'s path the day it comes closest to her. She says she can't bear the thought that I may come as close as 20 miles (32 km) only to steam away again. But we have had problems with the engine's oil pressure gauge, and I dissuade her from moving the boat. It's better to risk her staying another two weeks, or whatever it ends up to be, than to move now. I also inform Deborah that we have been trying to find another ship on its way to Palmer but have had no luck so far.

Beyond the issue of reuniting, there is no other conversation. Neither of us has enough energy left to pep the other, and toward the end of the conversation there is a weird emptiness in my chest. As much as we want to stay in touch, it also hurts to hear the other's voice. It underlines the frustration somehow. But because it would be worse to live in a vacuum, I suggest that we try to establish contact once per day.

The last evening on the Antarctic Peninsula, just before *Illiria* is to head out to sea direct for South America, the chef serves Swedish meatballs. My dinner partner, the ship's doctor, suggests that the delicious dish is perhaps meant as a consolation dinner for me. Whether it is or not, the meal becomes a starting point for a discussion about Scandinavia. For a little while the conversation splits my mind away from Deborah, and I wish it could have lasted longer. But before we've even finished eating, the doctor is called over the public address system and has to leave.

I push my plate aside and head for the radio room to contact Deborah. As much as she dislikes it, she has accepted that it will take another two weeks before I'm back. I'm in the middle of telling her, "There doesn't seem to be anything more we can do . . ." when the doctor flies into the room and asks to take over the radio. One of the chef's assistants has put his hand too far down into the meat grinder and has destroyed two fingers. The doctor needs a bone cutter. He hopes Palmer Station has one to lend him.

After a short silence, the voice of Palmer's doctor comes over the radio, and he confirms that they do indeed have the surgical tool. As the doctor rushes out of the radio room to confer with the captain, it clicks. Due to one man's misfortune, our situation may change for the better. Numerous thoughts swirl through my head. Everything goes so fast that I almost don't have the time to comprehend it all.

When *Illiria*'s doctor returns and informs Palmer that the ship is on its way there, I contact Deborah on the VHF radio to tell her the good news. But she has already followed the doctors' conversation. Before I even have time to say anything, I hear her sparkling voice inviting me on a date. "Couldn't I pick you up in a couple of hours?" she asks.

A little before midnight—thirteen days after we were separated—I am home again. The boat sits in ice-free water, just as I left it. Were it not for my incision still feeling tight, I don't think I would believe that these two weeks ever existed. The whole experience already seems like a most bizarre dream.

15

WHILE
THE CLOCK
RUNS

DEBORAH

■ ■ ■

After two weeks' rest under my watchful eye, not only has Rolf lost that post-op "gray around the gills" look, he's champing at the bit to get underway. But on the morning of our departure day, February 23, we find ourselves locked inside Hero Inlet. Not by ice. A westerly wind has picked up, and the pull of the Argentinians' dive boat on the hawser has raised the rope so close to the surface that *Northern Light* can't pass over it! One final request for help from the angel crew has Gail motoring out in Palmer Station's biggest dinghy. The plan is that without releasing the dive boat, she'll tow it into the wind far enough for us to gain clearance over the line.

While Gail's getting in position, I take care of things in the forepeak. When the last of the mooring ropes we've just taken in are hung in their proper places, I rearrange some sacks of onions and potatoes, moving them away from the anchor chain box in preparation for eventual anchoring. Rolf checks the placement and thinks the bags might slide around when we are sailing, bruising our "vitamins" in the process, and he suggests that I move them to a different position. Standing upright in the low space is impossible, so bent over at a right angle and with arms extended, I lift a 55-pound (25-kg) sack, twist, and feel something pop in my lower back.

I tell myself, *That was an exceedingly stupid move, Tall One*, and reflexively try to straighten up out of the painful position, but my head connects with the ceiling. Whammo! I cautiously back out of the small space. "Oooohhm," escapes from my lips as I stand up straight, and my eyes crinkle in the grimace. But I rub the small of my back and it doesn't feel too bad after time. I think, *You'd better be OK, Shapiro. Rolf isn't allowed any heavy work for some weeks yet.* The headline TWO CRIPPLES SEEK WINTER REST flashes through my mind.

We wave our thanks and good-bye to Gail. It's overcast and damp and starts snowing gigantic flakes. Palmer Station disappears quickly from sight. Not much scenery will be visible today either. We sail a compass course eastward toward the mainland, taking a modest 20-nautical-mile first step to Port Lockroy, where we drop anchor.

In sunshine the following day the majestic mountains reappear, and dazzled by the stark light reflected off water and glaciers, we dinghy to neighboring Goudier Island for a walk and a look around. On the rocky islet is a museum of sorts, a British weather station built in 1944 and abandoned eighteen years later. Since 1962 it's become a hideous mess: two buildings falling apart and one antenna tower falling down, and a little farther away is the traditional garbage dump. In addition, littered on the ground are at least 100 oil drums, rusted through and contents leaking.

One building was the group's living and working area. Another served as a food warehouse and in fact still contains hundreds of tins: Scotch oats, dried bananas, steak and kidney pie, all packed fifty years ago. Despite the age of the food, this could be a well-stocked refuge hut except that it's fallen into disrepair; the ceiling leaks badly and the cans are all rusting. Attached to the warehouse is one ten-foot-square, properly maintained room that has been recently used for parties. Empty liquor bottles are stashed here and there inside and others have been tossed out the front door, where they lie in smithereens. Just outside the door an up-ended oil drum serves as a trash can, although just who is supposed to empty it doesn't seem to have been decided: it is filled to overflowing. The last person to use it thought it a proper receptacle for an engine's used oil and oil filter. Of course, because the drum is open to the sky, during each snow or rainfall the oil has floated over the rim and run out onto the ground.

Here in Antarctica people often vie with indigenous creatures for the same snow-free rocks to use as building sites for their "nests." Port Lockroy is no exception. In the middle of and on top of all this manmade mess is a gentoo penguin rookery, a tern nesting area, and an elephant seal haul-out spot. Mixed in are carcasses and skeletons of birds and seals that have hurt or caught themselves on the trash and died.

The mess and its consequences are appalling, but according to the Antarctic Treaty, totally acceptable. The reason is that the treaty is more a club; the rules are drawn up for and administered by the participating countries who have better things to do with their budgets than clean up after themselves. Even worse, building and abandoning stations is actually encouraged by the Antarctic Treaty. Countries wanting to join are required to establish a station and man it for at least a year, then after just one year the buildings can be left to deteriorate.

On King George Island, one of Antarctica's most easily accessible spots just off the northern tip of the Antarctic Peninsula, are no less than fourteen stations, eight of which are abandoned. The treaty refers to these abandoned buildings as historical sites. I call them monuments to man's hunger for power and wealth as well as his selfishness and shortsightedness. Those countries that can afford to build stations to join the club do so in the interest of being able to share in the future exploitation of natural resources. Those countries that already have presence are happy to exclude those countries too poor today to be able to ante up according to the rules that the treaty signatories have established. What a power play! It reminds me of the Papal Bull of 1493 by which the Spanish and Portuguese divided up the world. In the same vein, treaty members seem to think that one day they will have the right to divide up Antarctica or its riches. Is that what's called learning from history?

Fortunately, at least it looks as if the issue of current environmental abuse isn't to be overlooked any longer. We have heard rumors that the peninsula is to be visited by a Greenpeace ship again this season. In the absence of an enforcement agency inside the treaty or a neutral one outside, Greenpeace has the self-appointed task of checking each station and tourist activity here to see how much environmental impact we all have; after all, no human is here without impact. Greenpeace investigates, makes immediate suggestions to those involved, and if necessary gives the public the downside of any environmentally damaging practices, such as when they exposed the Americans' lack of proper garbage disposal at their base on the edge of the Ross Sea. Then, where appropriate, citizens can raise their voices at home and use political pressure to get their countries' own programs managed properly and therefore help bring a quicker stop to the more blatant abuses.

At times, Greenpeace also tries to focus world opinion on human's operational policy in Antarctica, which becomes necessary when signatories act completely irresponsibly. This year they are taking the French to task. At their station Dumont D'urville at Pointe Geologie, the French wanted an airstrip immediately, so without bothering with the required environmental impact study, they started the project by dynamiting islands, including penguin rookeries. Yet are they kicked out of the club? No. The way we see it, they should have lost all right to even be in the Antarctic. One thing is clear. Inside the treaty, even though the countries have the right to inspect each other's operations, nothing further happens. And there is no protocol, not even in the face of outright abuse, through which a country stands to lose its membership.

Nor does the treaty directly regulate tourism. Although recommendations concerning preservation were drawn up in 1964 and were joined by conservation measures in 1978, all recommendations (seventy of them by 1988) are voluntary, unless a country effects its own law. What that means is that each person visiting or working in the Antarctic is only responsible to follow his or her own country's laws pertaining to the Antarctic!

In response to the lack of clear-cut procedures, tour operators as a group formulated their own regulations for visitors. The result? Each and every cruise passenger now undergoes education before stepping ashore. They are taught how to approach animals and what distances to keep, not to tramp on moss and lichens, and not to litter. In addition to the training, cruise ship tourists are ferried ashore in small groups, accompanied and policed by naturalists, to whatever extent the captain of the vessel requires.

A major problem with tourism in Antarctica today is that it has become too popular. Antarctica is now the cruise to take. Trip after trip is fully booked. More ships are therefore hustling to join the fray, and many are not suitable for polar cruising. As Captain Hasse Nilsson (the first cruise ship captain to Antarctica and through the Northwest Passage, and perhaps the most experienced in taking tourists to the polar areas) has explained to us: the preferred Antarctic cruise ship is a small, ice-classed ship. It can seek shelter in places a bigger ship cannot. A smaller ship also means fewer passengers. Hasse thinks that's important for multiple reasons: the passengers can get the attention they need and therefore be satisfied with their trip; smaller groups result in less harm to the wildlife; and fewer passengers means a better safety margin, because there are a manageable number of people to take care of and get back to the ship when the weather deteriorates quickly.

In addition to their larger ships, some operators now want to build airstrips and hotels. It's the sheer numbers of tourists tromping around that's worrisome. One operator has suggested that as numbers increase, cruise ships fan out, visiting different sites to lessen the impact on each place. We wonder if just the opposite—a fixed number of places to visit—isn't better until the impact of visits is understood. We propose that tour operators as a group invest in a study of the changes in animals' individual and group behavior at those sites. If the animals begin to abandon the sites or act strangely, then the cruise industry will have to respond and reduce the number of onshore visitors. The maxim in parks is that the more people there are, the more their individual access has to be limited.

Meanwhile, there is also good news. Based on Hasse's recommendations, a new generation of low-impact cruise ships has appeared. They run on regular instead of heavy diesel and therefore put out less smoke and make less noise than other ships. They have freezers for their degradable garbage and compactors for cans and glass; nothing is thrown overboard. In addition, these new ships have primary treatment plants for sewage. Surprisingly, not one research station does.

It's only natural to expect scientists, who are, after all, highly educated people, to know better than to run a station in a pristine area with no regard to pollution and trash. Unfortunately, that hasn't often been the case. Perhaps it's because the scientists don't run the stations and they prefer to not make waves with the administration. Perhaps it's because they understand only too well the budgetary implications of cleanups to the funding of their own project. Perhaps it's also because scientists concentrate on their own projects—after all, most are only here for the summer and it passes so quickly!—that they don't pay attention to anything else unless it directly affects their research, such as when the smokestack's discharge registers on their air-pollution sampling machine when they are supposedly monitoring pollution coming from much farther away.

We aren't alone in Port Lockroy a day before another sailboat comes in, disgorging its human occupants to spread like dry leaves before the wind. I guess the atmosphere hasn't been very good on board that boat; it seems that some folks have a little aggression to work off. Kicking rocks must hurt too much. Plump penguins serve the purpose instead, kicked airborne like footballs at a scrimmage line. Squawking in pain, penguins fly through the air, and outright chaos results when they land in another bird's territory and then try to get back home again. Another of the charter guests who wants to have his picture taken with a cormorant walks up to one sitting on its nest. Frightened for its young, the bird carries on the best defense it knows: wildly flapping its wings and hissing. But the display hardly scares the six-foot-tall tourist. He grabs the cormorant by the neck, lifts it off the nest and holds it there, while his buddy snaps a few frames. This'll be fun to show the friends back home, eh? Rolf runs toward the man, reading him the riot act. The tourist drops the bird, shrugs to his buddy and then looks at Rolf with disbelief, as if to say "If this bothers you, I can stop."

Some who read this will be as shocked as we are; others, like the man lifting the cormorant, will not understand what it is that upsets us. Respect for animals is still a new concept in many cultures. Today in Sweden, for example, there is legal punishment for maltreatment of animals. But we have a book aboard written only fifty years ago that chronicles the Swedish yacht *Fidra*'s round-the-world voyage. Among other things, they describe the fun they had shooting dolphins, taking potshots for the sport of it! They left dead and wounded dolphins in their wake, but you can be sure this idea would be repulsive to their grandchildren.

Group mentality does change; today, Swedish preschool children are educated by volunteers about how to behave outdoors. In Mulle School the kids are taught to be considerate of the wildlife and the surroundings and are taught not to litter. The schooling uses a negative example of a slovenly character who the kids come upon by chance during a walk in the forest. He sits on a trash heap and is as tragic and scary as he can be. By day's end, none of those kids wants to be a bit like him. Perhaps it is time for an international version? A little education at an impressionable age is all it takes to nurture respect for living creatures and for nature as a whole.

Kotic, another yacht on charter arrives, and we discuss with owner Oleg what has upset us. In turn, he gives us a rough draft of a guide that sailors Sally and Jérôme Poncet are working on. Oleg informs us that the guide addresses the problem that sailors do not necessarily know how to behave in the wilderness and gives guidelines for behavior. It represents the charter yachties' move to self-regulate, led by the Poncets who with their *Damien II* have been plying Antarctic and sub-Antarctic waters since 1977.

Oleg presents us with fresh food. I write to my mother and ask her to send him our first book as a thank you. How and where can I post a letter from Antarctica? Oleg will take the letter to Faraday, a British station a little farther south, that has a post office! Although by signing the treaty countries suspend any claim they've made to Antarctic land, each has its own methods of establishing that they operate there as if it is theirs, just in case. So starting with "political post offices," one-upmanship has ensued. The Argentinians, who also have a post office, brought pioneer families to settle their King George Station and then later even transported pregnant women to give birth there, all to have proof at a later date that they were the first to have actually colonized Antarctica. Every treaty country flies its flag as best it can. Do we see war brewing?

In steams *Abel-J,* an American expedition ship visiting old whaling sites, fact-finding for a museum in Massachusetts. The wind is rising and by nightfall screams off the glacier and through Port Lockroy. *Abel-J* is upwind of us, and during our anchor watch we keep an eye on it. Occasionally, the entire glacier wall is lit by the ship's powerful spotlights as they check for calving ice.

The shrieking wind takes different paths over the glacier, but no matter the direction, each time it hits, *Northern Light* is pushed until there's no slack left in the anchor chain. The links grind along the bobstay. The noise is abrasive, not in the least to the psyche. Just as I start to wonder if the anchor will hold against much more, the wind drops. A couple of breaths later, I hear the wind whining its approach until it howls and screeches from a new direction. The boat responds by skittering until it again finds the eye of the wind. Eventually, even this wild ride is perceived as its own pattern: swing so far in this direction, with this bearing to that landmark, then swing over to . . . , and my nerves calm as I simply watch and bide my time, waiting to react when and if the pattern changes or something goes wrong. To calm down isn't to imply that I can relax. There's something in the shriek of wind over 40 knots—like there is in a baby's cry—that grates and just doesn't allow a human the possibility or privilege of relaxation. This is part of the price Antarctica exacts.

When the wind dies, not only does it feel like Sunday, it *is* Sunday, and we are invited aboard *Abel-J* for brunch. Before we go, I have a chore to attend to: taking out Rolf's stitches. We're both pleased to see there's no sign of infection. Just a few more weeks of recovery and this hernia episode will be over.

Once aboard *Abel-J,* I offer to help with food preparation, but the owner's wife and a guest have relieved the cook for the day and tell me that I too am to take it easy. Rats: I really wanted to be able to stand up for a while. My back hurts when I sit, even though I am taking painkillers. By the end of the leisurely meal, I can barely rise from the hard settee. The captain wants to take us on a tour of the ship. Luckily for me, the first move is to the bridge, reached by going up a long, steep, narrow stairwell, where I can hold the handrails on both sides and stretch out a little, past the pain and ache.

Here we are, poised for the search for our winter harbor. Hamilton, the captain, is curious about what it is we will look for. "In Nova Scotia, where I come from," he says, "fishermen often let their boats freeze in for the winter. They have plenty of protected bays for the purpose. Their major problem revolves around the fact that they have wooden boats. . . . Ice freezes to the caulking between planks, and if the ice moves, it can pull the caulking out. More than one boat has sunk that way. Good you don't have that problem! On the other hand, the conditions are so much more harsh here. I've been wondering. What's your idea of the configuration of a secure Antarctic winter harbor?"

"Correct me if I'm wrong," Rolf answers, "but I'm willing to bet that fishermen in Nova Scotia let their boats freeze in much in the same type bay that their Swedish counterparts do, that is, a not-too-large bay where ice forms early all the way to shore. And they too probably freeze in, inside the line where the ice first cracks each spring."

After Hamilton nods his head, Rolf continues: "If only it were so easy here. But in addition to that type ice we freeze into at home, called fast ice, there are two more types here to consider: pack ice and icebergs. What I refer to as my 'perfect winter harbor' limits the dangers posed to the boat by those two types of ice.

"Start with the fact that we are certainly looking for a place where, just like at home, there *will* indeed be fast ice, as it will actually protect us, most importantly by creating a barrier to shield the boat from the moving ice, known as pack ice. The pack, driven by wind and current, is the most dangerous form of ice for us. It can crush any boat in its way. We consider getting caught in the pack a death sentence, just as it was for Shackleton's *Endurance.* Being inside a large island group is the best protection from the pack, which would have to creep up and over the islands to get to us.

"But I suppose," Rolf adds, as his gaze moves to the scenery outside, "that that can indeed happen in a very heavy ice year. The descriptions I've read from the Northwest Passage are hardly encouraging. Anyway, inside the island group we want to put ourselves in a shallow area. One reason is that it freezes first in shallow areas. Ideally, there will also be lots of shoals, just-submerged rocks, and uneven shoreline in the neighborhood to serve as 'attachment points' for the fast ice, which we want to stay put until it rots next summer.

"Being in shallow water also protects us from icebergs. The shallower the water the better, so that icebergs go aground long before they get close to us. The concept is, however, a double-edged sword," Rolf says through a half-smile. "It's also terribly risky to be in shallow water. And oddly enough, the factor that creates the biggest risk in shallow water is that very same group of icebergs, the big ones that can be up to 1,300 feet (400 m) deep that are actually miles away from the boat."

As Hamilton's eyebrows knit, Rolf's rise. "Yes, really," Rolf says nodding. "Even in winter, the underwater profile of a berg is eroding. Eventually, it becomes top heavy and capsizes. A wave forms. Out in deep water the wave is hardly noticeable, but as it comes up onto shallower water, its height and destructive power increase, just like a tsunami. In other words, we've got to find protection from huge breaking swells created by these capsizing bergs. We hope we will be able to tuck ourselves long inside an island group.

"But we cannot search for shelter in too-shallow water. The depth around the boat cannot be so shallow that at low tide the fast ice rests on any rocks or unevenness in the bottom contour, because then the ice can crack and heave. Water enters into those cracks, and when that water freezes, its expansion forces the ice to grow laterally. The resulting pressure is something no boat can withstand."

"Okay," responds Hamilton. "I'm with you so far: island group, attachment points, shallow, but not too shallow. *Northern Light* has about a 6-foot [2-m] draft, right?"

After Rolf nods affirmatively, Hamilton asks, "So what do you figure the depth of your anchorage should be?"

Rolf answers: "From the few statistics available, we expect the ice to build to about a half yard thick. Tide is about a yard and a half, but considering that the winter ridge of high pressure can extend this far north and lower the low-water level, let's say tidal difference can be as much as 2 yards, maybe even 2 plus. I figure that water of 4 to 5 yards depth, meaning 2 to 3 yards under the keel, will be perfect.

"Another aspect Deborah and I have to keep in mind as we search is that we have to find a spot where we can attach mooring lines ashore; we will not freeze in at anchor. The reason is that it's crucial to be able to control the boat's directional orientation as it freezes in. We want *Northern Light*'s bow facing the eye of the strongest wind direction through the winter. That's northeast, which also happens to be the most common wind direction. If the boat were swinging at anchor and froze fast on a southeast-northwest line, during winter she'd be beam to the northeast storms, pushed by the wind and heel, and would continuously mash the ice's edge. The hull might sustain cosmetic damage, but worse—and something we cannot risk—is damaging or destroying the rudder.

"We're lucky that the second most common winter wind direction is 180 degrees different: southwest, so it'll come from dead astern. Both winds, which we can expect to blow uninterrupted for days on end, will propel loose snow and build drifts on the lee side of hills and promontories. I expect that if it's anything similar to what I've seen in the Swedish mountains, the drifts can be so enormous that they could not only bury the boat, but the masts as well! We therefore will not tie up close to or behind land of any height. I don't want to spend my entire winter digging out. But you never know. We'll have to keep the deck cleared and maybe even keep a moat open around the boat. You see, the mere weight of a heavy snowfall can push the ice down. Over time, the ice may sink several yards, taking the boat—if it's frozen in—with it . . . down."

Rolf's shoulders and body have been sinking slowly during his description and his body language is mirrored by Hamilton, who slouches deeper and deeper into a console. But then Rolf brightens and both men stretch to full height again. "In other words, it'll be *very* far from the boat to land, both to the northeast and southwest!" he exclaims. "And we may get some exercise digging both snow and ice." Everyone, including me wondering about my aching back, nods.

"Last, but not least," Rolf says, nonblinking, as if staring into an imaginary crystal ball, "we hope to choose a place where the ice remains through the entire winter, but *not* the following summer. . . ."

During Rolf's explanation Hamilton has become more and more intrigued. I can see that he's anxious to get to the next round of questions. "Have you found any places on the charts that match your requirements? What area will you search?" he asks.

"The area to be explored," explains Rolf, "starts just south of here, where we can be 60 to 70 percent sure that it will freeze, and extends as far south as Marguerite Bay, where it's 80 percent sure to thaw. I expect to find several suitable places. But it isn't just the configuration of the harbor we have to consider in our final choice. Complicating the decision is that Deborah and I want to go skiing this winter. And, as long as the boat sits safely and the sea ice is good, we plan on skiing away from the boat once the light comes back. We therefore hope to have access to the mainland.

"And so, to your first question: Yes, looking at the charts, we have found possible island groups—Hovgaard, Pitt, and Fish—and also a few individual places like Horseshoe Island and Mutton Cove. Because the island groups are shallow and therefore not of interest to big ships, no one has bothered to chart inside them. We will simply explore, checking each one on our way south. Naturally, we'll have to adjust our search to the ice conditions we find en route. My plan is to search until March 20 or 25 and be back to the place we decide on no later than April 10. Later than mid-April, the daylight has dwindled too much, the weather has deteriorated, and snow may have started to accumulate, making attachment points on shore hard to find."

"Interesting, very interesting," says Hamilton, stroking his chin. "Listen, we are on our way south. As you know, this season looks pretty good. We hope to go south on the inside route and then into Marguerite Bay as far as the ice shelf, where Martyn is to check the status of Adventure Network's airplanes' fuel stash. If we can keep in touch, I'd be happy to apprise you of the ice situation we find."

We appreciate his offer. Information never hurts. Because Martyn has a regular radio sked with his office in Punta Arenas, it is decided that we should check in then if we can. Hamilton gives us his card and says, "Can't you please drop me a line next year and let me know that all's OK? Or, if you need any help, just get in touch. I'd be most pleased to do whatever I can." Rolf and I each get a big bear hug as we leave. Hamilton cares. He's concerned. And he's, yes, just a twinge jealous, methinks.

16

THE
LAST
BREATH

ROLF

■ ■ ■

A ntarctica is no sailing paradise. In the waterways between high islands, there is either no wind or too much. Besides that, wind flowing through these passages is channeled by the contour of the land. That means that it blows either on your nose or at your back. Nothing else exists.

As we leave Port Lockroy, the wind is out of the north. With our next harbor 30 nautical miles south, the wind is with us in the narrow sound between the needle-sharp 4,600-foot-high (1400 m) peaks of Wiencke Island and glaciated Doumer Island. Visually, it's an extremely dramatic passage.

Because the breeze is even and steady in direction, we pole the genoa out to port and wing the main out to starboard. The delightful sailing conditions underscore the excitement we feel at the prospect of beginning our search for a suitable winter harbor.

Dead ahead and 20 nautical miles farther away in the haze, lies Lemaire Channel. It was created millions of years ago when a crack developed in the mainland and a huge chunk of mountain shifted westward. Both sides of the waterway rise as straight as a plumb line, out of the sea and up a thousand yards. That's so high that the sun's rays only reach the water's surface when the sun passes through due north. At other times of the day the shadows cast are considerably longer than the waterway is wide. Lemaire is one of Antarctica's, if not the world's, most spectacular channels.

Toward such a destination I prefer to move slowly and whenever possible silently. At first it may seem that the silence itself has no value. But it functions as a catalyst, magnifying impressions. And isn't silence also a necessary ingredient for good health? Doesn't our ability to function properly diminish when there is too much external interference? My belief is that silence is so important a dimension of life that it is simply not allowed to disappear.

One evening at sea many years ago, I detected a very muffled humming much like a transformer creates, only far weaker. In fact, it was more of a sensation than a sound I could actually hear. At the time, there was very light wind. At first, I thought the noise came from a ship below the horizon. But through the night, and without ever seeing a ship, the sound became progressively more pronounced. I finally realized that it must be the sum of all the "voices" of people, cars, buses, sirens, music, and more emanating from the city of Rio de Janiero that I had started to detect from a distance of 70 nautical miles.

The cumulative sound had traveled through the air and was received by a human ear. It made me wonder how the noise we create affects other life. For example, how much low-frequency vibration does a seaside city of millions like Rio give off, especially from traffic on bridges, trains, and subways? How does that affect life in the ocean?

A city's hum includes 20 hertz, the same as generated by a large ship's propeller. According to Lyall Watson in the *Sea Guide to the Whales of the World,* Roger Payne (one of the world's foremost experts on the behavior of whales) has discovered that in water, a 20 hertz signal's strength only weakens 3 decibels per 5,000 nautical miles. Because the 20 hertz signal is also the frequency that fin whales use for communication, one can draw the mind-boggling conclusion that a whale located in the middle of the South Atlantic Ocean can hear a ship leaving Buenos Aires as well as the traffic in Cape Town! But the implication is scary: man-made sound can disturb a whale's ability to communicate with another, to the point where the whales may not be able to locate each other to mate.

The previous time Deborah and I visited Antarctica, we heard whales almost all the time. Inside the boat, we could hear them while they were still miles away. We soon learned each species' distinctive sounds. The killer whale made fast clicking sounds that were often followed by short muffled grunts, whereas the minke whale transmitted a repeated one-note signal. The humpback whale, the symbol for the living wilderness, is a master of song who's register extends beyond what a human ear can detect. Whenever we heard their melodies, our enthusiasm knew no bounds.

We often had whales close to the boat. But so far this time, we have only seen two humpbacks, which worries us. The huge number of engine-driven ships that now visit Antarctica each summer can be so disturbing that whales are avoiding the area. Beside normal ships, at least two ships this season are

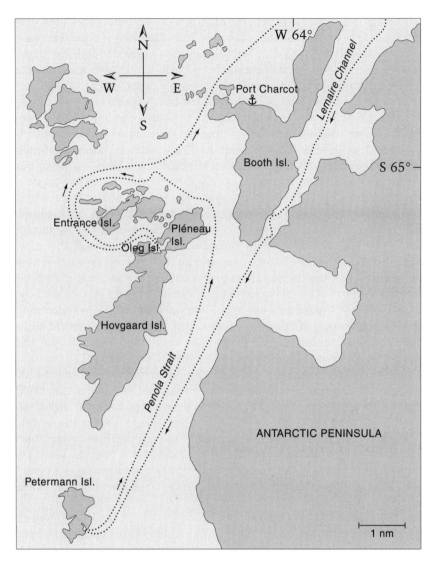

*The route to and from our winter anchorage. The area between Pléneau Is-
land, Booth Island, and the unnamed islands to the northwest is called "The
Iceberg Graveyard." Huge icebergs often went aground in the area, and sat
there for days and even weeks. The path marked on the chart—our only way in
and out of our winter anchorage—has not been charted. It can be a navigator's nightmare.*

conducting geological research by detonating explosives underwater. The shock waves from the explosions are most likely disturbing not just for whales but also for seals and penguins. Perhaps they even disturb the krill, the largest of the zooplankton and an important pillar in the Antarctic food chain. And this geologic research is undertaken even though treaty nations have promised each other to not exploit mineral wealth here for the next fifty years.

The possibility that whales would leave the area concerns us. We really don't want the same thing to happen here that has happened to the animals in the Swedish mountains. When Deborah and I took our long ski journey there in 1989, we hoped to relax for a while in what I, a couple of decades earlier, had experienced as northern Europe's most magnificent wilderness. I had hoped to show Deborah what I had seen: wolverine, perhaps on its way up along a steep mountainside taking newly caught food to its young; wild reindeer; snow owls; and, because it was an early spring, maybe also brown bear. But for the 140 miles (220 km) that we covered almost without sound, through the passes where the Saame had taught me to find animals, not only did we never see one single four-legged animal, we didn't even see a single track, neither fresh nor "petrified." (In contrast to what one might expect, heavy winds do not blow footprints away. Instead they blow the loose snow around the footprint away, leaving an elevated petrified print of the animal that's passed there.) In nearly three weeks, all we saw was one flock—five, to be exact—of ptarmigan. That was all. For all intents and purposes, the wilderness had died.

In the Swedish mountains Deborah and I did not meet one other self-sufficient person. The few others who traveled on skis had just food for the day in their backpacks. They slept in huts where they ate and picked up the next day's lunch. Their food had been transported there for them by snowmobile or helicopter. Most of the people we saw traveled by snowmobile. The engines' buzz had scared away all the animals; the only natural sound left was the wind. The feeling couldn't have been different had we skied across a deserted graveyard. It was horrible. We can't help but wonder if the same will happen to the animal life here in Antarctica.

Happily enough, in Antarctica, nature still sets some limits for humans' rampage. For example, Lemaire Channel is a bottleneck; no one ever knows beforehand if they'll make it through. Even in summer there can be so much ice that all through traffic is stopped, with the possible exception of an icebreaker. The ice has also been a hindrance to animals trying to expand their territories along the peninsula. Not until recently has it been possible for the elephant seal to make it with any regularity into areas south of Lemaire Channel, a move tied to the recent warming trend along the peninsula.

The closer we come to the narrowest part of the passage, the more excited we get. This time, it's our turn to be lucky. We make it through without much trouble.

Deborah and I have waited seven years for this moment. When we drop the anchor at Petermann Island an hour later, we feel like we're home. Everything in sight is familiar. We look toward the outcrops closest to the sea. Gentoo penguins still have claim to them. Their calls bounce off the snowfield that stretches to the top of the island. A couple of hundred meters north, Adélie penguins nest. A little farther away on another, steeper outcrop is a colony of blue-eyed cormorants. And this is all in the shadow of sculpted Booth Island. Deborah bubbles with glee.

The only thing "disturbing the peace" is a hungry leopard seal. Curious about us, it swims around the boat, repeatedly lifting its head out of the water to look at us. The eyes are lizardlike and therefore we cannot easily judge what its attention is fixed on. The seal is more than 10 feet (3 m) long and weighs approximately 770 pounds (350 kg). We're happy that it stays at what we think is an appropriate distance.

But suddenly the seal starts to move quickly and directly toward us. When it is just a yard from the boat, it lunges and stretches up so high that its jaw is level with our deck. The jaw muscle is as big as the muscle in my thigh. The leopard seal is the only seal in Antarctica that preys on warm-blooded animals, so we instinctively take a step back. What a beast!

It dives under the boat and comes up on the other side, where it lunges at us again. This time, the seal stretches even higher out of the water. Three times in a row it repeats this maneuver.

That this is the seal's territory is not in question. Although we had planned on inflating our dinghy to take lines ashore, we concur that we can just as well row when the seal has gone. We are in no rush; there are two more hours of daylight. We settle on deck to watch.

After it has given up on us, the seal moves toward a major gentoo penguin thoroughfare. There it dives. Within seconds, we see a group of penguins on their way back from feeding. When they only have some 50 yards left until their landing area, one of them suddenly disappears. It happens almost imperceptibly; there's not even a splash. All that remains are rings spreading on the water's surface and a small shiny spot where the penguin vanished.

Half a minute later, the seal shoots up out of the water, dragging a cascade of water with it. While the majority of the seal's body is above the surface, and with the penguin's feet in the vise of its huge jaw, the seal makes a rapid whipping motion with its head. The penguin hits the water with such force that its feather-covered body splits open. The whole belly tears and the skin peels off and turns inside out, rather like a hurried child would take off a jacket. The water turns red. The seal dives, and the surroundings are completely still for a few seconds.

Time after time, the leopard seal reappears to sink its teeth into the flesh that's left on the carcass and whip its head to the side. Each time the penguin body flies away, the seal swallows the piece of meat left in its teeth. For fifteen minutes, the carnivore savors its meal. It can take its time; the leopard seal has no enemy. It seems to me to be a very pleasant life.

It is now March 6. The sun already sets as early as seven o'clock, so we now have a reason for the first time in a long while to eat dinner by candlelight. Because it is too dark for any excursions on land after dinner, the meal becomes a little more drawn out than usual. The change and the candlelight-induced mood make us think about the approaching winter. We chat a little about how we think it will feel when we can no longer expect to see boats or people and how soon all our theoretical hashing will be replaced with reality. Just as Deborah asks if I would like anything hot to drink with dessert, our conversation is interrupted by the sound of outboard engines.

When we look out, we see that two boats carrying five men from the British scientific station Faraday are about to be tied up outside the hut on the island. Before the men disappear inside, we row over to say hello.

The hut is very simple. It has an entrance nook, a storage room, and a separate living room with a coal-burning stove, a couple of benches, and a huge, full-to-brimming bookshelf. Deborah presents the guys with a chocolate cake, which proves to be very cunning ruse. They offer to put on some tea. "Great," Deborah responds, "I mean, when experts arrive on the scene, why not take advantage of them?" Everyone laughs.

While we sit and talk, a discussion ensues about a tragic incident that happened here during a winter some years back. Three men from Faraday had skied to this same hut for a vacation weekend. The day after they arrived, a violent storm carried the sea ice away. The hut had a good supply of coal, and as they had plenty of food with them, the men were in no immediate danger. Because it was a cold winter, they assumed the sea would soon freeze over again. As they saw it, their only problem was that the other personnel still at the station had to assume their workloads until they returned.

After a week, the men thought the ice looked safe. They radioed to say they were leaving and figured to be back to Faraday within four hours. But they were never heard from again. It is assumed that the ice must have broken up so fast they never had the time to seek safety. But the whole episode is very strange. There was hardly any wind when they left. Their disappearance remains a mystery to this day.

When we row back, it is already midnight. The night is so calm that after just a few strokes Deborah simply stops. Neither of us really wants to go inside. For a long time we just sit quietly, enjoying the sight of all the stars that are visible once again. After our eyes adjust to the dark, we see that there are some icebergs in Penola Strait. On the other hand, where *Northern Light* lies is perfectly ice free. It's as peaceful as it can be. Not before Deborah hears me yawn does she pull the last strokes home.

There is no reason to even discuss standing anchor watch. We fall asleep immediately. But then, somewhere in my subconscious I hear a sound that I can't figure out—the rumble sounds like an avalanche coming toward us. Even in my dreamy state. I understand that's impossible. The nearest steep mountainside is more than 5 miles away, across open water.

I must have been sleeping very deeply. As I struggle to wake myself, I can't figure out if I am dreaming or on my way to waking up. It probably takes half a minute before I sit up, and the entire time the sound gets progressively louder. Finally, I come to enough to throw off the cover. The roar has increased to the point that it sounds as if we are about to be buried by the advancing avalanche. Even as my feet hit the cold floorboards and I wake up enough to understand that it couldn't possibly be an avalanche, I nevertheless cannot come up with any other explanation. For a fraction of a second I consider that I may be hallucinating; the sound is so unreal that my brain simply refuses to accept its existence.

On my way up the ladder, with Deborah right on my heels, I hear the shore lines tightening. Something is indeed up. The roar just increases. I can only assume that it's a breaking sea. But that can't really be possible; I haven't heard any wind. Perhaps this is a nightmare after all? I throw open the cupola and rush out in the cockpit. I *am* awake.

An enormous breaking sea is rolling toward us. The comber is over 100 yards wide and stretches over the entire entrance of the cove. Ten boat lengths ahead of us is a scene out of Dante. Reason tells me that we are not going to make it through this. In the weak light, I watch how the wave continues straight over the 2- to 4-yard-high cliffs on both sides of the entrance, without losing the slightest power. On its way it sweeps away hundreds of penguin nests. Everything: adult penguins, eggs, feathers, and newly hatched chicks disappear in the wall of water. I call to Deborah, "Turn the key!" As I close the cupola and hear the engine start, we are hit by the wave.

Even though there's no way I will be able to distinguish the rpms of the engine due to the rumbling roaring mass of water, I engage the gear and open the throttle fully. Still the boat is tossed backwards with such force that the granite pillar, thick as a man's body, around which we put our port shore line sheers off and the shore line goes slack. There's a risk of the rope being sucked into the propeller. As soon as I think that, I disengage the gear.

The purpose of having shore lines was to keep the bow pointing toward the anchor dropped at the entrance of the cove as well as to keep the boat from moving sideways. The cove is too small to swing freely on the hook and the holding is poor. Ten yards astern is a rocky shoal. There's a good chance that the wave will toss the boat back and up on to it.

In the dark, I cannot judge how far the boat has already been forced back. To my horror, I see that there are at least two more waves coming. They are not as huge as the first. But during the seconds it takes for the next wave to arrive, I become convinced that without help from either the rope on the port side or the engine, the anchor will not hold us in place. As far as I am concerned, the boat is already a wreck.

The starboard line shrieks, stretching to its limit, as each of the two waves hits us. Then the unbelievable happens: the anchor holds. We stay put. After two minutes of the waves reverberating inside the confines of the cove, it is calm again. The only sound to be heard is the penguin parents' nervous calling to their missing chicks. Very few answer. As the adult birds too become quiet, a ghostlike silence hovers in the bay. For the remainder of the night, worry hangs in the air.

I understood what was happening as soon as I got outside and saw the first wave approaching. At three o'clock in the afternoon we had seen an enormous iceberg move past Petermann Island. It was easily 60 yards high and a couple of hundred yards long. When we had rowed home from our visit to the hut, I had noticed that it was visible again; the tide must have brought it back. While we slept, that huge iceberg had lost its stability, collapsed, or rolled over, and the result was a swell that turned into a wave of enormous proportions when it reached shallow water. Had we tucked ourselves in to the very back corner of the cove, close to shore, as both *Porquois Pas* and *Kim* did when they wintered here, we would have certainly ended up smashed on the rocks or up on a snow-field. Before my cold sweat dries, I think about the men from Faraday who vanished. Their demise could have been caused by a similar occurrence when waves of a collapsing iceberg suddenly broke up the sea ice.

The next day we have radio contact with Oleg, who is on his way to Hovgaard Island. He suggests that we follow him. He has been there earlier and will show us the way through the uncharted part. Like Amyr, he is convinced that inside the archipelago there is a possible winter place for us.

While we wait for him to show up, Deborah and I chat in the cockpit. It's a sunny day and still perfectly calm. Not until we see *Kotic* approaching do we collect the shore lines, start the engine, trip the anchor, and put ourselves in his wake.

Less than a mile later, the engine starts knocking in a way that can only mean one thing: it's about to seize. Deborah immediately responds by easing the throttle and putting the gear into neutral, but just as she's grabbing the stop knob, the engine dies of its own accord.

The current sets us slowly north. There is no immediate danger. We could tie our inflatable alongside *Northern Light* and with the help of the 15-horse-power outboard transport ourselves at 3 to 4 knots. But Oleg offers us a tow, which we truly appreciate. *Kotic* is a 60-footer with a strong engine, so towing us proves to be no problem.

Our destination is only 5 miles away as the crow flies. But to get there, we must take a long detour through an archipelago consisting of twenty to thirty small islands and skerries, some of which are barely visible above the surface.

While Oleg slowly winds his way through, his wife, Sophie, and two others in the crew are sent to the foredeck to keep a lookout. More often than not, islands are hidden behind giant icebergs. When we leave the charted area, navigation becomes even more difficult. After an hour, we realize just how tricky it is. Oleg loses his orientation and slows down more to be able to avoid running up on any shoals.

Suddenly, there is a lightning-fast weather change. Storm gusts come roaring from astern, and from wind pressure on our rigging alone, we start to sail. The tow line goes slack. Lacking any means to slow our boat down, I can't keep *Northern Light* from catching up to *Kotic*. In the worst gusts, *Kotic* is forced beam to the wind. To keep us from running into him, Oleg has no choice but to increase his speed and go faster than he actually would like.

As far as boat handling is concerned, the best solution would be to tie the boats alongside each other. But because of ice that's not possible. All too often we must pass though barriers of brash ice. Were we side by side, it would be impossible to handle the boats due to all the ice that would collect between them. Besides that, the distance between some of the icebergs is sometimes just enough for us to pass between them the way we are attached. We have no choice. Our speed creeps up to 5 knots. The track takes us between two icebergs, each considerably higher than *Kotic*'s masts.

Suddenly there is a boom like a cannon being fired. One of the icebergs has cracked. The shock wave bounces back and forth between the ice walls, making it impossible to judge just where the sound originated. Slowly the echo dies away. I cross my fingers, hoping that no chain of events has been set in motion. But before long another iceberg, farther away, answers with a resounding boom. And when we hear even one more iceberg cracking and see a large chunk of ice fall with a tremendous splash, I find myself waiting for it to collapse and rotate. There is a lot of latent tension in icebergs, and it can very well be the sound from *Kotic*'s engine that is causing them to crack.

The wind increases, and to keep tension on the tow line, Oleg is forced to go faster and faster. The situation is nightmarish. During the half hour it takes to reach a little more open water, another two icebergs crack, but nothing serious happens.

After two hours of being towed, it starts to snow and visibility decreases. But we have already come so far that Oleg is sure he knows where we are. Before we turn east to enter a very tricky passage between two small islets, where Oleg absolutely must go so slowly that it is impossible to have *Northern Light* on a tow, we tie her alongside *Kotic*. But our only chance to make it through the passage together presents new problems. Because the wind now comes exactly from the side, the boats heel so much that half the topsides are under water. The risk that the rigs may hit or tangle is obvious, but luckily, *Kotic* responds with basically the same lean as *Northern Light*. Each time the boats heel, however, they pull to weather, but by differing amounts. It's nearly impossible to keep them on the same course during the gusts. Then, suddenly, the wind changes direction and comes from the opposite side.

The violent wind shift is because we now have Booth Island in the eye of the wind, where its 3,205-foot-high (980 m) mountainside acts as a dam. As the wind pushes on the windward side, the pressure builds, and when the mountain can hold no more, the northeasterly wind casts itself over the top and our two boats. Then it's calm for a minute or so. While the pressure builds on the windward side of the island again, there is a suction on the lee side. It's then that the southwesterly wind is at its strongest. For us, the result is a circus without comparison.

I try not to imagine how it would be if Deborah and I had been forced to sail our way in here. In conditions like this, we can just as well forget about using the outboard. If we don't manage to get our engine going again, it's not going to be easy the day we leave under sail alone.

But there isn't much time right now to think about the future. The wind is often so violent that I can't hear Oleg's instructions, and right where it is the narrowest—between a sheer cliff and a skerry—the wind changes 180 degrees for what seems the hundredth time.

The current now sets against us, and for the moment we also have the wind against us. That combination makes it possible for Oleg to progress as slowly as he wants with full control over both boats, but only as long as it takes to come through the narrowest part of the passage. Then the wind shifts again.

After another couple of boat lengths, Oleg signs to me that I should hold our boat away from his by compensating with our rudder. At the same time, he puts *Kotic* in reverse and lets down the drop keel until it holds fast to the bottom. He signals that we have arrived. For a moment we sit still, but the keel doesn't manage the task longer. To stop the boats from ending up beam to the current during the time it takes his crew to get lines ashore, Oleg reengages his engine in forward and runs it on a low rpm. After ten minutes, the lines are attached. I sigh with relief.

Immediately, one of *Kotic*'s guests comes aboard to take a look at our engine. Thierry explains that he is an agent for Perkins engines in Brazil. Could we have more luck? If anyone should be able to get the engine going, it's him. First, we remove the rocker cover and Deborah turns the key. A bang is heard, and for a fraction of a second we see the rods to the valves move, but barely. We try a second time, but the same thing happens. The start motor is simply not strong enough to get the flywheel going. When we try to move it with a crowbar, we can only budge the heavy wheel a tiny bit at a time. All we can figure is that the crankshaft has seized. Without a doubt, the engine is unrepairable, at least where we are right now. That the engine lasted this long after having salt water in it, Thierry attributes to Mobil 1, a totally synthetic oil that we've used for many years. Right or wrong, the engine now gets its death certificate.

Kotic has a tight time schedule. They have to get their guests back to South America in a week and therefore can only stay overnight. We are invited aboard for dinner. Sophie declares it's to be a celebration for Deborah and I having most likely arrived at our winter harbor.

Their boat was designed for big groups and has space enough for all eleven of us around the same table! As the main course, Sophie serves a mouth-wateringly delicious sweet and sour dish. It would be hard to find a more deft crew member than Sophie. Beside being mother to two young children aboard, she cooks for her family and guests and in between works as deck crew. Talk about putting your shoulder to the grindstone!

When they leave the next morning, Deborah and I watch while Oleg weaves his way through the most difficult area and out toward deeper water. Suddenly, the boat pitches. We hear the bang that confirms that they have run aground. For many minutes they run the engine in reverse, but nothing happens and then the engine sound dies. People rush under deck. Has the boat sprung a leak? We wait. Finally, we hear the engine again, and eventually the boat slides off the shoal. Our last view of *Kotic* is as she disappears behind an island. We are alone.

17

SETTLING
IN

DEBORAH

■ ■ ■

Northern Light is an outback bastion of free speech. Anyone and everyone on board is always welcome to express whatever opinion he or she may have and to feel as free to defend it as another may feel to challenge it. The practice is ongoing for Rolf and me. But just because we keep each other informed about feelings and ponderings, and always talk things over to the bitter end, doesn't mean that we rush into it.

Indeed, silence is a fascinating part of our conversation cycle. Allowing silence or maintaining silence is also a gift of space, mental elbow room as it were, living as closely as we do. Sometimes when I see that Rolf is lost in reverie, I try to guess whether he is musing abstractly, or figuring practically, or . . . , and I find myself waiting for the answer with the nervous anticipation of a teenager waiting for a date.

As *Kotic*'s engine noise dwindles and disappears, it's exactly silence that settles like a magic mist to envelop this crew of two as we stand frozen in place, gazing at a view we haven't yet dared touch. Both of us are lost in our own thoughts: organizing, prioritizing, analyzing, and, not least, savoring. Minute after minute passes, and neither of us budges. It is a time for sifting thoughts, preparing for metamorphosis.

Others, like the guests on *Kotic* who have left us to the realm of winter, think that after all that has happened to us recently, we are about to spin our cocoon or hibernate. But they are wrong. We are about to spread our wings. The exciting part is that for all our thinking, planning, and hypothesizing, what is about to happen is not to be conducted by us, but by nature—a raw and indifferent power—in a sequence of repetitive ticks of present time, each happening while we strive to understand the one that has just flown so we can add our own impromptu rhythm and song. Let it begin!

I finish thinking first. The turning point has sunk in, and I look around and do what I know I will be content to do repeatedly during the next months: drink in the scenery, light, and atmosphere of one of the most dynamically beautiful spots I have ever seen. My camera trigger finger itches.

Eventually Rolf is ready too. He sighs and asks, "Well, Deborah, what do you think?" Feeling like I am about to be consumed by my smile, I tell him: "Ever since we were here for our summer visit, I have dreamed about one day, maybesomedaymaybejustmaybe, being able to see a full moon rising over Lemaire Channel. If my estimation is correct, it's going to happen just in time to be our midwinter present. I simply couldn't be happier. *That's* what I think." Rolf joins me at the smile. Neither of us closes our eyes. The kiss affirms our pact and seals the mood of the future.

Although genuine, Rolf's smile is superimposed over a weariness that rules his face. The air is heavy with many "what ifs" already in motion from the engine's breakdown and our injuries. I believe that I have reached the point of competence where I can truly feel the weight Rolf carries on his captain's shoulders. But I also know that a "wonderful" winter will energize him and make it more than worth having lived on the edge for so long. The degree of wonderfulness will be—no, *is*!—built upon all the positive feelings and enjoyable experiences we can pump into it. For the moment, I too am weary. But much of that has to do with having had so many others around to deal with, interact with, answer questions for, and discuss our problems with, and I trust that everything, including feelings, will stabilize now that we are alone. Anyway, although my creativity isn't exactly flowing, I must do *something*, however small, to get the "wonderful" started. Just like doing light exercise when you're worn out, the payback will be much larger than the energy spent.

Oh, I have an idea. I invite Rolf to join me for an Italian dinner by saying, "The menu for this evening's meal is polenta-crusted pizza topped with mushrooms and sun-dried tomatoes and plenty-o-garlic, accompanied by prosciutto sliced so thin you can see through it and a glass of red wine from the bottle Amyr gave us. Couldn't you meet me in the salon, at our favorite table, around seven?" Rolf winks, and I grin. It's my simple way of showing that I think everything is going to be OK because, after all, everything *is* OK.

During dinner Rolf clears his throat. "I've been thinking," he says. "We don't really need the engine over the winter. We'll get electricity from the wind generator the entire time and some from the solar cell too, at least fall and spring. And if it isn't really enough, don't worry, we have plenty of kerosene for lamps, even enough to read by to our hearts' content during the darkest months." Rolf pauses for my response, but I stay as blank-faced as I can, and he continues. "The way I see it, as far as the engine—or lack of an engine—is concerned, it doesn't make much difference whether we sail away without one this year or next. In other words, there's no reason for us not to stay for the winter, especially since it's likely that we'll never get another chance to realize a project like this one. That we didn't get as far south as we had planned isn't so important to me." He shrugs. "And you know what, Deborah? I feel just like you do. Despite everything, I couldn't be happier! Finally," he says as he raises his glass, "our longed-for winter has begun. And by the way, my compliments to the chef!" We both sip the wine.

I can't help it. Skeptical me is just not convinced that Rolf is willing to drop the likelihood of our ski trip. Out pops one of my latest what-ifs. I say, "Rolf, if you want to go farther south and continue looking, I am willing. I trust that we can use the dinghy as a tow boat in calm weather. If we can trade some diesel for gasoline, then . . . " but I stop. Rolf is shaking his head.

"I've given thought to it Deborah, but it's less than two weeks to the equinox," he replies. "The nights are getting long and the weather's deteriorating. This place meets every last one of our winter harbor requirements. It's as if it were tailor-made to our list of criteria, including that . . . " (I love this about Rolf; sometimes his smile sneaks out whether he wants it to or not) ". . . there are no stations close by. Really, I don't see any reason to risk looking for another spot farther south without an engine. It seems that chance, luck, or fate, call it what you will, has determined where we will spend the winter."

I don't let an opportunity like this slide by. "Chance? Luck? Fate?" I say with an overly dramatic face. With knuckles against the edge of the table, I rise a little off my seat and lean toward him as far as I can before continuing. "You mean to tell me that it *never* occurred to you that the engine may have been sabotaged by your wife so she could spend the winter at the foot of Booth Island? Ha! Silly you!" Rolf plays along. He covers his face with his hands, rubs his eyes a few quick times, mocks the shivers, and then looks at me, smiles, and says, "Ha, ha, wise guy."

The next day we start looking for our permanent attachment points. The channel that we sit in, bordered by Hovgaard Island and an unnamed island we already call Oleg Island, runs almost northeast-southwest. Besides being the proper orientation, it also has the proper depth—3 yards under the keel at low tide—and the proper configuration. The channel isn't pin straight; 50 yards ahead of the boat where the channel zigs are some rocks and 200 yards astern where it zags is a shoal, so both brash and swell will be stopped before reaching us.

We have decided to put the anchor out ahead of the boat to the northeast because our $\frac{1}{2}$-inch (13-mm) anchor chain is actually the strongest "mooring

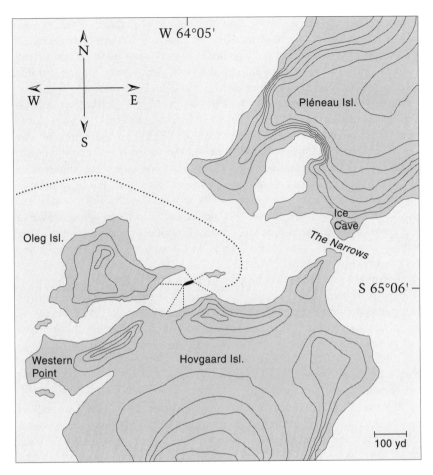

Northern Light's *winter anchorage. The places along the Antarctic Peninsula where it is shallow enough to anchor are not usually big enough to swing freely at anchor. Therefore "anchoring" usually includes taking lines ashore. Considering the oft-occurring violent winds, shore lines are often the only guarantee that the boat stays put.*

Unfortunately strewn with rocks and most often clogged with ice, "The Narrows" (our name) is not safely passable for boats.

line" we have. But because we don't want to have to trust the holding or risk that a small berg could tear the anchor free from the bottom, we don't anchor in the normal sense. First, we position the big dinghy under the anchor and then lower it and all the chain into the inflatable. While Rolf rows toward the rocks, I feed out the chain. Once there, we place the CQR anchor with its shaft between two rocks and its plow hooked around the most appropriate of the two, thereby locking it in place. "Wow, Rolf, that's great," I exclaim. "Yeah," he answers, shaking his head in near disbelief. "It's perfect. Nothing will disengage this anchor." We disconnect the line that's been holding us since our arrival, row back, pull it aboard, and pump up the slack chain. Next, we need to find one port and one starboard and two stern line attachment points.

After lunch, we start astern where the land is higher. On the port side, on Oleg Island, the snow-free rock slopes up from sea level like a huge dance floor. Try as we might, we find no crack deep enough for a boat piton. We can only look so far; the angle from the boat and the distance are both important. After all, we only have so much rope. There has to be something, somewhere, that we can use. Rolf takes off his hat and scratches his head. His brain is burning, I can tell, but there's no reason to talk to him when he's in a trance like this. No matter what I say or ask, he'd only mumble some negative answer. I have come to know that this actually means—temporary inconvenience, I am thinking—yet as it's more pleasant to avoid his nonanswer, I keep quiet and continue my own unsuccessful search.

Eventually, he snaps his fingers. "I have it!" he declares. "The tip of the plow of the spare CQR anchor will hook just fine into this 4-inch-deep V-shaped hole where part of the rock has sheered away. That'll be plenty strong. Let's go get it." This sure sounds less than fine to me. I, too, have dead giveaway behavior. For the moment, with my eyes crinkled and brows up to my hairline, I look just like someone who has smelled something sour. "You'll see," he retorts. "When there's pull on it, it'll be perfect. Oops, did I say that word *again*?"

We row back to the boat and root through what seems like thousands of kilos of stuff in the aft cabin for the umpteenth time. Moving things around is part of the overwinter job description. Finally, we row back ashore with the anchor and rope, and, as Rolf had anticipated, it is perfect. Naturally, I feel compelled to tell him, "It'll never—repeat never—hold." A bet is on.

We climb to the top of Oleg Island to look seaward to check today's crop of tabular seagoing icebergs. Daylight is dwindling. The sky is orange and the ice purple, a bizarre combination to our eyes. We turn back with yet another memory just made. That's it for today's outside activities.

The next morning we find one crack that will, maybe, support a piton for the stern rope that leads southwest. We put it in, hitting it with the hammer until at about the sixth hit the "donk" tellingly changes to "dink." That tonal change means it's in properly, but we'll have to watch it to see if it's trustworthy. For safety's sake, we decide to double it. We search around, scraping and shoveling snow off rocks (moving stuff again), looking for cracks and finding none. Instead, we eventually choose a decent-sized rock that's high off the water and take the second rope around it.

The morning has evaporated. In the afternoon we look for our forward points. As the tide is up, we head for the higher side, the Hovgaard side. There are huge boulders here and mounds of granite that look like gargantuan bread rolls, but the spaces between are far too wide for pitons. We ferry ourselves back to the boat for bigger gear, picking up the windlass handle and a crowbar. We each walk around searching, poking in cracks and holes, until Rolf shouts at me: "I found it. Check this out! The perfect cleft. In it the crowbar leans away from the boat, and the crack is longer than the crowbar. There's no way it can slip out. You see it down there?" he asks. I nod affirmatively. "Good. Now, can you think of any way we can get it out . . . ahem . . . so that we can attach the rope? It just sort of slipped." I peel off my survival suit and without losing too much skin, reach in until I can just grasp and pull on the forked tip of the crowbar. Yes, male plus female can be a good working combination!

It isn't really understood why, but high and low water in Antarctica do not occur according to any predictable schedule. Rolf's hypothesis is that the rapid air pressure changes due to fast-moving lows interfere with the tide. At any rate, because we need low tide to look for our port forward attachment point, we have to wait and watch for it to happen. When our chance comes the next morning, a gale-force wind is blowing. We wait again. The next day around noon we row over to look. There sits a wonderful free-standing boulder, high and dry at low tide. We wrap the piece of anchor chain around it that we cut for the same purpose in Hero Inlet, shackle the ends together, and attach the rope. Great! Finished.

We are pleased. Although we don't trust any of it until proven, we are quite confident that we've found and secured good attachments. Back on the boat we adjust the lines until the boat sits just the way we want. We shake hands. We're tied up for the winter! It's so pleasant it's hard to describe. There'll be a short respite from the constant consideration of the boat's safety and the need to keep an extrasharp twenty-four-hour eye on weather. There just isn't anything to worry about in the near future, at least not until the ice starts to form.

Now comes the second phase of getting settled. Approximately one and a half tons of gear is to be offloaded from the boat and stored on shore. Then, during the winter, as we use up supplies on board (food, kerosene, and diesel), we will continually move back the equivalent weight from our onshore stash. The idea is that come spring, the boat should have the same weight as it does when it freezes in. Were it lighter instead, as the sun melts the snow and warms the hull, the more buoyant boat could eventually pop up through what's left of the ice. In this process either the propeller or log would be damaged.

Off go fuels and other flammable liquids, plus all the unused tie-up gear. The five 26-gallon (100-liter) diesel drums are easy to lift out and off the boat using winches and halyards, but without a sky hook it will not be easy to get them out of the dinghy and up the hill on Hovgaard. Rolf comes up with the idea of building a cable car from the boat to land. Yes, we can take a line around the mainmast at the lower spreader and run it to a wire around a rock. An added benefit he perceives is that we'll also be able to use it to move ourselves ashore before the ice can carry our weight.

When we tighten up the line, the fallacy of this plan becomes apparent. It makes the boat lean 15 degrees. Although that poses no problem to getting the barrels or ourselves ashore, we can never leave the boat untended leaning like that. "Picture this," Rolf says. "As the tide rises, she will lean even more. And then if a gust hits, the line will act like a mooring rope. Masts are not intended to be used as bollards. At least it doesn't say anything about it in the manual. I considered attaching another rope in the opposing direction, but then both would have to be tended at every tide change. Plus the ropes would fight the boat's natural tendency to heel from wind. No, without an engine, we can't really afford to risk breaking the mast off at the first spreader. Let's get the barrels ashore and then take the rope away."

On shore, we place the diesel barrels at the piton end of the starboard stern mooring rope so that even after it snows they'll be easy to find. I take this opportunity to teach Rolf the refrain, "Follow the Mooring Rope Road." Then we ferry load after load of other stuff ashore, using the pulka to pull the supplies up the hill. Rolf's old bright-orange bivouac sack is sacrificed as the storage tent for all the small jerry cans of oil, the preheat alcohol for the Primus burners, and other items.

Without so much as calling our secretary for an appointment, an Adélie penguin suddenly launches itself out of the water, lands feet first on the snow next to our dinghy, shakes the water from its feathers, skwaawks its arrival greeting—actually, more like "auwk!"—and then, in all haste, drops to its belly and with the help of its wings and feet propels itself up the hill in our direction.

For fun, and in the hopes of communicating or at least prolonging contact with birds and animals, I have adopted the habit of imitating their actions and sounds. The practice began many years ago during my first solo watches outside Norway. By mimicking each beat of a bird's wings, for example, I was able to arouse the curiosity of kittiwake gulls to the point that instead of their normal circling of the entire boat, they would fly past me in the cockpit in between the masts, where they—whoops!—dropped altitude in the turbulence behind the mainsail. I've gotten pretty good at auwking. My first coup was in Deception Island during our 1984 visit. I was out rowing and taking abstract pictures when a gentoo penguin surfaced and auwked, presumably to locate its fishing buddy, who *should* answer if it too were at the surface. As no one else answered, I did. That gentoo zoomed full speed to the dinghy and tried repeatedly to launch itself up over the pontoon to join me or the other gentoo it assumed was in there. Luckily, the pontoon was too slippery for it to make it. I suddenly realized that I wouldn't have known what to do if it had indeed succeeded in getting in only to come face to face with a human. Probably both of us would have gotten hurt.

So, automatically, I answered this newly arrived Adélie's first "auwk." Rolf observes as the penguin and I converse the entire time it makes its way up the hill. I wish I knew what I was saying! It'll be interesting to see what happens if the penguin comes close. "Up close and personal" meetings between us and penguins usually go one of two ways. If we are upright, either walking or skiing, and come upon resting penguins or meet ambling ones, they scatter. I guess I would too if something five times my size suddenly appeared on the scene. But if it happens the other way around—if Rolf and I are sitting and the penguins come over a crest or around a bend—then they often continue toward us until only a few yards separate us. Most often, they then turn away or skirt around us. Sometimes, however, they have joined us, plunking themselves down in the snow a few yards away. Never, however, have they offered us any rocks.

Although we have been told that there is a gentoo rookery on neighboring Pléneau Island, so far we have only seen small groups of Adélies swimming in our channel or resting on the snow on either side. This must be a declared spot for regrouping after fishing forays; solo penguins arriving auwk and auwk, hoping to hear an answer and thereby locate other members of their group. I auwk whenever I stick my head out of the cupola to check the weather or look around, and to Rolf's delight, I am nearly always answered. Maybe this Adélie has heard me before and has simply been dying to meet me!

Rolf and I had both sat down quickly when this penguin had appeared on the scene, and I can hardly believe it . . . the little formally attired bird comes right up to me and insists on poking its nose into the sack as if it wants to know what's in there. I am afraid it'll panic if it goes in, so I don't let that happen, but Ms. Adélie hangs around, not bothered in the least that Rolf and I communicate to each other in a foreign tongue. Eventually, when Rolf decides to get back to work and passes me another jerry can to put into the sack, the penguin sees its chance and tries to dash into the sack with it. This is a real first. We are being "bothered" by a penguin! When it understands that I won't let it into the sack, it lies down in the snow beside me. I could pet it if I wanted. When I go down the hill to fetch another load, the penguin follows me! Then it follows me back up again and sits beside me at the tent.

Rolf suggests that we slow down and let the Adélie lead the working pace. "After all," he says, "we are the visitors." But when we pause, the penguin stands up from its resting position, auwks a few times, and starts to waddle down the hill, with its wings out for balance. I stand up and follow, doing my Charlie Chaplinesque imitation of its walk. But the Adélie doesn't dive into the water as I expected. Instead, it turns around. It stops in its tracks and about breaks its neck looking up at me. For a few heartbreaking seconds, I am afraid that the shock of my sudden increase in size will scare it to death. But no, the penguin just auwks again and decides to go back up the hill. It continues past me as though I didn't exist and disappears around a rock. "Rolf, do you think it'll ever come back again?" I ask. My partner shrugs before answering. "I guess it depends on what it was you actually said," he replies.

Once the gear is offloaded, *Northern Light*'s waterline is visible again, and we start phase three: restowing two tons of food inside for the last time. It's now to be stored according to temperature. Foods that can take subfreezing temperatures as well as dry stores that must remain in a well-ventilated area go into the aft cabin. (If flour and sugar get damp, they can spontaneously combust.) What can take refrigerator temperature goes to the forepeak. It's a little warmer there because the heater has some effect in the head, which in turn borders the forepeak. As always, cans and jars live under the floorboards in the bilges. Potatoes, onions and other things that have to remain free of frost go into the settee storage boxes in the main cabin and at the nav desk. Our 500 eggs now number 410. They and other daily needs live in a shelved food pantry opposite the engine room, in between the galley and aft cabin.

Finally, we move the four 75-amp-hour batteries from the unheated aft cabin to a spot near a radiator under the nav desk. The reason is that warm batteries release more available amp-hours than do cold ones. Considering that the wind generator will be our only means of creating "juice" during the winter, we can't afford to lock up any amps in cold storage.

When we're done, our heated space in the main cabin and nav/galley area is uncluttered and eminently livable. Not only is the boat's waterline visible, but she now sits evenly on it! It's one of life's small pleasures to live on the flat. Nothing more will slide off the table, including Rolf, who, after all, spends eight hours a day sleeping on it.

We return to the outside to start phase four. What's this? It must have been damp overnight with a light breeze because rime frost has covered everything in a delicate geometric design of white crystals that grow horizontally in defiance of gravity! These can't be disturbed. We postpone our work to watch them grow into longer and longer spikes.

The next day they are past beautiful; they are 3 inches of outrageous. We move around gingerly on deck examining a phenomenal decoration Mother Nature has given us, but then she takes it away. A steady breeze picks up and blows everything off bit by bit.

Now we can get back to work. We take off the sails and diminish the tension on the shrouds and stays. Rolf wants to reduce the tension on the lowers to 5 percent of breaking strength and the uppers to 10 percent of breaking strength. He opens the turnbuckles and detensions the wires until there is no humming or singing vibration left. As it has been explained to us, vibration of that type can change the wire's molecular structure. The wire fatigues—that is, it becomes brittle—and is therefore more likely to snap. As with any other material, stainless steel has its good and bad points.

We now consider ourselves settled. It's time for a day off and a celebration! "Rolf! Come look!" I yell. "You won't believe it. Look astern." Sure enough, through the snowflakes and the gray day we see a big colorful flag carried on the vague outline of a white sailboat. With binoculars I can make it out. I shout, "Prepare yourself for a real celebration Rolf, they're Norwegian!" I can hardly believe my eyes. There was nothing in the grapevine about a Norwegian boat on the Antarctic Peninsula and we've never heard them on the radio. Who could it be?

The yacht's name is *Sorgenfri,* which translated directly means free of sadness, the kind of sadness created by problems or sorrow. There are two young men from Oslo aboard, both in their early 20s! Johan and Peder are high-spirited and self-confident. Both were raised on boats and possess skill beyond their years. We are very impressed by them.

Over the next few days, we relish their company and hear about the gang that owns the boat and will in different combinations sail it around the world. These two hadn't originally planned on coming to the peninsula, but they got tips and encouragement from folks in the Falklands. That explains why they are here "after hours." After visiting their boat, we become concerned for them, however, when we see that it is really unsuitable for heavy weather sailing in tough waters. During the next visit, Rolf shows them the route we took north last time, points out the anchorages we used, and tells them our experiences. Their trip is likely to be slow going and tough. They'll have the wind against them, which means cold. The light now shares each day equally with darkness. I sure hope their youthful strength holds the hand of stamina.

In the middle of the night Rolf wakes only to see the strangest red glow coming through the skylight above our bed. He jumps up. Is *Sorgenfri* on fire? From the cupola he sees that the entire southern sky is aglow. Is Faraday, 20 miles south of us, on fire? It takes time for the night cobwebs to clear, but it finally hits us: this display can only be southern lights, aurora australis. But the magnetic pole is on the other side of the continent. We shouldn't be able to see the aurora here, but we can. What a wild place!

After a mild period with rain that melts most of the latest snow cover, we take the opportunity to ski all over Hovgaard and Pléneau, the highest islands in our group. The skiing conditions are quite horrible, but the purpose is important. We have to check the terrain to determine safe skiing routes, map the now-visible crevasses, and record bearings from different points and landmarks back to the boat.

Rolf is 100 percent recovered from his operation, and we both train to build strength and endurance for skiing. Although my back still hurts terribly when I sit, there is less pain standing and hardly any skiing. Whatever the damage, (most likely a pulverized disc), stretching my spine by cross-country skiing sure feels good, and that makes me confident that it will heal.

Hovgaard Island is a perfect training area. In a series of three hills and plateaus, it rises to the top at an altitude of 1,210 feet (369 m). That means a good two-hour warm-up climb to the top and wonderful slopes to ski on the way down, although I have to go easy on the icy parts. It's not only a pristinely gorgeous ski area, but it's uncluttered and uncrowded. The closest tree is 600 miles away, and there's only one other person to collide with on the way down.

And there are no lift lines! As we climb, I recall my folk's Swiss-born friend Maria, who used to visit us when we lived in the country. When we were all out skiing in the steepest pasture, she once commented how it reminded her of her childhood when they too climbed to get a downhill run. "You know," she said, "when you climb first, you warm up your muscles. You're therefore much less likely to fall and hurt yourself than when you ride up the mountain, freezing on a lift, like they do today." Beside the warm-up, from the top of Hovgaard we are rewarded with a view that spans 150 miles! "Just think, Deborah," my husband reports glowingly. "When this crystal vision freezes, it will all be your skiing territory."

On the calmest days we row around our immediate archipelago, exploring and filling in the blanks on the chart. Hardly anything has a name, including the island group itself. We decide on Hovgaard Archipelago and then continue to name the fifteen islands and even more skerries scattered over an area covering approximately 3 square miles (5 km²). If we ever finish here, waiting are 100 square miles of relatively shallow water to the west, home to myriad other similar island groups that all freeze together nearly every winter.

If you hear the sound of an outboard once you think you're alone, the first issue to clear up is that of sanity. I dash to look around, and for a change, I don't auwk. I sure am glad two big inflatables are almost to our bow. In them are, one, two, three, . . . no . . . sextuplets dressed in identical survival suits. The chorus of "Hello, Deborah" sports accents from all over the British Isles. It's a gang from Faraday, out for the last boat tour of the season, making a round to check all their "depots." The 1-yard-square red-painted wooden boxes, filled with food and survival equipment, are strategically placed for those out on trips away from the station in case bad weather should keep them out longer than planned. Unlike the Americans who are restricted to an area inside a 2-mile radius of their station, these guys are not only allowed out but are encouraged to use their time off during their two-year stint for outdoor activities like skiing, boating, and mountain climbing.

The weather isn't very promising, but they come aboard and we get in a short chat. I brew a huge pot of tea and bring out a cake. They add chocolate bars—my favorite vegetable—to the table. I quickly trade my piece of cake and ask if it's still the case, as it was in 1984 when we visited Faraday, that as part of their rations each man gets a giant-sized Cadbury bar every day. They fiddle and squirm and look at each other until Kevin the Chippie answers, "Yes, but in all honesty, we each prefer a pint to the whole bar."

A month after our arrival, on April 9, the Greenpeace ship *Gondwana* on its way between Faraday and Palmer stops outside Hovgaard and sends a four-man delegation to check out our setup. We give them all our statistics to date about fuel consumption and estimations for the winter; show them our clean-burning diesel heater's turbo, wind, and solar energy systems; and let them know we plan to take all garbage with us. We discuss sewage disposal. Unfortunately, we didn't know about a type of composting toilet they have at their Ross Sea base that we perhaps could have used so as to avoid discharging our waste into the water. Called a Rota-loo, it uses aerobic bacteria to reduce the volume of waste by 85 percent. We take them ashore to look at our fuel storage, all the while being questioned about our impressions and opinions about human presence in Antarctica. We promise to send them a report on our experience when we leave. I am rather surprised, but they make no direct comment about our presence or setup.

The days fly by. We want to see all the bird colonies before their occupants depart for warmer climes. Pléneau Island has a blue-eyed cormorant colony on its steepest promontory, chosen by the big birds for easy takeoff and landing. Now and again, some of them fly past the boat in a V-shaped formation. Migration has begun. On the farthest point away on Pléneau we find the gentoo rookery. Chicks have fledged and the last of the adults are molting. They too shall soon leave. On our way home, we sight a male fur seal on a rocky outcropping, sitting erect, nose into the air, long whiskers quivering. It seems that in addition to the winter anchorage being perfect, we have landed right in the heart of a living wilderness. The more we look around, the harder it is to believe. What luck we had to end up here!

18

A
CONTINENT
TO OURSELVES

Deborah

■ ■ ■

Many things point to the summer season being over. The average barometric pressure is falling. The lowest so far has been 958 millibars, the lowest ever measured on board! Outside ambient temperatures are below freezing except during warm front passages. The skuas are gone, off scavenging in friendlier latitudes. Arctic terns, forsaking winter, have also "terned" north. Of the mammals inhabiting the Antarctic Peninsula, however, the only to have left thus far are the summer humans. Their vessels visit no more and the final supply ships of the season have already been to Faraday and Palmer. Seals still abound and, oddly enough, so do whales. But whales react only to availability of food, which is regulated in part by ice conditions. We therefore assume that when the whales do disappear, the sea ice is due.

New fresh snow now covers the previously icy slopes and the crevasses, which we're glad we've mapped. We ski Hovgaard with a passion, memorizing contours and rocks, climbing nearly each day to the first plateau where there's a good view into Penola Strait and the glaciated mountain chain on the mainland. After climbing approximately 1,000 feet (305 m), it's time for a pause and a cup of blueberry soup. As our breathing moderates, we hear minke whales blowing and through binoculars find them swimming in between brash ice. The glaciers on the mainland have been calving a lot of late and Penola is full of bergs, bits, and brash glittering in the sun. I step over to Rolf and give him a long hug. "Thank you for bringing me here," I say.

I close my eyes to think for a second. When I open them, as I'm looking seaward, my eyes start their scan of the horizon. I can't help it; the habit is ingrained from the gazillion hours spent on watch. There's a particular technique: scan segment by segment, glancing back on the segment just finished to overlap the new one. Scanning that way helps us use our peripheral vision, which is important because the process of looking impractically tends to concentrate on pinpoints.

I have to laugh at myself when I realize that I am still on the lookout for boats. *Wake up, Deb!* I say to myself. No one is out there and no one is coming for eight, maybe even nine, months! I tell a momentarily confused husband, "When we get back to the boat, we can take down the 'do not disturb' sign." Our winter has begun. We are alone, with a continent to ourselves.

"Uhhh, Rolf? You awake?" I ask. "There's something walking on deck." "Mmm, I hear it," he says and rolls out of bed. "C'mon with me, Deborah, and stay close so we can keep the comforter wrapped around us both." To try not to scare whatever it is away or ruin our night vision, we do not light the lamps. We just squeeze up the ladder built for one and look out of the cupola. I see nothing new.

"Just above deck-level. Port side of the mainmast." Rolf whispers. "There's a black beak suspended in the air." I chortle, still seeing nothing. "Really," he continues, "there's no body." That it is a bird is not at issue, but not until it starts to move do I finally catch sight of the beak and an equally black pair of feet stepping toward us.

I flash back to one of the first days I ever worked on *Northern Light*, when Rolf had me paint the toe rail. I said to him then that although I thought the black rail framed the deck nicely, it would probably be a better idea to paint it a light color so that it would stand out in the dark. Rolf smiled and explained that it was actually painted black for exactly that reason: dark stands out best in low light. Although I found out long ago that what he said is true, never has there been a better proof than watching this bodyless bird moving toward me.

It must have noticed us, or our movement in the cupola, for it comes closer and closer until it is no more than an arm's length away. Finally, we see the bird itself, first as a grayish blur, like a diffuse fog. Then the moon comes out from behind a cloud. The bird's absolutely white feathers glow as though lit from within. Rhetorically, Rolf asks, "Have you ever seen anything so beautiful?"

The snow petrel taps its beak lightly on the cupola three times and then cocks its head to the side. I tap back lightly three times with my fingernail. The petrel backs and stiffens a little, listening, but then relaxes and pecks again. It gazes at us as if wondering who we are and what we are doing here, maybe wondering why it didn't notice us last year. The small bird, a mound of pure white fluff, could fit in the palm of my hand. "It looks too dainty to be able to survive the winter, but I guess looks are deceiving. It's tougher than I am. Let's go back to our cozy warm cocoon!" I say to Rolf as I move down the ladder, pulling the comforter with me to guarantee that he's not far behind.

The next day I turn to the *American Medical Association Encyclopedia of Medicine* to see if I can find out why we see black better than white at night. The direct answer is not there, but the first puzzle piece I find is: "As white light consists of a mixture of all wavelengths (colors), it stimulates all three classes of cone (that is: red-, green-, and blue-sensitive) to signal equally." Because cones don't operate in low light, I deduce that at nighttime, white, along with other colors, must also disappear. In low light, the rods take over. They "are highly sensitive to light but not color," the book says. If that means that rods perceive an object's degree of brightness, then I assume we see things in low light by their contrast to each other. Dark is the tail end of the gray scale, so it must stand out by its contrast to each adjacent brighter object. It is actually, the degree of darkness, not color, that is at issue. This makes sense to me, considering my original question is posed from the standpoint of night!

Another new noise, a raspy one, interrupts another night. "Whazzat?" we say in unison as we rush out of bed toward the cupola. Rolf sticks his head and shoulders out in the subfreezing air, but in the driving snow nothing is visible beyond the edge of the boat. I hand him the searchlight. He reports that a thin layer of ice had formed, but because of the wind picking up it's now on its move, cleaved by the bow and drifting past and scraping on the hull. It's just our first ice, that's all.

By May 5, fast ice has formed around the hull. When it's two days old, it's impossible to row through the mush, so to get ashore, we pull ourselves in the dinghy along a mooring rope as if in an inflatable ice breaker. We wonder how long we'll be able to use the dinghy this way. There's also a new daily chore: tending the lines and breaking those that touch the surface free from the ice. The lines are not allowed to freeze in or get buried in the snow on top of the ice because that layer will eventually get water-saturated and freeze, too. Were the lines to freeze in, they would surely snap when the ice starts to move in the spring.

The ice thickens, but before we can trust it to carry us walking, we pull ourselves along the rope in the dinghy, now on top of the ice. Finally, when the ice is about 5 inches (13 cm) thick, it bears our weight. I walk gingerly, behind Rolf. His weight pushes the ice down and sets a slight undulating wave in motion, but it holds. We wear our survival suits over our ski clothes . . . an ounce of prevention, you know. And because we pull the dinghy with us to use to get across the 20 feet (6 m) of open water along the shoreline, where the rise and fall of the tide keeps destroying the ice, we have it close at hand, to dive into, just in case.

Fast ice formation doesn't pose any problems for the seals thus far. They can easily surface to breathe as well as crawl in and out of the water in the ice-free zone along the shoreline. "*Iiii rrrrrr glunk*" is the sound that our predawn "Weddell seal alarm clock" makes as it swims out the channel under the ice to find breakfast and sonars in on *Northern Light*'s underwater body. Perhaps the trill "*iii*" sound starts above the human register because it's very high when we first hear it. The sound then changes to a gurgling character, descending note by note down to the bass register, followed by a pause, after which the resounding low register "*glunk*" vibrates through the hull with the force of a small explosion.

If Weddell seals have a lifetime territory, we have probably confused them terribly by adding new underwater obstacles—the anchor chain, for example—for them to avoid. I tell Rolf that we should keep our eyes open for birds and animals congregating in weird mixtures, because that could be a tribunal meeting to discuss expelling us from here. It could be comprised of the whales whose naps we interrupted, the snow petrel who flew into our rigging, and all the seals that must tangle now with the anchor chain.

Cold wind, blowing from the sector between east and southwest, had lowered ambient temperatures and thickened the ice in the channel, but now comes an interruption from north-northeast. The new wind starts the surging back and forth, as much as 10 feet (3 m) at a time, of the still-unattached ice in the channel. The ice plate and its steel prisoner move as one package. The strain on our lines is tremendous. This estimated 4-inch-thick, 80 by 165 yard (10-cm-thick, 75 by 150 m) ice plate weighs as much as 1,125 tons. The creaking, squeaking, and groaning of the lines as they stretch is met by similar noises from each of us. Any second, any one of them can snap. And this chilling feeling only gets worse.

Saltwater ice is not as tough as freshwater ice. Therefore, every time the ice surges it is cleaved by either the bow or the rudder, about 4 inches (10 cm) at a time. As the hole around the boat is enlarged, the ice can surge that much farther, and it gains more and more momentum until it's moving at perhaps a knot and a half. The plate slams repeatedly against the hull, the impact shaking the boat and reverberating through the rigging. Waiting has never been so tense. Rolf goes on deck to check the rudder, but he quickly realizes it's too dangerous to be there. The lines tighten hard as wire. A human body in the path of a mooring line that snaps . . . I don't want to think about it. The surge eventually has the ice pendulating 50 feet (15 m) every twenty seconds. If a line does snap, we can only hope that the ice surrounding the boat will act like a life ring and keep the boat midchannel. If the surge continues some hours after a line snaps and the ice edges mash on the sides of the channel, however, the whole cake will eventually break up and *Northern Light* will be on the rocks.

Luckily for us, the surge starts to diminish before our worst-case scenario occurs. The watch is called off and we collapse into bed. At daylight we see that one of our two southwest lines is no longer attached. We hustle on shore and find that it has not broken, but the enormous pull on the rope did move the rock and the rope ringing it slid underneath and off. At least that's easy to fix. First, we tie another rope around the rock like a package so it can't possibly slide off, and then we reattach the line. Since we saw long ago in Deception Island that *Northern Light* can pull boulders around, and we don't want that to happen to this lesser rock, we build a ramp in front of our attachment rock. To move, our rock would have to climb up and over the other rocks. That's impossible since the pull on the rope is downward. We both wear wraparound grins because the other southwest line's piton held. When we check the other attachment points, they all look like the surge never happened. Rolf is really pleased. The anchor in the crack held, so he won the bet, and the test period is over. "No wind in the world, not even hurricane force, can exert as much pressure on the ropes as that surging ice sheet did. Although we may get a repeat performance come spring, we don't have to worry about the ropes until then!" he exclaims.

The way the boat is positioned is not good for the antenna's angle of radiation to Boston, so at Andy's recommendation we have been planning to run a new long-wire antenna for the winter. We wish we could; we're on the low side of the eleven-year propagation cycle and any improvement would be appreciated. The plan of running a wire from the boat to a fixed position on land has to be abandoned, however. Surge like we just experienced would surely break it. Plus, we are beginning to see that this spot has the potential to be *very* windy. Booth Island has been an efficient northeast wind barrier so far, but in the "surge gale," 50-knot northeast winds spilled over the dam, often in gusts of 70 knots. The boat heels as soon as the wind isn't dead from the bow. We don't think the antenna wire could take it, but if it could, the attachment point on the boat would be too strained. As good an idea as the cable car was, the antenna idea has to be discarded. When we tell him, Andy is disappointed—he's been looking forward to running propagation tests during the winter—but there's no way we can do it. As our sked winds down, Andy relays the information he's finally received about the storage temperature of the GPS components. The antenna can't take more than $-41°F$ ($-41°C$) and the "brain" $-31°F$ ($-35°C$). Luckily, it hasn't been that cold yet.

So that people in the Northern Hemisphere won't worry about us, we are not disclosing that our engine has broken down. On a "need to know" basis, we did, however, inform Faraday and Palmer and other yachts so that they would understand why we could no longer be counted on for help in search and rescue operations, for example. But there's no reason that the information be passed any farther.

So I can hardly believe my ears when, after I sign off with Andy, the captain of a research vessel that left these waters not long ago contacts him and passes along the scuttlebutt that *Northern Light*'s engine failed. "Oh, really?" Andy says. "That's news to me. Well, let's see if N1CCA is still listening. Deborah, you there?" I pick up the mike and say: "Yes, I am, and yes, we had a problem with oil pressure, but all's OK."

Boy, are we angry. The captain, who probably overheard one of our VHF conversations, has broken the code of radio ethics: that information one overhears on the radio is never to be repeated. Naturally, Andy has no reason to believe a stranger instead of me. The issue is dropped.

Next, a maritime net in South America gets into the act. The net controllers, who have heard about our engine failure, have taken it upon themselves to contact the Argentine Navy to arrange transport of spare parts or a new engine to us. Now we really see red!

Swedes have an expression "björntjänst" (a bear favor), which means that someone does something for you that he perceives as a favor but that carries negative side effects he can't or didn't anticipate. The net result of the good intention is worse than if the person had done nothing at all. The net controllers are doing us a bear favor. Not only are they infringing on our right to conduct our expedition as we see fit, but they have also started what would be a very expensive chain of events. Sure, they *want* to be helpful . . . but they are organizing help we neither need nor requested. This is one reason why we had decided to not inform the outside world about the engine. Nets are inclined to commit bear favors such as starting unnecessary search and rescue for boats "behind schedule." The side effects are that other people's lives and property are put at risk unnecessarily and funds are wasted. Such misappropriations could lead to a navy or coast guard to not be able to help others who actually are in need.

I am forced to use precious electricity to go on the air, introduce myself to the net controllers, clarify our position, tell them to cancel whatever they have started, and inform the Argentine Navy that we are not in need of any help. We've never actually "worked" this net, so they were not aware of our modus operandi. Andy, Frank, and all in our group are, or so we think.

Propagation really deteriorates. For a few weeks, although I hear Andy and Bob, their signals are very faint and they don't hear me at all. We generally meet twice per week on the Pacific Maritime Net on the frequency of 21412 at 22–2300 UTC. This net is small enough—with eight operators spread from Los Angeles to Halifax following only twenty boats—that they can take the time to handle me specially. When the net opens, they call me. One of them nearly always hears me, and if the Boston group doesn't, then that operator relays for me.

During the few weeks while the propagation is terrible, I listen to the net every day but am unsuccessful the few times I try to contact them. Finally, I hear the net control Bill (KA6GWZ) well and he hears me. He phones Frank, who is on the air in just a few minutes, just in time, as it turns out.

Although Frank and the group knew they didn't hear me due to bad propagation, they had nonetheless begun to worry that just *maybe* something had indeed happened to us. This is exactly the downside of having an agreement to keep in touch. People can't help it; a sked builds expectations and if not met causes worry. It's ironic that something meant to ease worry can cause it instead! Frank tells me they were just about to call Palmer Station via satellite telephone to find out if we were OK. But as I inform him, we aren't in touch with Palmer, so they have no idea if we are fine or not. We don't keep any radios on, so Palmer would have no way of contacting us immediately. The only thing the Palmer radio operator could do is put a message into an electronic mailbox and wait to see if I ever pick it up. Meanwhile, until I were to answer the message, people at Palmer might worry, and we want to avoid that. In fact, that we specifically want *not* to burden them is one of the reasons we wanted to winter far from stations. We made it clear to both Palmer and Faraday station managers last summer that they were not to ever even think of risking anything to try to get to us, no matter what.

To reiterate our philosophy to our ham contacts, I tap everything into the computer and when propagation allows, I link up in a digital mode with Frank and send the file to him. It reads in part: "Propagation is lousy now and you all must have known our silence was due to that. If, on the other hand, propagation is good and you don't hear from us, then you must assume that either we have no electricity or that there has been an electric or radio system failure. That is what you must believe and the explanation you must pass to others. If anything happens to our ham gear, we will let you know as soon as we can. Perhaps we can VHF to Palmer and one of their ham operators will contact you. If that's impossible, someday we may be able to ski to Faraday and contact you. If not, then next spring we will watch for the first ship to come through Lemaire and have them pass you a message. You will have to help everyone stay cool in the meanwhile." Frank responds in total agreement.

Still, I have come to the point that I would like to cancel the sked, to silence the radios for the winter. We have come here in part to experience solitude, and radio communication disallows that. We will probably never do this again, so why not do it 100 percent? Be alone, get no outside information, hear no other voices, have no skeds to keep, sink into our own world.

Rolf and I sit down to examine the pros and cons for the others involved. I think I've actually done our family a bear favor by having a weekly sked from the boat. Whereas they were used to waiting to get the letters we'd send when we arrived somewhere and would therefore have blocks of time where they could shut off the worry and carry on with their own lives, they now have a weekly reminder of our mortality. The negative effect of my good intention is that I have created constant worry, a terrible burden. In that respect, shutting down the radio is in the family's pro column. The cons have to do with agreements we've made. First, we'd take the enjoyment and payback away from our radio friends. Second, we have not discussed the idea of radio silence in person with them or our family. We, after all, are the ones who started this weekly communication from the boat, and even if we've come to realize that our family members would be better off not to have to wait to hear each and every

Northern Light *approaching the Antarctic Peninsula. Ice is a constant hazard to navigation.*

Autumnal equinox at Hovgaard Island. We have just arrived. The mooring lines are in place, but the final re-stowing of gear has not yet been accomplished, so Northern Light *sits heavily on her stern. The starboard mooring lines are attached to Hovgaard Island, the largest island in the group. The low, glaciated island ahead of the boat is Pléneau Island. Behind it (actually sepa-*

rated by a mile of open water) is the cockscomb ridge of Booth Island. Visible just between the masts, the 150-foot-high glacier wall marks the southeastern corner of Booth Island and the opening of Lemaire Channel. Above the masts, the flat-topped dark mountain is on the Antarctic mainland. Note how the rocky perimeter of our island group keeps the brash ice in Penola Strait at bay.

Rime frost forming

Chinstrap penguin

The fast ice has formed. Time is now our own.

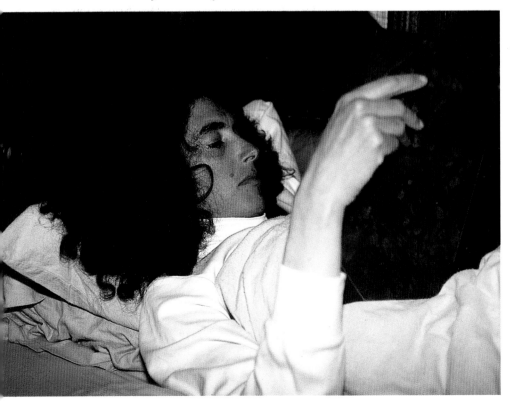

George Washington's birthday

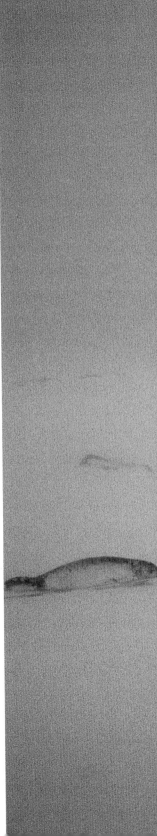

(RIGHT) *An unexpected and unusual encounter—the only crabeater seal seen during the winter approaches Deborah. In hurricane-force wind, Deborah is padding the edge of* Northern Light's *ice cradle with snow to protect the hull from impact and lessen the noise inside.*

A morning chore

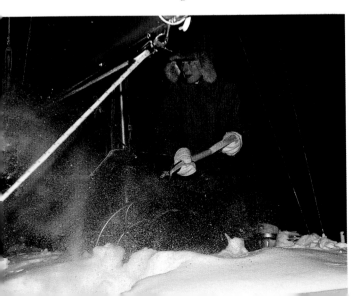

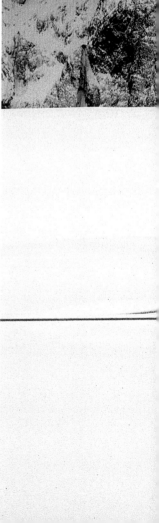

(ABOVE) The "oh-so-well-marked" fuel stash
(RIGHT) Two months until midsummer
(BELOW) Adélie penguins

(ABOVE) Homeward-bound from the Gentoo penguin rookery, Rolf approaches a favorite downhill slope on Pléneau Island.

(LEFT) Weddell seal "power sleepers"

(OPPOSITE PAGE) Lunch break near the cormorant colony
(ABOVE) Wind-chiseled icescapes on Pléneau Island

With the thaw in progress, Deborah checks the tuning of the mainmast, in preparation for sailing away.

week if there's been contact, we should have discussed it in person and secured their agreement first. We decide it's unfair to simply stop.

As always, the pendulum swings. We've been taping animal sounds and other Antarctic noises for the sound track to our video program, and when propagation picks up we play some over the radio for Bob. He tapes them and turns a cassette over to his girlfriend, Judy, who then takes it and our first book into her preschool classroom. She shows the kids pictures of the animals in the book and plays their sounds and our voices, too. The children are enthralled. Bob has added a new dimension for us, allowing us to share meaningfully, almost in real time. He keeps us informed of the kids' reactions and relays their questions. Rolf is surprised that the children never ask us about winter, but Bob explains that they don't have to—they live in Boston! No, their questions are, naturally, mostly about penguins.

Then comes the dividend. During a sked, Bob tells us that earlier that very day Judy watched as a pair of five-year-old preschoolers rearranged the classroom chairs in a long string of pairs and then sat down in the first row. Roger was in the left chair and Heather was in the right, holding the globe in her lap. Intrigued, Judy asked what they were doing.

"We made a bus," Heather answered. "Roger is the driver."

Judy asked, "Where do you plan to go?"

Heather pointed to a large patch of white, at the top of the globe as she was holding it, and replied matter of factly: "We are going to Antarctica to visit Rolf and Deborah! Want to come with us?"

No, we won't stop our skeds.

The heating system is working fine, and it seems as if our insulation calculations were correct. We can't say the same of our fuel calculations, however. Because 68°F (20°C) is too warm for sleeping comfortably, we turn the heater off an hour before bed and will continue the practice as long as the cabin temperature is above freezing when we wake up. We never leave the heater on when we are gone from the boat, so it is in use at the most 14 hours per day. So far, we are using a half a gallon (2 liters) of diesel per day for heat, instead of the calculated 0.85 gallon (3.25 liters) for twenty-four hours.

Even though we are running the heater on the lowest pilot setting, were it not that some of the heater's Btus are used to melt snow into water, it would be altogether too hot inside during the day. The Danish Refleks heater is tubular with a flat top; it's the perfect platform for a large saucepan that we keep refilling with snow all day long and pouring the melt off into jerry cans. It's no problem to create the 1.3 gallons (5 liters) water per day needed for drinking and cooking, but we have to melt and save another gallon per day for washing clothes, bedding, and towels.

We use salt water for brushing our teeth and for bathing. If you towel off salt water before it has a chance to dry on your skin, there's no residual sticky feeling. Because saltwater usage is unlimited, we are allowed to bathe as often as we want, but we find we don't have to very often. After all, there's no dirt or pollution in the air. We sponge bathe whenever we want, but we take real baths, in the plastic tub we also use for washing clothes, about once a month.

At first, this schedule may not sound adequate to those who bathe at least once per day. But dead skin is all the "dirt" we have to get rid of, and that transfers mostly to the nubby inside of our beloved Triple Function long underwear when we ski. And, as everyone knows, it isn't good to wash your skin all the time, especially not every day, so I figure, we're actually doing ourselves a favor. There's no pressure here to smell anyway else but the way we naturally do, so there's simply no need, perceived or otherwise, for daily bathing. Whenever one of us decides our smell is too concentrated to be able to change clothes without grimacing, then it's bath time!

Although we don't subscribe to the British idea of dressing for dinner— formally, that is, like sporting a tux on safari (did they *really* do that?)—we do spruce ourselves up and we keep our hair and teeth brushed. No one arriving on the spur of the moment would think we look like wild animals, except perhaps that I am letting my hair grow out over the winter.

My hairdo already had diameter enough during the summer to lead the gang at Palmer to nickname me "Deborah with the big hair." Now I believe that my bristles will not actually lie down until they're more than ten inches long. It's outrageous looking, but then Rolf cut my hair once. . . .

That was back in 1983, in the Roaring Forties, on the way from Pitcairn to Chile. Rolf insisted on using his own system for cutting curly hair. He snipped here and there where he thought it looked too long. The result was stub in some places and no cut in others. A chimpanzee probably would've done a better job. Although I'm not the most vain female, that haircut reduced me to tears. For the next few weeks, I felt lucky that hats were necessary in Chile's chilly weather. Needless to say, Rolf has never been allowed to come near me with shears since. On the other hand, thanks to me, Rolf always has his hair and beard in good trim. Yes, you could transfer him to Madison Avenue any day. In a straitjacket, that is.

19

CHANTERELLES
AND
BLUEBERRIES

ROLF

■ ■ ■

The midwinter month opens with the best weather imaginable. At sunrise the sky is almost cloudless, it's 14°F (−10°C), and only a zephyr puffs from southwest. The air must have been dry and cold during the night because, for a change, the thin snow cover around the boat is completely dry. The ski conditions are ideal to start charting the local waterways. Our goal is to locate a safe route out of here for next summer.

While there was still open water, we tried to find the shoal that Oleg hit, but were unsuccessful. The sun was already so low that from land, the water's surface looked black and impenetrable. Even from the dinghy, the visibility through the water was poor. The most we could see down was a few feet. Besides that, only on one odd day was it calm enough to row ourselves around. All in all, and not the least because we felt compelled to save gasoline for towing Northern Light next summer, we discarded the idea of searching for shoals in that manner.

The technique we'll use now is to look for cracks and vaks (a Swedish word that rhymes with hawk meaning a hole in the ice that remains all winter). Cracks and vaks exist where the ice rests on or near a shallow area or shoal at low tide. Where the ice remains crack-free, the depth of the water at low tide is greater than the thickness of the ice.

Because the tidal difference between high and low tide equals the boat's draft, we are looking for a *vak*less lead. There the depth is sufficient for us to get out at least three hours on each side of high tide. We are starting our search now, as soon as the ice bears our weight. Later, when there's more snow, we can't be sure that we'll see cracks or *vaks*, and both are dangerous traps for us. During these early reconnaissance outings, we will also map safe ski routes over the ice to be used for the entire winter.

We start by measuring the thickness of the ice just a couple of yards away from the boat. It is half a foot (15 cm) thick, which is safe for us to travel on with skis. But over the past few weeks we have noticed that, as quickly as the ice formed, in some places it has been eaten from underneath by the comparatively warm bottom water brought in by the tide. Even when the air temperature was well below freezing, these same ice sections kept disappearing and refreezing.

Especially when new snow has fallen during dark hours, it is practically impossible to determine exactly where the ice is only one night old. The resulting uncertainty has been countered by a new dress code for skiing: life jackets. In addition, stuck into our vests at chest level are "ice studs." Standard Scandinavian safety equipment for anyone out on ice, ice studs are a pair of screw driver–like tools sharpened to a point. If you happen to go through the ice, you grab your studs and jam them into the ice edge. Without them, for all intents and purposes, it is impossible to pull yourself out of the water.

The first time out in life jackets we discover an unanticipated side effect. The "Mae Wests" puff out so much that it is impossible to use our ski poles properly. Our arms are forced almost straight out from our shoulders. As we wobble away on our skis, we look like two penguins masquerading as skiers. We laugh so long that we have to stop and rest. The mood at the beginning of the darkest month of the year couldn't be lighter.

Once finally underway, our first business is to try to find the shoal Oleg hit. Because the ice looks best far out from land, we stay to the middle of the channel. Halfway over to Entrance Island, we find a *vak*. It is almost high tide, so we can't see the shoal itself; all we see is a large gaping hole in the ice one yard in diameter. Deep down there somewhere is the rock itself. When we take some bearings they confirm that just as we thought: this *vak* lies considerably farther away from land than where Oleg went aground. Thus there is more than one shoal in this area. But today's search stops here; the ice is getting too thin. Even though we must turn around, we consider our first trip out on the ice a success. Most important is that we learned it is really possible to find shoals using this technique. Satisfied but concerned that we still don't know how many shoals there may be, we ski back toward the boat.

As always when we are out, we keep track of the number and species of birds we see. On the way home, we spot two giant storm petrels, four gulls, and three Antarctic terns. Earlier in the day we saw more than fifty blue-eyed cormorants. When the cormorants were on their way out to sea to feed, they had to work their way upwind. To facilitate that, they flew in V-formations, with fifteen to twenty birds in each of the three groups. It's wonderful to watch animals cooperate. When we see them again, on their way back to the rookery, they fly individually; with the wind, they can make it alone. We hear one penguin. Assuming it's just Ms. Adélie, we don't even bother wobbling over to check. We don't want to give that penguin the opportunity to laugh at us.

When Deborah and I first began planning this overwinter expedition, we thought we'd offer to collect data for scientific use. When we approached the Joint Ice Center, coadministrated by the U.S. Navy and the National Oceanic and Atmospheric Administration (NOAA), and asked if we could do something for them, they suggested the following: record the daily minimum and maximum air temperatures, measure the ice thickness periodically, count icebergs, determine current direction and strength, note the outer limits of sea ice, and make a comparison of the relative safety of navigable routes.

At first glance, it all seemed interesting. As we collected data and information others could use, we could learn something that we otherwise would not have thought of. But as time progressed and we pondered the consequential uses of the facts that we had been asked to collect, we declined the proposed project. None of the information gathered would benefit Antarctica's wilderness or its wildlife; in fact, just the opposite would happen. The groups most likely to benefit from the information are interested in increasing shipping, building harbors, or researching the possibility of offshore oil drilling.

Deborah and I did, however, accept one task. At the request of an ornithologist, we agreed to record bird sightings and, as best we could, collect facts about their behavior. We see no harm in sharing such information. Indeed, as curious as humans are, the search for information and understanding will never stop.

Isaac Newton stated that for every action there is an equal and opposite reaction. This statement implies that for each scientific discovery that humans use and call progress, there is an equal and opposite reaction. We typically think progress means that things have gotten better, because for most of us individually they have. But, Newton's law means that the net gain can never be just improvement. The net gain is change: improvement and its side effects.

Lifting the lid of Pandora's box, even just a crack, bears immense consequences. Parallel to our search for pure knowledge, it behooves us to develop the wise and ethical use of it. It is our responsibility.

Some time during the night it begins to snow very heavily, and the snowfall continues even while we step off the boat and down to the ice to go ashore. A little too late, we realize that the snow has weighed down the ice so much that it's now under water. Even though it's well below freezing, only the very uppermost of the snow cover is dry. Under that is 6 inches (15 cm) of saltwater-drenched mush. We climb back aboard with soaking wet feet to change to rubber boots, wondering if we should dig out the dinghy again.

When the ice surrounding the boat became so strong that we were sure we would no longer need the inflatable to get ashore, we buried it under the snow above the high-water mark. We had many reasons for doing so. First, due to the low temperature, we couldn't get the aluminum floorboards apart, and without disassembling the dinghy there was no way to get it under deck. We didn't want to have it on deck, where it would interfere with snow shoveling, and we didn't want it on the ice, either. The perceived risk of the latter option is that when the dinghy gets covered with snow and that snow turns to slush, it would eventually freeze into the ice. All things considered, the only choice was to bury it ashore. There, under the snow, the wind couldn't take it. Besides, given the likelihood that the ozone hole will reappear come spring, the snow cover will protect the dinghy from getting blasted by too much ultraviolet radiation.

Indeed, we do have a spare dinghy we could inflate. But to make it across the 4-yard-wide (3.7 m) tide zone, we decide instead to fill the gap and build a snow bridge. It takes a couple of hours, but then we can ski directly from the boat to land. Suddenly we feel as if we are living on shore! We can come and go as we wish. If only one of us wants to go out for an exercise loop, we no longer have to coordinate our schedules. It gives each of us a feeling of independence that we haven't had for a long time.

At every low tide, the edge of the ice rests on the seafloor just at the beach. Over the next few weeks, the ice that forms during high water cracks a couple of feet from land. The thicker the ice gets, the farther out the ice cracks. The colder it is, the more clearly we hear, especially inside the boat, when it cracks. When it's colder than approximately 14°F (−10°C), the noises sound like gunshots. Sometimes tension develops in the ice that makes it crack parallel to the shore. Then we hear a *zing* that passes by only to disappear somewhere far away from us. Absolute quiet inside the boat is rare.

During the wee hours of June 9, we hear the wind slowly increasing from west. The onshore wind carries ice with it and therefore speeds up the freeze. More ice makes it possible for us to extend our ski excursions farther and farther afield so we can visit new islands. That's made westerly wind our favorite. Easterly wind, on the other hand, always breaks the ice up and carries it out to sea. So far, only the ice between *Northern Light* and Pléneau Island has stayed put.

Yesterday, there was open water 220 yards (200 m) aft of the boat. As soon as there is some daylight, we ski to Western Point to look. During the night so much brash has been blown toward shore that there is now a continuous ice cover all the way to the farthest islands in the next island group, some 5 miles (8km) distant. Considering our long ski trip, this is a good development.

Now if the brash would only freeze together! Inspired by the turn of events, we use the rest of the day to build a little more endurance. First, we ski up to the 490-foot-high (150 m) plateau on Hovgaard and then downhill to the Narrows, over the ice to Pléneau, up and over the island, and then around it; we take the opposite direction back. When we arrive home after three hours, we are nicely tired.

We both prefer to stay outside as much and as long as we can. The next day, we trudge through almost a foot of soft snow to climb all the way up to the top of Hovgaard. On the way up we broke through the cloud cover, so from the top we cannot see the boat; it's hidden under a cloud bank that stretches all the way to Anvers Island. But we can see that all the neighboring islands' highest peaks, including Booth Island's cockscomb ridge, are colored bright red by the season's barely rising sun. On the northern side of Hovgaard is a light updraft that forces a single cloud to rise. Like a flame, it shoots many hundreds of yards above the gray surroundings. The sight is bizarre.

Through the only opening in the cloud cover we can see that most of Grandidier Channel is covered by ice. Because it's the first time that has happened this season, we cross our fingers. If we are lucky, it won't be long until we can ski as far as we want.

"What an amazing world we live in," I shout to Deborah, standing nearby. "Yes! And I wish we could stay here forever," she answers. Then she turns around and heads downhill. Last night's new snow makes the skiing the most enjoyable so far. Wide turn to the right, to the left, and so a little tighter, and so a little faster . . . and then I increase my speed as much as I can and pass Deborah. That accomplished, I start showing off a little too much, lose control, and dive in face first. When I look up, I see a cloud of snow, which I understand must encapsulate my partner. "Imagine, being able to play as much as we want," I call out. "Yes, isn't life wonderful?" she says through a smile. Then we lie still a long while, half-buried in the snow, enjoying simply being.

The next day we start building an igloo. We must have an alternate shelter in case a fire forces a quick evacuation from the boat. Fire is an omnipresent risk in Antarctica; the air is exceedingly dry. In fact, the humidity can be as low as 1/1,000 of the average at the equator. Anything that overheats can all too easily end up in flames. In addition, during the winter it can be difficult to have access to enough water to extinguish a fire. Although the ice has not clogged our saltwater intakes so far, if they do freeze, we will have to maintain a hole in the ice where we can bucket up water. Water or no water, we think it's prudent to build an emergency shelter.

We begin by laying a ski pole on the snow. Deborah holds it firmly by the leather strap, and I grab hold of the pole's basket. As I walk around Deborah, I push the basket down in the snow, marking a circle. The track the basket makes is to be the diameter of the igloo. Then we saw snow blocks, approximately 27 by 20 by 12 inches (70 by 50 by 30 cm). Because the snow is very dry, it is difficult to keep the blocks intact, but before it gets too dark, we have managed to manufacture over fifty snow blocks, finish the foundation, and start the second round of the spiral.

When Deborah sees how far I lean the blocks inward she challenges: "Just what do you think you're doing? The next layer will certainly collapse!" But I explain: "If we don't lean them, we'll end up with a lighthouse. To make a dome, each circle of the spiral has to be narrower than the previous one. To accomplish that, the first blocks have to lean in quite far. Finally, the last turn will exist of just two blocks and then you can put on the lid. Bingo!"

But Deborah is not impressed. On the way back to the boat she tells me in a nonending stream: "It will never work. As a matter of fact, I don't believe that even the first turn will still be standing tomorrow." Now, I know that teasing me is one of Deborah's favorite methods of entertaining herself. But at the same time, it's been more than twenty years since I last built an igloo, so it's possible I may have exaggerated the lean a little too much. I therefore don't bother to defend my design.

The next morning it is 7°F (−14°C), and when we arrive at the building site we find that the first layer has frozen solid to the snow. Great! That makes it very easy to continue. The mere presence of the second layer, just as we left it, makes us both smile. Deborah hauls and hands me one block after another. I stand inside the circle and cut each block to fit snugly to the previous one. After two hours the spiral is as high as I am tall. The uppermost blocks meet precisely where they should, and in the end, Deborah hands me the lid. Wow, is she ever proud.

To let me out, Deborah shovels a long tunnel. She digs deep at first and then on an upward slant so that the upper part of the opening is at ground level inside the igloo. That specific design creates a slide where cold air will escape. As long as the cold can fall or run out of the igloo, it can become "warmer" inside. When Deborah eventually makes it inside, we cut and dig a center path all the way to the far side of the igloo. That creates a bench on each side where we can sit or sleep.

To both Deborah's and my surprise, our creation actually looks like the real thing! The building technique is ingenious. Each block in an igloo is equally important; each and every one is a keystone. And the blocks create a beautiful pattern inside. A narrow band of opalescent blue light seeps through every crack where each block nudges the next. But best of all, according to Deborah, is that the finished building doesn't have any sharp edges or corners. Round shapes appeal to her. She has told me that if she ever builds a house, she wants to have a bedroom shaped like an observatory and constructed entirely in glass. She has two reasons why it should be see-through: to be able to see stars and to always have a "window" facing the sunrise. Morning light should slip in no matter what time of the year.

To seal any and all chinks, we shovel snow over the igloo. Then we move in all the equipment we think we would need in an emergency, including survival suits, sleeping bags, a tent, Therm-a-rest air mattresses, the spare dinghy and pump, alcohol and kerosene camping stoves and fuel, matches, a hundred days' food and toilet paper, utensils, a solar panel, a handheld VHF radio and rechargeable batteries, an emergency sled, knives, repair kits and tools, clothes, and a notepad and pencils.

As a surprise for me, Deborah has made a colorful nameplate for our igloo. She has decided it should be called Inn Casa Fire. She also brought a thermos filled with hot apple soup. We stay in the igloo a long time, toasting our new building and celebrating its housewarming. When we come out, the moon has already risen. It hangs a hand's width over Lemaire Channel, where the sky is dark blue. The nearest mountain peaks are rose-colored. Those that lie farther away are iridescent purple. The snowfields and glacial tongues that reach to the sea vary in shades of green. The sky is still orange where the sun disappeared a little while ago into the ocean, but it is starting to shift to red. No matter where we look there are shimmery pastel colors. It is the most magnificent dusk we've ever experienced. For a long time we stand perfectly still. Then I feel a hand finding its way in under my hood, and Deborah whispers: "Let's ski back home. My feet are cold. Wouldn't you massage them?"

Our midwinter month just continues to be wonderful.

The next morning I am awakened by an unusually strong crack reverberating through the ice. The thermometer shows 3°F (-16°C). Looking through the cupola, my gaze can follow the Milky Way from the high mountains in the east across the dome of the sky to the west, where it disappears behind the horizon. It's half past six. Although there are four hours left until sunrise, the night sky is too special to consider crawling under the blanket and going to sleep again. I light the heater and grind coffee.

The clear sky is due to a high that started to develop June 10 and that has strengthened a little each day since. This is the sixth consecutive day of amazingly gorgeous weather. Prior to this high there have been on average a mere three days per month when we glimpsed the sun. There's no way we would let fine weather like this slip away. At eight o'clock in the morning we ski away from the boat. Each time we plant a ski pole is the telling creaking sound of dry cold. The moon makes it almost as light as day.

Our destination is Pléneau Island. First, however, we detour over to the Narrows and Entrance Island to see if there are any Weddell seals on the ice or in the snow farther up on land. Weddells are the only seals we're likely to see. Crabeater seals are most likely somewhere on the pack ice far south of us; we haven't seen one for months. Both fur seals and elephant seals have migrated north. We look all over, but there are no Weddell seals to be seen today. It's probably too cold for them out of the water.

Around nine o'clock dawn's light begins to shimmer. Anvers Island shifts in color from green to lilac. An hour later, while we are coming around the northern side of Pléneau Island, the sun rises. As the first rays reach us, the snow that we ski on is pink. With each glide, our shadows dance like long dark ghosts over the layer of rime that covers that hard surface. The sun is at our backs, and when we turn around we see that half of that giant ball of fire is still hidden behind an island at the horizon. Yet it seems disproportionately large. The phenomenon must be due to great temperature contrasts in the atmosphere.

The terrain on this side of Pléneau is hilly with soft slopes, and we steadily progress up one. At the top, we suddenly catch sight of big, reddish, steamy clouds rising beyond the next hill. Neither of us can come up with a possible cause. We are very curious, to say the least.

Finally, we see that some thirty elephant seals have gathered on land. Never before has a sighting been reported this far south wintertime. There's a tremendous bellowing competition going on between the seals, and it's during those exuberant exhales the vapor is generated. In the cold air it hangs like haze over several hundred square yards.

Every so often, one of the male seals raises its upper body off the snow, stretches its neck, and with its head held high in the air, rushes another one. The one that's about to be assaulted responds by raising itself as high as it can on its foreflippers to prepare for the attack. The seals then hit chest to chest, and sometimes, one succeeds in biting the other. Still, for these young, sexually immature males, this is only training. The real test will start when they get a little older and are trying to build harems of thirty to forty females.

We follow their competition at a safe distance. These 3- to 4-ton animals have a completely different presence than those we saw during the summer. Then they were carrying extra weight for the purpose of being able to remain on land, lying in one spot for the weeks it took their fur to molt. Now, however, they are impressive bundles of muscle and exhibit both a strength and suppleness that we could never have imagined them to have. The last few yards of their attack, they rush a lot faster than we are able to run, so the viewing distance we keep is greater than summertime's. The only one that takes this all very calmly and isn't at all afraid to get close is the sheathbill. This bird is always at hand where there is something to eat. It is so pretty that it is difficult to imagine that it feeds mainly on carrion and excrement.

We are so taken by these enormous animals that we can't pull ourselves away. But it doesn't matter that we don't start to ski back home before dusk: it will never get really dark. In the light of the full moon we can see well enough to ski through the whole night.

After having been frozen fast in the ice for a little more than three weeks, we realize that *Northern Light* has started to lean to port, 1.5 to 2 degrees. At first, I believe that contrary to my original assumption, the ice is indeed lifting the boat. But when we measure the ice thickness, it is thinnest on the starboard side. Were there any lift it should have been thicker there. We therefore conclude that wind must be causing the lean. Even though it has felt like the boat has been sitting fast in the ice, the wind has had the power to push her "down" on the lee side. It is not enough lean to make anything slide off the table. So far, it's only been bad when we pour too much milk on our morning porridge.

The next day it is more important than ever that everything on the table stays put, because there is to be a feast! It's June 21; from now on, the days will get longer and longer. At 1035, right at sunrise, we establish radio contact with both Faraday and Palmer Stations to wish everyone present "Happy Midwinter." It is the first chat we've had with them since we froze in. Also on the air are the men at the British research station at Signy in the South Orkney Islands. We find that although it is nice to talk with people who also enjoy being here during the winter, it feels a little strange to admit that we already have half the winter behind us. Time is moving too quickly.

To cheer ourselves up and become more celebratory, we ski over to view an ice cave on Pléneau Island. We arrive there just when the sun is at its highest in the sky. Because today's highest is barely above the horizon, the light reaches farther into the cave than at any other time of the year. Through the opening we look in at the outermost chamber. Its floor is five times as large as our boat's deck, and Deborah wouldn't be able to reach the ceiling even if she were to stand on my shoulders.

It is tempting to enter the cave, but too often we hear snaps and pops coming from the ice. We judge that the risk of getting hurt by ice pieces falling down from the ceiling is too great. But just looking through the opening is enough to transfer us to another world. An amazing blue light spreads through the whole cave. Farthest in, some rays from the sun refract in a pool. And, despite the cold, last summer's rainwater still drips there. Some drips, having worked their way down through the snow, fall in shallow water; others fall in deep. Each drip creates its own tone and echo, and the resulting music casts its enchanting spell over us.

We walk along the cave's mouth, looking at each icicle hanging there. Some of them are more than 3 yards long, and many branch out like giant crab claws. The enormous icicles bend the sun's rays to color the shadows in the snow with sparkles of all the colors of the rainbow. It's a midwinter fireworks display, better than any other. As the sun sets and the colors dissipate we turn for home.

When we get back to the boat, Deborah and I start to prepare our banquet together. First, we put on a pot of wild rice and slice leaf-thin slices of prosciutto. Then we decorate the dinner table with an embroidered cloth Deborah's sister Lisa made for us and light some candles. When the rice is nearly ready, we prepare an omelet with wild mushrooms that Mats and Eva picked and dried. The chanterelles' aroma transfers us to a Swedish birch forest in late summer. For dessert we serve cheesecake topped with a layer of blueberries.

For evening entertainment, we listen to Smithy's tape. It's a present from Mats and his band, a recording that we have long saved for this special occasion. What we didn't know was that Mats composed the first tune especially for us. It's called "Rolf's Song." The style is blues, and the recording sounds like it was made around 1930 in a New Orleans cellar. Mats sings and plays harmonica. The first verse starts: "There's a red boat in the harbor. And it ain't leavin' tomorrow. Just one more door to be varnished. . . . "

The melody is almost as wonderful as the idea behind its creation. We had no idea that Mats followed our work in Fiskebäckskil so closely that he could compose a song about it. For the duration of the song, it feels like he is with us. When the tape is over we replay it from the top.

This is not the first time I have the feeling that some other person is visiting. Hearing Mats' voice is, of course, special and a little out of the ordinary. But even when I have read a book that a good friend has given us, I sometimes feel a strange emptiness when I put the book down, as if that person's just left the boat. I suppose the feeling is because the person who has given me the book has also indirectly given me information about himself or herself. The choice of book mirrors a person's interests and personality, an insight that can be difficult to gain through normal social interaction. To read a book that I've gotten from a friend therefore gives our friendship a deeper dimension. With distance between us, it's a way to be together.

Spontaneously, the face of my friend Åke pops into my mind. We have known each other since first grade. Over the years, he has presented Deborah and me with many books written by earlier polar explorers, books we have appreciated to the highest degree. Åke has spent days, maybe even weeks, prowling antique stores, locating original editions for us. I open one and read aloud for Deborah the description of Roald Amundsen's and his men's midwinter feast before they became the first to reach the South Pole.

What a party! To end our evening, we play the song Mats wrote one last time. As the music dwindles, the presence of our heroes and friends dissipates, like the last wispy threads of the aurora disappearing from a polar night's sky.

The day after midwinter is cloudy. The northeasterly wind is back and with it a rise in temperature. By afternoon it's 35°F (2°C). The following day it's 19°F (−7°C). The morning thereafter it's 34°F (1°C). That evening it's 21°F (−6°C). And so the temperature continues to yo-yo. On June 27 it's 33°F (0.5°C) and raining. The sun's been behind cover over a week.

Suddenly, while eating lunch, we hear the wind increasing very rapidly. When we look out, the air is full of spindrift. But it's clear over Booth Island and east of the Lemaire Channel. Above the updraft sways a large nacreous cloud. A phenomenon seen only in the polar regions, the cloud displays all the colors of the rainbow, swirling, fluorescent, like a mother of pearl shell.

Neither of us has ever seen anything like it before. We rush; this is a photo we simply can't miss and the sight can disappear any second. We each grab a camera and jump down on the ice. Because we both have the idea that the boat must also be in the picture, we run behind it, but in slightly different directions. Just yesterday, we measured the ice thickness around the boat and found it to be 16-inches thick (40 cm). So neither of us considers it necessary to don a life jacket.

When Deborah is four, perhaps five, boat lengths away, I watch her sink through the ice. I immediately change direction to go to her aid but manage only a few more steps before I also go through. Luckily, I sink so slowly that I manage to turn around and pitch myself toward the edge. I end up with my chest on the ice and get wet only up to my waist. On my belly, I slither back a few yards in the direction I came, then pause. When I look around I see that Deborah has also escaped getting completely wet. She is lying on the ice, already starting to snake her way back to the boat.

As the spindrift eases momentarily, I realize that a huge section of ice in the channel behind the boat has disappeared. Less than 200 yards away is completely open water! Now I also realize that there is some swell traveling under the ice. It's heaving. I get the impression that the whole ice sheet around the boat is about to break up. But it remains intact as long as it takes for Deborah to make it back to the boat. Then I start my approach. Eventually, I also make it aboard.

We have not lived up to our maxim: keep adventure at bay. Obviously, there is no such thing as being too careful.

20

DARKNESS, DESPAIR, AND CABIN FEVER

DEBORAH

■ ■ ■

If I've said it once, I've said it a thousand times: "The thought of killing Rolf has never occurred to me." Why would I ever say such a thing? Well, I had to answer *something* when people asked: "You two live in that sardine can? What happens when you have a fight? And I hear you're going to freeze into the ice and be in there all winter? You'll kill each other."

Yes, I heard it at least a thousand times, and I never learned. My gut response was to chuckle under my breath, mostly from the discomfort of not knowing exactly where to start explaining to people how they misunderstood our life. But time after time, when I saw that the person didn't understand that their proposed scenario wasn't the only possibility, it was my turn to question: does the majority of the married population actually hate his or her spouse?

In my case, were murder an acceptable solution to being aggravated with someone, I would have killed myself long ago; all too often I don't measure up to my own mark. And isn't it true that the majority of people who stood on the dock insinuating that Rolf and I would one day look at a winch handle as a murder weapon aren't actually aggravated by their spouses either, but by themselves, or something else outside their relationship, and simply take it out on their spouses?

I've been thinking about it. I decidedly prefer the self-improvement plan. The better I feel about myself—including for having the guts to immediately and directly counteract things that bother me—the less aggravation I have to vent and therefore the better I can treat those I have chosen to have around me. Murder may be easier, but it's *so* messy.

OK, Rolf and I do live in a small space and we can't get away from each other. Counteracting that, unlike most two-income couples in the Western world, Rolf and I actually depend on each other for basics, all the way down to survival. When you truly, honestly *need* another person, the idea of murdering them must be found somewhere way off the behavior continuum.

Perhaps those who comment that our home is too small have an issue with space that Rolf and I don't. The only time we have thought that maybe *Northern Light* was indeed too small was when we overloaded her for the trip down here from Mar del Plata. Otherwise, for our usual needs, and so far this winter, she's just right. If, instead of confronting me with their preconceived notions, people were to frame an open question about our living space, I would respond with something like: a boat may be a confined space, but from it the horizon is endless . . . this small space can take me anywhere there is as much water as I am tall . . . and because it's small, my commute only takes five seconds.

Cabin fever is a mental disease that occurs when you perceive that the small space you live in is confining or cramped, that itself bothers you, and the resulting irritation eventually finds expression in destructive behavior. People cooped up in shared spaces have killed over seemingly petty problems, like here in an Antarctic station where one man flared up during a chess game and killed his opponent. The final straw always seems to be some trivial incident, the "you don't put the cap back on the toothpaste tube" murder. It seems as if we humans can be quite spontaneous creatures under stress. Unfortunately, the chosen method of expression can be very inappropriate.

Rolf thinks there is another type of cabin fever that can happen when just two people live confined to close quarters and lack the feedback that group social interaction normally provides to keep us in check. Although one person sees that the other *is* indeed another person, he eventually perceives no separation. He comes to expect his partner or roommate to act as an extension of himself. When the person doesn't, it's as if he himself were ill; after all, "his" body is no longer carrying out his brain's internally initiated messages. In that case, murder is a cleansing process, a way of getting rid of the part of himself that isn't operating as it should.

The scary part is that crossing the border into psychosis isn't perceived by the person it's happening to. That implies that you can't talk them out of it or reason with them. If either of us were to cross that line this winter and attack the other, I figure that the one attacked would be justified to kill in self-defense. Swedes have an expression that is all too applicable in this case: He who lives, gets to see.

Although neither of us thinks that two people who plan to spend the rest of their lives together are as likely to get on each other's nerves as easily as men thrown together for a relatively short period of time, we have long planned how not to get cabin fever. We counteract the cabin part simply by being outside as long as possible every day. While we're out, we counter the fever part by getting exercise. We perceive that burning off excess energy and feeling physically tired is important. After all, nothing is as easy to misdirect as unused energy.

During these darkest months, outdoor time has occasionally been limited to as little as a half hour. If there's a whiteout—when there's so much snow in the air that you can become disoriented and lost only feet away from your destination—our outdoor area is restricted to *Northern Light*'s deck, where we shovel snow or simply stand in place and exercise. But only when the weather is so bad that it's dangerous do we not venture out at all. Some days, like today, it has simply been too windy. But there is another even more dangerous condition in this maritime region of Antarctica. Just a few weeks ago it rained. The rain filled the spaces between snowflakes with water, saturating the upper layer of snow, and then froze. Swedes call this surface ice *skare* (pronounced scar-reh). If you fall on *skare* skiing and your jacket sleeve is pushed up in the process, it can cut you badly. *Skare* can be as much as 2 inches thick. Wind can lift sections of it and blow it around. Once, when we were on our way for a ski but hadn't yet left the boat, the wind suddenly picked up from about 20 knots to 75 knots. In no time flat, 5 to 10 pound (2–4 kg) chunks of this ice layer came flying at us. We beat a hasty retreat inside and watched through the portholes as the killer discs either bounced off or self-destructed in our rigging. Rolf said to me: "Remember when Steve Christian once told us that his home island, Pitcairn, is no place for amateurs? Well, ditto here."

Yes, there are some days when we gladly remain inside our sardine can, drinking hot chocolate.

When confined inside, we have ways of creating space for each other. The systems we've developed over the years we've lived aboard now serve us well against the onslaught of cabin fever. Any person thinking, reading, writing, or listening to music is (with the exception of boat-related needs or emergencies) left alone, uninterrupted to concentrate, mull, dream, get lost, travel. Then when we meet, it's as if we haven't seen each other for simply ages. Long time, no see!

Another illusion of space is maintained by a "let it be" attitude. Especially since everything we do that is sailing-related has to be done identically, we have always seen to it that we keep our personas as separate as possible. That is to say that although we must both belay the main halyard on the same pin and in the same manner, we can squeeze the toothpaste tube however we choose. We like different types of music, dress as we wish, and let each other have moods, be they silly or bad. If, for example, Rolf is in a bad mood, I don't call attention to it. As long as I am not the cause, I don't take it personally, get involved, or comment, and I certainly don't try to reverse it. Pressure from the outside only makes it worse. Assuming we are otherwise healthy, bad moods pass in an acceptable amount of time. We all must be able to be.

A step up is the control of negative behavior by the person himself. Or herself. I, for example, never knew I had a temper before sailing with Rolf. But when we were in Spitsbergen in 1982, anger was oddly enough released as a response to fear. Was anger inappropriate or appropriate?

Here's what happened. I started getting shaky when told to: "Take this camera and get into the dinghy. Trust me. The ice is no problem and I'm quite sure those seals will not bother you. While I sail, you take pictures." When I started muttering, Rolf reminded me that we had agreed long ago to do this. But I did not like being left behind in an inflatable while Rolf sailed away with everything, including my actual life support. I came up with every possible excuse of why we shouldn't go ahead. When none was accepted, I got foot-stomping mad and said things I couldn't believe would ever come out of my mouth! Very soon I saw that I had to get myself under control. Rolf already had enough problems. Besides, I found I couldn't be upset and work creatively at the same time. I couldn't even hold the camera steady.

When I realized that anger was a way of mustering energy to deal with fear (appropriate) but that the expression of anger was counterproductive (inappropriate), I decided to allow myself to feel however I did but simply not engage my mouth; I would work it through privately instead. OK, self-discipline is a simple idea, but it isn't always easy. Yet it gets easier with each passing year.

The same self-control has also been successfully applied to other bad moods, such as being cranky due to being hungry or tired, or being disappointed and aggravated from working with gear that fails, or feeling sorry for yourself for some kind of physical or mental pain, or being sad over a memory. This is not to say that either of us has perfect control over our personal Pandora's box. When we're really worn down and lose the control, we hope it's only happening to one of us so that the other can meet the outbreak with compassion. A little compassion goes a long way. Trusting that your partner really is a good person but having a bad time makes it easy to react compassionately. That's love. But if the other of us is also worn down and responds instead in kind, then trouble could erupt. So far, either a project has demanded attention or something about the boat has reminded us that we have a duty to operational safety and we soon turned our energy to some work, with the result that we drop our problem. It seems there's a system for everything on board boats.

But in the worst scenario, when we're both worn out, and I mean really worn out, there'll be no energy left, not even to be misdirected. If that ever happens, I hope we can make it to shore, because it'll be time to stay there permanently.

Specifically, what do we do all day long, through the long winter's night? We start with an hour-long getting-up routine. Rolf, who wakes with a zing, jumps out of bed, immediately starts with the weather observations, lights the heater, and puts on coffee, chattering all the while, planning the day. I am the opposite type, hitting the snooze-button two or three times preferring to wake incrementally. Mostly I need to extricate myself from a dream-state quagmire by thinking about the dream that was interrupted by the alarm clock, then processing the previous few. Slowly but surely the cobwebs clear, but sometimes not until after the first half of my cup of Swedish-style very black morning brew. I have also been known to doze back off between sips.

That Rolf can twist me around his little finger these days is partly because of this gift he is giving me each and every morning. So many years of difficulty of getting up—for school or work or, even worse, for the umpteen times I have had to force myself out of bed to go on watch in a very few minutes, or even faster to help out on deck—are slowly unwinding during this slow-dance awakening in Antarctica. I relish it to the point of bliss, and I adore Rolf for his repetitive gift.

After breakfast—usually oatmeal or rye porridge with fruit, but replaced at whim by French toast or waffles—I tend to farming our alfalfa fields and the kefir in the dairy barn while Rolf works with gear. As soon as possible, we head outside to see which of the 200 nuances of morning light is playing, to ski and look around, to tend to the lines, to shovel snow, to film. Lunch is a picnic.

Midafternoon finds one of us cooking, and probably baking. We bake two days out of three, alternating bread and goodies. We're eating more than ever; our metabolisms are by no means depressed! Cooking as we do, by beginning with raw ingredients, takes two to three hours per day.

If Rolf and I have experienced difficulties in our relationship due to having grown up in different cultures and with different mother tongues, one of the pluses comes when we look at the same ingredients and come up with different meals. The cooking competition is fierce; after all, the dinner guest, although always appreciative, is as food savvy as any gourmet! Today, we are to be "in Sweden" for the traditional Thursday dinner: pea soup. Whole yellow peas (still recognizable, not green split pea mush) are the base, and tiny salted pork pieces add flavor. It's served with mustard on the rim of the bowl to dip into with each yummy spoonful and is accompanied by cheese, hard bread, and hot punsch; in our case, we drink just a few symbolic sips of punsch, a sweet Swedish liquor blended of rum, ararak, and vodka. Dessert to this wonderful winter meal will either be crepes or an apple-topped egg soufflé.

While one of us cooks, the other does as she or he pleases: reads, writes, or plans and researches for our documentary work. Most of the evening we interact and entertain each other. This is nothing new to either of us; reliance on family members for survival as well as fun was a big part of our training as kids. Rolf spent summers in the country; I grew up there. So we solve the "Gee, Mom, I don't have anything to do" syndrome the same way as we did when we were kids and there was no free entertainment: we play games together, talk about things, read aloud, tell stories, mess around. The only thing that I must say is missing is that neither of us can play an instrument. It would be super to listen to Rolf strum a guitar while I bake cookies, but. . . .

The past few months I've been reading to Rolf in the evenings. He got tired of hearing me erupt in laughter while reading Kurt Vonnegut's novel *Galapagos*, so I started over, aloud. Vonnegut's commentaries are a great kick-off for discussion, especially since he often fuels us with a laugh.

Had those folks on the dock in Fiskebäckskil been able to read my brain, they would have seen that the largest question looming in my mind about the winter was not getting on each others' nerves but, "Will Rolf and I run out of things to discuss?" If we do, *then* we've got a crisis on our hands.

It's only natural that we are always discussing things. We have a lot of decisions to make. Indeed, if we have a profession, I guess it is "decision making." Not only where to go, and when and why, but also tending to the sailing itself. Sailing's medium is not simply the tangible—the water and sky we move through—but one stage of decisions after another. The same applies to any wilderness activity.

Discussion ensues around here at the drop of a hat. As part of our mental health plan, we have adopted a normal debate system. Free-for-alls are never allowed. Our favorite type of discussion is a thought exercise originally called What if? that now goes by the name Putting Time on Ice. The name change came recently, when we started using the opener What if? to discuss solutions to current global problems. We understand that we are not the only ones thus engaged. At Palmer Station, a similarly oriented discussion group is referred to as the Benevolent Dictator Society. Perhaps the interest in global problems is because we are so far removed in this climate zone from all that is nurturing to humans that we look at Earth the way astronauts do: from the outside.

Rolf and I have been considering, for example, what if humans could come up with a fair system for the sharing of Earth's nonrenewable natural resources. What if each person on Earth was granted, at birth, an equal right to those resources? Say that each and every person would be a shareholder in a global partnership. Some individuals or groups might choose to buy more than their share of the resources. Others might simply choose to receive the dividends from their shares. What would the world look like then?

Another favored type of discussion is to take our simple understanding of a subject and try to figure something out by ourselves. For example, both of us are fascinated by meteorology. Our understanding of it is surface (pun intended). We know that a low spins counterclockwise in the Northern Hemisphere, but why?

Each of us is allowed to put forth our guess and challenge the other's. We may go into round two, three, four. And sometimes we come up with the answer, sometimes not. We came up with all kinds of theories about how lows and highs form, but in the final analysis were sure that none was correct.

Once upon a time, my brother Mark sailed with us from the Caribbean to Tahiti. He'd listen to this type of discussion until Rolf and I talked ourselves clean, then he'd say, "Now are you ready for the answer?" His knowledge is encyclopedic. It caused problems for me when we were kids; I was just a class behind him in school, and the teachers' expectations were always sky-high when I came tromping into their classrooms after him. But when Mark was our crew, I came to appreciate his knowledge. For three months we exercised our brains and if we didn't get it, got it anyway.

Not long after that, Rolf and I married. As a present, perhaps at Mark's suggestion, my family gave us the twenty-six-volume *Encyclopedia Britannica*. We had to ship the 165 pounds (75 kg) of answers to Sweden. "What a coincidence," Rolf said at the post office. "This is not only weighs exactly as much as Mark, but its 6 feet 6 (2 m) is as long as he is!" In Mark's absence we yack and yack and then hit his shelf replacement for "the" answer. Sometimes it's right, sometimes we accept it as so, but sometimes it's wrong. Of that we're sure.

Because Rolf and I hail from different countries, we get another type of discussion for free. No cultural precept can be taken for granted. It can take time to explain to Rolf why what Mark's wife, Linda, wrote in the books she gave to us in Florida: "To *Northern Light*'s to be red library" is funny. I had to start by explaining the series of jokes that evolved from "what's black and white and red all over." Cross-cultural relationships probably lose most where humor is concerned.

As far as spelling is concerned, I feel sorry for us all, but especially for anyone who, like Rolf, has learned English by speaking it. The rules as it were of English spelling are all but impossible to pick up that way. Not long ago I figured that playing Scrabble could be a good way to teach Rolf to spell and be an interesting challenge for the winter. He was willing to play along, so we modified some of the rules. For example, when he misspells a word, I tell him, he learns it and he gets to go again. Thus far, the spelling continues to confound him. Rolf lives by logic, you see; ergo, English spelling is crazy to him. A poem he wrote illustrates the problem:

WINDSONG TWO
FOR YWO

The gusty wind
has Northern Light pind,
heeling 15 degrees
if you plees.
The incline this morn is such
that our porridge bowls we must cluch.
And since we find it so rude

to have to hold on to our fude,
out into the blow and snow
we shortly will gow,
to be upright! and ski
through the wind and the li.
We'll get our daily exercise
(wearing goggles to protect our ise)
and we'll work up a good sweat,
I beat.

The next day, when we can actually get out of the boat and go skiing, we see that a big iceberg has collapsed during the night. On the Penola side of Hovgaard and Pléneau the fast ice has been broken up by the resulting wave and the evidence on the snowfield tells that the wave was no less than 10 feet (3 m) high!

In mid-July we ski for the first time over the ice as far as Entrance Island, all the while checking the ice's thickness. The 12-inch to 15-inch-thick (30–38 cm) iceway effectively doubles our skiing territory. This is great! During a pause, when we turn our faces away from the biting wind a while, Rolf realizes that we haven't seen any seals resting on the ice during this last cold spell either. Do we detect a pattern? Is it so that when the ambient air temperature falls below 14°F ($-10°C$) Weddell seals are better off—that is, use less energy—by remaining in the water at all times? If that's so, we may not see more than their faces in breathing holes until October, when the pupping season begins.

But a mere two weeks later, coming over the crest of a hill, we almost ski over the carcass of a stillborn Weddell pup. We are lucky to ever see it. Within minutes, six giant petrels arrive for the feast. Although only 2 feet (0.6 m) long, the pup was fully formed. We wonder how big they get in utero. Maybe this one was conceived early, maybe the pups will be born bigger than we anticipate, or maybe the reference information is wrong again?

Although it's already more than a month after midwinter, there isn't any noticeable increase in light yet. All the way back in the planning stages of this project, I wondered how the lack of light midwinter would affect our circadian rhythm and general mood.

I have never found winter depressing. Sure, there are fewer daylight hours than in summer, but I love snow and always accepted that snow is coupled with less daylight. But in Sweden I heard about the darkness and the despair and dread of winter. Swedes talk a lot about light and weather as if they could do something about it and as if they were controlling factors in life. Granted, light and weather are part of the fabric, especially in the high latitudes where the seasonal differences are so striking, but I have never seen any reason to dwell on them much. But John Doe (who in Sweden goes by the name Sven Svenson) seems to appreciate bestowing martyr status upon himself for living through the dark each year, even though the magical payback of a nightless summer always makes him lyrical, and makes the light distribution fair.

Pick any two points on Earth, or any hundred for that matter. Each and every one of them has the same number of hours per year when the sun is above the horizon. Those hours are just apportioned differently. At the equator, there are twelve hours of daylight followed by twelve hours of darkness each day year-round. At the poles, there is a six-month day followed by a six-month night each year. In between, there is a sliding-scale distribution of dark and light, changing with latitude.

Is one situation better than the other for humans? Although humankind was most likely born in the Tropics, there have long been people living from the equator to within a few hundred miles of the North Pole. That alone is proof for me that humans can adjust to any of the light situations on Earth. After having lived with degrees of darkness, I think Swedes aren't actually complaining *because* of, or even *about*, the dark, even though that's what they talk about. What bothers them is that they aren't allowed to respond naturally to it. More darkness than light each day triggers the body to want to slow down, to hibernate. But modern humans aren't allowed to alter their pace. One is expected to work as long and as hard in winter as in summer. One has to get up at the same time, wake the kids and dress them and bundle them off to day care—all in the dark—and then spend all the light hours in an office. The drive home, the reversal of the morning, is again in the dark. No one is allowed to slow down to an appropriate winter pace. I propose that's what leads Sven and Svenessa to feel poorly and to complain. Is it not an irony of modern times that we have to work too many hours and accept feeling poorly in the name of having a better standard of living?

Before we came here, I had expected that, when we froze in and had even less light than I'd ever experienced in southern Sweden, I may indeed become depressed. What I've found, however, is that neither of us are depressed in the psychological sense; we are as up and happy as always. Only in the physiological sense are we depressed. I believe, in general, that we operate more slowly here (although that's hard to tell without an outside observer) and our bodies want close to nine hours of sleep. When we can determine our use of the day and its pace without any outside interference or control, those are the only changes we can detect.

I have a solution to offer people in the cities of the high north. Because I know they won't do what they should—that is, cut back the daily number of working hours in the dark period and slow down—my suggestion is that they adopt a radically different winter schedule. Start work when it gets dark; in other words, work from three to eleven P.M. Go home. Sleep nine hours. Wake up when it's light, be outside, ski, play in the snow with kids. Use the daylight rather than hide from it. Why not? If the march of time itself isn't controllable, isn't the time of day at least arbitrary and meant to be arranged to suit our needs?

There's even more to consider about the haves and have-nots of light distribution. Although every spot on Earth has the sun above the horizon an equal number of hours per year—the cumulative twilight in the high latitudes is much longer than at the equator or in the Tropics, where the sun sinks and disappears quickly. Because of the increased twilight period, the total number of hours of *light* per year is actually greatest in the high latitudes!

Twilight is important to navigators, and we see it as having two stages. The time when the sun is just below the horizon to 6 degrees below the horizon—on its way either up or down—is called civil twilight. During that period, although the sun itself is not visible, the light is bright enough to read by. The time when the sun is 6 to 12 degrees below the horizon is called nautical twilight. Then, stars are visible, but there is still enough light to see the horizon. This is the time celestial navigators like best because we need to be able to see the horizon to measure the height of the celestial body above it.

We have a book aboard, *The Nautical Almanac,* which contains the data necessary to celestial navigation. From it Rolf and I have gleaned some figures concerning the yearly apportioning of light on Earth.

DAY OF THE YEAR		EQUATOR	POLAR CIRCLE
WINTER SOLSTICE	Sun above the horizon	12 hr 07 min	2 hr 19 min
	Civil and naut. twilight	1 hr 38 min	6 hr 14 min
	Total daylight	13 hr 45 min	8 hr 33 min
SPRING AND FALL EQUINOXES	Sun above the horizon	12 hr 07 min	12 hr 18 min
	Civil and naut. twilight	1 hr 29 min	3 hr 59 min
	Total daylight	13 hr 36 min	16 hr 17 min
SUMMER SOLSTICE	Sun above the horizon	12 hr 07 min	24 hr 00 min
	Civil and naut. twilight	1 hr 38 min	0
	Total daylight	13 hr 45 min	24 hr 00 min
TOTAL DAYLIGHT ON THOSE FOUR DAYS		54 hr 42 min	65 hr 07 min

But that's only four days out of 365, you say. What's the yearly cycle like? Imagine for a moment that you live on the Arctic Circle. As early in the year as February 24, there is already exactly the same amount of light from the start of twilight through the day and to the end of twilight, at the Arctic Circle as there is on the Tropic of Cancer, and there is either an equal amount or *more* light at the Arctic Circle from that day until October 16. The conclusion: During four months of the year the Arctic Circle has fewer hours of light than the Tropics. But during eight months it has more, and as you see from the pattern started in the table, the total hours of light per year are more. Odd as it may seem, if it's light you crave, the only logical conclusion is to move closer to the pole!

Many people living in the north will look at the preceding table and scoff. "She says we have more than eight hours of light on the Arctic Circle midwinter. Pshaw!" But it's true. Those folks just don't realize it because city light, the bright light inside a house, or car headlights obliterate the twilight. Our eyes can't perceive gentle twilight when already stimulated by bright light. The physiological reason is that the receptors in our eye that, according to the *Britannica Macropedia*, receive the most light tend to inhibit those that receive less." This difference, of light perceived from a light place or a dark one, used to get us in big trouble as kids. In the summertime, we were always supposed to be home by dark. Mom, looking out from a lit house, thought it was dark, when we—in the "dark"—found it still light!

To test the phenomenon for yourself, go outside at night. Walk slowly away from a fully lit area into the darkness. Proceed so slowly that your eyes adjust to allow you to walk around safely. After ten minutes your night vision takes over. You can see detail previously hidden, yet your sensitivity to low light will continue to improve for twenty minutes more. At that time you have full use of your night vision. Impressively, your eyes will now be 10,000 times (yes!) more sensitive to light than when you started.

For total appreciation of winter light, to the sun's twilight you must add in the light from that tremendous reflector of sunlight, our moon, which (still at our reference point of the Arctic Circle) is higher in the sky at midwinter than the sun is at midsummer. During half of each winter month there is enough moonlight to ski by; the natives of Scandinavia's high north call it the "second day." And don't forget the reflective power of snow itself.

Light is the substance of Rolf and my photographers' existence. Blue starlight, silver moonlight, or the muted midwinter pastel twilight—when snow is pink and clouds lilac, or a second later when they trade colors—is a source of never-ending work, to say nothing of beauty. We don't have to hibernate. If this winter, when each brushstroke is our own, is either boring or filled with despair, we'll only have ourselves to blame.

21

MONTH
OF
THUNK

ROLF

■ ■ ■

With both arms outstretched, Deborah schusses *up* the slope of Hovgaard Island. The wind at her back is so strong she doesn't even need to plant her poles. She moves very fast, especially in the gusts. It's a new sport: ski-sailing! I check out her technique. To turn, she just leans her shoulders a little in the direction she wants to go. With one arm high up in the air, she looks like a storm bird playing in a whirlwind. The distance between us increases quickly, then she disappears in the spindrift. When I reach her, as she waits for me on the first plateau, Deborah radiates pure glee. She says, "That was the first time I ever managed to imitate a bird so well that it actually felt like flying!"

Together, we continue up and over the crest to Western Point. The wind has been increasing the entire time we have been out. We decide to head back. To be sure not to lose our bearings, we keep to the channel where *Northern Light* sits in the ice. With steep hills on both sides, we can't get lost. That's not to say we see the boat: we can barely see as far as our own skis. This upwind leg does not go fast. The wind funneling between the hillsides is ferocious. To progress, Deborah leans so far forward it looks like the law of gravity has been suspended. Whenever a really heavy blast hits while I am trying to advance a ski pole, it feels as if someone is holding onto it. Sometimes I find it near impossible to move my arms forward against the force of the wind. In the worst of the gusts, we go nowhere. Instead, we are forced to hold ourselves in place, with both poles dug into the snow, or we'd be blown backwards. Not until we find ourselves caught in the V of *Northern Light*'s stern ropes do we know that we will soon be home again. The boat itself isn't visible until we are less than 10 feet away. To say the least, it is very exciting to be outside in weather like this.

Thanks to the fact that the wind has finally picked up seriously, our wind generator now spins full-speed around-the-clock. For the first time this entire winter the batteries are fully charged and we can use as much electricity as we want. That was never the case during June and July, when the wind generator provided a mere fifth of the current we had counted on. Power was a valuable commodity and we rationed it, with personal use lowest on the list of priorities. We read as much as we could by the light of kerosene lamps. Only when our eyes became so fatigued that we had to read by electric light did we roll out the double berth and sit together under the comforter, sharing the light of one single halogen bulb. Those were nice evenings. But it's better for our backs to be able to sit as we can now, each in our own corner of the sofa, our teacups on the table between us. Reading is mainly what there is to do. In the worst gusts it howls so much that it's impossible to carry on any real conversation.

One evening in the beginning of August we realize the lights are dimming. The meter shows only 11.6 volts. I investigate. The generator is spinning and its fuse is intact. Something must be wrong with the generator itself. Even though it's close to bedtime, I know I won't be able to sleep before I have diagnosed the source of the problem, so we dress to go outside.

It's 10.5°F (−12°C), snowing, with a full gale-force wind blowing out of the southwest. We have never disassembled the wind generator before. While trying to catch the fin and depower the generator, I wonder if it will even be possible to take the lid off without the whole interior of the generator filling with snow. But because the wind is coming from astern, we can rotate the generator so that when the lid is in the lee, it faces our only possible working position on the aft deck.

While I work on the first of four screws, Deborah holds the flashlight. She also has to hold the wind generator perfectly still and keep it facing in the right direction. Poor Deborah; the generator blades provide a lot of windage, and more often than not, the wind hits so hard that it shakes her. Try as she might, she seldom manages to hold the flashlight steady enough for me to see the notches in the heads of the screws. It takes an eternity before I can even loosen the first one, and then the head of the screw is so frustratingly small that I can't possibly grab it with my mittens on. In the end, I am forced to work with one hand bare. After just a few seconds' exposure to the bitingly cold wind, my fingers lose all feeling. When I finally get the screw out, I drop it. It would have been lost in the snow behind the boat, but for Deborah anticipating what could happen. Cold as the flashlight must be, she lodged it between the hood of her anorak and her cheek so that she could place her now-free hand under mine. I scream, "Nice catch!" When she shakes her head and points to her ear, my second try to compliment her is a simple smile.

It takes ten minutes to open the casing. Then we see what is wrong. Inside, three of the cables going to the rectifier and a fourth one to the choke have been ripped away from their contacts. Checking closely, it also seems as if the generator shaft can slip in the rubber-lined brackets. How the rest is constructed cannot be determined in the dark. All we can see is that there's a second shaft inside the one that spun and that the cables in question come out through that inner shaft. We cannot tell if the cables inside the shaft have been damaged. The only action we can take is to reattach the contacts, put the lid back on, and then check the meter to see if the generator charges.

It does, for five minutes anyway, at which point it quits again. Now we are convinced that the shaft is indeed spinning. We check the manual to see how it is constructed, but the drawings are not detailed enough for us to determine how the different parts are mounted. And, disappointingly, there is no enlarged view of the interior workings. If we want electricity, we're going to have to figure this out by ourselves.

Back out into the driving snow we go. We decide that the most obvious and reliable repair—drilling a deep hole through to the inner shaft and securing it with a long screw—is too risky: we could ruin the cables. To stop the shaft from being able to spin, we decide to place a fixed wrench on a nut that sits at the end of the shaft and lock the wrench in place by putting a hose clamp around both the wrench and a support post next to it. After a short run, the hose clamp snaps.

The forces are stronger than we thought. Our second try is to wedge a screwdriver between the foundation and a nut on the end of the shaft closest to the blades. But after just a few seconds that also fails. We pause to regroup. After some contemplation I have an idea: let's take advantage of what happens when a rope catches on a spinning propeller shaft. The rope wraps, then winds itself tighter and tighter until it eventually jams and everything comes to a dead stop.

We put a $\frac{1}{6}$-inch (4-mm) stainless steel wire around the shaft and wind it as hard as we can. To finish it off, we wrap the wire around the support piece five times. Then, an eye splice in its end is hooked over a screw we put in the foundation. This repair job works. But without being able to work out the shaft's torque, we don't know if or how long it will hold. We start rationing electricity again, saving enough for our next radio sked when we ask Frank to please call the manufacturer.

A week later, Frank tells us that they don't know the forces generated either. Now we understand why the generator fell apart in the first place. Moreover, the manual states we should use a 15-amp fuse, which had led us to believe that the generator should be able to take wind speeds up to what it takes to make that much charge. But now they have told Frank that we should not let the wind generator charge more than 7 to 8 amps. The blades should be tied off at that point. That's their "judgment" after hearing that the generator had broken down.

After the conversation with Frank we hear two other radio amateurs talking. During the conversation, one asks the other what kind of antenna he has, and he gets a straight answer: "My antenna is what I call Modified to Work." The man who asked the question laughs. We do too, sort of.

So, "Modified to Work" has become a brand name! What a world. After we shut down the radio we aren't sure if we should laugh or cry. Deborah takes a broad-tipped permanent black marker and reinforces the paint job she did long ago over all the brand names visible inside the boat. The first time around, it was done for aesthetics; this time it's to work off a little steam. When she's done, she promises to make up new nameplates in all shapes and sizes so that we can put an MTW logo onto anything we've modified.

We turn to serious discussion. If the wind generator really does die, we will not be able to continue our video documentation because without the generator we cannot charge the batteries for the one camera that still works. The solar panel does no good now in the dead of winter's low light. It may possibly still work when the sun comes back, but when we last used it, it didn't charge as well as it should because moisture had followed the cables into the panel.

As far as video filming has been concerned, our goal has been to come back aboard each day with fifteen minutes of taped images. If we're lucky, from those 900 seconds, we will be able to glean twenty seconds for a program. Filming in cold temperatures has its own problems, obvious and otherwise. We have learned to take along thermoses filled with warm towels to warm the lens of the underwater housing so it won't condense and freeze. And that's after we doubled the lens by gluing on a spare lens filter. Including the time spent on board preparing each morning and out in the field waiting for the right light, we have so far spent 500 hours taping. If halted now, in the middle, the video project is as good as over.

At this stage we wonder how much of the equipment we brought along will make it through this winter. There's not much left that functions as it should. For example, all the steel edges on our skis are about to fall off. One of mine already has, and when it went, so did the bottom layer of the ski. Technically speaking, there was no chance that the edges could stay attached. There are neither barbs nor holes in the steel edges by which they could be melded to the ski itself.

The first thing to go wrong with our ski poles was that they lost their studs, which were only stuck into place. When we poled in a hard icy surface, the studs pulled out and stuck in the ice. We manufactured new studs and epoxied them in place. The second problem was that the poles' baskets were only held in position by being snapped into a little depression in the plastic. They probably stayed on fine in the heated factory and store. When the first basket fell off, it took us a whole hour to find it. We had spares, but what about people who don't? Even a short trip in the mountains or hills close to home can be tiresome or even dangerous when a significant part of one's gear breaks. The job of modifying the attachment—drilling a hole in the pole to secure the baskets with a cotter pin—only took four minutes per pole and should have been done by the factory. These poles are, after all, that manufacturer's best mountaineering ski poles.

Then our backpacks lost their function. The nylon fittings that hold the pack on the frame cracked. Then a jacket pocket fell off because there was too little seam allowance. Then . . . well, I won't bother continuing with the list.

We have learned that what Roald Amundsen said after living with the Inuit, where he built his skills for his successful attempt to be first to the South Pole, seems to be just as true today: to survive in the polar wilderness, you'd better learn from those who do.

The month continues to be windy. On August 12, we wake in the middle of the night with a feeling that the Booth Island "weather dam" has just broken. Until minutes ago the boat was frozen fast in 3-foot-thick ice, but now it's vibrating so violently that our mattress is moving around. It feels like a giant has grabbed our mainmast and is shaking the boat as hard as he can.

As I get up, I think about how unusually high the barometric pressure was a week ago: 1,015 millibars. Since then, the pressure dropped continuously for six days, a fair warning that a lot of wind was on its way. I turn on the spreader lights, but I can't see well through the cupola because it's almost entirely snowed over. I can only see out aft, and there everything is a gray haze. The wind is coming from dead ahead at an average well above 60 knots, and the roar generated in the rigging is deafening. I wait until the wind finally decreases a little before opening the cupola to look forward. Through the driving snow I manage to see that the cause of the shaking is the forestay swinging from side to side, moving almost 3 feet in each direction.

While I dress to go outdoors, layering on the warmest of my winter gear, I think about how we felt two months ago when the boat froze fast. Deborah and I figured we had a long vacation ahead of us; we neither could nor needed to do anything for the boat. The thicker the ice became, the safer and more secure we felt. For weeks now the boat has been sitting so steady in the ice that we could have let the shore lines go and still stayed put. It felt like living on shore. Until just a few minutes ago, our dream about a long, relaxing time without boat responsibilities was fulfilled in every respect. That's not to say that it hadn't been windy already, but nothing like this had occurred.

By the time I have my anorak on, the shaking has become so violent that it is apparent I need to hurry. Something in the rigging will soon give up.

As I wait for the proper time to open the cupola, my mind races. I assume the swaying begins when the forestay profile's leading edge is turned into the wind and its aerodynamic shape develops lift. If my theory is correct, then turning the profile sideways to the wind should stop the phenomenum. But outside, as I am hit by the first gust, I recall that long ago, to make it easier to shovel snow, we removed all lines leading to the cockpit, including the one from the furling jib. To turn the profile, I'll have to make my way out to it on the bowsprit.

There is so much snow in the air that I have to make my way by feel. To avoid the bone-chilling wind, I lower myself into a crouch. The last bit across the foredeck can only be safely accomplished on all fours. I eventually get out on the bowsprit and turn the profile. The swaying does stop, but not for long. The wind is never so constant in direction for there to be one perfect resting position for the profile. No matter how I position it, it's just a matter of time until the swaying starts again.

I look around. Despite the deck lights, it is impossible in the dark to judge what is below me. I can barely make out the teak grating my knees are resting on. The driving spindrift makes it look as if the boat is rushing through the darkness at a dizzying speed. The cold is numbing, windchill hastening its effect. I begin to have difficulty thinking. As soon as I look up, snow stings my face. Time and motions start to seem dragged out.

The force of the wind and shaking become so violent that the whole bowsprit starts pumping. Finally, I come up with a possible solution. What if I attach the genoa halyard to the pulpit on the starboard side? Perhaps that's the answer.

Surprisingly, I manage to open the frozen hank. I unwrap the halyard from the profile and then take a couple of turns around the pulpit and secure it. Then I work my way to the mainmast, where I tension the line with the help of the halyard winch. The result of running the genoa halyard almost parallel to the forestay profile is that a slot effect creates a low pressure and the halyard and profile are drawn toward each other. The swaying stops. But the peace doesn't last long this time either. In the next gust, the wind shifts again, enough to start the pumping all over again.

Still, I believe I'm on track. To complete the arrangement, I release the spinnaker halyard hank from the mainmast. My plan is to attach it dead ahead of the furling profile and by doing so create a similar slot effect to the genoa halyard's. I pull at least 4 yards more slack in the halyard than necessary for the distance, but the wind grabs the rope with such force that I can only pull it as far as the bow. There, I wrap the halyard around the cutter stay a few turns and use both hands to hold on. When the wind finally "eases" momentarily, I continue out onto the bowsprit. Eventually I fasten the halyard where I want it. Back at the mast, I winch it tight and all the swaying stops. I wait a few anxious minutes before I am certain the problem has indeed been solved. Satisfied, I make my way aft to the cockpit and down into the boat.

"That was an unexpected maneuver," Deborah says, then she takes my arm and smiles. She is just as relieved as I am that I am back safely. "But gee, it took you a long time. Just tightening up two halyards took four times as long as it used to take you to change headsails," she says. I look at the clock. "Whew, that actually took me a whole hour?" I ask.

I should've known better than to take the bait. Deborah nods and says, "Yes, you must be getting old." I don't bother commenting. I'll show her how wrong she is.

A few hours later nature interrupts our sleep again, this time with a terrible jolt. Before we even understand what is happening, the boat heels so much that I roll into Deborah, and together we continue gliding off the mattress up onto the side of the hull. An eternity passes before the boat ever starts to righten, and during that time we try our best to crawl out of bed. But at the same speed we crawl uphill, the mattress slides farther to the lee. When we finally reach the floorboards and are on our way out into the galley, the boat is almost upright. Then it's forced over again, this time to starboard, with such force that both of us are nearly knocked over.

The floor is suddenly covered with items that have been standing on counters for months. It is difficult to know where to put our bare feet. We must be particularly careful to not step on anything sharp. When I eventually reach a light switch, we see on the clinometer that the boat is heeling 25 degrees.

It takes half a minute before the boat starts to righten, but this time it never comes all the way up. One violent gust is quickly replaced by another. As soon as wind comes from 5 to 10 degrees off the bow, the boat is completely knocked over again. The force this wind must have is difficult to fathom.

Each time the boat hits the edge of the ice, anything that can move inside the boat does. Saucepans, utensils, glasses, and plates shift in lockers and drawers. The cans in the bilge roll. The cumulative cacophony is amazing. It sounds like no one thing will survive intact. The wind must have increased to far over hurricane force. The worst gusts shriek somewhere between 90 and 120 knots.

There's nothing else to do but crawl back under the blanket. But it's impossible to sleep, and not just because of the noise of the thunks and crashes each time the boat twists or lurches in its ice cradle. We start to wonder what kind of damage the boat may be incurring. We know it would be insane to go out now to try to look, but we hope that by the time it gets light the wind will have decreased some. What worries me most is that the log propeller and the rudder can break or bend as the boat rolls against the ice.

That thought is not more than finished before we hear a terrible bang. This time the noise comes from the stern. Each time the boat heels, it bangs again. We recognize the noise; the tiller is hitting a bollard. That means that the steering wire connecting the wheel to the tiller has snapped.

In the early part of the winter when the ice sheet still moved continuously, we positioned the rudder amidships and then locked the wheel with its mechanical brake so that it would not be exposed to more stress and strain than necessary. As soon as the ice became so thick that both the boat and the ice sat perfectly stationary, we loosened the brake again so as to not overload the wires. But, apparently, there was still too much tension.

To put an end to the banging, I get up, dress again, switch on the deck lights, and crawl out to the aft deck. I tie a rope around the tiller and secure each end to a bollard. I leave some slack in the rope. Were there no play, the tiller would bend when the boat gets knocked over. I wonder about the rudder, but I won't be able to determine if anything has happened to it until this wind moderates.

The following morning there's a message in our electronic mailbox from Jim, the winter radio operator at Palmer Station, informing us that their biggest antenna was knocked down by the 80-knot wind they measured last night. Our estimation of the wind speed here must have been right; Palmer is nowhere near as exposed as we are in this wind direction.

When it gets light, we go out to inspect the extent of the damage. The paint has sustained two small scratches just above the waterline, but there is nary a dent in the hull. Unbelievable! It's still quite windy, and each time the boat heels, we watch the steel plates scrape against the ice, but the rounded hull never gets stuck. Any hard-chine boat, or one with more flared topsides, would certainly have been damaged. The part of the rudder visible above the snow is neither twisted nor bent. To inspect the rudder itself, we dig up the ice around the stern. The ice is 2 feet (0.5 m) thick and the digging takes a couple of hours, but then we see that the rudder has not been damaged either. What a relief.

Still, we don't want to expose the rudder to any risk for the rest of the winter. We dig until it can swing freely in both directions. We let the pool freeze overnight and then shovel loose snow on top of the newly formed ice cover. As long as the snow insulates as we expect it to, we figure that to keep the rudder safe we'll only have to remove a half a foot of ice each fortnight from now on.

At midday the blow is over and it's almost calm. *Northern Light* sits completely still in her ice cradle, but she has still a fairly heavy lean to port, between 5 and 6 degrees. It seems that after the final knockdown, she never straightened all the way up; there is after all some friction between the hull and the ice. To bring her back on an even keel, we borrow the spinnaker halyard from the forestay's antisway system, lengthen it with an additional line, and then attach it as far as possible along the starboard forward shore line where it disappears into the snowbank. While I watch along the mast to check that it doesn't bend too much during the process, Deborah winches.

The ice crackles, but nothing seems to happen. We pause. Suddenly, the boat lurches. It straightens up a bit, and we continue. Each time the boat straightens up a bit, the rig shakes. But because the mast still shows no tendency to bend, we can continue. Slowly but surely, we pull the boat out of the lean.

By dinnertime it's totally calm. For the first time in over a week, it is so quiet in the boat that we could have whispered to each other. But now our habit is to talk as loudly as we can. Not until Deborah starts laughing, wondering if we haven't suffered an occupational injury and suggests that we actually *can* lower our voices until the next storm, does peace settles over the dinner table.

That there will indeed be a new storm is now obvious. During the past week, the barometer needle has continuously rotated counterclockwise, more than half a circle! The barograph arm on the other hand is stationary. It has bottomed out.

During the entire night it is surprisingly calm. Ditto the next day. But because the wind will arrive sooner or later and with a punch, we stay close to the boat. From Oleg Island, we can view what happened to the ice past Entrance Island. We ski over. From the top of Oleg we see that the overwhelming majority of the ice has been blown out to sea. That's a bad sign as far as our long ski tour is concerned. We ski back to the boat, disappointed. We eat an early dinner, read for a while, and go to bed earlier than usual. Our low moods are also partly the result of the exceedingly low pressure. The barometer shows 948 millibars, which is lower than we have ever measured previously. And it's still falling. . . .

During the night there is a little wind whistling in the rigging, but it only sings now and then. The wind hasn't managed to fill the Booth Island dam yet. Suddenly, the boat moves. It seems to be lifted straight up, as if the tide rushed in so quickly that the ice couldn't keep pace. I am immediately wide awake. My first thought is that an iceberg must have collapsed and that the same thing is now about to happen here as at Petermann Island! On my way out of bed, I feel even more clearly how the boat is still rising. Finally, it starts to sink back down. As I put my feet on the floor, the boat hits the ice with a crash. A kerosene lamp's glass chimney falls on the bed. On my way into the galley and up the ladder, I feel how the boat heaves. When it falls, it thunks again.

To my surprise, when I get the hatch open and look out, the entire sheet of ice looks just like it did earlier, and there is still no wind. Only after watching the boat be lifted a foot (30 cm) and fall back into the ice cradle do I figure out what is happening. Although its wind has not yet reached us, the storm blowing out at sea is generating such enormous waves that the resulting swell continues like seismic waves under the ice, all the way here. At its worst, when the boat slams into the ice, the crash sounds as if we had run aground. As soon as it becomes light outside, we lessen the impact of each thunk by shoveling snow between the hull and the edge of the ice. It works for some hours, then we must go renew the padding. The thunking continues two days straight, during which we get neither rest nor sleep.

When the wind finally does reach us, we must tie off the wind generator; it can never be exposed to too much wind again. Whenever the wind increases, no matter the time of day, we must go out and stop it from spinning. As soon as the wind diminishes, we must go out and free it. Otherwise, we don't get the electricity we need. It's like tending to a sick child.

For ten days the barometer continues to drop. On the morning of August 13, it bottoms out to a record low, 933 millibars, after a continuous fall of 82 millibars! In the last hour, it has dropped 8 millibars and the northeasterly wind has died completely. The silence is heavy. Deborah and I anxiously wait to see what will happen next.

Wind suddenly blows from the opposite direction. Snow whirls in through the galley hatch, which was open a crack for ventilation. We slam it closed and lock it. A glance to the barometer shows that in the last ten minutes the pressure has risen 3 millibars. Here we go. The boat quivers. We watch while the wind grabs the snow from the 4-foot-high drifts that have formed on the lee side of big boulders during the past days. Another gust shakes the boat. Suddenly, the wind intensifies to a deafening roar. This wind carries enormous amounts of snow, and within a few seconds the visibility is totally obliterated. As a matter of fact, looking out through the cupola I can't see the mizzenmast. The feeling that something completely incomprehensible has happened is so overwhelming that for a few seconds my brain refuses to function. Logically, the mast must be there, but . . .

There's nothing for my eyes to focus on. There is no up or down. All reference points have been wiped out. It has become such chaos that a long while passes before I realize that a dark segment I keep glimpsing and assume to be the cliff a couple of boat lengths away on the starboard side is actually the genoa winch! At best, the visibility isn't more than a couple of feet. The wind shrieks steadily for ten minutes before decreasing any. Slowly but surely, visibility increases. That has to have been the most violent cold front passage we have ever experienced.

Were something similar to this to happen while we were out skiing, our only possibility to survive would be to dig ourselves down into the snow. The distance to the boat wouldn't matter. In such conditions, one simply doesn't travel another step. Knowing that we can be caught for some time away from the boat, we almost always take a pulka, loaded with shovels, cooking gear, and enough food for a few days. But now, after seeing what can really happen, we question the likelihood of ever getting shelter in the snow. The slightest carelessness could cause the shovel to be ripped from our grip to fly like a projectile through the air. If it hit the other person, the blow could easily be fatal. We must have the same attitude to the weather here as we do at sea. In wind strengths above 70 knots, one can never be sure what will happen. During the most extreme conditions, it may be a struggle for survival.

This time, it was far more than 70 knots of wind, but just how much is difficult to say.

The next day it's practically calm again. The only thing left of the storm is an aftereffect, a signature of a sort. *Northern Light* sits in what looks like a scene of an agitated sea that has been frozen in place. Oddly, because the wind came from astern, the snow wave the wind created along the boat gives the impression that the boat is sailing backward. There's a typical bow wave at the stern, and off the bow flows a stern wave, big enough to look as if we made 8 knots. It seems strange at first, but with snow and water being different forms of the same thing, the wave isn't really anything weird. But to see it is still amazing, as is anything one has never experienced before.

Lucky me. Because Deborah and I talk about what it's like to experience something for the first time in life, I suddenly remember that it will soon be her birthday. On August 21, she'll turn forty. I say nothing, but am I glad I remembered!

Before we left Mar del Plata, Deborah in her inimitable way, sent out birthday party invitations. For some reason, I was the only one to RSVP. Imagine what a catastrophe it would have been if I didn't show up! On the invitations she wrote that people were welcome to stay forever, as long as they brought their own food. Maybe that's what turned them off. Anyway, I'm going to bring a really big cake with me, that's for sure.

At seven o'clock in the morning of her birthday I start a Swedish-style celebration, waking Deborah and presenting her with the *World's best chocolate cake.* "World's best" means that not only does the cake itself have more chocolate per volume than in any other ever baked but it's also covered with a layer of pure dark chocolate, a quarter of an inch thick. Well, not really pure chocolate; for the topping to be shiny, the chocolate destined to be the icing was melted in butter before being spread on top.

I baked the cake and iced it before I went to bed, and then I had a hard time getting to sleep, That's how delicious the cake looked. Anyway, now all the candles are lit, and when Deborah sees the cake, her mouth also waters. After her first taste, I am told, "This is the best breakfast I'll ever have!" It should be: there are at least 1,000 calories in every bite.

I try to make Deborah's fortieth as memorable as possible. Even so, I'm not the one who springs the greatest surprise on her. How the guys at Faraday got to know about Deborah's birthday is a mystery to us, but via the electronic mailbox comes congratulations from them. When we print it out, she gets an almost 2-foot-long banner saying HAPPY BIRTHDAY DEBORAH!!! Deborah turns the radio on to thank them, and it immediately feels like the boat is full of people cheering and singing. While I applaud, Deborah clangs some pots and pans together. When Gavin, the radio operator, asks what the noise was, she tells him that she was just putting on her armor so that she would be dressed properly for the Middle Ages! There is laughter and more calls of happy birthday from those assembled in Faraday's radio room. Deborah is truly moved. It's a wonderful party.

When she switches the radio off, she turns to me, looking slightly disturbed. Half joking and half serious, she wonders aloud, "Just what do you think happens to a person who turns forty without any reason for a crisis?" That's a question to which I have no answer.

The barometer climbs back up to 980 millibars by the following day, and the temperature hovers around 14°F (-10°C). To our delight more than a foot of new snow fell while we slept. When we ski around Pléneau Island, it looks as if there has never ever been any wind. There isn't a ridge of wind-packed snow (sastrugi) to be seen. There are no sharp edges anywhere, and everything is soft and billowing. We travel over a sea of cotton. There are no tracks from seals or penguins, nor is there any sound. There is a peace that occurs only when nature rests. This is the time of the year that I like the best, the time just before the hectic spring season begins.

22

THE
PLEASANT
SETBACK

DEBORAH

■ ■ ■

From the height of the second plateau on Hovgaard the news of the day is plain to see. *All* the sea ice is gone. After scanning the horizon Rolf turns to me and says: "It comes, it goes. That's the cycle so far. The only conclusion to draw is that it is too dangerous to be out skiing on it for any length of time. I'd considered trying as long as we took the small inflatable with us, but it's just too heavy; it represents too high a percentage of the weight we can pull. I'm sorry, but I just don't think we should look forward to a long ski trip anymore."

I have three reasons why his decision is not crushing. First, the times we've been outside our archipelago's iceway to measure and check the sea ice, I had seen that although it carried us on skis, it undulated from each glide. Watching the wavelets we set in motion was enough to give me the shudders. I couldn't imagine any happy ending to a story that started with going through the ice harnessed to a 145-pound (65-kg) pulka, wearing skis.

Second, even when I pull a pulka loaded only with daily needs, I can feel that my back is still weak. Every time the pulka accelerates faster than I do and pushes on me, my lower back responds with a wince. The concentration required to keep my injury from worsening leaves little room to enjoy either skiing or scenery. I always thought I would be able to pull on smooth, flat sea ice, but the sea ice so far could never be described as smooth or flat. It's always been composed of frozen together pack ice, and that means hauling up and down over bumps. My back couldn't take that.

Those two thoughts are completed privately. I'll voice them only if they are still valid at the time the trip could actually happen. I turn to Rolf and tell him the third reason why I don't find it hard to stay put. "Were this island group void of animal life, the cancellation of the ski trip would be a loss, but actually, as interesting as it is here, I think that leaving would be wrong. We'd never know what we missed if our 'neighborhood watch' were interrupted. And we'd never come to understand the cycle of life that occurs in exactly *this* place," I say.

I know Rolf has always looked forward to this ski trip, in part, I believe, because he expected to be bored when confined to one spot. But there is as much stimulation here as any person can take. I know he agrees because he's been nodding his head, he hasn't broken eye contact with me. Neither of us feels a need to take a vacation from this place or to change for sake of change. In fact, staying put has a plus: it has been a hiatus, allowing us the privilege of feeling settled and at peace.

For years now, a constant in our lives has been "watching the scenery change." But that has taken on a new meaning while frozen in one spot. Instead of views continuously changing because we are sailing past them, the changes here float through, past, and over the scenery itself. We watch changes in temperature, humidity, and the height of the sun and moon superimposed on already beautifully formed majesty. I have come to love watching highlights temporarily gracing craggy landscapes and frozen glacial rapids. And what would I do without being able to keep my eye on Hovgaard's top? It's amorphous bowl-like shape, in itself pleasing, plays continuous tricks with the ambient light. Most often, in soft or low light conditions it appears to glow from within, radiating a muted light of its own, different in hue and intensity than the other snow below or behind it many miles distant on the mainland. It's always intriguing to look at two overlapping landscapes that are actually separated by miles of airspace and figure out how to best capture it on film for the future appreciation of other people in only two dimensions. Lately, Rolf has had to caution me to control my shutter finger to save some film for the summer.

I have more to say to Rolf about staying put. I'm surprised, but I find I have to clear my throat before I start. "Rolf," I begin, "I know it'll sound a little wild, but this year is one cycle, next year's will be different. Maybe next year, a little farther sou . . . ? Well, I may as well just say it: I'd like to stay a second year. We'd really be in synch with this place. We would appreciate things on a deeper level, see if animal behaviors are repeated, how the weather differs, and what it is we start to think about when our thoughts are more our own. The second year would be the more interesting, don't you agree?"

"Oh, Deborah," he answers. "To be honest, I have also entertained the same dream. But realistically, as interesting as it would be to spend two years or five years, we can't do it this time. There will be other trips. Maybe even a return here. Who knows?"

Maybe even a return here. I can't imagine leaving. This experience is so all-encompassing that I can no longer be sure I've ever been anywhere else. We *belong* in a place like this; it's become home. But then, departure is still months away. I tell myself not to think about it; it will only interrupt what's in progress. Enjoy this now.

"Hey Rolf, wanna race?" I ask. He nods. "OK, first one to the rookery on Pléneau!" I shout. Just as I thought, that was guaranteed to get him to laugh. He'll be there an hour ahead of me. But I beat him in Scrabble every time and have to let him win at something!

Race or no race, we have a lot of energy to burn after being cooped inside the boat a couple of days during the last week. The daytime temperatures had hovered around freezing, and twice during the first week of September it actually crept above and rained. The skiing conditions were not the best! So today, we take the opportunity to fly down the hill and continue lickety-split over the ice to the rookery.

Just prior to the rain, we'd been very surprised to see 2,000 gentoos hauled out on the snow at the summer's most popular landing spot. Today we are rewarded with the sight of 500 penguins sitting there. It's still a couple of months until mating season. What penguins actually do over the winter is unknown; observations are scarce. Are they so territorial that they actually like to stay as close to the rookery as possible all year? From what we have seen, they don't seem to go any farther than necessary. But then, why would they?

Many times when we're skiing, I like to drop a couple of hundred yards behind Rolf. That way, I don't hear him or feel his presence, or the snow he kicks up, for that matter. Instead, I get to feel the magnificence of the place. I can pause to look without worrying about the pace. But not today. Today is for the exercise, to exercise myself until I'm really tired, so even on the return trip I stay close on Rolf's heels.

Waxless skis track well going up these little hills, I think to myself, and then I gasp. There's a round blood stain on the snow to our left. Rolf's head is also turned, drawn by the unusual color. We stop dead in our tracks. We hear a low mooing sound. We continue a couple of yards to the crest of the hill and look down. Just 50 feet in front of us are a huge glistening Weddell seal mama and her pup.

The mother is asleep. Neither our noise nor smell arouses her in the slightest. She doesn't stir. But the pup is wide awake and notices us as we notice it. It looks up at us with a face cuter than any stuffed animal manufacturer could ever design: an almost heart-shaped face that sports a wet button nose and quivering whiskers, but that is oh-so dominated by big dark liquid eyes. Even the most hardened heart would melt at this sight.

The little creature must already be at least a day old. It's fur is dry and fluffy. It shows no "dizziness" from the birth procedure. The fur around the mother's teats is compressed and wet so that issue has already been settled. Temperatures in the high teens (around $-7°C$) pose no problem to the pup; it doesn't even have to stay snuggled up to its mother.

The pup is obviously curious as to just who or what we are, so we back off. We most certainly don't want to draw it away from its sleeping mother only to have her wake to a distressing situation. Since we won't play, the pup decides to make a round trip around mountainous Mom. When we came upon the pair, the pup was lying nose to nose with its mother and then turned toward us. The first stop on this circumnavigation is get back face to face, sniff her, and moo. So that's what we heard! The little guy had been trying to get Mom's attention, to make her wake up!

So far, the pup's excursion has been easy. It only had to roll over from looking at us to get back to its mom, but now it wants to move forward. Adult Weddell seals move like inchworms, hunching up, then pushing forward when flattening out. But this little one hasn't developed the needed coordination yet. When it rolled over it caught a flipper under its body and now can't extricate it. Talk about frustration! The seal pup whimpers, flexes, jerks, but nothing happens. Mom wakes up and nudges her pup free. She also sees us. *Uh-oh*, I think. Now what?

She raises her head, looks at us a few seconds without making a sound, puts her head back down on the snow, lows to her pup, and closes her eyes. Talk about blasé!

The pup gets underway, exploring every inch of its mom, sniffing, looking for the teats. They're here somewhere, or so it thinks before it's experienced enough to tell the difference between Mom's back and front. Around Mom's flippers, the pup searches inch-by-inch, its every bone showing through the fur. It looks like it was born in a coat that's a few sizes too big. We find it hard to tear ourselves away, but when the pup finally finds the food source and starts feeding, we decide we should disappear and leave them in peace. We ski some strides away before we talk, through our grins. "Let's call it Sunny," I say. Rolf nods.

"Yow, I didn't expect the mother to be so huge! She looks twice normal size," he says. Both of us know from reference material that seal mothers fast while the pup is suckling, so I respond: "I guess we'll be able to watch Sunny fill out that skin and then some as Mom shrinks back to her normal svelte state. I sure hope the weather holds so we can watch a long time tomorrow. Whaddya say?"

"Of course," answers Rolf. "This is part of the reward for spending the winter. We can bring food and sleeping bags and binoculars and cameras and plunk ourselves down and watch all day if you like."

I smile and sigh. "Rolf," I say, "isn't it grand that we had already decided to not go away on a long trip? Just think if we had missed this! As far as I am concerned, September 8 has just been added onto our permanent birthday cele-bration list."

Four days later, just a few hundred yards from Sunny's nursery, we ski past another mom and pup, only this pup is still wet and the pair are still lying beside the pool of blood. The mom is attending to her newborn pup, licking and nuzzling it, lowing softly. She soon gets the pup moving, inching it away from the birthing scene, knowing that the sheathbills and giant petrels will soon be there to clean up. We ski home, side by side, chattering gleefully. Rolf names this one Cloudy, and so we continue, during the next week, happening on new pups and naming the 4-foot, 50-pound (122-cm, 23-kg) furballs after the weather conditions when we find them: Gray, Windy, and Warm Front.

Although the weather would never lead us to believe that spring has ar-rived, animal behavior does. Beside the pups appearing, the gentoos that heretofore have stayed clustered at the landing spot are spreading out over the rookery. First come, first served, perhaps? The very few visible rocks surfaces are soon staked out, but because there aren't many, the majority of the birds sit on the snow. Some have started courting, bowing to one another. Cormorants and the first few cape pigeons are also back.

Another sign of Antarctic spring—silent and imperceptable, but deadly—is the reappearance of the ozone hole. We're therefore thankful to the men at Faraday who measure ozone levels for putting a message into our mailbox on September 9 alerting us that the ozone has already fallen from the normal 300 Dobson units to 200. With a loss of a third of the protection the ozone normally provides, Faraday's base commander Iain cautions us to diligently protect our skin and eyes from the increased ultraviolet radiation. So far, our faces are the only part of our bodies ever exposed to sunlight. We apply 100 percent sun-block, although its perfumy smell makes us both nauseated. Then the glacier goggles go on. These glasses, which we always use during daylight, have very dark lenses with a reflective coating, UV protection, and side blinders—leather patches—that block out the light reflected off the snow. We don't want to sport cataracts one day as a souvenir of our time spent here.

During a six-day high pressure with its attendant cold (average about 14°F or −10°C) no pups are born. Can the Weddell mothers control when they give birth? It appears so, for as soon as the temperature climbs again to hover around the freezing point out pop five new pups in a twenty-four-hour period! So as not to double weather descriptor names, these in the second batch are called after the geographic locations of their place of birth: Ice Cave, Lake, Glacier, Glacier II, Entrance. There are already so many that we can hardly check up on each one each day to make sure their mothers are treating them "right."

Cloudy's mom, for example, is not living up to the reference books' job description. After we hear the voice of a crying, whining pup, we come upon Cloudy, wet and shivering on the ice with its nose over an open pool of water. Mom is nowhere to be seen. Cloudy inches closer and closer to the water, until its balance is upset and it slithers once again into the water. Poor thing; its downy baby fur isn't meant to get wet and offers no warmth when it is. On its way out of the water, Cloudy notices us and starts squirming in our direction. Perhaps it figures that at least near us it won't be alone, but we back off and head up a slope it can't possibly negotiate. Eventually the mother—who clearly has decided that fasting is not for her—shows her face in the open water and calls for her pup. Cloudy answers in a nonending stream of gurgles and blurts. That seems to be good enough for the mother, and she disappears again. Cloudy is scared, disturbed, call it what you will, and lies shivering at the edge of the water. We stay and watch.

Five, maybe six, minutes later Mom appears again. This time, she sees us and lets out a long, mournful cry, sinks down under water, and then shoots herself up onto the ice to rejoin her pup, who by this time needs her warmth desperately.

Glacier's mom is Cloudy's mom's soul sister. She also abandons her week-old pup and slithers into the water through a tide crack for a feed. When we come upon Glacier, it is whimpering, staring down into the dark pool of water, looking like a drowned rat. The pup eventually has too much weight over the hole and just like Cloudy, bloop! slides in. It doesn't have much energy left and can't get back out. But suddenly, Glacier is launched skyward by an overly enthusiastic nudge from its underwater mother. She also wants to come out. She tries, but can't; the hole's too small. Her girth must have been compressed by the ice's edge when she slid down, into the water, and evidently she can't create the force necessary to do the same thing on her way up and out of the water. Under the watchful eyes of her pup, she starts to enlarge the size of the hole.

The *Encyclopedia Britannica* says that Weddells "gnaw with canine and incisor teeth" to maintain their breathing holes, but Rolf saw one enlarging a perfectly round breathing hole just aft of the boat, and as he described it, the Weddell sunk its canines and front teeth into the ice and propelled itself, both upward and around, so that, spinning like a drill bit, its teeth went through an inch of ice in a matter of seconds.

Glacier's mom, however, has a bigger, odd-shaped hole to work on and she employs another method. She sinks her teeth into the ice and with a sideways sweeping motion grinds away layer after layer. She works on one side, with her pup's nose almost touching hers. Then she sinks down into the water and attempts to squeeze herself up through the hole to get out but is unsuccessful again. She goes to work on the adjoining section, and the next, and the next. Each time she disappears, Glacier slides into the water, but fortunately can get out more easily now that it can use the ramp its mother is forming. The poor little pup is tired and shivering madly. Mom never gives up, but it takes her a half hour of frenetic labor to extricate herself. When she makes it up, we hightail it out of there.

We start to run out of names again. Because the ham operators on the net have enjoyed hearing about the seals, we decide to name pups after them and then to continue with other friends' names. All in all, inside our island group and within skiing distance of the boat, twenty-six Weddell pups are born, all a month earlier than the references led us to expect.

Of course, these pups were not born early; they're born right on time. And although we appreciate researching to anticipate wildlife behavior and schedules, nothing beats watching in situ. Yes, firsthand learning is a pleasure.

We never know what to expect around here from one day to the next. On the night preceding the spring equinox on September 23, we have the coldest ambient temperature so far: $-1°F$ ($-18°C$). Then westerly wind brings the pack ice in *again* toward shore. From the plateau we see ice all the way to the horizon with the exception of one small ice-free zone at the southern end of Lemaire Channel.

The penguins take no chances. They leave the rookery, marching over the ice that formed overnight. You can't blame them. As strong as their desire may be to inhabit the rookery and get on with procreation, they can't afford to expend an excessive amount of energy walking miles each day to get to open water for a feed. On September 25, easterly wind dominates, which pushes the ice offshore again and gives a 37-degree (20 degrees on the Celcius scale) rise in temperature in twenty hours! No gentoos return, however. We interpret their absence as a long-range weather forecast: it's going to remain cold.

On September 26, Rolf calls to me from on deck, "Come check this out!" He wipes his index finger over the snow-free galley hatch and shows me. "It's some kind of dust. And look around on shore," he adds. "There are patches of it everywhere!"

A month ago, the Hudson Volcano in Chile erupted. We've heard amateur radio operators in the Falkland Islands talking about the ash that was dumped on them in the week following the eruption. It was so dark at midday during the fallout that they had to use headlights while driving. The accumulation of ash on the ground made it hard for their sheep to find food. But can this really be the same dust? We suppose it is. Plenty of it could have been circulating in the upper atmosphere these past weeks before swirling down with some weather system.

I fire up my radio and break in on a conversation between England and the Falklands to ask a woman to describe the dust. "It's fine, very abrasive, and somewhere in between a gray and sandy color," she tells me. That perfectly describes what we have. I put a note in Palmer's and Faraday's mailboxes. Faraday replies that they take snow samples on a regular basis to measure levels of radioactive isotopes anyway, so they will look around and take a special sample to send to England for analysis.

We will be long gone by the time they get the answer. But the news from Faraday that they are measuring radioactive fallout here gives me pause. Besides being deeply disturbed, I find it ironic that Rolf and I came all the way to Antarctica's winter wilderness only to draw the conclusion that there is, in fact, no wilderness left on Earth. Considering the natural exchange of air in the atmosphere, and of water in the oceans, and in the freshwater systems, no matter where on Earth humans generate or put their pollution, it eventually spreads out over the entire planet. An example is that ozone depletion in the Antarctic has been proven to be caused, at least in part, by the use of chlorofluorocarbons as a propellant and refrigerant, mostly in the Northern Hemisphere. Shall we rename Brownian motion "brownout in motion"?

Nuclear testing and disposal of radioactive waste is forbidden by the Antarctic treaty. That sounds great, but only member countries are bound by the paper, and some signatories, like the Americans who once set up a nuclear reactor at McMurdo, prefer to interpret the rule rather loosely. Member nations that do keep their testing in the allowed area (that is, north of 60° S) don't have to consider the side effect—fallout inside the treaty area—at least as far as the treaty is concerned. Like the French, who we heard plan to open a nuclear test area on a subantarctic island in the Southern Indian Ocean, all people seem to care about is keeping their testing as far from home as possible. Although humans may be smart enough to understand, harness and use nuclear energy, they lack common sense. It's clear and obvious that nowhere inside the same atmosphere can ever be considered far away. It's myopic and perfectly mad to think otherwise.

Early October is cold. Nighttime between October 3 and 4 we record −6°F (−21°C) and the day after the windchill factor is −22°F (−30°C). When it's time to go skiing, Rolf takes away the piece of insulation under the cupola only to find that the hatch's rubber gasket is frozen to the aluminum frame. We have to wait for it to thaw before we can get out, but meanwhile we get to see the morning light illuminating the swirling frost patterns in the cupola, changing from blues to reds as the sun rises above Anvers Island.

Daylight is increasing by leaps and bounds. Midwinter's little more than two hours of daylight became twelve hours by mid-September, and by the end of this month we'll have twenty-four-hour daylight. Due to longer daylight hours, more *vaks* are opening. We now know where every rock is. That knowledge will come in handy when we sail away; that is, *if* we can sail away. From past statistics, we expected the thickest snow cover in September, but now it seems to be coming in October instead, and the snow that falls on the ice still gets water-saturated and turns to ice. On October 8, both vertical and horizontal distance to open water is more than ever before. Sea ice spans all the way to the horizon and is 7 feet thick (2.1 m) around the boat!

We have a book aboard about a group of men who overwintered 50 miles north of here, on Brabant Island, and while reading it during the winter, we laughed at their not being able to find the fuel for their snowmobiles at this time of year. But the last laugh is on us. . . .

The system for finding our stash has worked all winter: go two ski lengths in a specific bearing from the mooring rope attachment point and dig. It worked as long as there was no more than 3 feet (0.9 m) of snow, but since these latest snowfalls have drifted, they've covered not only the attachment point of our mooring rope but the entire hillside *and* the ice halfway to the boat! It takes us two hours of trial "I think it's here" digging in seven different spots before we hit the blue barrels, 5 feet (1.5 m) below the surface. Ha! I'm reminded once again not to laugh at other people's problems.

During a particularly heavy snowfall, we ski past the seal nursery. Sunny is already grown and has gone. We continue to Pléneau; cormorants fill the summer roost. We arrive at the gentoo rookery, but it's still empty. Oh, well. It was a hard upwind slog here with the wind propelling the soft fine powder horizontally, but the wind will be at our backs on the return trip. We decide to take the high track, up and over Pléneau to get to the slalom hill on the other side. On the slant above the rookery, with just a few yards' visibility, dozens of heretofore invisible penguins suddenly stand up, one after the other, like popcorn popping. They've been totally buried under the snow where they've enjoyed protection from the wind and cold.

Oddly, these gentoos don't flee from us. So far, our experience is that groups of gentoos resting on the ice or snow get skittish and scatter when we come within 75 yards of them. Does their behavior differ today because of the poor visibility or inclement weather, when regrouping could be difficult?

We refer to these small groups of twenty-five to fifty birds as "advance guards." They've been coming and going all September and October while the sea ice has been extensive. But on October 21, a northeast storm hooting and hollering over Booth Island breaks up the ice and the very next day 500 penguins arrive and spread out over the entire rookery. They are here to stay.

There aren't many visible rock surfaces here and there's a rush to claim them. After all, the fastest nest builders get to put down the first eggs. We are rather surprised, however, that the gentoos that don't get rocks aren't sitting together in a big group; instead, they spread out over the entire rookery, looking like lonely sentinels in the snow. We wonder if they are perhaps already positioned "on top of" their old nests? As Rolf remarks, there are no rock contours visible where they have plunked themselves down, yet from having seen the place last summer we know that the entire hillside will eventually be nothing but rocks and pebbles.

To see if our hunch is correct, we choose a couple of birds that sit in snow but close to easily recognizable rocks or contours. Within a few days, as the snow melts from their body heat, the birds sit in hollows that progressively become tubes as deep as 2 feet (61 cm). I don't think they could get out even if they wanted. And, right on! They eventually end up smack dab on nests. How's that for navigation? All that's left for them to do is rearrange the piles of pebbles to personal satisfaction!

Within a week of their arrival, the gentoos begin mating. And once enough pebbles appear for the penguins to fight over and steal from each other, we've come full circle in our visit here.

Compared with other birds, penguins get a late start at nest building and mating. But, naturally, those that can fly over the ice have an advantage. Cormorants, for example, started building their nests around October 9. That day, while we were maintaining the hole in the ice around the rudder, a cormorant flew past us with a strand of seaweed in its beak. We headed directly to the roost after it to look. Sure enough, the building season had started. The air was full of the heavy signature noise of cormorant wings flapping as they came and went.

Cormorant roosts are strategically placed on steep outcrops, favored to facilitate takeoff and landing. But such sites are also exposed, and as we see over the next few weeks, nests have a tendency to be blown away as they are being built. Pairs of birds have an easier time than single ones. One of a pair can dive for seaweed while the other stays and acts as an anchor in the nest, responding to each gust by poking down any strand that works loose and in the meantime scraping up mud (a buildup of dirt and guano) to cement the seaweed in place. Some, try as they might, do not get their nests to stay put, especially those on the perimeter of the roost, but the nests in the more sheltered interior soon take on the shape of a high-sided bathtub.

When it comes to landings, cormorants are not the most sophisticated flyers. They have a hard time touching down where they want, especially in strong wind. In fact, when one is coming in for a landing, it's impossible to predict exactly which nest it's aiming for. There's a wild flapping of wings then a clumsy touchdown and crash landing, often followed by half a takeoff to "jump" a few nests and avoid the hissing neighbors. Finally, the cormorant can pass the treasured seaweed to its mate. The mate quickly pokes it into the place it wants. Then the thank you comes. Their heads weave back and forth on top of long necks, bending in complex curves, like a Balinese dancer's fingers. As we see it, the pair's necks undulating and overlapping in open air look like a moving mobius strip. Their motion is hypnotic.

On October 27, darkness disappears from the Antarctic Circle, not to reappear until February 15. The light is a nice birthday present for Rolf, a.k.a. Mr. Fix-it. He won't have to bother repairing the kerosene lamp chimneys again. Good thing too, as far as our eyes are concerned. The chimneys have cracked and been repaired so many times that they are now more opaque Instaweld than glass.

Twenty-four-hour daylight has us mentally and physiologically poised at winter's end, but any ideas about sailing are still on ice. *Northern Light* is firmly ensconced in a 6-foot-thick (1.8 m) molded cradle. The average temperature remains below freezing and the snow still accumulates. Fresh snow has covered the dust patches. That's good as far as we're concerned. Dirty snow absorbs seven times more heat than clean snow does and would therefore soon melt, ruining our ski trails to the birds. It now seems that our guesses made back on midwinter's day that we'd be in open water by late November were very wrong indeed. How exciting!

Sunlight means that krill production has started again. We know it for a fact: first, because the little shrimplike creatures have come into the sink when we pump salt water to do dishes, and second, because the minke whales are back! We heard, then sighted, two on October 14 in Penola Strait.

Sunlight gives shadows, something the locals don't seem to understand very well. They don't seem to understand what ropes are either. While tending our lines, digging them out of last "night's" drifting snow, I see two Adélies on their bellies, working their way up the channel. I alert Rolf of their presence. When they get to the rope, which sags almost to the snow's surface, they don't know what to make of it; it resembles nothing they know. They stop, stand, look left, look right. They lie down again and wait. Maybe it'll go away? Nope. They stand up. Finally, they decide it would be better to jump over the rope than go under it. Within a microsecond of each other, they launch their bodies up and away! Their bellies clear, but they don't have their technique together— that is, they don't flip belly up at the highest point of their trajectory—ooops! both birds catch their long toenails on the rope. Used to being graceful, they are both discombobulated by the experience. Rolf consoles them: "Don't worry guys, you made it. That's more important than style." As if encouraged, they stand up and continue. But then they come to the rope's shadow.

Both birds put on the brakes and come to a full stop. Nothing in their genetic material, training, or experience has prepared them for this. They don't know what to make of the shadow and can't decide how to negotiate it, especially after the last fiasco. I guess their pride has been wounded; they decide not to even try to jump "over" it. They turn and walk all the way to the shadow's end before turning back onto their original course.

Speaking of shadows, Rolf has turned into a real Scrabble aficionado over the winter and has improved faster than I ever would have guessed. He zoomed through the first barrier, breaking 200 points, and today, he scrabbled, on his first turn no less. Not to be outdone, I responded in kind. I can't believe it!

And I am the shadow of my mother, the champion Scrabble player in my family. I know she'd have loved being in on this game. I tell Rolf, "Wait till Mom hears about this!" We can't call her exactly, but in my bubbly mood I have to tell someone. Before I even think about what I'm doing, I raise Palmer on the VHF radio and tell the radio operator what happened. In his unflappable professional radio voice, Ajo answers, "Well, I guess you can stop playing now."

We chuckle and continue our game. Little do I know, but the worst is yet to come, history is about to be made. Rolf beats me! I congratulate him, pump his hand, and then reiterate Ajo's words: "I guess we can stop playing now."

23

EVEN
MORE
BIRTHDAYS

ROLF

■ ■ ■

While I've been digging out the ice around the rudder, Deborah has taken a ski trip over to Pléneau Island. She comes flying back, and between shallow breaths says to me: "Rolf, there's a track in the snow that looks like nothing we've ever seen before. The part I saw starts at the Narrows and continues all the way up and over Oleg Island. I'm going to follow it. Want to come along?"

I put on my skis and join her. Up on the crest of a 120-foot (40-m) ridge on the eastern side of Oleg Island we intersect the track. It is patterned, so it's not a Weddell seal's. Theirs is almost always smooth and shiny, and besides, Weddell seals never travel this high up on land. The track is far too wide to be from a fur seal. It is certainly not an elephant seal's. . . .

The elephant seals' track we saw in midwinter were sometimes so wide that Deborah and I could ski next to each other in one and still plant our ski poles inside its outermost edge. The mammoth concave tracks were very smooth and had parallel marks outside them that looked like oar strokes, which were actually made by an elephant seal as it dug its flippers into the snow. To move on land, the hind half of its body was dragged forward as it raised its back into an arch. Then the seal threw its chest forward as far as possible and took a new stroke. Despite the mighty effort and huffing and puffing it took to move its bulk along, an elephant seal would often shuffle as far as 400 to 500 yards, up to heights where it could then rest undisturbed.

The track we see today indicates that the seal that made it moves in a completely different way. This seal hasn't left any imprints from foreflippers. It snakes its way forward. The track's outer contour is straight, but a rhythmic and beautiful overlay of a zigzag pattern made by its hind flippers spreads out past the edges of the track. Most likely, this is the track of a crabeater seal; that is, after all, the only track we've never seen yet.

It's apparent that this seal has an easy time traveling over land. Downhill it has glided as we would have on skis. It also had a clear idea where it was heading and is a real long-distance traveler. We realize this when we see how its track disappears over the thin ice to Entrance Island and straight up a 300-yard-long and very steep snowfield where Deborah and I would have needed climbing skins. If anyone truly has waxless skis, it's the crabeater.

To our delight, we spot two crabeater seals the next day resting on the ice only a hundred yards in front of the boat. The female's fur is a light cream color with a touch of silver. Were not the snow in Antarctica whiter than any other place on Earth, it actually would have been difficult to spot her. The male's fur is longer than the female's, and because it's mottled gray, he is easy to see. His neck looks like that of a poodle-clipped sheep.

Compared with the female, the male looks very rough and worn out. He has many scars and wounds, some of which are still bleeding. He must fight a lot with other males. But now, both are sleeping sweetly. The female lies stretched out in the snow; next to her lies the male, with his head resting on top of her "shoulder." They look like lovers should look in spring.

By examining their tracks, we determine that it was the female's Deborah discovered yesterday. Today, each made their way to their meeting point from opposite sides of our channel. Somehow, they had decided to meet here. Perhaps they wanted to be alone. It's hard to say. But why not? The other crabeaters are still on the pack ice farther out at sea.

Continuing around our ski territory, we come to a flat rock on the northern side of Oleg Island where we often eat our picnic lunch. But today, the sunny, warm spot is already occupied by five of this year's Weddell seal youngsters. They now live on their own. Here, as well as everywhere on Earth, the "teenagers" have gathered in the spring sun at their favorite hangout. Apparently the rock is their equivalent to a street corner or pizza parlor. It's thought-provoking to see what similar needs all animals have.

Each passing day, the ice becomes more porous and unreliable. Our ski territory is shrinking. Because we don't know how much longer our iceways will last, we take advantage of the lengthening daylight and are usually away from the boat ten to twelve hours at a time. On our way home the evening of November 7, while still several kilometers from *Northern Light*, we are shocked to notice that the masts are tilting forward, very far forward. Something is wrong.

Any tiredness immediately vanishes. With our hearts in our mouths, we speed up. When we eventually get close enough to see the hull, we realize that the bow has been pulled down so far that less than half of the topsides are visible.

While we have been gone, the tide has gone down almost 10 feet (3 m), 3 feet (0.9 m) more than any previous time. The result is that the bottom of the ice now rests on a rock two boat lengths ahead of the boat. The ice has cracked there and a piece of ice as big as the boat is standing on its edge. That ice block has pinned down our anchor chain, and that, in turn, is pulling down the bow.

The anchor chain is stretched almost to its breaking point. We have to feed out more chain, and quickly! To our dismay, the capstan will not turn. It sits to one side of the windlass, and the tremendous load has bent the shaft. Within seconds we tie three different ropes to the anchor chain, all forward of the windlass. We then lead each rope to a different winch. Cranking, we load each one as much as we dare. When we have successfully managed to release some load from the windlass, we use a sledge hammer and our biggest screwdriver to hit the capstan. It finally gives, and we can feed out more chain. Whew!

It really would not have mattered if we had not had more chain to feed out; the end of the chain is *not* shackled directly to the steel structure inside. Instead, it is secured to the boat via a piece of rope that is long enough to allow the last link of the chain to come up above the deck. That means that we can add more chain or rope whenever we want, or (after tying a buoy to the end of the chain) cut the rope and let the anchor chain go in an emergency.

Still, the experience gives us thought. Had a different ice situation made it possible for us to undertake the six-week ski journey, we would have been gone now. This episode could have ended in disaster.

Each day more species of birds return. The Antarctic tern, which stayed a little north of us the entire winter, is back. We also see, or more often hear, the Arctic tern. Its nerve-wracking, high-pitched screech overpowers practically all other sound.

What a fantastic long-distance flier the Arctic tern is. Every year it migrates between the northern and southern polar regions' summers. Because of that, it lives almost its entire life in daylight. Only when it passes through the Tropics, on its long journey of 8,000 nautical miles does it experience darkness.

The skua has also arrived. We actually saw the first one back on October 31, and now, any time we reach a high ridge or point that they claim, we are attacked. The skua often sits on a snow-free rock. As soon as one spots us trespassing, it takes flight, usually long before we have spotted it. The skua is a master strategist. Whenever possible, it attacks with the sun at its back, knowing that the "enemy" will have difficulty seeing it against the light. When we're outside we must remain extremely aware. Skuas arrive so fast that if we aren't paying close attention, we only hear a sudden short whoosh before getting hit in the head.

The bird attacks with its feet. After one knocked my hat off, we took to protecting ourselves by holding one ski pole over our heads any time we see one. We pull the pole away just before the bird reaches us. But it is a tiring game, at least for us. No skua ever gives up until we and our sore arms have left its domain.

Each skua, or skua pair claims a territory for the nesting season and defends it around the clock. When another skua enters the airspace, a fight ensues. In an attack or escape maneuver, skuas can fly at speeds exceeding 60 mph (100 km/hr). If it's a calm day, we can hear the special whining sound that that speed creates from more than 500 yards away.

The South Polar skua isn't only a fast flier, it's also an incredible long-distance flier. In April when they leave the Antarctic Peninsula and cross Drake Passage, some of them follow the west coast of South America and others the east coast to continue north. Some make it all the way to Greenland, others to British Columbia or Japan, before returning here.

From what we saw when we visited Palmer Station, the skua can also be tamed, especially if fed when it's young. Perhaps it was such a bird that landed on our deck last Thursday while we were eating dinner. It walked around in repetitive circles, pecking on one Plexiglas hatch after another. "It wants to come in. It must smell the food. Perhaps it migrated to Sweden this last winter where it cultivated a taste for Thursday's pea soup," Deborah suggested, laughing. Although the skua didn't get any food from us, it stayed for two hours. We appreciated the visit, but the bird probably thought we were the most inhospitable people it had ever met.

The number of blue-eyed cormorants in the roost are also increasing. On November 16, the first cormorant of the approximately 250 birds inhabiting the colony has two eggs in its nest. On the same day, one out of every ten gentoo penguins also has eggs. The birds don't seem to care that it is cloudy and either snowing or raining most of the time. Of course, they are well adapted. But we visitors aren't, and there's no way to stop our clothes and ski boots from getting soaked every outing.

We do our best to not get bothered by the discomfort. But something that really *does* bug us is that none of the birds' spring activities can be documented. Our second video camera has also failed. The breakdown came as no surprise, but it has us feeling down nonetheless.

The gloomy weather and the breakdown are not the only things that make November a dark month. On the last day of October, I injured my right eye while digging out the oil barrels from under 7 feet (2.5 m) of snow. It was quite dark at the bottom of the pit, so I took off my sunglasses while I hacked away at what was most ice. In the process, a sliver of ice ricocheted and hit my eye.

At first I thought that the cornea had been scratched and therefore expected it to heal in a couple of days. But the pain increased instead, and I had to assume the injury must be something more serious. Perhaps a small piece of the shovel's aluminum had lodged at the outer rim of the iris; there was an ulcerated spot there.

As long as I was inside the pain wasn't too difficult to deal with, but outdoors it hurt like snow blindness. Whenever the light became bright, I had to double up my sunglasses, but that made it hard to ski. A couple of days later, I tried a black patch over the injured eye, but with only one eye functioning, I lost depth of field. So I went back to two pairs of sunglasses.

When my eye didn't seem to improve after the first week, we radioed the doctor at Palmer Station. He advised Deborah to take a syringe needle and use its scooped edge to scrape the ulcer away. If there was indeed an aluminum splinter in it, it would then be gone, too. He agreed that it could be painful. And even if it bled, Deborah should continue scraping until she came to a harder surface, but not deeper.

After the conversation Deborah and I discussed if we really should go ahead with the "eye surgery." A major problem was that we didn't have any anesthesia other than snow blindness eyedrops. Without something stronger, we felt there was a high risk that I wouldn't be able to hold still enough. Deborah was also concerned that she may not be able to properly discern when she should stop scraping. She voted against trying.

For a while I entertained the idea of performing the procedure myself. I figured that I'd be able to judge better than Deborah what was happening and therefore be able to stop when the pain became too great, before I recoiled, I hoped. On the minus side, I would have to work using a mirror. I was concerned about having difficulty judging the distance between the needle and the eye correctly or having the mirror fog up.

That plan ended up being just an exercise in thought. Deborah, who knows better than to disturb me when I have a smart idea, didn't say anything until I had decided not to try. Then she said that she thought that the idea was idiotic. Yeah, maybe.

What worries us most is that my eye may not heal before we start sailing. Getting salt water in it will really hurt and so will wind blowing on it. Wearing ski goggles or a diving mask is no solution because as soon as those get splashed, they're impossible to see through. One missed handhold in Drake Passage could be catastrophic.

It's now two weeks since the incident happened and the pain has not eased in the slightest. Even so, it looks like there is some hope. Today I noticed that some blood vessels have started to grow from the white of the eye into the cornea toward the ulcer, and a haze has developed over the area. We figure that when the blood vessels reach or surround the ulcer, my body may take care of dissolving the metal piece. At least that's the self-healing capacity we hope for.

There is plenty of time to wait. *Northern Light* still sits in snow up to deck level, and it's clear we won't be getting underway before New Year's.

Despite the pain, I refuse to remain inside. Deborah, who's back hardly bothers her at all anymore, leads the way around Pléneau Island to inspect the bird colonies. Nearing the gentoo penguins, we see an interesting behavior we've never seen before. It is performed by two adult penguins standing next to each other in the snow, nowhere near any nest. Suddenly, one starts to beg for food from the other. In the same manner as a chick begs, one adult taps its beak against the other's and soon thereafter is indeed fed. Then the beggar walks full circle around the "parent." The procedure is repeated a total of five times. We wonder what the behavior means.

On November 26, the first cape pigeon arrives. We see it sleeping on a rock just a few yards away from the blue-eyed cormorants. We have never seen cape pigeons except at sea. When we passed the convergence on the way down here, groups of ten to twenty birds flew circles around the boat. Sometimes they stopped midair and looked at us, but they never came very close. I always thought they were black with white patches, but now I see that they are brown and white. Each day, I learn something new.

During the entire month of November, we only see the sun for a total of four hours. But just as if to leave us with a little brighter impression, it shows itself at noon on the very last day of the month. As this is the first time since the middle of October that the snow has sunk so far that the topsides are visible again, the sunshine is very timely. For the entire winter, the diffuse blue-gray light made the boat look purplish brown. When the now high-in-the-sky sun strikes the hull, the boat looks redder than we remember. The bright color is an unreal contrast to the white snow.

But the snow is not white everywhere. There are areas where the volcanic fallout has surfaced after being covered for two months. The dust certainly makes skiing interesting. Whenever we come out on a large brown patch, it's like suddenly hitting a newly sanded road. Because the dirty patches are either wet or saturated, we sink down to our boot tops, if we are lucky. When we fall, our arms disappear into the muck and we become quite messy all the way up to our elbows. The only thing we find that the mush *is* good for is snowball battles.

In tonight's dinner preparation, we use the last onion. There are only five potatoes left. That our supplies are coming to an end gives us the feeling that we've been here for a long time. It's almost an omen, because the next day, summer arrives without warning, exactly as it always does in the high latitudes. The sudden shift from below-freezing temperatures to shoveling out the shore lines shirtless is indescribable!

The sun shines for five days in the longest continuous period of clear weather since June. It's warm and nice, but we also welcome the summer for another reason: it is the time of the year when the ozone layer recovers. Had the ozone hole lasted just one more month, I don't believe that we'd have had any outer garments left. The cotton in our jackets has been particularly weakened.

The fact that materials deteriorate due to overexposure to ultraviolet rays leads me to think about my eye not healing. It has already been two weeks since the blood vessels reached the sore, but nothing has improved. Scientists have proved that too much UV light hinders or halts cell development in plankton, so perhaps too much UV is also the reason the healing in my eye hasn't started. I put the black patch on again. Three days later the pain is completely gone.

I can't tell for sure if the "blackout" allowed the wound to heal in the time it should have taken from the start or not. But it is certainly scary that international agreements still allow the use of chlorofluorocarbons, which we know precipitate the ozone depletion.

This year's final ozone statistics are that on October 15, the ozone density dropped to its lowest value, 147 Dobson units, or half of what it should be. At that time we were exposed to thirteen times more UV than we are in Sweden on a sunny summer day. Or perhaps I should say "should have been exposed to." Now the Northern Hemisphere is developing an ozone hole as well.

In the beginning of December, while we are sitting on deck with a cup of evening tea, Deborah hears a very deep, low-frequency pulsating sound and climbs the mast. When she reaches the lower spreader, she tells me that a cruise ship is steaming out of Lemaire Channel. I hear how disappointed she becomes. "Oh, Rolf, our honeymoon has just ended," she says sadly. I feel the same rather melancholy reaction.

The first trip that Deborah and I did together—sailing from Sweden to the pack ice north of Spitsbergen and then to Antarctica and back—was actually a declaration of love from my side. I wanted to give her something that she most likely would never have been able to experience otherwise. But during that voyage, and especially at the beginning, I was often forced to ask far more of Deborah than she ever thought she would be able to accomplish. Because she was so unused to being at sea, she often suffered much more than I, both physically and mentally. The life we lived wasn't nearly as romantic as folks probably thought.

Not until much later did I realize that a more gentle treatment of my wife wasn't perhaps such a bad idea and that there were better presents to give her than sandpaper and varnish. It was then that I suggested that we should sail back to the Antarctic Peninsula, let the boat freeze into the ice, and have our honeymoon. We have, and we're both thankful. It's just that the peace could have lasted a little longer.

Three days later, we see another cruise ship. This time we raise them on the VHF radio. Captain Aye proudly tells us that his ship, *Frontier Spirit*, is specially built for cruising ecologically fragile areas. A rather small ship, it can take 164 passengers. But because the first trip of the season is only filled to 15 percent of capacity, it feels rather deserted on board. He's doing all he can to spice up the twenty-six lives in his care. He asks if we would consider coming aboard to entertain the passengers.

Taken by surprise, neither of us knows what to say. But then I tell the captain that we decided long ago that we would not go aboard any ships this summer. We haven't been around any other people for eight months. His passengers have come from all over the world, and there's no telling what kind of infectious illnesses they may be carrying. We'd hate to end up like Greenland and Canadian Inuits who always got sick after they had been on board the first ship of the season.

Perhaps Captain Aye is not used to thinking about his passengers as walking germ boxes. At any rate, he changes the subject. He asks some questions about our winter and how it was. But then I understand that he hasn't given up his idea of a visit. He asks when we last had a fresh apple or a tomato, and without turning the conversation over to us for an answer, continues by promising that we will get a whole box full of fresh food as a thank you for our visit if we would only come out and tell everyone about our winter. In the end, we acquiesce, if for no other reason than it will certainly be interesting to meet Captain Aye! We feel we can limit the risk of being infected by keeping our distance from other people. After all, there aren't many of them.

We ski to the edge of our ice, where we are fetched and ferried out to the ship. To meet people so suddenly and unexpectedly is strange, to say the least. We hold a short spontaneous lecture, telling why we wanted to spend the winter here, what our intentions were, and how we perceived our stay. Most listeners sit perfectly still and stone-faced. We can't tell if they are bored or shocked, but when we are finished, silence prevails. No one has any questions for us. As a matter of fact, no one even moves.

The ship is about to turn north. That means that the passengers are almost on their way back home. Maybe they have seen enough ice. Perhaps they would never want to spend more than a week or so here themselves, so they don't have anything to ask. One woman finally speaks. But when she asks us if we had actually planned to stay the winter, I don't know where to start. Haven't we just explained that? Deborah and I look at each other, and under my breath I say, "Maybe we are skinnier than we think." Our dumbfounded silence lingers. None of the other guests says anything either. Eventually, Deborah simply confirms that we did indeed plan to winter. Our first meeting with other people is odd, to say the least.

Captain Aye comes to take us to eat lunch. While walking for what seems forever, through umpteen corridors, we talk about fuel consumption and compare numbers. When his ship is fully booked for a nine-day cruise, it uses the same amount of diesel per passenger that the two of us will burn over a period of sixteen months.

The dining area is huge and open and has windows all around. How unsettling it is to look out and all of a sudden see the mainland loom so closely. How weird it feels to be moving. And I can't get used to looking at faces other than Deborah's! So it goes when a frozen perspective thaws.

And yes, Captain Aye is a man of his word. When we leave the ship, he presents us with an entire carton of delicacies. The next day we have bacon, lettuce, and tomato sandwiches for lunch. To the day, it is one year since we left civilization. To really celebrate the anniversary, we also scramble four eggs from our "Don Carlos supply." The one-year-old eggs still taste just like fresh eggs. It's unbelievable. All we did was leave them in their cartons on the shelf in the passageway to the aft cabin, where the temperature has been between 23° and 41°F (−5° to +5°C).

In mid-December the melt really gets underway. Each day there is more open water between the hull and the ice. The number of really big cracks is also increasing, and for each passing day, there is less ice that bears our weight.

Up on Hovgaard's first plateau, so much meltwater has collected that what was once a valley is now a small lake. For weeks the snow holds the water back, but when the dam breaks one night, enormous amounts of water come rushing down the slope toward our channel. There is never any danger to the boat, but in the morning we see that the landscape a couple hundred yards astern is completely changed. Land contours that we haven't seen for nine months have surfaced again, and some of the ice in the channel is gone. It can only be a question of days before we no longer can ski on the ice. We wish we didn't have to sleep.

Midsummer day, December 22, we discover that some of the cormorant nests have chicks. We only see five small heads but think we hear more peeping. The ones we can see seem to be between one and three days old. The older ones have already become strong enough to hold their heads up in the air and harass their parents for some food. It seems to be very important that the young birds get strong neck muscles as soon as possible because it can take many minutes before some parents even respond. We can't tell if it's the more experienced parents that wait and the first-time parents that spoil their chicks, or vice versa, but there certainly is no end to the youngsters' demanding.

The smallest cormorant chicks seem absolutely helpless. Their heads seem to be unproportionally large; they can't even manage to hold their heads up long enough to work their way out from under the feathers of their parent's wing. They just lie there hidden, peeping, getting less food than their older siblings.

On December 25, gentoo penguins have chicks. The first we see are "twins." They must have hatched at almost the same time, and it must have been recently. Without any trace of feathers, both are completely dependent on their parent's warmth. Two days later, of the 900 nests that exist on the northern side of Pléneau Island, one in ten has at least one chick. The sound in the colony is unmistakable. A very hoarse-sounding *a . . . a . . . a . . . Ahh . . .* is repeated without pause. I close my eyes. Like time has stood still, it could just as well be one year ago when we arrived at Cuverville Island.

Each day we spend as much time as we can visiting both the gentoo penguin and the cormorant rookeries. The more we learn about their behavior, the more we come to understand that each bird has its own temperment and behavior. Some parents treat their offspring with kindness; others seem to be more nervous and irritated, especially when the chicks are begging for food. It was the same with the Weddell seals. Some mothers stayed with their pups the whole time they were suckling and made sure they always slept close to their pups so that the young could get shelter from the wind when necessary. Other mothers carried on as if they had no responsibility. Just like people, each animal is obviously an individual with its own unique behavior and needs.

This is the first time in my life that I have had the possibility to study wild birds and animals so closely. The contrast between those I see here in the wild and those I have seen in zoos suddenly becomes so apparent that I start to wonder what right humans have to deprive animals of their freedom.

The first zoo ever to open to the public was in Vienna in 1752. At that time in Europe, one still had the right to buy and sell people as slaves. Before we developed the concept of humane treatment of people, it's no surprise that there was no thought given to decent treatment of animals.

Recent research erases some of the boundaries we have long maintained separate us from all other animals. Apes, although they can't speak, do understand language. They and other animals use tools and have emotions. I don't think that anyone can disagree with the statement that animals removed from their family groups and deprived of their natural habitat, to be confined in zoos and parks, suffer. Or the statement that all too many die in transport. Although those are reasons enough to challenge the existence of zoos, there is another concept to consider as well, one that pertains to the human visitor.

It is often said that a visit to a zoo is educational. Yes, but what is learned there? The frightening thing is that people who take their own freedom for granted bring children to look at animals living in unnatural, undignified conditions. That some animal parks today keep animals in larger spaces than in the past makes no difference. A child learns that our culture still reserves the right to deny other life forms their freedom. Accepting that as a norm can lead to another cruel behavior. From not showing respect to animals because they look different to acting with cruelty toward people who look different from oneself is certainly not a big jump.

Abolishing slavery has been considered human's first step into civilization. Why not walk farther?

"Rolf!" Deborah's voice interrupts my thoughts, and I look in the direction she's pointing. About 3 miles south in Penola Strait, something immediately catches my eye. Even though the object isn't wider than a strand of hair when held at arm's length, or higher than the width of a matchstick, the manmade object stands out clearly from the scenery. It's a sailboat mast.

Slowly but surely the stick grows taller. After half an hour, the boat has come so close that the people on board spot us sitting on shore. One of them jumps into the dinghy and comes rowing frantically toward us. Halfway to us, he starts yelling, "Hello, Rolf! Hello, Deborah! Won't you join us for lunch?"

"Sure!" we answer in unison, and when he reaches the shoreline, we jump into the dinghy and he rows us out to the boat. On its stern is the name *Teake Hadewych*. The people introduce themselves as Eerde and Hedwig from Holland and their Canadian guest, Richard. They have just visited Faraday and have been asked to deliver a present to Deborah and pass along regards from the cook. We look at them dubiously.

The reason for our confusion is that, during one of the first radio contacts we had with Faraday, Deborah really put her foot in her mouth, at least as far as the cook was concerned. Now, not sure if this is some kind of a joke, she opens the package anyway and sees that, among other things, it includes two rolls of English McVities Digestive biscuits. Deborah and I chuckle, then she tells the story.

During a conversation with Gavin, the radio operator, she asked him where he was from. Hearing that his hometown was Edinburgh, Deborah mentioned that we had been to Scotland in 1986 and transited the Caledonia Canal. She didn't hesitate to tell him how pleasantly surprised we were when we found delicious food in Scotland, considering how tasteless—well, actually, disgusting—we think food is in England.

Toward the end of the conversation, Deborah asked if they might have a recipe for Digestive biscuits, which we think is the exception from the above-mentioned rule. "I'll ask," responded Gavin, tittering. "The cook, who is here with me in the radio room, is from England." Absolutely aghast and ashamed for probably having hurt his feelings, Deborah had a short exchange with the cook, who promised to look for a recipe. But, of course, none ever appeared in our mailbox. Opening the package of Digestives, Deborah laughs. She knows she is being teased and she knows she deserves it.

The gift package also includes six large Cadbury chocolate bars, which we understand must be from Kevin, and a bottle of rum, which is great! As we explain to our hosts, our vanilla extract is almost gone. To make new extract, we can pour this rum over the vanilla beans we bought in Tahiti back in 1983. In five months the extract will be ready to use.

I turn to Deborah and say, "But he who waits for something good, cannot wait too long, eh?" Nodding, she faces Faraday and yells out, "Thanks lads!" By her expression I can tell she thinks it's nice to put the faux pas behind her.

24

THE ICE
COMETH
NOW?

DEBORAH

■ ■ ■

Three heads poke up above the crest of the hill on Oleg Island. Then down schuss three purple-and green-jacketed people, shouting, "Allo! Bonne Année! Happy New Year!"

Although we've been expecting them, and even though they're not the first people we've seen, as unaccustomed as we still are to having humans as part of this scenery the sight of them is a pleasantly shocking, colorful experience.

The trio has come from the 135-foot French schooner *Antarctica*. The ultramodern aluminum ship, its walnut shell–shaped hull designed to pop up if caught in pack ice, is anchored 5 miles away at Port Charcot, where a French television crew is filming a segment for a twelve-hour series. From the anchorage, Criquet, Hélène, and Eric have ferried themselves in a dinghy to the edge of our ice and then skied the final few miles in our tracks to bring us two replacement video cameras that have been sitting at Palmer Station.

Bill, the ornithologist for whom we've been logging bird sightings, was kind enough to bring one camera with him from the United States. It has been sitting at Palmer "only" 25 miles away since before the second camera even broke. Oh well. When the second died, Robin, a marine biologist, was "volunteered" to bring the second replacement. *Antarctica,* the first yacht to visit Palmer this season, was—luckily for us—heading this way, and the crew was kind enough to help us out.

One of our visitors is Eric, a deck hand on *Antarctica*. He expresses his surprise that our boat looks so good after the winter. We are surprised too in a way; we had expected the four-year-old paint to have faded to rose or pink by now and the waterline at least to have been scraped away by the ice. But the two-part polyurethane paint, made by the Danish company Hempls, is tough as can be. The boat is still candy apple red and shiny, and the waterline is nearly intact. We smile our pleasure as well as our thanks and invite our visitors in.

Criquet, an expert in polar history, is the project leader for the series being filmed here for French educational TV. His eye is immediately drawn to the old texts in our bookshelf, and though he can't understand Swedish or Norwegian, he caresses the leather-bound volumes and pages through them during his entire visit, looking at drawings and photos. He asks Rolf to teach him how to pronounce "Nordenskiöld," the Swedish polar explorer's name.

Ah, but we are creatures of habit. I find myself watching our visitors the way I'm used to watching other animals. Sliding into a reverie, I remain as still as possible while examining a face, a hand, a movement. The result is that I often lose track of what it is they're saying. The mere sight of other human faces and their expressions is captivating, and the emotional pleasure of encountering my own species is heightened by the novelty that such a simple, normal meeting can feel so foreign. To add to the confusion, we are not only *allowed* to interact with them, we are expected to! Yes, I can see that we have entered a new phase of this experience: a curious, tickling adjustment as we come out of seclusion.

Hélène is the cook for the thirteen people on board. She has brought a New Year's present she's made for us: chocolate truffles. That goes straight to the heart! To warm up our visitors after their excursion, we treat them to a Swedish specialty they've never had before: blueberry soup. And as a thank you for the link they provided between us and Palmer, I have baked for them. Hélène carries home the biggest loaf of braided egg bread ever baked in our oven and a baker's dozen of Chinese sesame cookies, one for each person on *Antarctica*. Eating the cookie guarantees that the coming year will be lucky. It's a tradition Rolf and I have that will from this day on be twinned with chocolate truffles.

After they leave, we tear into the packages. From no cameras to two cameras. Rolf raises his eyebrows. "Do we dare try them?" he asks. "Do we dare not?" I counter. Within minutes we know that everyone in the transport chain has been careful. Both cameras work.

It took three skiers to transport two cameras because that's not all that's been sent. Friends at Palmer have also included presents. One is a recent—well, recent enough—news magazine. Its cover is a montage. Each and every minute detail of it is of the greatest interest, but the jammed clutter assaults us. In fact, that cover and the full-page ad on the back are all our nervous systems can handle the first day. After all, they represent other peoples' creativity and display color, plus information and new images. And, of course, we need to discuss every nuance.

Later, I write a note of thanks to Ajo, in part saying, "It's been quite an experience to thumb through a magazine, when no longer conditioned to them. The ads blare so, they keep us from the news. Color! Pizzazz! What are those Joneses up to? I'm sure that when I'm used to the ads, I don't pay so much attention to them. Or do I?"

Packed with the cameras is mail, including a batch of pictures of the three newest additions to our family: granddaughter Emma, nephew Sam, and niece Elena. We look through the photos umpteen times. The children all look beautiful to us: healthy and full of expression. There's also a stack of drawings made by children in my nieces' fourth-and sixth-grade classes after they read our first book. My father sent an article about six men who recently dogsledded across the whole of the Antarctic continent, a 220-day, 3,741-mile jaunt.

The next day, one of the supermen from that very article steps off the page and onto our ice. Jean-Louis Etienne, sports medicine specialist from Paris who skied alone to the North Pole before becoming one of the six-man crew to traverse Antarctica successfully and is now the narrator for the French TV series, is coming to visit us! We are flattered, to say the least.

Before we left on this trip, I made Rolf promise me that upon our arrival he would not even think of asking me to ski to the South Pole. Yes, it was said in jest, but knowing Rolf, also to make things very clear. So my hat goes off to Jean-Louis and his teammates for the sheer determination they must have to accomplish such a feat. To arrive at the finish line before the onset of winter, they were forced to start from the northern tip of the Antarctic Peninsula on July 28 and travel all August and September along the peninsula, months I now know are storm-filled beyond description. No matter how long Rolf and I were out during those days, no matter how cold or wet we got, we came back to a dry and, soon, warm boat. Jean-Louis and his teammates were out slogging against wind and driving snow, and at the end of each day they took shelter from hurricane-force winds in tents that were cold and worse: damp.

Yet, as it always is with amazing physical accomplishments, Jean-Louis explains that the toughest part was mental. He tells us that during the seven months a-ski, he not only ran out of memories to mull over, he even ran out of things to think about. Monotony became his prison, yet he skied on. What people *can* accomplish is amazing. Think, dream, plan, execute. Anything is possible.

Partway into their trip, after struggling for 138 days to arrive at the southern axis of Earth, Jean-Louis was dismayed to see flags flying: one for each treaty member nation and, at the pole itself, the American Stars and Stripes, an odd statement as he saw it because Americans have specifically not claimed any of Antarctica. Jean-Louis had experienced enough of the continent already to understand and know that the bitter cold heartland of the Antarctic interior is not mankind's place. He asked that the flags be removed. People tittered uncomfortably, hoping he was joking, but he was not. And he told them: "Flags do not belong here. And I'm sorry, but the world does not turn around the United States."

He and his five teammates, each from a different country, had as a goal to accomplish an exceedingly arduous task, but not just for the sake of their own selfish reasons. Jean-Louis tells us that to finish, they had to believe that they were accomplishing something that others could benefit from. In part, they wanted to draw the public's eye to Antarctica, to interest populations enough that they would convince their governments to drop their partisan interests and offer Antarctica to the world.

The sun seems to think that it showed itself enough during the month of December. The gray is back. The fog steals the yellow light to which we have become accustomed, swallowing it and leaving us blue. *It's downright bluetiful*, I think to myself as we're skiing Entrance Island's long sloping back with Booth Island's cockscomb ridge towering smack dab ahead of us. Booth's immensity dwarfs us, giving the impression of skiing without gaining any ground. If I'm not careful, I could probably ski the smooth slope watching the light play on Booth and fall off the edge on the other side. It's that beautiful.

Oh, how I wish that a wish could come true for every time I've said or thought *beautiful* while we've been here. Is it possible that we humans have an intrinsic need for beauty? That we find peace and satisfaction in looking at natural shapes, forms, or designs that we perceive as beautiful? Don't we mirror beauty; aren't we actually nicer when there's beauty around us? If there's a plane of life I experience out in nature that I wish everyone could experience, it is the simple happiness, or contentedness, of sinking into beautiful.

People certainly create oases of beauty, but for each oasis there are who knows how many abominations. We've come so far from the umbrella principle itself—of having the energizing, seemingly conflicting combination of comfort and stimulation of natural unadjusted scenes around us—that I think we've become accustomed to the beating we take from ugliness. Some people will oppose my opinion, arguing that cities are beautiful. They will tell me that they can look at what's messy without seeing it, just like I thought I could look past the ads in magazines. Knowing that we humans can be so easily conditioned to the point that we believe in the untrue fills me with a quaking sadness. Fooling ourselves means never questioning, never examining, which in turn means never looking for solutions.

The fog swirls out of Lemaire Channel and licks Booth Island's highest contours. We know it's one of our very last skiing days around the archipelago, and we both just simply must watch the thick steam stream for a while. That

Rolf and I share the same wavelength means no decision has to be negotiated. The pulka is soon unpacked and the tent set up to give a modicum of shelter from the damp wind. We lie on our tummies with our heads outside the flaps, eat our lunch propped up on our elbows, and then just lie there, looking.

The appearance of the fog is like the pleasure of a good friend stopping by in that unexpectedly, superimposed on the day, is a gift, entertainment, variety. *Fog could be called "nature transient,"* I think to myself. And Jean-Louis would certainly agree; equally as pleasing as its appearance could be the mere thought of it, even though a thought is, by nature, transient.

The final stage of the thaw is in progress. Patches of ice are darkening, a sign that it is rotting from underneath. A few weeks ago, by the end of December's sunshine, the majority of our paths were already gone. Only the iceways that formed first remained. In anticipation of eventual need, the dinghy was dug out of its snow hangar on January 2 and returned to the mother ship. On January 3, we picked our way carefully ashore; the ice along the shoreline was deteriorating fast.

Now, on January 4, we can no longer ski away from the boat! We reckon that we have skied more than 1,000 miles, "about as far as Sweden is long," Rolf tells me. OK, but if we had left here and skied toward the South Pole, how far would we have come? We measure. Merely halfway. . . .

Yacht after yacht takes shelter inside the Hovgaard archipelago. The majority of them have charter guests. We start to think it's fun to meet people, to give them tips about the area and what we've learned about bird and animal behavior. Some people drop by to visit us. Sergio, from Milan, is here to birdwatch. Specifically, he is hoping to see snow petrels and their nests. He has many questions for us.

Another man, very cosmopolitan, looks at me as he climbs aboard and then at the scenery, or rather the heavy clouds hiding it, and in a derogatory tone sneers, "So, this is your universe." A knife pierces my heart.

On January 7, the last of the rotten fast ice floats down the serpentine channel on the tide without so much as a tug on our shore lines. *Northern Light* is in her natural element once again, free to sail after ten months in winter quarters. But her crew is busy filming birds and sees no reason to move from the 100 percent safety of this anchorage.

An American yacht with a Swiss woman aboard as crew heads toward our archipelago. "Surprise," she says after raising us on the VHF. "It's Sabina!" Before we left Mar del Plata, Sabina had graciously given us some Swiss chocolate from her private collection. Each bar was marked with the occasion on which it was to be eaten: midwinter, first day of spring, and her birthday. I give her a kiss on the cheek for each one and tell her how happy I am to be able to reciprocate now. I promise to bake something and share it in the evening with her and her shipmates.

Later, while we are eating the cake I baked, Rolf scares everyone by telling them it's been made with penguin eggs . . . but it wasn't. The very last of Don Carlos's 500 eggs have been used to bake it! Sabina and the others are stunned. They'd thought the cake was scrumptious, only to be told that it was made with eggs slightly over 400 days old!

Although we assume that there's not much nutritional value left in the eggs, the only change we ever perceived was that, over time, the whites became progressively runnier. We never tasted any difference, and the eggs always performed as expected in recipes. Sabina's crewmate Tom snickers slightly and adds that his brother, the owner of a grocery store, once informed him that considering production, warehousing, and transport to the stores, the average American "fresh" egg is laid six months prior to being taken home from the store. So the question remains: How long *do* eggs last?

The wind turns southerly and the pack ice moves in, jamming—yes, totally blocking—the archipelago. *Betelguese* can't get out! Sabina is especially pleased to be around and socialize with friends a little longer. She borrows my ski equipment and entertains herself on Hovgaard's slopes. After a few days, as the novel situation of pack ice has everyone antsy on board *Betelguese*, they give it a try and go. The owner offers us a tow, but trusting that the wind will shift, we decline, to stay and film.

The third time is a charm. After two tries, we finally connect with the cruise ship *Ocean Princess* at Pléneau Island. We collect the 10 gallons (38 liters) of gasoline they've brought for us to have as a safety reserve for the outboard engine in addition to the 15 gallons (57 liters) we already had. It's nice to see Lars-Eric and Ruriko again. Lars-Eric is pleased to see us in good shape after the winter and to hear that all his arrangements for Rolf's hernia surgery went well. Then, on my mother's request, he asks to check our teeth to see if we are suffering from scurvy. That's my mom!

Up on the bridge, the ice master, Swede Kenth Grankvist, corners me. "Now tell me," he demands. "Whatever *did* you two do all winter?"

Oh, boy, where should I start? Wait, I know! I tell him, "We drank champagne and made love." Kenth and the others within earshot start laughing. Rolf puts his hands on his hips and harrumphs. In a very serious tone that quickly puts a damper on my joke, he, ever-so-straight and honest, says: "De-bo-rah. Why do you say such a thing? They'll get the wrong idea. I want people to know the truth. We didn't have any champagne." Kenth and his crewmates collapse in laughter, then so do we.

As we load the two jerry cans of gas into our dinghy and are saying good-bye to Lars-Eric, Kenth comes flying down the corridor, yelling for us to wait. "I have something for you," he says breathlessly, and out of a bag comes a magnum of real French champers, with the note: "Enjoy making love after this bottle. With best wishes from your friends aboard the *Ocean Princess*."

That night the very odd smell of burning wood wakes us up. Because there is another yacht in the Pléneau anchorage, our first thought is that perhaps they are in trouble. We flip on the VHF. But there's no distress call. Quite the opposite. Someone who's having a party thinks we should all have the privilege of joining in, so they have turned channel 16 into a radio station, broadcasting music over it. How juvenile. "OK," says Rolf as we turn off the Top 40 music and go back to bed. "There's no emergency anyway. The yacht probably has a wood-burning stove. At least I hope so."

The next morning we foray past the outer edge of the archipelago to the pack ice and find an ice floe bearing a dozen crabeater seals. One male has had a serious encounter that's left him with severe neck and face wounds. An empty eye socket and his badly torn mouth are infected and dripping puss. While the other seals on the floe sleep, this poor guy squirms and writhes. It's reported that crabeaters often die of infection, so I suppose the encounter that led to these wounds may have been his last.

The other yacht is just off the path home. We are invited aboard for coffee. On our way out, we see that they have had a fire on the rocks next to their boat. My heart sinks. Oh, no. That's what we smelled last night. They've been burning wooden crates and garbage, and now there's a fresh orange peel sitting on top of the remains, all in the very same spot where, just a week ago, we'd found and picked up a bunch of trash.

Rolf confronts the crew. They exonerate themselves with statements like: "Everyone does this. And you have impact here too."

Rolf answers, "Of course we all have impact. That's why we have to do what we can to minimize it. But your behavior is abusive. Weddell seals haul out here. They can get badly cut on the staples from those crates. And skuas nest all over these rocks. Their chicks peck at everything. We just spent two days cleaning up this area. We picked up nails and staples from burned crates, glass shards, hundreds of bits of unburned foil from food packages, oily rags and corroding batteries, a wood carving, cans, and a sheet of masonite we fished out of the water. I have no idea who's mess it was, but as you have clearly proven that you don't know how to behave in the wilderness, you don't belong here. I suggest that you leave Antarctica immediately."

We row home, indescribably depressed but not really surprised. After all, inside the categories of people here—scientists, their support crews, military, yachts' and ships' crews, and tourists—only a small handful of individuals come to absorb a wilderness experience. One yacht's charter guest who came with just that intention told me, with bitter disappointment in his voice: "I came to see Earth's last wilderness. But I am too late. There hasn't been one day, not one bloody day, when we haven't seen at least one ship, and we've yet to have an anchorage to ourselves."

Cruise ships keep in radio contact to make sure they don't cross paths with other ships or visit sites at the same time. They do so to give their passengers as much wilderness feeling as possible. In the same vein, it's odd that a charter skipper doesn't see the point of keeping garbage aboard, unseen. What's to say that this one doesn't have a dump at each anchorage he frequents? Do guests appreciate being sailed from one dump to another? Imagine if we sailors, who have everything to gain from keeping our "back yard" beautiful, aren't willing to take the little time and energy it takes to leave no glaring sign of our presence behind. I had always thought that sailors could lead the way, could show that even with small space and small means, an environmentally conscious lifestyle and presence can be accomplished. Am I too naive, too optimistic? If charter crews and their passengers who make the effort to bring themselves to this "last wilderness" see nothing wrong with spoiling it, what hope is left?

The next day, another sailor stops by to relay the information that the mess will be cleaned up and to ask us to work positively to help spread information to sailors about how to behave in the wild. If we relate the negative incidents instead, we could ruin it for yachts in Antarctica. We are given a copy of the recently published *Southern Ocean Cruising*, a guide that Sally and Jérôme Poncet wrote. The messenger says that it's moves like this guide that will hopefully allow yachting in Antarctica to continue. I hope that's right.

I study the booklet. The Poncets have clearly put a lot of time and effort into it, first gathering information from every country that claims and administers subantarctic islands and then distributing it in draft form to various organizations and sailors for their suggestions before suggesting policy in the final version. The booklet has four sections: guidelines for visitors, a list of off-limit areas, a cruising guide to the subantarctic islands, and a list of the yachts that have plied the Antarctic Ocean.

A basic premise in the guidelines, and what I see as a policy statement, is: "Visitors are not always a threat to Antarctica's wildlife or ecology, providing they are adequately informed about the environment and how to minimize their impact upon it when passing through."

It sounds good, and I wish that were true. Yet because humans are a nonindigenous species, our presence always carries a latent threat. And the second half of the statement is only true if the person *wants* to have minimal impact.

Some stations are now starting to follow Antarctic Treaty regulations to the letter. For example, to not run the risk of introducing disease or bugs, Americans have sent decorative houseplants and potting soil back north, and the British are about to ban sled dogs. Still, some stations and sailors, despite regulations and risk of being fined $10,000, insist on having feline pets.

Cats can introduce bacteria and illnesses to indigenous animal life against which they have no resistance. Besides that, a cat can also cause major disturbances in bird colonies. Last summer, an Italian ornithologist told us that he had once seen a cat closing in on a penguin rookery. When the cat was still a few yards distant, the first penguin got scared and rushed away from its nest. In the process, it disturbed other penguins, which in turn disturbed more. As the cat continued toward the mass of birds, frightening each one that saw it, panic spread through the whole colony. Many penguins, including a high percentage of chicks, were trampled to death.

Another serious problem is that if cats are left behind on the subantarctic islands, they *can* actually survive. If the worst happens—that is, that a suitable mate is brought to the island—the result can be the same as has already happened on Kerguelen, Marion, Macquarie, and Crozet Islands. There, visitors' cats left behind have multiplied. Today they survive on bird eggs. The summer of 1949 to 1950, five cats were brought to Marion Island. They multiplied until, in 1965, there were an estimated 2,000 cats that killed 450,000 petrels that year. On Kerguelen Island, the cat population kills 1,200,000 prions each year. No one knows how to get rid of the cats. The problem started with selfish humans.

It is often said that Antarctica belongs to us all. As an umbrella concept, that leads us to think that we can use it in whatever way we like. I would therefore contend the opposite: Antarctica belongs to no one. If you accept that instead as a basic operating premise and follow it with another—that our presence is a threat to the environment and the indigenous life—then perhaps you will be dedicated to pass through with as little impact as possible. You will study and plan accordingly before you go. When in Antarctica, if questions arise that must be answered, or if situations occur that you must work your way out of, then the basic premise (and not what suits you or is easiest) can be used as the frame inside which you formulate your solutions.

Another subject in the cruising guide that warrants further discussion concerns disposal of garbage. In the draft we got last year, the Poncets proposed that yachtsmen (who they say are used to indiscriminately dumping their trash overboard) be allowed to dump their trash—including food, sewage, paper, wood, bottles, and cans—in the water while cruising in Antarctica. In the final guide, that idea has been amended to dumping food and sewage only. Why should we be allowed to dump garbage? What's the difficulty of keeping food scraps aboard for the weeks we're here? After all, food garbage never has more weight or volume than the original supplies, and due to the cold, it never smells. And what about sewage? What impact does it have? Do we, by dumping sewage, introduce harmful bacteria or disease? Do we have to have holding tanks for sewage on yachts and primary or secondary treatment on cruise ships and at stations? What will happen if salmonella is introduced here?

Furthermore, whereas the draft laxly stated that open burning is not recommended, the final says in one paragraph, "Paper and wood are also to be kept aboard," only to later repeat the draft's "Open burning of materials is not recommended." Not recommended implies that under certain conditions it's OK. What conditions could those be?

With the exception of vulcanism, fire and smoke do not exist in Antarctica. Fire confuses and frightens wildlife. In addition, like anything dark, ashes landing in the snow lead to undesired melt. The rule has to be no open fire allowed. And that means, as Captain Aye instituted on *Frontier Spirit,* not even smoking outside the confines of the ship or any other manmade structure. His passengers face a $50 fine for any infringement!

Thinking about *Frontier Spirit* leads me to another important point missing from the guide altogether. As cruise ships' captains do, the captain of any yacht must have the responsibility to both educate passengers and oversee that all—captain, crew, and passengers—live according to the rules.

The weaknesses in the guidelines tell me that the sailors and station administrators who contributed to the final text have a dilemma: to choose between what Antarctica needs and what people can easily cope with. As a statement of policy, it's sad and disappointing. This guide could have been the beginning of a change in the political atmosphere here. Instead of following the established suit, yachtsmen could have led the way.

As I read Poncet's guide I note all my comments with the intent of sending them to them, to start a dialogue, to continue the political process. But when I reach the very last page, I just wish for once that I didn't care, because I see the magnitude of the task ahead and even perhaps the folly of my hopeful thinking.

Our neighbors—who burned trash, who allowed their charter guests to collect rocks and other Antarctic souvenirs, whose paid crew tossed his filtered cigarette butt into the water and whose skipper tossed his match into the water after lighting his cigarette, practices either disallowed or to be avoided according to Poncets' guide—are on the final page thanked for their input to the very guide itself. So we can't say that they never had a chance to learn the precepts of wilderness behavior. No, we know now that we're seeing typical human behavior: say one thing to politic yourself into good light, then do as you please. The only conclusion to be drawn from this experience is that any group self-regulation is a sham.

We were told that we should write to teach people about wilderness behavior. That may be well and good and that's always been our plan, but what about people who don't want to learn or, worse, who don't care? Who is going to get tough on anyone who breaks the rules? Finally, what was that message about us "ruining it for yachts in Antarctica" if not totally twisted?

As we see it, there has become far more cause to worry about us ruining it for the Weddell seals and skua chicks than there is ruining it for fellow humans or their interests. Perhaps it's a sign of the beginning of the end: the world's gone topsy-turvy. After generations upon generations of people protecting themselves from the elements, those elements now need protection from humans.

In Antarctica's case, I hope the protection comes quickly. Rolf and I took it upon ourselves to talk to the skippers on most of this summer's yachts about people's environmental impact in Antarctica. About half, including some of the charter skippers, hoped that Antarctica would be kept pristine and were indeed already doing their part to keep it that way. The other half thought we were too extreme and called us self-righteous. Those charter skippers soon referred to us as the "harbor captains." Doesn't that imply that when we leave they will heave a collective sigh of relief and go back to business as usual?

Bright light overpowers shadow; in the spotlight, we can't but help seeing things as they really are, blemishes included. Every group here is more concerned about their image than their behavior. Cruise ship operators, yachtsmen, treaty members with and without stations, all have written their own operating procedures for the Antarctic. It's like letting the comptroller of a steel mill write up the company's environmental regulations only to find that, oddly enough, the environment takes a backseat to the bottom line. Every group here looks to spend the lowest amount of energy and money to accomplish their goals, and they will as long as they can. It's what has led to the demise of every other wilderness area on Earth.

We want to take a stand on the other side of the continuum from short-sighted, selfish behavior and speak up to stop the deterioration and despoiling. In Antarctica, an outside regulatory agency, a politically neutral group, needs to investigate all activities and bring their findings to a forum where a comprehensive environmental protection program and procedures for preservation can be drawn up. It must include an enforcement system to make sure people comply with the rules and quotas. Similar systems already exist in the Galapagos Islands, Himalayas, New Zealand's subantarctic islands, and an array of other sensitive ecological areas. Perhaps they work well enough to be used as models.

It has been proposed that Antarctica become a park or a preserve. We agree. All nations united should declare the patchwork treaty, created by a few nations, null and void and start again. Forget about jockeying for position. Realize that Antarctica belongs to no one, not even those who got there first. Declare exploitation forever off limits; take no resources. Tourism should be limited and regulated, as should science. Scientific stations should be park territory rather than belonging to individual countries. To avoid today's unnecessary duplication, a committee should determine which projects should be conducted and where. Each study should have an international group working on it. It's then that we have international cooperation and we leave a "breathing hole." Isn't that what Earth needs today?

As much as I hate to think of it, another alternative is to accept the Antarctic Convergence as a circular "Keep Out" sign beyond which no human intruders or interlopers are allowed. If negotiations start there, perhaps the concept of Antarctica as a regulated territory doesn't seem very bad.

Every twenty seconds a new human being is born. Earth's population has tripled in my lifetime. Overpopulation is already a fact, and there is no place for us to run. Our planet is finite. To manage it, to use it wisely and not ruin it, the number of regulations will remain in proportion to the size of the group. The more people there are, the more rules become necessary to keep everything under control. Instead of more rules, I would love to see the population start a voluntary downward turn. Until we again have elbow room, however, human's access to both places and things will have to be limited. Just how much is dependent upon the chosen amount of industrialism of the total population. It's our decision. I hope our global planning will be based on decisions made the way Native North American tribal leaders did, with the next seven generations in mind.

On February 5, we eat the last piece of salt pork. It's the first category of meat we've managed to work our way through. There's enough pastrami left that I believe we'll have it all the way back to South America. Other dry and canned goods will probably last all the way to Sweden.

On February 6, we bring the blue barrels and what's left of the stash back on board. Not one plastic or metal container ever leaked a drop. On February 7, we bend on our sails. It's the day we had originally planned to leave Antarctica to be able to sail across Drake Passage without darkness, but there's still so much filming to be accomplished!

Late in the evening we hear another yacht arrive, but it ties up down the channel, around a bend and just out of sight. My guess is that it must be the last yacht to arrive on the Antarctic Peninsula this season. In just a little while I hear the putt-putt of a little outboard, and even though the sound makes me sour, I go on deck into the special summer cold that settles in the channel after the sun goes down. A man in a dinghy is examining our Monitor windvane. We have never met, but I believe I have heard him on the radio. In the same breath I both take and give a chance. My "Hello, Clark" is matter of factly met by "Hello, Deborah" and a slight smile.

We make a date for tomorrow's midmorning coffee. When Clark and his perky partner climb aboard, they introduce themselves starting with the last chapter first. They—Michelle Poncini and Clark Steed—built a new boat then sailed off on its maiden voyage from Germany to Greenland and westward through the Northwest Passage.

"Although we had the necessary food and equipment with us," Clark explains, "rather than spend the winter, we jumped an 80-mile band of pack ice by being lifted aboard an icebreaker, so the unaided transit record in a yacht is still to be claimed." They then proceeded south along the coasts of North, Central, and South America and will soon be turning north again until they meet their outward track. A circumnavigation of the Americas; what an accomplishment!

It's easy to imagine that they have stories to tell. Clark, a German freelance photojournalist who had taken up sailing to transport himself to stories, met Michelle on her home turf in Australia. Without knowing how to sail,

Michelle joined Clark. She took along her working tools: video and sound recording equipment. Both are determined individuals, working hard on their separate projects. Each has a knack for storytelling, and I certainly look forward to their productions.

There is Pacific-blue depth to their personalities. I relax with them, learn from the conclusions they draw from their lives, and therefore feel free to share the deepest of our winter thoughts with them without feeling that I am faltering, stumbling, or feeling my way through the dark. We describe the comfort and meaning of the seclusion, the time in "iceolation" when our thoughts sifted and conclusions became more our own, and we feel appreciated for doing so.

We are invited aboard their impressive, immaculately maintained, aluminum *ASMA*, a 44-foot boat with an open interior outfitted for two. We sit in front of the wood-burning stove, share dinner, and then talk for days. As far as our adjustment to being around people goes, it's very fortunate to make new friends just now; otherwise I think I may have joined the ranks of the Flying Dutchman. And Clark, through a very small incident, restores some hope for the future. While skiing Hovgaard we happen upon him filling water jugs in a meltwater stream. About to finish a cigarette, Clark takes out a small glass jar in which he stamps out and deposits the butt. He is the first smoker I have ever met who carries an ashtray with him outdoors. I have always wished that cigarette packages had an extra compartment at the bottom for butt, ash, and match storage, but lacking that Clark has come up with his own solution. To my kudos Clark shrugs. He says simply, "My bad habit doesn't have to be left in the streets, on sidewalks, in the snow, or floating in the water."

Abel-J reappears this summer on charter to the BBC, captained again by Hamilton. We hear his ever-cheerful voice on the radio and join in for a chat. He gives us an updated ice report: "The pack ice covers nine-tenths of the water from Hovgaard to Faraday, and from there south it's a complete stop for all ships except icebreakers. Had you made it down to Marguerite Bay last year and wintered there, you wouldn't have made it out this summer . . . "

The moment the wind shifts to northeast, *ASMA* leaves to go south as far as is possible. We ski up to the plateau to watch their progress and see that Penola is not navigable more than 5 miles south. Clark and Michelle work their way into the edge of the pack ice. It's too thick for us to even think about trying to go farther south without an engine. We have to consider ourselves lucky that the wind has pushed the pack ice south to allow us to scoot out of the Hovgaard archipelago.

It's time to prepare to leave. The first step is to get the anchor and chain back aboard. Wouldn't you know, a tubular ice chunk about 4 yards in diameter and about 5 yards high has grounded on top of the chain, at high tide, no less. Rolf climbs up on it with an axe and starts to hack in cracks, enlarging them until 25- to 100-pound (10–50-kg) chunks fall off. Piece after piece falls in the water until he thinks that the berg's light enough to float away at next high tide, which it does. We collect our anchor and chain and remain in position now with shore lines only.

To be able to leave, it must be windless and the tidal stream must be against us in the channel. On February 18, the conditions are met. The anchor is reset, out just 15 yards ahead of the boat. Hanging on the hook in the stream, we take away the shore lines, lash the dinghy to the port side, give each other a hug, have a final appreciative look around, and, finally, with the help of the 15-horsepower Yamaha, prepare to tow *Northern Light* out of our winter anchorage.

Rolf goes into the dinghy and engages the outboard while I pump up the anchor. It's an exciting moment. Instead of going forward, the boat starts to turn port, even though both the rudder and the outboard are turned fully to take us starboard! So much for having a non–middle-line engine.

Pumping up the anchor is the only thing that pulls the bow in the direction we want to go. I pump as fast as I can and as we gain speed—ghosting barely a half knot—Rolf puts the outboard amidships, jumps on deck, loosens the wheel, and reports we've got steerage. When the anchor is aboard, I jump down into the dinghy and incrementally open the throttle until we reach 2.5 knots, when I move to the bowsprit to keep a lookout. With Entrance Island abeam, our local knowledge comes to an end, and there are 15 miles to go before we're back in charted waters.

25

A GLASS
OF WATER
PLEASE

ROLF

■ ■ ■

Entrance Island slips astern. It was a year ago, almost to the day, that we reached our winter quarters. At that time, we felt like temporary visitors, but that changed. What we are leaving is an important place and part of our lives. I don't look back.

In uncharted waters, my attention is focused on navigation, progress; my concern is finding safe passage. There is no wind, and I am glad for that. Wind-created ripples on the surface of the water could make it impossible to see rocks or shoals in time. While Deborah continuously looks for hazards and searches the water's surface for any eddies that could indicate shoaling, I jump down into the dinghy and open the throttle incrementally. To my satisfaction, the twelve-year-old outboard sounds just as it should. As a matter of fact, when *Northern Light* eventually reaches a speed of 4 knots, I can even ease the throttle a little. There can't be much growth on the hull.

But even though the outboard works so well in calm conditions doesn't mean it will have power enough when there's a lot of wind. For the immediate future, the worst scenario I can imagine is a nighttime wind shift that leads to dragging anchor. The coal black nights only make getting under sail that much more difficult. There's no question about it: the safest plan would be to leave Antarctica immediately. But because my injury made it impossible to film any sailing sequences last summer, we have decided to do just that during the upcoming week. We will work out of Port Lockroy, reanchoring there every night after filming. The way that anchorage is situated, we can leave whenever we want, even if the outboard shouldn't start.

If the current doesn't set too hard against us today, I figure we'll be in Port Lockroy within eight hours. Maybe we'll even sail part of the way there. The mere thought that we will soon be able to sail—when and wherever we want—eases my worries some.

But then I remember that there's a small snag. When Robin, who brought one of our video cameras to Palmer Station, was packing to leave the United States, she asked Deborah's mother if there was anything *really* special she could bring us. Because Deborah's mother knows her daughter as well as all parents know their children, her spontaneous reaction was: "Oh, yes! Deborah loves turtles, the chocolate-covered variety." As kind as Robin is, she didn't just buy one or two of the chocolate-covered pecan and caramel confections; she bought a two-pound box. But did the treats come with the camera? No! Included in our care package was a note informing that she had brought turtles for us but that she and Maggie had decided to keep them as bait to ensure that we would stop by for a visit. It's a nice thought, but the question is whether or not stopping there will be possible. It is not easy to get to or from Palmer without an engine. If the wind is too strong or from the wrong direction, or if the outboard quits, there won't be any stop, turtles or no turtles.

Suddenly, Deborah shouts, "Rolf, look!" My immediate concern is that we are about to hit a shoal and instinctively I turn the rudder in the direction she's pointing. Just as the boat starts to turn, I hear the releasing word: "Whales!"

Among the brash, north of Booth Island, I see a spout of fine spray and vapor, indicating at least one whale. It's about a third of a mile ahead of us, just to starboard. If we want to see it up close, we'll have to go into the ice. Considering how difficult it is to tow ourselves through areas of brash and how much wear and tear it means to the dinghy, we decide to pass.

There is only one way for us to make it through barriers of brash ice. We fully open the throttle on the outboard to gain speed before we reach it. Then just before the bow drives into the ice, one of us jumps down in the dinghy, stops the outboard, lifts it up so that the propeller is out of the water, and then, as fast as the thought itself, jumps back aboard the mother ship again, hopefully before the dinghy has reached the ice. Then *Northern Light*'s 15 tons does its thing; the momentum plows her through the ice. The din created is without comparison.

To try to make it through the ice with the help of the outboard would only destroy its propeller. On top of that, were one of us forced to remain in the dinghy to handle the outboard, the dinghy would most likely be squashed between the hull and the edge of some ice piece and punctured. Without our weight in it, the dinghy bounces like a rubber ball on top of the ice. Not that we really know what's happening to the bottom of the dinghy from our chosen method. So far, anyway, it doesn't leak.

We follow around the edge of the brash for a while. There are at least two whales. When they move, they move very slowly, which indicates that they are humpback whales. Sometimes they lie still. We couldn't wish for a better opportunity to get closer to them. Because this could well be our last chance to film whales, when we find a lead opening into the ice we decide to go ahead. While Deborah prepares the cameras, I take us in. When we are about 50 yards behind the whales—the appropriate courtesy distance—they start to swim a little faster. My first thought is that, courtesy distance or not, I may have scared them. Then, instead of continuing on their path, they turn around and head straight for us.

Ever since we entered the ice, we have only made between 1 and 2 knots, but even so, it is impossible to decrease our speed quickly by putting the outboard in reverse; its propeller is far too small to have any effect. To avoid colliding with the whales I therefore turn port as hard as I can, then jump down in the dinghy and stop the outboard. When I look up, the whales are only a couple of boat lengths away and we are still steaming toward them. Our speed was too low for the rudder to make any difference to steerage. Instead, the random position of ice chunks determines where the boat goes, and the path is straight for the whales. I feel awful. It was a terrible mistake to even approach them.

At the last possible moment, the whales calmly give way to us. They have perfect control over the situation. Amazingly, they don't seem to be at all scared; it is as if they realize we don't mean them any harm. Instead of diving, they swim a full turn around the boat and then come to a halt, resting on our starboard side. The closest one has stopped only 15 feet away. We can see down into its huge blowhole. Seconds later, Deborah and I get soaking wet from the spray. The exhaled air carries such a heavy smell of krill that we both gag.

After the whale inhales again, three minutes pass before it exhales. During the two-second-long exhale, the whale blows out $1\frac{1}{2}$ cubic meters of air. That is 2,000 to 3,000 times more than a human breath! Then, in a second, the whale inhales all the air it needs. The draw makes a whistling sound on top of an even more dominant deep metallic sound, as if the whale is breathing through a tuba. My chest vibrates from the sound.

After a while it appears as if the whales are sleeping. Each time they exhale, they sink down in the water until only their breathing holes remain above the surface. When they then inhale again, they float up so that half their backs are above the surface. While they rest, we can see how huge they actually are. The one that's closest is considerably longer than *Northern Light*. Between 16 and 17 yards long, it's most likely the female. The male is $1\frac{1}{2}$ yards shorter.

Through the clear water we can also see their huge flippers, which are almost a third as long as their bodies.

After a half hour's pause, the whales start to move. We start the outboard and follow. In the beginning they move without haste, like a pair of locomotives slowly building up steam. They swim close to the surface for a couple hundred yards, then increase the pace, taking five to six breaths at about twenty-second intervals. The female shows her impressive flukes as she dives and disappears from sight. What lithe motion! The whale handles her 30 to 40 ton body like a high jumper gliding gracefully over the bar.

Deborah has been sitting on the bowsprit, and through the camera I watch the whale's enormous flukes spread like a plume behind her head and then slowly sink into the sea. Then the male dives without showing his flukes. It is as if he doesn't want to compete with the remarkable sequence that I managed to capture on video. Instead, he lets his mate take all the applause. "Isn't this wonderful?" Deborah shouts out through a smile.

The whales are also heading north, so we continue in their company for more than two hours. When they dive, they are sometimes gone as long as fifteen minutes, during which time we continue the course to our anchorage, but the pair always surfaces within a couple hundred yards of the boat. We would have liked to stay with them longer, but at six o'clock in the evening, the whales turn northeast into Gerlache Strait and we continue into Peltier Channel. It's a little sad. Deborah grabs my hand and we wave good-bye to them. We don't really want to think about it, but this is most likely the last time we will see humpbacks. "So long guys," Deborah calls out. Her voice echoes back from land. The whales blow. Their sound also reflects off the high cliffs bordering the passage.

As we head into the craterlike bay of Port Lockroy, dusk has already settled. To be sure that our anchor really sets, we execute a maneuver against all the rules. Because we are not able to set the anchor as we usually do by going reverse, we let it go while the boat still has 2 to 3 knots' forward speed. It sounds terrible as 55 meters of chain drag along the hull, but we have no choice. I tighten the capstan and then we wait. To my satisfaction, the boat comes to a dead stop. I sigh with relief. It seems we found the clay patch we anchored in last year. I had hoped I would remember the bearings to it.

Now there's just one more concern; will the outboard work properly until we visit Palmer Station? If it had been just one turtle it hadn't mattered too much, but two pounds!

The next morning the sun shines from an almost cloud-free sky. It's perfect for filming. We take the opportunity to sail up Neumayer Channel and into an alplike landscape that must be counted as one of Antarctica's most majestic. The mountainsides are not quite as vertical or barren as in many other places, so the snow remains on the slopes, making the surroundings very dramatic yet at the same time mild and welcoming. For two consecutive days, the sun illuminates a sculpted scene so breathtaking that we will remember it for the rest of our lives.

On Leap Year's day, it's snowing and blowing a gale-force wind. We remain anchored in Port Lockroy, and using eggs that Sabina and her friends gave us, bake bread and cookies for the first days out in Drake Passage. Due to all the recent skiing and sailing, we feel in fine form and figure that a rest day will build up our energy reserve. We know it will come in handy when we put ourselves out into real ocean swell for the first time in over a year. Listening to tapes we've received from Mats and other friends create some longing for home. We need it. Closing in on the moment of departure is not easy for either of us.

On the next day, a nice northerly breeze and less cloud cover swings our decision in favor of heading for Palmer Station. There's nothing in the weather situation that bodes ill for the immediate future. During the last two weeks, the barometer has only moved very little, hovering around 1,000 millibars. If the breeze remains, this will only be a overnight stop, then we'll be off.

As soon as we have secured the boat in the inlet just off Palmer Station, we are invited in for dinner and to see all our friends. It's especially nice to meet Robin and thank her in person for the help she gave us. But because we want to leave very early the next day, we excuse ourselves after dessert and say our good-byes. On our way out, Ajo gives us the latest weatherfax chart he's pulled in from Australia. The prognosis is that a north-northeasterly gale-force wind will arrive tonight, reach storm force by early morning, and probably last two days. If we head out into Drake Passage tomorrow, according to the prognosis, we'll have onshore wind coupled with tremendous sea right on the nose. The combination would not make for a very good start.

We immediately regret our decision to come here. Had we not, we'd already have been well offshore. Right now, the wind strength is 25 to 32 knots. But in this wind direction the station is in the lee of Anvers Island. There's no way here to get a clear idea about the wind's direction or strength at sea. At daybreak, the wind is stronger. Uncertain of the offshore conditions, we stay put.

For the next two days, we are confined for the most part to the inside of the boat. When we leave it's never for more than a half hour at a time; we're concerned that if there's a rapid wind shift, the boat will be very unprotected. We truly wish we could sail away. The longer we wait, the darker the nights and the higher the risk of storms.

Because this depression has become almost stationary, there's no judging how much it will intensify. But as far as leaving is concerned, it's not the wind speed that is our major concern, it's the wind direction. We must leave just as the center of the depression is passing us; then the wind direction is most favorable for departure.

Time after time, we look up to see if the characteristics of the sky have changed or knock on the barometer, but nothing much ever happens. After four days of caged waiting, we are both decidedly antsy.

By 0400 on March 5, the depression's total barometric drop has been a mere 10 millibars. But as best I can tell, it looks as if it may be starting to flatten out. This is the moment we've been waiting for. We want to get going during the calm, before the wind shifts and increases. If we wait until the barometer starts to rise, the wind will have shifted to southwesterly, and in that wind direction, we can't get out of this cramped position. While waiting for twilight, we eat a substantial breakfast, set up the sea berth, and double check the navigation and bearings already marked on the chart. Then we start the outboard.

At 0630 we start to collect our shore ropes. Half an hour after leaving Palmer Station, we move out of the island's wind shadow. The wind increases slowly from northeast. That doesn't bother me. I take the fact that the wind has not yet calmed or shifted as a sign that we got underway in time. As a matter of fact, because our intention is to head almost due west until we've passed the continental shelf, it'll be just fine if the northeasterly wind remains for some hours. That will enable us to take the shortest possible passage through the iceberg belt that parallels the coast.

As soon as the wind stabilizes around 7 knots, we set sail. Nonetheless, the dinghy with outboard still mounted is kept in tow and will be until we have passed the last skerries. We may yet have use for it if, for example, the wind dies before we reach open water. There's a lot of current here, and I don't want to take any risk of being set up on any shoals. Happy to be underway, we keep the boat going as best we can in the light wind.

Half an hour later, we are hit by such a forceful downdraft from Anvers Island that *Northern Light* heels until the toe rail is being dragged through water. Just as quickly as the gust came, it disappears. The boat rightens. It's absolutely calm, but we can see that more gusts are on their way. Clouds of loose snow rush toward us from the mountainsides.

While I reef, Deborah takes the wheel. It's extremely difficult sailing. In the worst gusts, the wind strength is more than gale force, then there is no wind at all. It's crucial that Deborah drive the boat as efficiently as is ever possible, because less than 500 yards to the lee is a strip of violently breaking sea that continues as far as we can see. We wish it were possible to gain some height in the gusts, but it isn't. Ice trailing off an outcrop of Anvers Island keeps us from being able to do so.

On top of everything, it starts to snow. We sometimes lose sight of the dangers that ring us. In the space of a very few minutes, the conditions have become the worst imaginable. Besides, the swell now rolling into the sound is a clue that farther out to sea the conditions must be ferocious. Deborah also starts wondering if it was right to leave. "Typical Antarctic weather," she mumbles.

What worries us most is just how we are going to get the dinghy up. We wish we could have taken care of it earlier or that we had enough sea room to heave to here, but we don't. Nor can we turn around and do it in the lee of Anvers Island. There is no way to guarantee that the gusts aren't just a local wind phenomenon that will soon peter out. The only thing to do is continue another 10 miles. Once well out at sea, we will haul everything aboard. It will be a nightmare of a job.

Reaching open water, the wind speed is at least 30 knots and the sea is rough. To take up the dinghy, it would be best to heave to with the staysail backed. That way, with the bow into the wind, the boat would sit nearly still. Unfortunately, that's not possible. Because the dinghy can only be hoisted up onto the foredeck, that space has to be clear of sails and sheets. In other words, the staysail has to be dropped and the genoa furled. To reduce the likelihood of an accidental tack, we put *Northern Light* almost beam to the sea and continue sailing at 1 to 2 knots. The boat rolls violently.

We tie the dinghy along the lee side of *Northern Light*, with its painter belayed around the forward bollard, preparing to take the outboard up first. One second the dinghy is level with the upper lifeline, the next it's in danger of being punctured by the log propeller. Nevertheless, I make it into the dinghy and attach the cutter staysail halyard to the outboard.

During the time it takes me to get back up on deck and help Deborah lift the outboard off and secure it on the lifeline, the dinghy fills with water. We can hardly budge it, let alone lift it by its painter to drain the water out. I have no choice. I'll have to make it into the dinghy again to attach the staysail halyard to the bracket I mounted long ago on the aluminum floorboards. Then we'll be able to winch the water-filled dinghy up on deck.

This move into the dinghy doesn't go as well as the first time. As my feet touch the floorboards, a sea grabs the dinghy and lurches it away from *Northern Light*. The tether of my safety harness is clipped onto the lifeline, but it's much shorter than the dinghy's painter. I quickly realize that I am about to be pulled out of the dinghy. Instinctively, I grab for *Northern Light*'s toe rail with my right hand, but I don't stand a chance. Pain shoots through my shoulder, and as I lose my handhold, I hear Deborah scream my name.

My upper body hangs outside the dinghy, dragging in the water. Thoughts swirl. If my feet leave the dinghy, I'll be dragged in my safety line along the hull, and when the dinghy gets drawn back in to the hull by the next wave, it'll push me down under water. But my analysis is interrupted. My head hits the topsides.

It takes a few seconds of struggling to get my head back above water. I am still hanging onto the dinghy by one leg and have also maintained a cramplike hold around the staysail halyard. Shaken and disoriented, I somehow make it into the dinghy, attach the halyard to the dinghy's lift system, and crawl back aboard *Northern Light*.

Both of us feel drained by what has just happened. All the energy we have left is used to hang on and remain on deck. The second we feel able, we winch the dinghy up on deck. But the floorboards are frozen in place and won't come out. I go below to get a handful of screwdrivers and chisels, then I hammer them between the floorboards and the two longitudinal support stringers. The idea is to try to create enough play to be able to lift the floorboards straight up. But it doesn't work. We can't budge them. We're too tired. Deborah suggests we reattach the halyard to the bracket and tighten up on it until the dinghy is slightly airborne. Then we'll throw ourselves on top of the semideflated pontoons.

We're successful, in a manner of speaking. The dinghy and each of us land on deck with various thuds. All the floorboards and stringers lie in jumbled confusion inside the dinghy, except the one attached to the halyard. Like a pendulum, it swings away far outside the deck, only to come back a couple of seconds later and crash into the mainmast. It bounces away but gets penned in by the forward shrouds. I grab a corner. Simultaneously, Deborah slacks the halyard. The floorboard falls on deck, with me on top of it.

The cold makes it impossible to roll the dinghy tightly enough to pack it in its case. We roll it as best we can, stuff it down through the companionway, and pull it into the crawl space where we leave it lying in a crumpled mess. We shove the floorboards in under it. Everything is out of the way as far as boat handling is concerned. For the moment, that's all that matters. We just want to get back under sail and out to deeper water as quickly as possible.

The work with the dinghy, which normally takes ten minutes, took over an hour. During that time the wind has increased to more than 40 knots. The sea is terribly steep, so we set less sail than we normally would on a beat in this wind speed. The boat labors slowly. The conditions won't improve until we are off the continental shelf, but we don't care. We are free from land.

We sit together in the cockpit, and both of us start to feel nauseated. When it gets dark, Deborah chances going to bed but she can't get any real rest. She is continuously disturbed by the noise of me throwing up. I was never able to recover from the heavy work it took to save the dinghy and have become terribly seasick. I freeze and break into a cold sweat while repeatedly retching. Eventually, I have only bile left. Never have I been this seasick.

When it becomes too dark to spot growlers or icebergs, I furl the genoa and mainsail and then tack. Without resheeting the staysail, it backs and the boat heaves to. I reef the mizzen a little. With this sail combination we can make speed again in just a couple of seconds, if necessary.

It will be dark for eight hours, and we decide to divide it into two-hour passes. Deborah takes over the watch. As soon as I put myself into the seaberth I fall asleep, but I awaken soon after. Deborah has gotten sick, too, and it doesn't take long before she is wracked by dry heaves. This must rate as the most unpleasant beginning of a long voyage we've ever had.

The next evening it is snowing so heavily that we decide to heave to before it's really dark. The sea conditions are still frightful. Waves have been breaking over deck so often that we have had to take away the heater's chimney and seal the intake. The only heat in the boat is that created by the kerosene lamp at the nav desk. It is damp and cold. The thermometer shows 37°F (3°C).

We are both still seasick, but Deborah is in really bad shape. She can't eat. Worse is that she's on the verge of becoming dehydrated. The most water she can keep down is a tablespoon at a time, and that only when she drinks it and immediately lies down. Otherwise, it comes back up again. She's shivering continuously but can't even get a little extra heat from drinking a cup of tea. We have lengthened our watches to the usual four-hour pass. Poor Deborah moves around as if she has a ton of lead in each leg. All the work she has to accomplish is done by adding pure willpower to old routines. Time moves very slowly. Watches are drawn-out torment.

On the third day out, everything takes a sudden turn for the better. The southwesterly appears with a clearing. We are freed from seasickness. We've come so far now that the ice risk is minimal, so we can continue sailing through the night. To be on the safe side during the darkest hours, we sail with a trim reef in both the genoa and main. That way, if we have to avoid some ice, we can gybe in the 20-knot breeze without first loosening the preventers; they are dimensioned to withstand a lot more strain than that. It's also important that the one off watch knows that everything is under control and can relax enough to get the best possible rest. We have some catching up to do in that department.

By the fourth day out, our gray faces start to regain some color. The water temperature rises to a comfortable 45°F (7°C), and for the first time in a long while, water bubbles and fizzles around *Northern Light*'s bow as it only does north of the convergence.

As wonderful as the frothing water sounds, it also serves to remind me that we have left a wounded Antarctica behind us. In the space of one lifetime, offenses have been committed against Earth's most important wilderness that can only be described as a show of disrespect to the planet's future. Humans seem to lack the cleverness to not cut off the branch upon which they are sitting. The water flowing away from the bow could just as well be tears of sorrow.

The southwesterly wind blows steadily for more than a day, then it shifts slowly to southerly and increases a little. Most of the time, it's blowing 22 to 27 knots. With the wind in a little aft of abeam it only takes two days to cover the 360 nautical miles left to reach the latitude of Cape Horn. We never see the cliff itself; it is too hazy. Just after midnight, five and a half days after leaving the Antarctic Peninsula, we have a wind shift back to southwest. In it is the sweet fragrance of the forest on Tierra del Fuego.

At five o'clock in the morning, as first light appears, so does Staten Island. It pops out of the haze a little on our starboard side. Although that's right where we expect it, it still comes as a shock. The hills look as smooth as if they were created purely from moss. The island contours shift continuously in shades of green, radiating colors we haven't seen for such a long time. It is as if it isn't the same cold and inhospitable island we passed a little more than a year ago.

The genoa is poled out to port, the main and mizzen are out to starboard, and the staysail is sheeted amidships as a stabilizer to keep the boat from rolling. With the help of the tidal stream, we make 11 knots over ground. After a half hour, the island is again swallowed by the haze, as if it were only a mirage.

During the night we pass 60 miles west of the Falkland Islands. To take full advantage of the Falkland Current, we continue on a course running basically parallel to the South American coastline, just outside the continental shelf, about 200 miles out in the Atlantic. The sailing conditions are the most comfortable imaginable. The continent gives us full protection from the swell coming from the South Pacific, the offshore wind is mild, and it's sunny and warm. Ten days after leaving Antarctica, it's 68°F (20°C) at the nav desk. We sailed from full winter to full summer in just a little more than a week. Earth is certainly not very big.

For six days the wind remains between southwest and northwest. With the exception of two weak fronts that bring a few hours of northerly wind to stir up a little sea, the ocean is almost flat. The conditions are ideal to enter Mar del Plata. But it's almost annoying; the splendid weather doesn't last all the way there. During the afternoon, just as we spot the high hotels, the barometer starts to drop rapidly. The sky turns suddenly dark, heavy with rain clouds. As the first drops fall, the wind shifts to due easterly. At dusk, it's blowing 20 to 24 knots. Because we still have 7 miles to go and know that there is poor holding in the outer harbor, we decide to heave to for the night and continue our watches as usual.

While we prepare our evening meal, the wind increases further. Rain pours and the sea builds rapidly in both height and length. But it doesn't worry me very much. *Northern Light* is on port tack, heading away from the coast at the pace of 1 knot. Besides, easterly wind is ideal to surf in on between the breakwaters.

Just before midnight the barometer flattens out and starts to rise. The rain stops a couple of hours before dawn. The visibility improves and I see lights on the shore. Just the thought that we will soon meet people that we haven't seen for a long time builds excitement.

As daylight comes we get underway again. At sunrise, the clearing comes with a wind shift, unfortunately to the southwest. We have to beat our way back toward shore. But we knew it had to happen; it's the wind pattern of a rising barometer in the Southern Hemisphere. During the two intervening hours it takes before we see the harbor entrance, the wind shifts even more, to pure southerly. But we have planned our tacks to get slack in the sheets, and the last little bit is downwind. The wind has decreased a little too much for my liking— down to 8 knots—but the sea isn't worse than we can still sail wing and wing.

The only maneuvers remaining to enter the harbor will be gybing the genoa at the right moment and then rounding up.

To understand the wind direction farther in, we have been watching the smoke coming out of a tall industrial chimney situated at the back of the huge harbor. So far, the wind there remains the same as here. All indications are that we'll get a beam reach after the gybe and all the way in. To get an idea about the status of the tide, we sailed the last half hour as close to the beach as we dared. It's appears to be almost high tide. That means that the current between the breakwaters can't be very strong. The conditions could not be better. Nonetheless, Deborah and I have decided on a final decision point—where we either continue in, or go back to sea—500 yards outside the shoaling sandbank in the harbor entrance. A likely reason to have to turn around is if any ship is leaving the harbor. They need the deepest area to themselves.

Shortly after the genoa is gybed, I start to feel ill at ease. So slowly that I haven't paid conscious attention to it, the wind has decreased further. We have passed our point and have come so far that we no longer have enough sea room to gybe back and gain speed on a new tack to sail back out into deeper water. Our speed sinks below 2 knots, and the boat becomes difficult to steer. From just outside the harbor entrance, I see that the current there is considerably worse than I expected. Without being able to do anything about it, we are being set toward the end of the arm of the giant breakwater, less than 200 yards in the lee.

Were it not for the unpleasant experience lingering in the back of my mind since leaving Antarctica, I would probably have inflated the dinghy and put the outboard on, just in case. But now I am glad I didn't. The sea has grown so rapidly that I realize it would most likely have submerged the dinghy had it been tied alongside in towing position.

To my horror, I see that there are at least three breakers rolling toward us from the shoal. The first, which is probably 3 yards high, is only a couple of boat lengths away. If it hits us beam to, we will come to a dead stop, and then I don't know how I will be able to avoid drifting into the long breakwater. All I can hope for is that we still have enough speed so that I can turn and take the first wave from dead astern. That means I will have to steer straight for the breakwater and then try to steer away at the very last moment! My mouth is parched. I don't have any time to explain my decision to Deborah. I simply say tersely, "If I tell you to do something, do it fast." She responds with a swift "OK."

Any movement of its rudder makes a boat's speed decrease, but I have no choice. I turn the wheel to almost full starboard rudder. As I feel the stern being lifted by the wave, I ease the rudder. We gain speed. I have no idea if I will be able to hold the boat on a straight course or if it will broach.

Suddenly, it feels as if we had set the spinnaker in gale-force wind, but in reverse. As the wave tosses the boat forward, there is a tremendous bang in the rigging. Deborah instinctively ducks. The boat lurches as it suddenly gains speed. With all sails backing, we surf at 9 or 10 knots straight toward the break-water.

With 150 yards left, I use the speed to bear off as much as I dare. If I can maintain the course without the boat being knocked down, there is actually a possibility that we can clear the inner corner of the breakwater. But with only a hundred meters left, the boat no longer managers to hang onto the wave. It's probably making over 20 knots. At the bottom of the valley, we nearly come to a dead stop.

Although the wave didn't take us as far as I expected, it did put us in quite a good position. While I struggle with the wheel to take the next wave from the best possible angle, the boat starts to lean forward. It feels as if we are about to somersault. When this steeper breaker reaches the stern the impact shakes the boat. As she's gaining speed, the rigging reverberates. My mouth is so dry I find it difficult to breathe. I must have something to drink. While the boat is surfing and the spray on either side of the boat makes her look like she's taken flight on white wings, I yell to Deborah that I must have some water. While she's down in the boat and we slide down into the next valley, the wave contin-ues its path and slams into the end of breakwater.

As Deborah comes on deck, the third wave has just gotten a grip on us. The breakwater fills our field of view. The people fishing from it are reeling in their lines as fast as they can. I can't make out a word of what they are scream-ing down at us.

With only 50 or 60 yards left to the corner of the breakwater, I put the huge stone wall out of my mind. Instead, I concentrate on steering toward an imaginary rounding mark I set 10 yards to the left of the breakwater, inside the harbor. Without even realizing it, I take the glass that Deborah proffers and empty it while turning the wheel hard to port. Then I scream, "Hang on!"

This can only go one of two ways. Mere seconds after I think that, I watch the windvane swish past the inner corner of the breakwater, with 4, maybe 5, yards to spare. The people standing on top of it cast out their lines again. They are hooting and hollering, but I can't tell if they are angry or having fun. At the same moment, I feel the wind increasing from forward of abeam. Before I even manage to say anything, Deborah is sheeting in the genoa, matching the pace with which I steer to windward and sheet the mizzen and main.

Concentrating fully to use the little drive the wind provides, I cannot af-ford a glance astern to see what happens with the next wave. But a glimpse of Deborah's smile tells me that it will never reach us. She announces: "You made it! Welcome to Mar del Plata!" Then she jumps over to me and clasps her arms around my neck. It's the finest hug I've ever received.

26

CLOSING THE CIRCLE

DEBORAH

■ ■ ■

Yesterday evening, while we were hove to at sea, Rolf pulled out his black leather briefcase just to check that all our ship's papers were in order and ready to present to the Argentine authorities. Except for a little dust, all was just as we had left it a year ago. Paging through his passport nostalgically, Rolf got to thinking about his trip to the hernia repair shop and, for the first time, actually looked for the stamp he got when he left Argentina aboard *Illiria*. But there wasn't any. He's never been stamped out of the country!

I can only assume that the hair-raising experience of surfing between the breakwater arms is about to pale in comparison to that soon to come in the officials' office when we arrive with clearance papers from the same office, now yellowing with age, that declare us bound for Chile (although we never checked in there) and with a captain who appears to have been inside Argentina for more than a year already, while his crew, on the same boat, hasn't. As we walk toward the first office, I rather dejectedly tell Rolf, "I wish we'd studied more Spanish over the winter. Explaining this is far beyond our capability."

But it seems we have had the luck to arrive on a Friday. Never are people as busy at their work—their *own* work, that is—as they are Friday afternoons; the sea of desks has nary an attendant. Ringing the bell on the counter gets us no response. We wait patiently, figuring that someone has to show eventually to lock up, if nothing else. When one man finally appears, he's in a rush. We recognize him, but if he has any even vague memory of us, he doesn't show it. What he makes very clear, however, is that we should hurry up. His hand cuts the air like a knife, nonverbally demanding that we temper the opening formalities and just hand over the papers. If he has any questions they are surpressed. He can't locate all the stamps fast enough, as he bam-bam-bam processes us in. All those gray hairs for nothing.

Soon after we return to the yacht club, Mariano and his family show up. They've been pouncing on each boat to arrive the last month, asking questions concerning our whereabouts, expecting us. After a warm welcome and tears of happiness, they whisk us off to their neighboring motorboat club's restaurant. "You must have ice cream immediately!" says Mariano. What a reputation we have!

Then we have a promise to make good. As there was neither time nor energy available for more than verbal thanks for all their help and hospitality before we left for Antarctica, we had promised that upon our return we would have Mariano's whole family over for a celebration. But fall weather has already arrived, and because it's too chilly to eat on deck and there are too many people to sit comfortably inside *Northern Light*, we suggest that the dinner be staged at their house. Rolf and I bake rolls and dessert on board, then shop for all the dinner ingredients en route to their house.

Cooking in their kitchen becomes a party in itself. Mariano's mother, Raquel, gets quite a kick out of watching the Swedish chef invade her domain. She dances around us, watching every move we make, giggles, asks questions via Karina about the cooking, and gets so bubbly that she reaches for the phone, calling her best friend to describe the event as it's happening. Then she repeats everything, blow by blow, for Mariano's sister, Marina, when she arrives home from school. The entire scene is purely and simply delightful.

The day before takeoff, Hector shuttles us to the wholesale district to buy fresh vegetables. He'd planned to go to one particular stall, but after pulling up in front of it, he puts the car in reverse, explaining that we'll go instead to one of his fellow motorboat club members at *Establecimiento Los Muchachos*. I love the name, and that it's painted atop an overflowing cornucopia of vegetables on a gaily colored sign bodes well I think, at first.

Juan, the boss and a bear of a man, gets our list; Hector tells him that our *loco* plan is to sail from Mar del Plata all the way to Sweden without stopping. Juan's first response is to hit himself in the forehead with the heel of his hand. "Ha!" he shouts and then spins around and whistles for a couple of employees. With the tone of a drill sergeant and without as much as a glance to the list Hector handed him, Juan shouts out names of different vegetables and his men carry the assortment—crate by crate!—to the door. It is much more than we had planned on buying, but we don't seem to be able to get that idea across.

This man's exuberance must somehow be tamed. Getting Hector's attention, I revert to sign language. Palm up, I rub my thumb across the tips of the other four fingers. "Money, Hector, Money!" I say. "We won't have enough money." In response, his shoulders rise to ear level and a big question mark covers his face.

I don't know what to do. Why buy more than we can eat? "Half of this will go bad in the heat of the Tropics," I say to my equally confounded husband. "How can we get it across to him that we only want what is on the list?" But it's already too late. Juan grabs me by the arm and half drags/half dances me across the dirt floor toward the front door of his *establecimiento* and outside into the glaring sun. He motions for me to get into the car and sit in the backseat. "*Klaro!*" I tell him, but *OK, OK, get your hands off me* is what I'm thinking. Another whistle to his men and out they come out in a procession, carrying gunnysacks of carrots, cabbages, onions, and potatoes; crates of tomatoes, eggplant, lettuce; and a rainbow assortment of peppers. They pack the trunk, then pack me in. Rolf is unceremoniously shoved into the passenger seat and buried under a crate of broccoli. Then Juan waltzes around to the back door, leans in, and in the wafting smell of dirt and fresh produce kisses me on both cheeks. He smiles the winning smile of a big heart, and from inches away yells, "*Buena suerte!*" Perhaps he thinks I need the extra volume to understand.

All assembled—Juan, his men, and by now the bookkeeper as well as others who have gathered to the commotion from neighboring shops—are standing outside the car with Hector, all having a good laugh . . . and it dawns on us what is happening . . . how this man is becoming part of our trip by bestowing what he has to give as his best wishes for our voyage. Hector puts his four-wheeled overflowing cornucopia in gear and drives off. If I could turn around, I would. Second best will have to do; I put my arm out the window and wave good-bye.

On April 22, at 1530 local time, under a semiovercast sky and with wind out of the north at 4 knots, Mariano, his brother, Martin, and Karina tow us from the marina to the outer harbor. Another motorboat zooms towards us. Gabby and Jorje, live-aboards and happy owners of a 12-volt fridge unit Rolf "discarded" when we were here last time, didn't know we were leaving and have come out to say good-bye. They pass us a letter that arrived today from Akemi and Yoshio, the Japanese couple we met here on our way south. It includes a note congratulating us on our successful overwinter and a beautiful watercolor Yoshio has painted for us. I'm getting easy to reduce to tears, I find out.

Everyone is waving and tooting horns. Above it all, Mariano shouts: "Good-bye, my friends. Remember that you will always be welcome here." Then he lets the tow rope go. It's an easy departure through the breakwater's arms this time in the northerly breeze.

As the crow flies, the track from Mar del Plata north and around Scotland to the windmill in Fiskebäckskil is 7,300 nautical miles. A few generations ago, captains of square-rigged ships en route from Australia to England planned on seventy to seventy-five days to get from this latitude to Plymouth. The time this segment takes for our engineless ships is more dependent on the "stickiness" of the doldrums than anything else. We figure we'll make it through faster than any heavy sailing vessel could, but because we're going farther than England, we estimate that it'll take us those seventy to eighty days before we sight Sweden.

Just moving ourselves from point A to point B is not enough, however. We want these two-plus months to be meaningful, a time to be remembered with pleasure. Neither of us gives a thought or worry to the idea of being bored on the passage. After fifteen months in Antarctica, almost nine of which we were as alone as two people can be, we are time-usage artists. First, there are plenty of tasks to accomplish when just the two of us sail. Exactly one half of the time the voyage takes, I will be on watch. The responsibilities, chores, and work watches entail ensure that twelve hours of each day will fly. Beyond that, we'll strive to keep our creative gears engaged: writing, filming, and inventing new menus. There's a prize to be won this trip by coming up with a meal that's never before been served aboard. Thanks to Juan, there's no decision to be made about the first twenty main courses I'll be preparing for dinners; they'll include eggplant in one form or another. But how many will be award winners remains to be seen!

Clicking off the miles, northbound through degree after degree of latitude and thereby fast-forwarding ourselves through seasons will be stimulating, especially to bodies that have lived in cold storage the last fifteen months. I'm sure that just for the sake of change itself, the climate change will be appreciated, and ditto for the sailing tactics this oceanic transection involves, a challenge that demands study, analysis, and planning. No, boredom will not be an issue. On the other hand, we have to watch out for boredom's cousin. On such a long voyage, the repetitive drone of our four on, four off watch schedule holds the promise of tediousness, the growing ground of a dangerous fiend called monotony.

Were we to stick to a pure four-hour watch system, each of us would have three watches each twenty-four hours and our watches would be the exact same time slots every day. To change that, we each stand a two-hour watch in the afternoon, thereby jogging the time schedule. It also means that we have three watches one day and four the next. In a voyage of seventy days, that's 245 watches. Two hundred and forty-five times I will go from standby to on duty, have wake up and dress, and then undress and sleep. Yes, monotony is likely to be the devil to keep at bay.

The longest time we've ever been at sea is forty-one days. That length of time presented no specific problem. But this trip may be twice that long. All I know from experience is that we will be tired for the first seven to ten days until our bodies adjust to the new sleep pattern, then all can be fine for at least thirty more days. After that, it will be interesting to see what happens. I plan to check on myself and Rolf, watching for either complacent or lackadaisical attitudes or behavior. My guess is that the droning repetitiveness of the four on, four off schedule can seep into, or superimpose itself onto us. The implied danger is a dulling, numbing effect, leading to disintegration of analytical, cohesive thought, an invaluable capacity for sailing and safety as well as creativity, which is so very important to the time-usage artist. Of course, the big question is whether, when dulled and numbed, one can realize it oneself. With that problem in mind, I've added a reminder to the fortieth day's line in the logbook to make sure to start checking.

Rolf seems to have caught the cold that was circulating in Mariano's family. It's a bad one and will ensure that the first few days drag, but when it's over there'll be no more illness; there are no bugs to catch out here. It's actually amazing to think that since coming out of isolation we have never gotten seriously sick, not from contact with folks on cruise ships, stations, or in Mar del Plata.

Unlucky me drew the 2200–0200 watch. It's a toughie the first night out, so when dinner is done, I lie down for a nap. After what seems like five minutes' sleep, Rolf nudges me. "Please get up right away," he says. "There's a fishing boat nearing on a collision course. Put your jacket on and stay in the cupola. You probably won't have to do anything, but I want you to be ready, just in case." He disappears quickly. I jump up and look out. Sure enough, there it is, coming dead against us. I lift the cupola to alert Rolf that I'm in position. He describes the situation. "I don't think he's seen us. I'm steering as deep downwind as I can, and showing him our red lantern, but he just keeps bearing down on us. We just have to wait and see if he forces us to gybe."

Of course, it's always difficult to be woken up like this, to come from dreamland to stark reality. But, once again, I think that it's no problem really; as long as we keep a strict lookout, there's always enough time to maneuver out of the way. It's the dance of the high seas for us little guys today.

The fishing boat never makes an exaggerated move, the signal between ships that are too close for comfort that means: I see you and, if necessary, this is the way I will turn. No, there's no sign from him of any intention to move or that he even knows we are here. With just a few boat lengths between us, he passes right by, the manifestation of the symbolic ship in the night. We never see anybody aboard: not a person on deck, not a shadow in the wheelhouse. Maybe it's their dinnertime? There are lights burning inside and we hear music playing. It's an eerie sight, an eerie feeling.

During the first five days we adjust smoothly and get our sea legs back without any seasickness, thanks to having slack in the sheets and cool, sunny, pleasant weather. The constellation Scorpio is overhead. This trip is so long that any indication of covering distance is appreciated. Scorpio doesn't help any. It looms so large, spreading over the dome of the sky, that it feels like it will take forever to move out from under the nasty spider. Our daily noon positions show that so far we have 1 knot current against us, slowing our progress. On the positive side, perhaps due to that current, the water is already getting warm. It's 82°F (28°C), 2 degrees warmer than the pilot chart leads us to expect this time of the year, and it's alive with dolphins! After numerous sightings of small groups, today we had no less than 100 bottlenose dolphins, including babies, cavorting around the boat! They crisscrossed behind, under, and in front of the boat, leaping, spinning, bellyflopping, for five minutes. We were ecstatic. Suddenly, a "call" sounded, and within one second, every last one of them zoomed away in the same direction. They could have stayed around longer, I pouted. At least the memory lasts forever.

By day six, the wind has shifted against us, coming from the northeast, and then, in a typical pattern, increases to 28 to 36 knots then pauses. Overnight it increases steadily until it's blowing 60 plus knots out of the north. The barometer has dropped during this time from 1023 to 1001 millibars, and we find ourselves in a full storm, now atypical. Indeed, this is the strongest storm we have ever experienced at sea.

By the end of my watch, the lee portholes are once again under water. *Northern Light* needs a final reef. Rolf begins his watch by furling the tail ends of the yankee and main to continue under our storm sail configuration: staysail and double-reefed mizzen, heading about 60 degrees off the wind. It's as high as we want to point in this wind strength and, fortunately, is only 15 degrees off course. Four hours later, when Rolf wakes me for my watch, he tells me that there is no reason for me to get up. "What? Surely you jest! Not stand watch? Unheard of!" I exclaim.

"Well, have a look," Rolf says to me. I have to climb slowly and carefully out of the sea berth, which is now tilted to the max to compensate for the 20 to 25 degree heel of the boat. Each move toward the ladder has to be timed to the severe pitching of the boat in the big sea. I move slowly from handhold to handhold and climb the ladder up to the cupola. What do I see? Nothing, nada, zilch. Not the moon, nary a star. I cannot even see as far as the next wave; the crests are being blown off so mightily that the air is full of spray. It's like looking through a waterfall. My captain says: "See what I mean? You don't want to be out there. As a matter of fact, it's not even worth the risk of trying to stay on the ladder. You'd never see a ship before it was too late anyway. We might as well rest this one out."

What? Rest? When I should be on watch? My body is awake and ready to work, my mind trying to cope with this strange turn of events. I hold myself in position on the ladder a few minutes. The noise and motion is amazing. Considering the situation, the boat is riding nicely; so well, in fact, that she can still be sailed with the wheel locked. *Northern Light* balances so well that, close-hauled, we can sail without using the windvane and can thereby save the Monitor's servoblade from the pounding it would otherwise take in this pitching.

Ah, one can love a boat one trusts. But trust luck? That's a new one. "I think you misunderstand me," Rolf replies. "The one on watch, although prone, is to stay awake, listening for changes in the wind, for any funny noises, and especially for ships. Lying on the floor you will most certainly hear the cavitation noise from a ship's propeller long before you would ever see the ship by looking out through the cupola. The idea is that since you can't see anything you can't be *on lookout*. But you'll be *on listen*."

Now I understand. Rolf takes over the sea berth and I move some cushions to the floor. Thus we alternate floor to sea berth over the next twelve hours. What energy is being unleashed! It blows and blows as if there is no other wind strength beside full storm available. The sea builds, getting higher and steeper, yet *Northern Light* can still hold her own 60 degrees off the wind. That's not to say she's not taking a pounding, dropping off wave crests, becoming airborne each time for nerve-wracking seconds, then free-falling into the troughs until landing with resounding, bone-shaking booms. I listen closely for any change in sound or noise, especially one that signals the approach of a freak wave. The gusts are true shriekers. One has already snapped the wooden windvane. Wow. Well, I always thought that in a storm like this we'd have to turn and run with it. Instead, we're making 5 knots against it. What a boat!

The wind finally begins to diminish. Then, during the morning of April 30, the cold front arrives. In a flash, the wind shifts from north to southwest 35 knots. With the new wind direction blowing across the old sea, it gets so very confused that it looks at first as though wind will cancel wave, but that's just my wishful thinking. The corkscrew motion the boat takes on, coupled with the din, is beyond description. Yet even more decibels are added. The cold front sports a percussion section as well, in the form of thunder. It's as if we are living through the personification of a symphony conductor's nightmare: a cacophonous movement where every musician plays any old tune, full speed, full volume. I become convinced that this passage can only end in "cymbolic" destruction, obliteration! The knot in my chest twists tighter. Then an albatross wheels and cavorts through the scene. Backlit by a bolt of lightning, I watch it glide up the front of a 25-foot wave. Reaching the breaking crest, it soars upward until it *just* clears the mass of spray speading before the wind. That bird, perfectly at ease, balleting through the midst of this chaos strikes a final, rich, and harmonious chord at the end of the movement. My perspective can't but change. With the realization that we aren't dancing too badly ourselves, I find myself laughing.

The day after the storm we catch a perfect-size fish, by which I mean one that we, who have no refrigerator, can devour before any of it spoils. The dorado has a robust flavor, the perfect accompaniment to, what else? Ratatouille a la muchachos.

On May 3, we find the northeast wind. The tactic is to sail east now so as to stay away from the northerly wind and current against us at Cabo Frio, just east of Rio de Janeiro, and then continue easting until we find the southeasterly tradewind. Six days later (twenty-one watches, but who's counting?), the wind shifts counterclockwise to southwest, giving us a little slack. With the boat upright for the first time in a long time, Rolf takes the opportunity to check around. Hanging over the lifelines he notices that a patch of paint is missing from the bow, about the size of his head and shoulders. It *was* blowing after all, enough to chisel off paint. Now that's a story!

The wind continues around. Within twenty-four hours, on May 10, we get southeast. It should stop there, but it seems the trades are not as reliable as they used to be; this time they are blowing more from the east than southeast, but that's fine for those of us who are in a hurry because it means a beam reach (a little faster point of sail) north to the doldrums. But, unfortunately, the shift continues counterclockwise as far as east-northeast, and here we are almost close-hauled again against 15 to 18 knots. The hatches have to be closed because of the spray *Northern Light* kicks up, and it's hotter than I remember. My body is not used to this, that's for sure. I'm very happy that, at 8 degrees south of the equator on May 14, the wind shifts back, going to east-southeast 16 to 20 knots. We can now get more airstream inside again. Otherwise, I think I should have expired!

Our course is naturally a little more zigzag than any motorized vessel would take. Studying the pilot charts, one can check the shipping lanes between any two points to see what the Great Circle route is. We're glad to have a chart that shows those routes so that we know when to keep an extraspecial lookout for shipping. It may sound ridiculous that we look both ways before crossing a shipping lane, as if we are pedestrians about to cross a highway, but that's exactly what shipping lanes are today. Modern ships, relying on GPS navigation, can keep precisely to the lanes and take the absolute shortest route: a fuel-saving, therefore cost-conscious, method. Here, near the eastern bulge of South America, we first cross the lane that goes to and from Cape Horn, and then, closer to the equator, we cross three lanes that lead to or from the Cape of Good Hope. We meet ship after ship. Little do I know, but the entire way north through the Atlantic we will see at least one ship on each and every lane! How many thousands of ships are there in operation, I wonder?

Just after midnight on my watch, I see the flash from the lighthouse on the island of Fernando de Naronha—just where it should be—10 miles to starboard. After passing it, I resheet *Northern Light*. The tactic now is to steer a course 5 degrees east of north until the doldrums.

On May 16, Rolf proudly relates to me that during the previous week we made 1,021 nautical miles. "So far since leaving 'Marianotown' we've averaged 127 miles per day. If we can keep this speed, the total trip will only take 63 days!" he says. Do I hear "the racer's if"?

The next day at 1956 UTC we cross the equator, at 32°14′ W. On May 19, we cross above the Mid-Atlantic Ridge, its 6,000-foot-high mountains rising off the seafloor. Even without any means of fixing our position we'd know we were coming off the plains; we can feel the upwelling even though the mountains are a third of a mile underneath us! The turbulence makes the sea roil and gives *Northern Light* a peculiar jerky motion.

Rolf sighted the first man-o'-war on his watch, which he sadly told me was sailing almost as fast as we were. Yes, the southeast wind is getting lighter and lighter. At 5°40′ N we hit the doldrums. We work hard, trimming and trimming, to claw our way through what can be a very trying place. We play every puff, trim through every wind shift, and especially love the furling sails here! It's so easy to unroll them that I never hesitate to try to use a puff, and I can quickly furl when the wind dies. That saves the sails from the tremendous wear and tear of flapping and flogging when becalmed. When it's calm, the surface of the ocean looks oily and mercurial. The mix of airs builds lots of squalls and we use them to fill and top off our water tanks so that we once again have an eighty-day supply. Then we take showers and launder sheets and towels. The rain also brings us bad news, however. It has started dripping in the aft cabin and engine compartment. Our cockpit is leaking. The "marine plywood" is delaminating.

After just one day and a mere 75 miles in the doldrums, with variable winds of 0 to 5 knots, a heavy cloud line brings a thirty-minute tropical downpour followed by three hours of light rain. I'm confused. Where are the heavy gusts, lightning, and thunder? When it clears, the wind stabilizes from the north-northeast at 10 knots. That wasn't a squall. We've passed through a barrier zone into a new weather system: the Northern Hemisphere's tradewind! We certainly got through easily this time.

The tactic now is to stay relatively close-hauled, taking the wind 50 to 55 degrees to starboard for speed's sake, steering 350 degrees magnetic. Our next target is a point 150 miles west of the Azores, to be adjusted any time the position of the windless mid-Atlantic high-pressure cell shifts. We've already started to keep track of the high's center by listening to two maritime nets on the amateur bands, both of which cater to boats in the North Atlantic. One is the Trans-Atlantic Net on the frequency 21400 at 1300 UTC. Each person who checks in gives their position and reports the weather there. From that we can sketch the true North Atlantic weather picture, along the milk run we will soon cross. The second net, the UK Maritime Mobile Net, on 14303 at 0800 and 1800 UTC, reads both the British and French weather synopses and forecasts for the North Atlantic and reports the position of the center of the "treacherous" high, now sitting directly in our path just west of the Azores. We may just have to make a radical swing west. Florida? There goes our hope for a seventy-day passage!

Without an engine, we do not want to get stuck inside the windless center of the high. Thus, during this entire segment it's crucial to keep the center to starboard. It's fun to keep track, and what we learn is that the French meteorologists know what they're doing. Day after day, the high moves exactly as they predict.

Poor Rolf lost another fish today. So far it's three to two in favor of the fish. But mileage wise we are doing fine. Today, May 24, thirty-two days out, we are halfway to Fiskebäckskil! It's still hot and sunny, and we've had good wind—between 12 and 20 knots—for the last three days. On May 28, we sail out of the Tropics. It only took twenty-two days and twenty hours to sail from the Tropic of Capricorn to the Tropic of Cancer, equivalent to one-eighth of Earth's total circumference. At that speed, it would take us 184 days to sail around the world. No record-breaker there!

I can hardly believe it, but we still have one of Don Juan's eggplants left. The skin is little bruised, marked by the strings of the hammock, but the flesh is still fine. We won't lose one! It also seems as if we'll have cabbage for a few weeks yet and onions and potatoes the entire time.

Passing time. . . . Adjusting the position of the solar cell every ten minutes to keep it exactly 90° to the sun. We might as well keep it working at maximum effectiveness; it's the only source of electricity we have during this trip. I have been penning letters to the children in our family, each one about a different aspect of life at sea or an event on this particular voyage. I also talked on the radio to Bob and Frank today and gave them an update. And I baked a cherry pie, although even without the oven on it's too hot. On May 29, we see an adult and a cute baby pilot whale. On May 30, with the wind westerly at 6 to 8 knots, Rolf wakes me to help set the spinnaker. Such pleasant sailing now. We cross the Great Circle route between Panama and Gibraltar. Yikes! There are ships everywhere, and with light, variable wind, I am extremely glad to have a VHF just in case a ship comes too close and we don't have enough wind to maneuver. On June 2, we start our favorite week. There are no less than four birthdays to celebrate, so there's no monotony around here! We've now been out for forty days, averaging 125 miles per day, which keeps us to the *Northern Light* norm for long passages.

On June 7, the barometer reaches a record high for this voyage: 1,044 millibars! With it comes a little cloud cover. I'd nearly forgotten clouds exist. On the next day, the wind shifts to south. According to the pilot chart, southerly wind dominates this region from 40° N, and we got it at 40°24′ N. These pilot charts are amazingly helpful. The wind direction means that we can finally steer for the next marker: the northwest corner of Scotland, only 1,695 nautical miles away.

Ah, luck has been with us. As we drew close to the Azores, the center of the high started to move, taking a dramatic swing north to a position west of Scotland! With the Azores 200 miles to starboard and the high pumping, we got easterly wind, shifting to southeast and now south and we . . . are . . . flying! June 9 brings southwest wind at 15 knots, June 10 brings southwest 8 to 10 knots! On June 11, it's southwest at 18–20 knots; on June 12, west at 10 to 12 knots; on June 13, south-southwest at 20 to 25 knots. To the clouds, add fog. The lads at faraway Faraday taught us that foggy weather is to be called "mank," and because we're close to their home waters, we name the region

Mank Bank in their honor. June 14 brings north-northwest wind at 18 to 25 knots; June 15, north-northwest at 15 knots. We made 1,147 miles last week! On June 16, it's west-southwest at 16 to 22 knots.

We're so happy. I know this will sound odd, but we broke a block today. It's a Rutgerson block, which we switched to when we changed the rigging four years ago. The block was on the main boom's preventer, which on *Northern Light* also functions as a vang. We had the block under too much load for the sea condition and the shackle broke. In other words, it was our own fault. What made us happy was that after examining the broken block, we found that every single part was deformed and about to give up. That means that the block was actually well engineered; each individual part was properly designed to take its share of the load for which the block is rated. Kudos to you, Mr. Rutgerson!

On June 19, we reach the northwest corner of Scotland. We are northing no more! Turn east! At noon, only 484 miles are left to the windmill. At 1430, land ho! Fair Isle abeam!

It's a good thing we don't have too far to go. We'll make it, but there's been a warning sign that monotony has indeed taken the upper hand. Complacency has reared its ugly head.

It's been foggy for more than a week now. I was making lunch and woke Rolf from his nap. The fog had thickened from what it had been on most of my watch, so I should have asked him to keep a lookout while I completed lunch preparations, but I didn't. Suddenly, I heard the unmistakable sound of a propeller. Sure enough, as embarrassing as this is to admit, there was a fishing boat on an opposing course already abeam; it was perhaps 200 yards away. My heart stopped. What a shock!

I've got to do better than that, I tell myself when I realize what has happened. Right now, we're coming into the most crowded water of the entire voyage. The North Sea is the worst place I know. Hidden in the fog are lots of fishing boats, and oil fields, and there's always a continuous stream of ships moving hither and dither.

The next day, it's Rolf's turn to make lunch. He wakes me from a short nap, which has spin cotton candy in my skull. I sit silently at the nav desk, rubbing my eyes and staring at nothing, waiting patiently. Rolf turns from the stove and tells me I'll have to fork over the prize because the dish he's made has never been served on board before! That gets my attention. He passes me my lunch. It sure smells good.

I look at it and start laughing. The food, a variation of a dish from northern Sweden called *Lappskojs,* is a mashed potato and turnip mixture with meat chunks in it. Restated, it's an orangy mush with brown bits in it that I—I can't help myself—I think looks like puppy poop. Through laughter, I tell Rolf what I think is so funny. I get no response. Still, try as I might, I can't stop laughing. That Rolf doesn't see the humor only makes me laugh more. That the dish is called *skojs* adds to the joke, because *skoj* means "funny" in Swedish, and whether it is funny or not, I still can't stop laughing. You can't tell me that people are meant to keep a four-hour schedule forever.

When the giggle attack finally winds down, Rolf and I look at each other. "Don't worry," he tells me. "We'll soon be there."

Presently, at the latitude of 57°23′ N, just before midsummer, I can't really call my night watch "night watch" any longer. I imagine showing my nieces and nephews this latitude's light at midnight when only the brightest of the stars are visible, something they've never experienced. It naturally follows to write to them about it. It's nice to share some time with other people, even if it's in spirit only.

A steady mild wind out of the southwest blows 18 to 20 knots and I've got *Northern Light* sailing wing and wing with the genoa poled out. I am thankful that the fog's finally gone. At the risk of winning the understatement of the year award, I can say that this area, just before we become sandwiched between the coasts of Norway and Denmark, is very heavily trafficked. In perfect visibility during the last thirty hours, three ships in sight has been the norm. If ocean sailing is a wilderness experience, then the North Sea is civilized. Monotony is no longer an issue.

A ship comes up over the horizon astern, steaming slowly toward our port stern quarter. From my favorite watch position inside the cupola I take a bearing of the pinpoint-sized lights over a winch in the cockpit. I hum softly as *Northern Light* pulls at hull speed, about 8 knots. It's fine sailing. Time for a cup of tea, and a walnut and soybean pate and sprout sandwich on a fresh roll. Not a bad midnight snack! The ship comes toward us slowly, slowly, on the same bearing. After twenty minutes, I wake Rolf and explain the situation. I know it's with reluctance that he climbs out of his cozy seaberth. He looks through the cupola, then says, "Since you say he's gaining on us on a collision course, I'll dress. He's still plenty far away, and probably plans to pass us on our port side."

I put my foul weather gear on. The ship has yet to change direction or give any sign that he will. My nerves prickle. I think Rolf isn't dressing fast enough. "I'm going out on deck. I'll take preventers away in case we have to make a quick course change." Rolf shuffles along. I tell him: "Please call the ship on the VHF. Now." Rolf calls but gets no answer.

You can imagine what it's like when the call "Eastbound ship, this is the sailboat on your bow" goes out over channel 16 in the North Sea (even on low power, with only 1-watt output). Anything from one to who knows how many ships' watchkeepers have to look outside.

Two minutes drag by and we still get no reply. Instead of looking out at the ship, I am beginning to have to look up at it. Damn, it's a big, black, ugly thing. Its broad bow begins to fill my field of vision. If I knew he would turn, I would be able to lower my gaze and consider the phosphorescent bowwave beautiful. If we had an engine, we'd be able to pull a last-second maneuver. And if wishes were horses . . .

Rolf's the captain, but I'm the watch captain and this is my responsibility. Lifting the cupola I order: "Call him again. If he doesn't answer, it's time for us to move out of his way." The man who eventually answers our call is still half asleep. You can hear it in his voice. He says crackily, "Yes, I see you and I will turn port."

Whew, it's over. Wait, no it isn't. The ship's going starboard! It turns so hard that Rolf is afraid it will loose steerage, slide sideways, and mow us down. But it doesn't. With a margin of maybe a hundred yards it passes astern.

I say to Rolf, who is also quite awake now, "Well, it's 100 percent sure that the captain of that ship just rolled out of his bunk, so no matter how you cut it, Mr. Sleepingonwatch is in deep trouble." Rolf squints, knitting his eyebrows as he turns his gaze to the ship. "I just hope that wasn't the Captain we spoke to," he replies.

The following night I get a repeat performance. A ship rises from the horizon over the very same winch. But after last night's episode, we have decided to call any ship on a collision or near-collision course that comes within 2 miles of us and ask them to declare their intention. The law dictates that the overtaking vessel is to make any course change necessary to avoid collision. We reason that if they have already seen us and have a plan, then we'll hear it. If they don't have a plan, 2 miles gives them ample time to make one.

Our call is answered immediately. "Yes, yes, I see you on the radar and the computer tells me that I will pass you at a distance of six cables," is the reply. It's difficult to tell from the disdainful tone whether the man is bored or finds us bothersome. Rolf says simply, "OK, thank you," and clears off the air. But then we agree that with only a few degrees' course change, he could stay at least a mile away. After all, any wind shift or wind increase could bring us a lot closer than six cables. We start to wonder whether ships' crew actually understand a sailboat's maneuverability in various sea conditions and on different points of sail. There's no reason to assume they do. Although we say nothing more to the ship, it steers a little more to port and parallels our course until well ahead of us before crossing our path.

The following night, on the starboard bow, I see two white lights come over the horizon. One is right on top of the other and they are soon flanked by a red and a green. Here we go again. But even before I finish suiting up, the ship makes a sharp port turn and arcs around us at 3 mile's distance. I scream into the night, "I love you, whoever you are!" and think to myself, *Seamanship is not dead.*

During the remainder of my night watch, I ponder modern folks' reliance on instrumentation and wonder how destructive it is to the judgment that underlies the art of seamanship. For instance, the man last night knew (because a computer told him so) that he would pass us at six cables' distance. Reliance on that information displaced active analysis on his part, and furthermore, accepting information as fact deterred him from making any judgment, such as whether the distance was or was not enough. The result of machine-generated information being accepted as a fixed truth is that margin for change or error crimps; danger therefore expands. The absolutely unpredictable hazards that we are now experiencing occur inside situations created by people. Interacting with nature, even in its extremes, is for the most part predictable. *This* is adventure. Welcome back!

Within a few hours, we are in a force 8 gale. I listen to the weather report. Because it's Sunday, I am pleased there is one; it's still a novelty after being in South America so long, where weather reports don't exist on Sundays. But this report is peculiar. The English coastal stations and oil rigs just upwind of us don't report more than a breeze, and the gale we have is forecast for tomorrow. Odd. The British Shipping Report is usually quite good. But because it's important for us to remain as active as possible now, near the end of this passage, I suggest to Rolf that we even stop listening to the weather reports. After all, our tactics from here to the finish line only depend on what the weather is and we can get that information by looking.

A good portion of my watch is spent wondering what excitement to expect tomorrow if we close the lee rocky archipelago in a full gale without an engine. I reacquaint myself with the charts of *Northern Light*'s home waters and make my own contingency plans for entry in different wind directions. I know Rolf has already made his.

In the shallow Skagerrak, waves build steeply. I keep a constant 360-degree lookout; the distance I can see is certainly not more than $1\frac{1}{2}$ miles. I don't trust that any other boat will see us. It used to be the law that each ship had to have two people on lookout: one to port, the other to starboard. But that is no longer the case; people have been replaced with radar. In this breaking sea, when the radar's sensitivity is turned down to reduce the clutter that breaking waves make on the screen, the radar echo that little *Northern Light* creates is also tuned out. I am concentrating, watching, busy, and hungry, but I ignore the last fact. Time passes quickly.

A ferry comes up from our starboard quarter. I lose sight of it for long periods in the high sea and therefore cannot determine its exact course, but it'll be coming close. In broad daylight, we can see the ship's color and flag, which makes it easier to call just him. He answers immediately: "Yes, I see you. I will turn port so we can pass each other starboard to starboard." I see the shock register on Rolf's face.

Rolf replies: "Do not turn port. I repeat. Do not turn port. We are just on your port side, not more than a quarter mile away." We rush out on deck, just in case. The ferry alters course slightly to starboard and passes ahead of us. That man had "seen" some other boat on his radar, not us.

On June 22, although we can't see land, we smell a wood fire from Norway. As if on cue, the wind starts to diminish. At noon, with only twenty miles to go, we sight land. The low pink granite coastline of Sweden—lovely Bohuslän—creeps up over the horizon. The GPS continually updates the course to steer, compensating for the heavy current, to deposit us at our waypoint: the buoys closest to our home harbor. The wind becomes light, southwest 5 to 8 knots, which allows us to enjoy the sights, the feelings, and a leisurely lunch; the last meal of this passage if things go according to plan.

Sailing wing and wing, we cross all the summer sailors' north-to-south along-the-coast paths. Inside the shelter of the outer archipelago, the sea calms. Delightful! Our longest ocean voyage is over. The total elapsed time at sea to cover 7,937 nautical miles was sixty days and eighteen hours. It took us only thirteen days from the latitude of the Azores, averaging 162 miles per day. Not bad! We're going to take the entire village by surprise.

The very last plan necessary for this expedition is now to be played out. We'll sail right up to the mouth of our home harbor, drop the hook, inflate the dinghy, attach the outboard, and tow ourselves to the dock.

Just after we sight Fiskebäckskil's windmill and are chattering about almost being there, a small motorboat comes up astern. We don't recognize it, but after trailing in our wake for a while the boat's occupants pop up. The first Swedish faces we see belong to friends! Happy tears form. Bengt and Cilla take a rope and tow us to Lyckans Slip, where we gently place *Northern Light* alongside the very same dock she left nearly three years earlier. It's so easy that the arrival takes on the air of an anticlimax.

Our thirty-four month 28,000-mile voyage, and that *Northern Light* has become the first Swedish vessel to ever winter in Antarctica, is brought to the attention of the mayor of Göteborg, and he wants to welcome us back by celebrating in a big way. It is his suggestion that we have *Northern Light* towed the 40 miles to that city and then be led into the harbor by fireboats spraying arches of water, greeted at the city wharf by a band, and formally welcomed home by the mayor himself! Rolf, spontaneous fellow that he is, says "Sure!"

I want to talk about it, but our mail is delivered. The bundle includes a card from our Japanese friend Tate! He tells us that he completed his trip as planned, in three years, to the very day. The message that sums up his feelings is "Concentrate Gratitude."

Rolf and I both smile. I tell him that yes, indeed, I think I can do just that for a while, lying in a field somewhere, listening to bugs buzzing, and chewing on a blade of grass. I certainly feel grateful. I might as well think about it and let it blossom as the weariness dissipates. To the mayor we say: "Thank you, but no thank you. The trip to Göteborg is too dangerous as tired as we are. That you wanted to do it is good enough for us."

A

APPENDIX

■ ■ ■

Northern Light: History and Lines Drawings

N*orthern Light* has sailed a total of 139,000 nautical miles, the equivalent of 6.5 times around the world at the equator.

Northern Light's Voyages
1977–1981 **"Around the World"**   Sweden via Cape Horn and Cape of Good Hope to Sweden. 65,000 nautical miles.
1982–1984 **"Arctic–Antarctic"**   Sweden, north of Spitsbergen to the pack ice, reaching 80°25′ N, Greenland, Panama, Chile, Antarctic Peninsula, United States. 33,000 nautical miles.
1986 United States, via Scotland to Sweden. 4,000 nautical miles.
1989–1992 **"Antarctic Winterover"**   Sweden, United States, Bermuda, Azores, Madeira, Canary Islands, Brazil, Argentina, Antarctic Peninsula, Argentina, Sweden. 28,000 nautical miles.
1994 **"Around Scandinavia"**   Sweden, Åland, Finland, Denmark, Sweden, Norway. 3,700 nautical miles.
1995–1996 **"Winterover on the Arctic Circle"**   Nordfjord, Norway, to Sweden. 1,000 nautical miles.
Northern Light's Records
1977 First Swedish sailboat around Cape Horn
1981 First Swedish sailboat to complete a trip around the world without transiting either the Suez or Panama Canal

1984 First Swedish (also first Scandinavian) sailboat to Antarctica

1984 Covered the longest north-to-south-distance ever achieved in a sailboat in one continuous voyage, with the same crew

1984 First sailboat in the world to have sailed in all oceans and visited all continents

1992 First Swedish sailboat (also first Swedish vessel) to spend the winter in Antarctica

Awards

1986 The Cruising Club of America's "Blue Water Medal"

1986 The Swedish Cruising Club's "Ship's Bell" Award

1986 The Solander Plaque

1987 The Seven Seas Cruising Association's Award

Designed by Jean Knocker

Steel hull, deck and superstructure built by META in Tarare, France, 1973–74

Rigging, interior etc. done by Rolf. Ready-to-sail 1976

Length on deck 39'7" (12.07m)

Beam 12'01" (3.68m)

Draft 6'01" (1.85m)

Displacement 14 tons

Sail plan: Main 385 square feet (35 square meters)

Mizzen 154 square feet (14 m²)

Genoa 616 square feet (56 m²)

Cutter staysail 165 square feet (15 m²)

Mizzen staysail 330 square feet (30 m²)

Spinnaker 1232 square feet (112 m²)

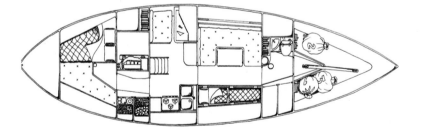

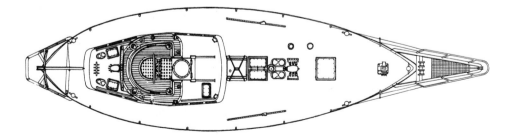

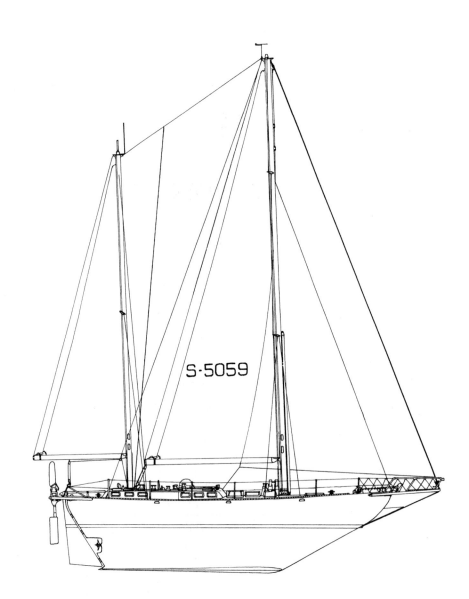

S·5059

B

APPENDIX

■ ■ ■

Weather Observations

Weather observations on board *Northern Light* at Hovgaard Island

Around any mountainous coastline, weather conditions are very local. Therefore, what we recorded at Hovgaard Island may not represent the weather 5 miles away.

MONTH	AMBIENT AIR TEMPERATURE		
	HIGHEST	LOWEST	AVERAGE
APRIL, 1991	39°F/+4°C	18F°/−8°C	28°F/−2°C
MAY	36°F/+2°C	12°F/−11°C	23°F/−5°C
JUNE	33°F/+0.5°C	5°F/−15°C	16°F/−9°C
JULY	39°F/+4°C	9°F/−13°C	19°F/−7°C
AUGUST	36°F/+2°C	5°F/−15°C	19°F/−7°C
SEPTEMBER	37°F/+3°C	0°F/−18°C	23°F/−5°C
OCTOBER	43°F/+6°C	−6°F/−21°C	19°F/−7°C
NOVEMBER	41°F/+5°C	23°F/−5°C	28°F/−2°C
DECEMBER	45°F/+7°C	27°F/−3°C	30°F/−1°C
JANUARY, 1992	41°F/+5°C	28°F/−2°C	36°F/+2°C
FEBRUARY	36°F/+2°C	27°F/−3°C	30°F/−1°C
MARCH	43°F/+6°C	23°F/−5°C	30°F/−1°C

MONTH	NUMBER OF STORM SYSTEMS	HIGHEST GUST (knots)	NUMBER OF DAYS WITH A MINIMUM OF 3 HOURS OF NINE-TENTHS CLOUD COVER OR LESS
APRIL, 1991	4	70	5
MAY	1	36	7
JUNE	2	30	10
JULY	5	80	5
AUGUST	4	70	5
SEPTEMBER	4	44	5
OCTOBER	3	56	5
NOVEMBER	5	40	3
DECEMBER	3	40	13
JANUARY, 1992	4	36	3
FEBRUARY	3	40	8
MARCH	6	44	2

Extremes of "temperature recognition" on bare skin:
 Coldest, with windchill factor: −77°F/−60°C.
 Warmest, in direct sun: 77°F/25°C.

C

APPENDIX

■ ■ ■

Provision List

	Food Consumed by Two People			
	Total in 16 months in lb. (kg)		Amount per month in lb. (kg)	
MEAT				
Vacuum-packed corned beef	80	(36)	5	(2.25)
Prosciutto (2 legs)	44	(20)	2.8	(1.25)
Salt pork	38	(17)	2.4	(1.10)
FRESH VEGETABLES				
Potato	222	(100)	13.9	(6.25)
Onion	166	(75)	10.5	(4.75)
Squash	44	(20)	2.8	(1.25)
Cabbage	44	(20)	2.8	(1.25)
DRIED VEGETABLES				
Squash	22	(10)	1.4	(0.62)
Spinach	11	(5)	0.7	(0.31)
Potato	22	(10)	1.4	(0.62)
Leek	11	(5)	0.7	(0.31)
Carrots	11	(5)	0.7	(0.31)
Tomato	4.5	(2)	0.27	(0.13)
Mushroom	2	(1)	0.13	(0.06)

	Food Consumed by Two People			
	Total in 16 months in lb. (kg)		Amount per month in lb. (kg)	
FRESH FRUIT				
Orange	89	(40)	5.6	(2.50)
Apple (Granny Smith)	89	(40)	5.6	(2.50)
DRIED FRUIT				
Prune	18	(8)	1.1	(0.50)
Raisin	22	(10)	1.38	(0.62)
Apricot	22	(10)	1.38	(0.62)
Apple	11	(5)	0.7	(0.31)
Peach	33	(15)	2.1	(0.94)
Pear	33	(15)	2.1	(0.94)
DAIRY PRODUCTS				
Butter	144	(65)	9	(4.00)
Cheese	89	(40)	5.6	(2.50)
Powdered whole milk	166	(75)	10.4	(4.70)
Fresh eggs (500)	78	(35)	4.9	(2.20)
BAKING NEEDS				
Bleached flour	444	(200)	27.7	(12.50)
Whole wheat flour	71	(32)	4.4	(2.00)
Corn meal	33	(15)	2.1	(0.94)
Wheat berries	22	(10)	1.38	(0.63)
Dry yeast, baking powder, spices	55	(25)	3.5	(1.56)
MISC				
Matches (16,000)	11	(5)	0.7	(0.31)
Toilet paper (70 rolls)	40	(18)	2.5	(1.13)
Dishwashing detergent (4 liters)	9	(4)	0.55	(0.25)
Laundry detergent	6.7	(3)	0.42	(0.19)
Personal hygiene articles	4.4	(2)	0.28	(0.12)
HOT DRINKS				
Coffee	69	(31)	4.3	(1.94)
Tea	6.7	(3)	0.42	(0.19)
Cocoa	16	(7)	1	(0.44)
Blueberry soup	22	(10)	1.4	(0.63)
Rosehip soup	18	(8)	1.1	(0.50)
MISC FOOD NEEDS				
Vegetable & olive oil (8 liters)	18	(8)	1.1	(0.50)
Sugar	133	(60)	8.3	(3.75)
Salt	15.5	(7)	1	(0.44)
Golden syrup	9	(4)	0.6	(0.25)
Molasses	4.5	(2)	.28	(0.13)
Honey	4.5	(2)	.28	(0.13)
Vinegar	18	(8)	1.1	(0.50)

	Food Consumed by Two People			
	Total in 16 months in lb. (kg)		Amount per month in lb. (kg)	
CANNED MEAT AND FISH				
Mackerel (86 × 280 gr)	53	(24)	3.3	(1.50)
Tuna (70 × 200 gr)	31	(14)	1.9	(0.88)
Fishballs (16 × 400 gr)	13	(6)	0.8	(0.40)
Cod roe (16 × 400 gr)	13	(6)	0.8	(0.40)
Corned beef (52 × 350 gr)	40	(18)	2.5	(1.14)
Clams (70 × 300 gr)	46	(21)	2.9	(1.20)
Ham (16 × 500 gr)	18	(8)	1.1	(0.80)
Bacon (8 × 400 gr)	7	(3.2)	0.44	(0.20)
Roast Beef (8 × 400 gr)	7	(3.2)	0.44	(0.20)
CANNED VEGETABLES AND FRUITS				
Tomato paste (70 × 150 gr)	24	(11)	1.5	(0.66)
Tomatoes, crushed (35 × 400 gr)	31	(14)	1.9	(0.87)
Red cabbage (16 × 400 gr)	13	(6)	0.8	(0.40)
Spinach (18 × 400 gr)	16	(7)	1	(0.45)
Zucchini (20 × 400 gr)	18	(8)	1.1	(0.50)
Mushrooms (30 × 100 gr)	6.7	(3)	0.4	(0.19)
Lingonberries (10 × 1 kg)	22	(10)	1.4	(0.63)
Cranberries (17 × 400 gr)	16	(7)	1	(0.40)
Blueberries (20 × 700 gr)	31	(14)	1.9	(0.88)
Applesauce (16 × 1 kg)	36	(16)	2.2	(1.00)
FREEZE-DRIED DINNERS				
7 different main courses				
(165 × 0.47 kg)	173	(78)	11	(4.70)
CEREAL				
Oatmeal porridge	100	(45)	6.2	(2.80)
Rye porridge	16	(7)	1	(0.44)
CARBOHYDRATES (dry stores)				
Mashed potato	44	(20)	2.8	(1.25)
Mashed parsnip	44	(20)	2.8	(1.25)
Soybeans (incl emergency rations)	80	(36)	5	(2.25)
Brown beans	40	(18)	2.5	(1.13)
Yellow peas	78	(35)	4.9	(2.18)
Garbanzo beans	22	(10)	1.4	(0.63)
Brown rice	51	(23)	3.2	(1.44)
Spaghetti noodles	64	(29)	4	(1.81)
Lentils	38	(17)	2.4	(1.06)
Barley	18	(8)	1.1	(0.50)
Hazelnuts, almonds, walnuts	33	(15)	2.1	(0.93)
Diverse extras	222	(100)	14	(6.25)
TOTAL	3,936	(1,773)	246	(112)

Fuels Used by Two People		
	Total in 16 months in gal. (liters)	Amount per month in gal. (liters)
Kerosene for cooking:	56 (210 liters)	3.5 (13.00 liters)
Kerosene for lamps:	16 (60 liters)	1 (3.75 liters)
Preheating alcohol:	8.5 (32 liters)	.53 (2.00 liters)

Notes:
1. The food list reflects what we actually consumed in sixteen months. For safety's sake (in case of spoilage, etc.) we had 10 percent extra with us. Had we needed to, we could have rationed to make the supplies last twenty-four months.
2. Prior to our departure for Antarctica from Mar del Plata, we were fortunate to buy a variety of sun-dried fruits and vegetables. But even fresh fruits and vegetables last for weeks, and some for months, without cold storage. That holds true even in the Tropics, as long as nothing has ever been stored at a temperature lower than it will be stored on board. To buy fruits and vegetables that have never been refrigerated, we buy directly from small growers, either from farms or in outdoor markets and stalls.

GLOSSARY
OF SAILING
TERMS

■ ■ ■

Note: Any word used in a definition that is also in the glossary is set in italics.

Backing (a sail)   When the wind fills a sail from the wrong side. Done on purpose if one wants the boat to go reverse or *heave to*, usually accomplished by tacking without re*sheet*ing the sail.

Batten/fully battened   A batten is a long, flat piece of wood or composite material that supports the *roach* of a sail. A fully battened sail has battens that extend from the roach all the way to the mast.

Beam reach   Wind in from the side of the boat (at a right angle).

Bilge   Commonly, the area between the floorboards and the keel.

Broach   When a big following sea forces the boat to change course suddenly, so it ends up with its side to a wave. The potential results: a partial knockdown, or the mast hitting the water, or in severe cases, the boat rolling 360 degrees.

Broad reach   Wind coming in aft of abeam, halfway between a *beam reach* and *downwind*.

Cable (measurement of distance)   One tenth of a *nautical mile.*

Cleat   A belaying device, that keeps a rope from slipping.

Clew   The lower aft corner of a sail.

Close-hauled   Sailing into the wind, with the bow pointing as close to the *eye of the wind* as possible.

Displacement boat   A boat that cannot plane due to its weight-to-size ratio, that is restricted to a speed that equals a wave's speed, where the distance between wave crests is equal to the boat's waterline length.

Double-ender   A boat that has a pointy bow and stern.

Downwind   Wind in from astern (dead aft).

Ease   The action of increasing the angle between a sail and the wind. The opposite action is *sheet in.*

Eye of the wind   The direction the wind is blowing from.

Fluxgate compass   An electronic compass with a microprocessor that senses the Earth's magnetic field.

Foot   The lower edge of a sail, between the *tack* and *clew* (closest to the boom).

Frames   A steel boat's ribs.

Furl   Originally, on board sailing ships, furl meant binding a sail onto a yard or a boom for the purpose of stowing it in harbor or at sea in response to too much wind. We use the word to mean taking in a sail completely.

GPS   Global Positioning System. A navigation instrument that works out its position from data it receives from satellites.

Gybe   While sailing with the wind, swinging the boom from one side of the boat to the other.

Halyard   The rope or wire with which one hoists (raises) a sail.

Heave to   Make the boat lose its forward motion by *backing* one or more sails. When heaving to, the boat slowly drifts to leeward.

Height/high   Steering toward the *eye of the wind*. "Steer higher" means closer to the eye of the wind. "Steer as high as you can" means as close to the eye of the wind as the boat is able. (No boat can sail directly into the wind.)

Leech   The outermost aft edge of a sail (the hypotenuse of the triangle).

Leeway   A boat's propensity to slide sideways. The amount of leeway is the difference (measured in degrees) between the direction in which the bow is pointing and the boat's true heading (usually 3 to 5 degrees when sailing *close-hauled*).

Lifeline   Wires attached to *stanchions* to create a "fence" around the perimeter of the deck.

Luff (noun)   The forward vertical part of the sail.

Luff (verb)   Steer to bring the bow nearer the wind.

Meridian   Any Great Circle that passes through Earth's North and South Poles.

Nautical mile (nm)   A *meridian* is divided into 90 degrees between the equator and the pole. Each degree is divided into sixty minutes; one minute is a nautical mile. (A nautical mile is equal to 2,025 yards.)

Noon position A boat's position at noon. Aboard any boat without electronic navigation equipment, the latitude is ascertained by observing the *meridian* passage of the sun (measuring the sun's highest altitude with a sextant).

Pilot chart A "chart" used to portray information of use to mariners for route planning. Each ocean has a chart for each month that displays wind direction and strength, wave heights, water temperature, percentage of fog and gales above force 8 on the Beaufort scale, depression and hurricane tracks, direction and strength of surface currents.

Plot Marking a boat's position onto a chart.

Preventer A line used to "prevent" the boom from swinging by holding the boom forward, opposing the pull of the *sheet*. (Our system also allows us to use the preventer as a vang—a mechanical device that holds the boom down—to control the sail's *twist*.)

Reef (noun or verb) When there is too much wind for full sail, reefing is the action of reducing the size of a sail to match the wind strength. (As the wind decreases, one "shakes out" a reef.)

Roach The area of a sail that extends aft of a straight line between the head (top) of the sail and the *clew*—in other words, a rounded part added on to the hypotenuse of the triangle—needing the support of *battens*.

Scupper A hole in the *toe rail* where water can run off the deck.

Sheet (noun) The line used to adjust a sail's shape and angle to the wind.

Sheet in (verb) The action of decreasing the angle between a sail and the wind. The opposite action is *ease*.

Shroud A wire (or rod or rope) that supports the mast sideways.

Spear (pole out) When the mainsail is fully eased, out to one side, using the spinnaker pole to hold the headsail out to the opposite side. Done when sailing with the wind, dead *downwind*, or with the wind no more than 30 degrees off the stern. This sail combination is called "wing and wing."

Spreader Structural "arms" on a mast through which the *shroud*s pass (that "spread" the shrouds), thereby creating a more favorable angle for mast support.

Stall (verb) When the wind enters a sail at too great an angle, the wind traveling across the lee side of the sail becomes turbulent, destroying lift and causing the sail to lose its driving force. The term *stalling* can also be applied to a rudder or keel (or an airplane wing).

Stanchion The metal "fence posts" at the edge of the deck that support the *lifelines*.

Stay A wire (or rod) that keeps the mast from falling forward (backstay) or aft (forestay).

Stern quarter An angle approximately 45 degrees either side of the stern.

Tack (noun) The lower forward corner of a sail.

Tack (verb) Changing course by moving the bow through the *eye of the wind*.

Telltales   Lightweight ribbons attached to a sail that indicate the wind's path over the sail. The information is useful for trimming the sail.

Toe rail   The low vertical rail rimming the deck (what you brace your toes against when the boat heels).

Twist   The shape of a sail should be "twisted " in a continuous outward twist from the boom to the top of the sail so that the wind enters the sail at the same angle at the top of the mast as it does at deck level.

UTC   Universal Time Coordinated. The time on the zero *meridian* of longitude (without adjustment to daylight savings time). We need to know the UTC time to work out our longitude. UTC is also used as a reference point when setting radio schedules. Formally called GMT, Greenwich Mean Time.

Windex   A mechanical wind indicator at the top of the mast.

WWV   A radio station (on 5, 10, 15, 20, and 25 megahertz) that broadcasts information to mariners: a continuous report of the correct *UTC*, interrupted at specific times for navigational warnings and weather reports.

Yankee   Outside the United States, all Americans are referred to by the name Yankee. In the United States, Southerners call Northerners Yankees. In the North, only New Englanders are called Yankees. In New England, only those whose relatives came on the Mayflower are Yankees. Then there's a baseball team called the Yankees. It can be very confusing when one word means so many things. On a sailboat, a yankee is a high-cut (off the water) foresail. Used when sailing *close-hauled*, against the waves, when the bow would tend to force too much water into a lower-cut sail.